CATALOGUE OF THE
JAIN MANUSCRIPTS OF THE BRITISH LIBRARY

Including the holdings of the British Museum
and the Victoria & Albert Museum

VOLUME I

Candrabhāl Bh. Tripāthī (1929-1996)

CATALOGUE OF THE JAIN MANUSCRIPTS OF THE BRITISH LIBRARY

Including the holdings of the British Museum and the Victoria & Albert Museum

By Nalini Balbir, Kanhaiyalal V. Sheth,
Kalpana K. Sheth and Candrabhal Bh. Tripathi

VOLUME I

INTRODUCTION, BIBLIOGRAPHY
APPENDICES, INDEXES, PLATES

The British Library & The Institute of Jainology
London
2006

Published jointly by:

The British Library

96 Euston Road
London, NW1 2DB
U.K.

www.bl.uk

Institute of Jainology

Unit 18, Silicon Business Centre
26/28 Wadsworth Road
Perivale
Greenford
Middlesex UB6 7JZ
U.K.

Samay Apartments
B-101, 1st Floor, Nr. Azad Society
Nr. Vastrapur Telephone Exchange
Behind Bimanagar
Ambawadi
Ahmedabad 380 015
INDIA

www.jainology.org

Printed by:

Thomson Press (India) Limited

104, Kamanwala Chambers
Mugal Lane, Mahim (West)
Mumbai 400 016
INDIA

www.thomsonpress.com

Distributed by:

Hindi Granth Karyalay

9 Hirabaug, C P Tank
Mumbai 400 004
INDIA

www.hindibooks.8m.com

First Edition, 2006 ~ 500 copies

Set of 3 vols and 1 CD (not to be sold separately)

ISBN 0 7123 4711 9

Table of Contents

Contents of Volume II

Contents of Volume III

Blessings

The root of human knowledge is the alphabetic character which is defined in three ways in the Nandi Sutra *of the Jain scriptures: as a symbol, as a sound and as a power of meaningful expression. Jain sages, using the art of writing, have expressed their knowledge through the creation of abundant literature in Jain and other religions.*

Such literature has been preserved in many collections in India and abroad and their contribution as the pride of India's glorious past is noteworthy.

The publication of this Catalogue of Jain Manuscripts in the collection of the British Library by the Institute of Jainology *will be an important contribution for use by the researcher, teacher and student alike.*

With auspicious blessings,

Pujya Acharya Mahapragya

****

It is commendable that the Institute of Jainology *is dedicated to the noble cause of bringing awareness of Jainism worldwide, through the publication of this catalogue and other channels.*

Original manuscripts are of utmost importance as references to avoid and correct inaccuracies in printed versions of scriptures which usually get propagated.

Jain institutions in India and abroad should co-operate with the Institute of Jainology *in their efforts to expand and extend their activities for which I offer my blessings and best wishes.*

Pujya Jambuvijayaji Maharaj

****

Today's turbulent world needs peace most. Three principles of Jainism – Ahimsa *(non-violence),* Anekantvad *(non-absolutism) and* Aparigrah *(non-possession) can be the basis of world peace.*

Jain manuscripts contain the essence of Jinvani. *By publishing catalogues of the manuscripts, the* Institute of Jainology *will help propagate the philosophy of peace to mankind in the world at large.*

My blessings to this project of heritage and knowledge.

Pujya Acharya Vidyanand Muni

****

Religious manuscripts are like the rays of the sun and, throughout our life, give us 'light'. The scriptures show the path which people can 'walk' and gain true inner 'sight'. Thus, the project undertaken by the Institute of Jainology *of cataloguing the Jain manuscripts in the collection of the British Library and other such organisations is a commendable activity which you have completed successfully.*

My blessings are with you for this activity to expand in the UK and extend to other foreign countries in the future.

Pujya Sadhvi Dr. Divyaprabha

List of Plates

Plate I: Opening pages of Jain manuscripts

- Full illustrated page with floral motifs as opening (*Śrīpāla-rāsa*, Or. 13622, fol. 1A, **Cat. No. 737**)
- Mahāvīra in padmāsana (*Śālibhadra-caupaī*, Or. 13524, fol. 1B, **Cat. No. 747**).
- Goddess Sarasvatī (*Nāmasāroddhāra* on the *Abhidhānacintāmaṇi*, Or. 13806, fol. 1B, **Cat. No. 1351**).

Plate II: Types of numbering
- A palm-leaf manuscript from western India with foliation in letter-numeral and number (*Jītakalpacūrṇi*, Or. 1385B, fol. 9B, **Cat. No. 159**).
- Two pages of a paper manuscript of the *Kalpasūtra* with double foliation and inlaid illustration (*Kalpasūtra*, Or. 13455, fol. 22B and 46B, **Cat. No. 106**).

Plates III-IV: Artistic forms of writing
- Instance of calligraphic script in a manuscript of the *Sāmāyikapratikramaṇavidhi* (I.O. San. 1564e, fol. 1B, **Cat. No. 274**).
- Ornamental designs around folio numbers (*Igyārasa no tava*, Or. 15633/126, fol. 1B, 2B, 3B, 4B, **Cat. No. 1117**).
- Diagrams illustrating figurative poetry (Vāgbhaṭālaṁkāra, Or. 2146C, fol. 2A, **Cat. No. 1378**)
- Instance of *citra-lipi* (*Upadeśamālā*, Or. 2114B, fol. 53B, 54B, 55A, 55B, **Cat. No. 527**).

Plate V: Vignettes inlaid in the text
- Triśalā's dreams in a *Kalpasūtra* manuscript (Or. 13701, fol. ṣ5B, **Cat. No. 122**).
- Deities in a *Saṁgrahaṇī* manuscript (Or. 2116 C, fol. 4B, **Cat. No. 337**)
- Sun and moon in a *Saṁgrahaṇī* manuscript (Or. 2116C, fol. 13A, **Cat. No. 337**)

Plate VI: Jain manuscripts in scripts other than Devanāgarī
- A *Kalpasūtra* in Bengali script from Dr John Leyden (I.O. 2879, **Cat. No. 108**).
- A Jain manuscript from South India in Kannada script (I.O. San. 3532)
- A Digambara treatise in Prakrit with Persian commentary (*Pancāstikāya*, Add. 25,022, fol. 132, **Cat. No. 1201**)

Plate VII: The two oldest Jain manuscripts in the British Library
- Last page of the *Śālibhadra-caupaī* by Sādhuhaṁsamuni (Harley 415, composite manuscript with twenty-five texts in Gujarati, fol. 39A, **Cat. No. 750**).
- *Anekārthasaṁgraha* by Hemacandra with commentary (Sloane 4090E, fol. 220A and 220B: **Cat. No. 1354**).

Plate VIII: *Kalpasūtra* leaves
- Golden script on crimson background (Or. 14262 (2), fol. 41A and 41B, **Cat. No. 141**).
- With Lakṣmīvallabhagaṇi's *Kalpadruma*, informal style (I.O. San. 1622, fol. 63A, **Cat. No. 116**).

Plate IX: Instances of Scribal Remarks
- Manuscript of the *Sālibhadra-caupaī* (Or. 13524, fol. 39A, **Cat. No. 747** and Appendix 1).
- Manuscript of the *Ṣaṣṭiśataka* by Nemicandra Bhāṇḍagārika with Sanskrit commentary (Or. 13179, fol. 8B, **Cat. No. 586**).
- Father and sons as manuscript-collectors, *ex-libris* Jain style (*Praśamaratiprakaraṇa*, Or. 2098 A, fol. 67B, **Cat. No. 517**; Or. 2098 B, fol. 12A, **Cat. No. 516**; *Anekāntajayapatākā*, Or. 2111, fol. 244A, **Cat. No. 670**)

Plates X-XI: Formats of manuscripts and commentaries
- The smallest Jain manuscript in the collections (*Ārādhanā-vidhi*, MSS. Guj. 6, fol. 1B, **Cat. No. 288**).
- A fine manuscript (*Puṣpamālā*, I.O. San. 2112B, fol. 4B, 5A, **Cat. No. 537**).

- Instance of pancapāṭha: text in the centre, commentary on four sides (*Jīvavicāra*, Or. 2112 E, fol. 5A, **Cat. No. 487**).

- Sanskrit text with interlinear Gujarati commentary (*Ratnākarapancaviṁśatikā*, Or. 15633/197, fol. 3B, **Cat. No. 906**).

Plates XII-XVI: Variety of texts illustrated, religious symbols

- Different groups of ascetics in a cosmological work (*Saṁgrahaṇīratna*, Or. 2116C, fol. 22B, **Cat. No. 337**).

- Siddhacakra in a manuscript of the *Śrīpālarāsa* (Or. 13622, fol. 72B, **Cat. No. 737**).

- Yantras accompanying each verse of the *Bhaktāmarastotra* (Or. 13741, fol. 2A, 7B, 20A, 20B, **Cat. No. 884**).

- Illustrations in a manuscript of the *Bhaktāmarastotra* (Or. 13478, fol. 1B, 3A, 5B, **Cat. No. 876**).

- Jina images (*Caturviṁśatijinastavana*, Or. 13623, facing fol. 64 and fol. 76).

- Palm of the hand with symbols (*Sāmudrikaśāstra*, Add. 26,461 D, fol. (93A), **Cat. No. 1416**).

Plate I: Opening pages of Jain Manuscripts

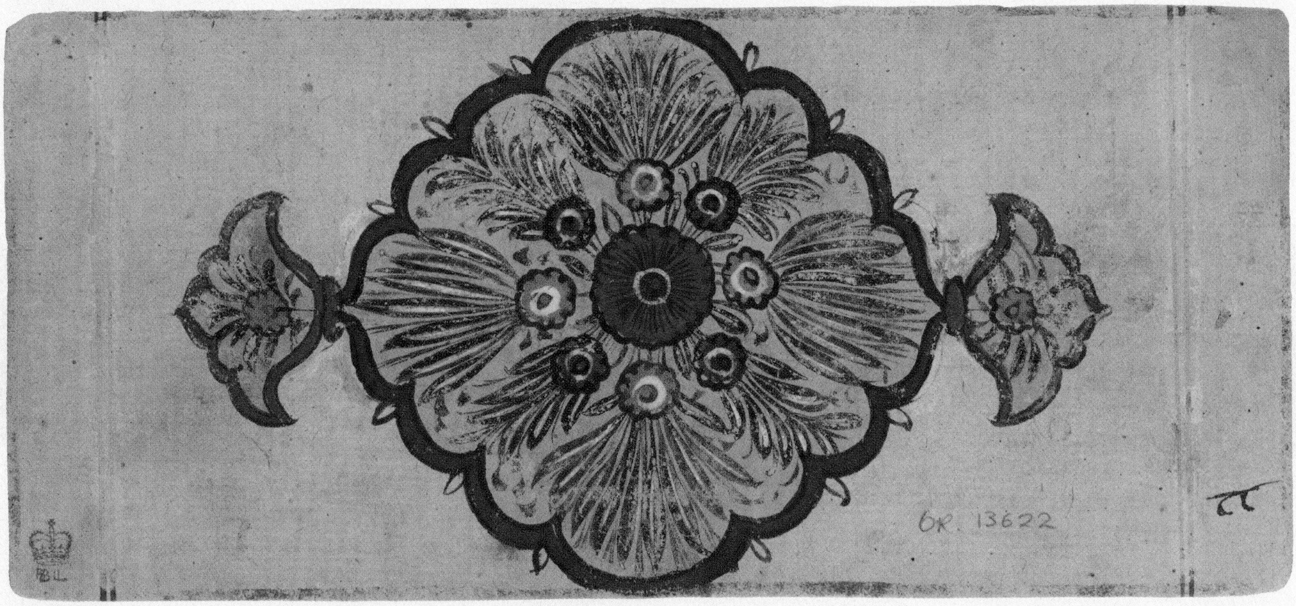

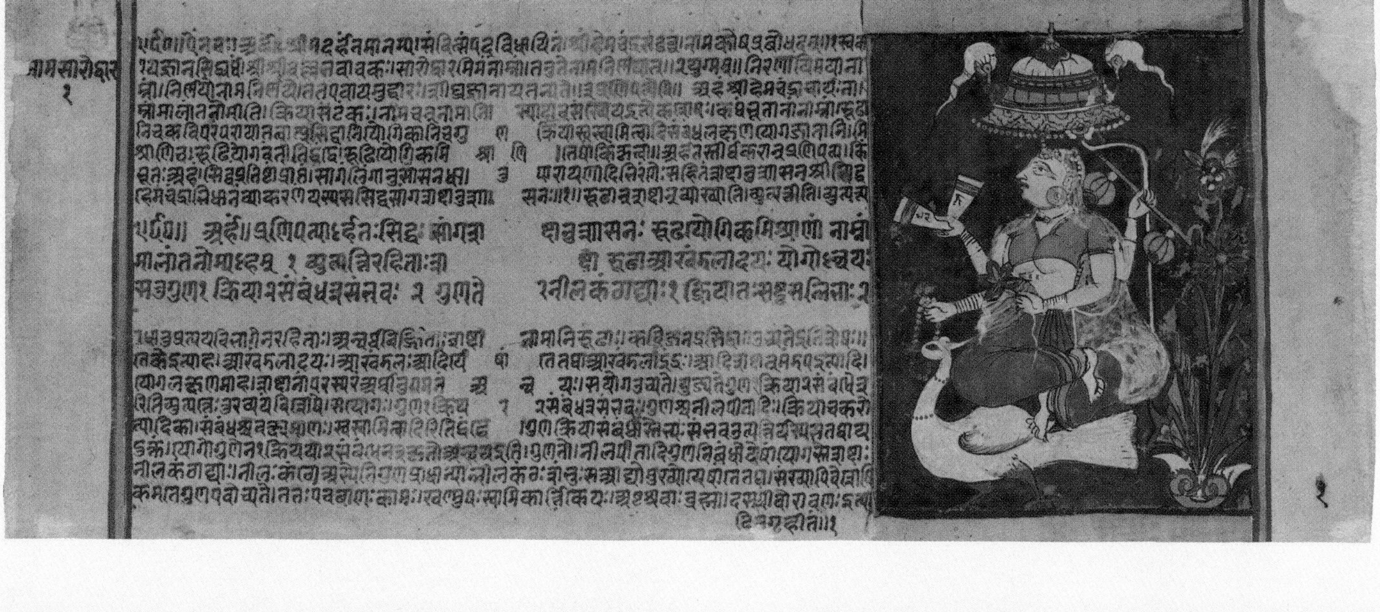

Plate II: Types of Numbering

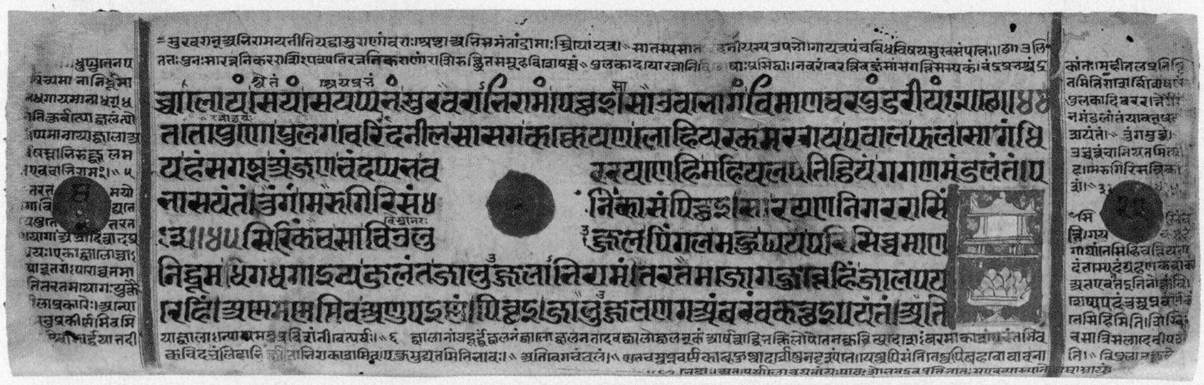

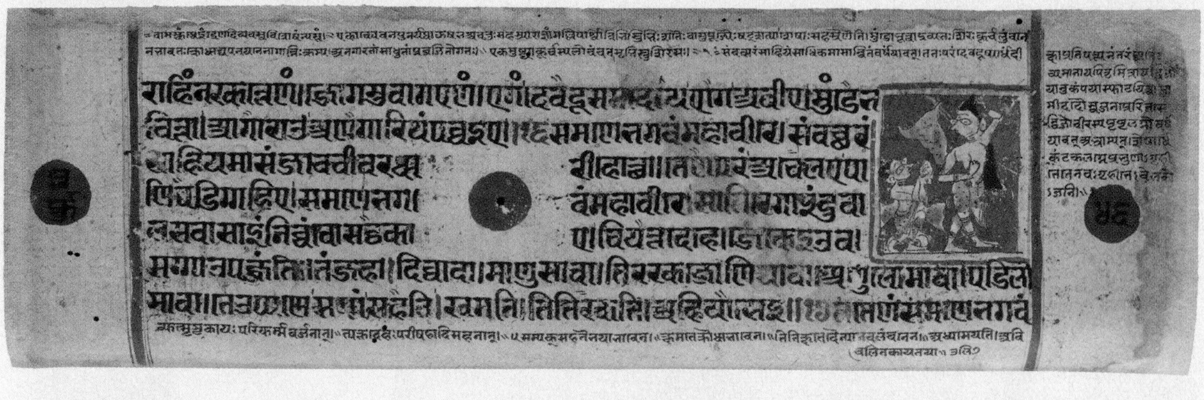

Plate III: Artistic forms of writing (1)

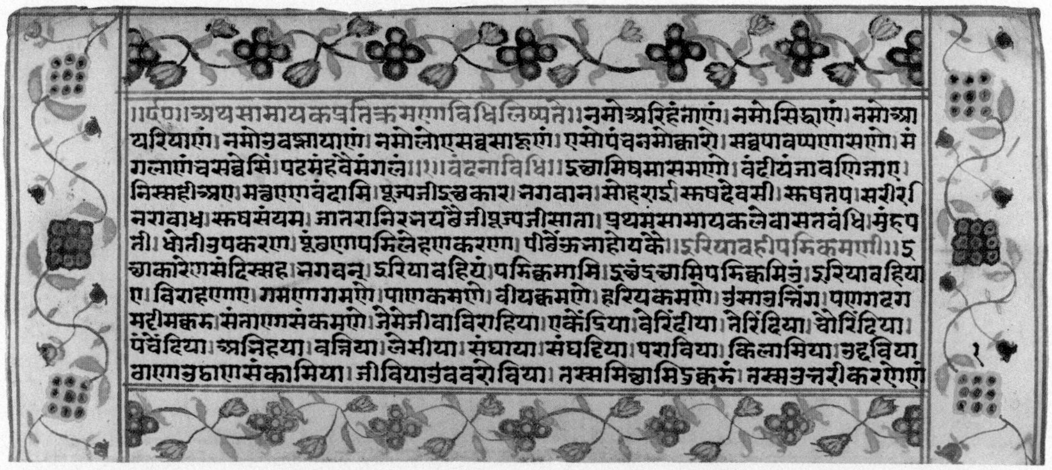

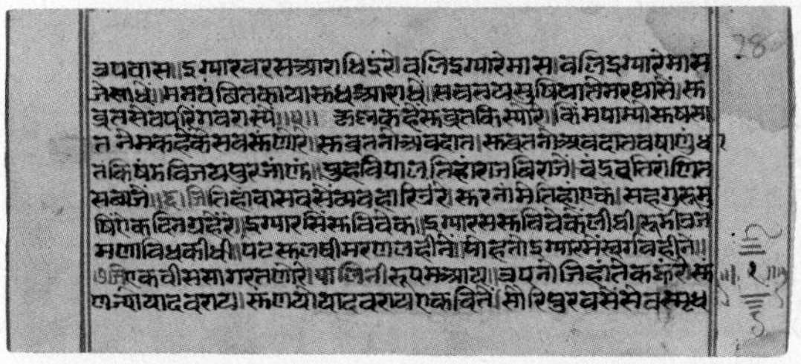

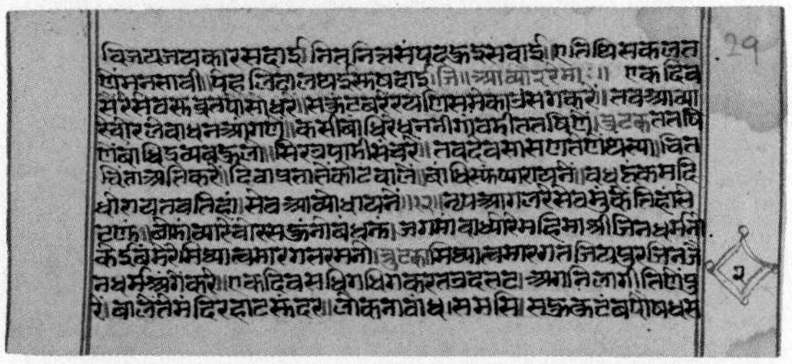

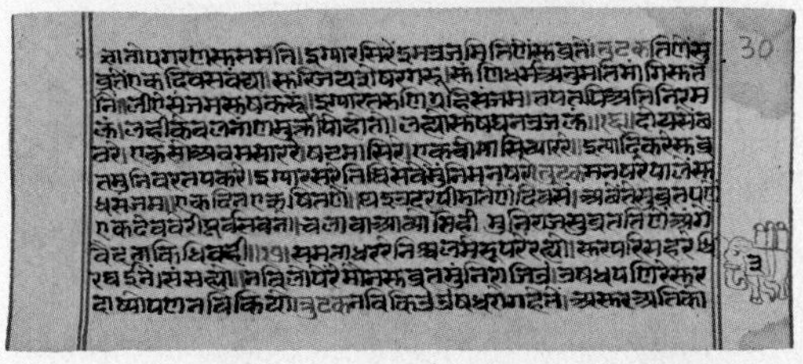

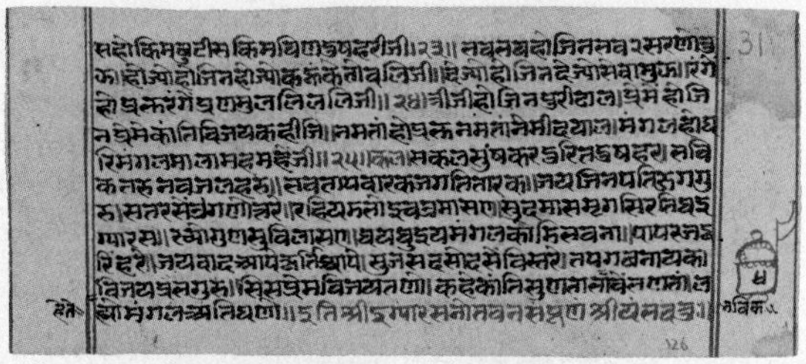

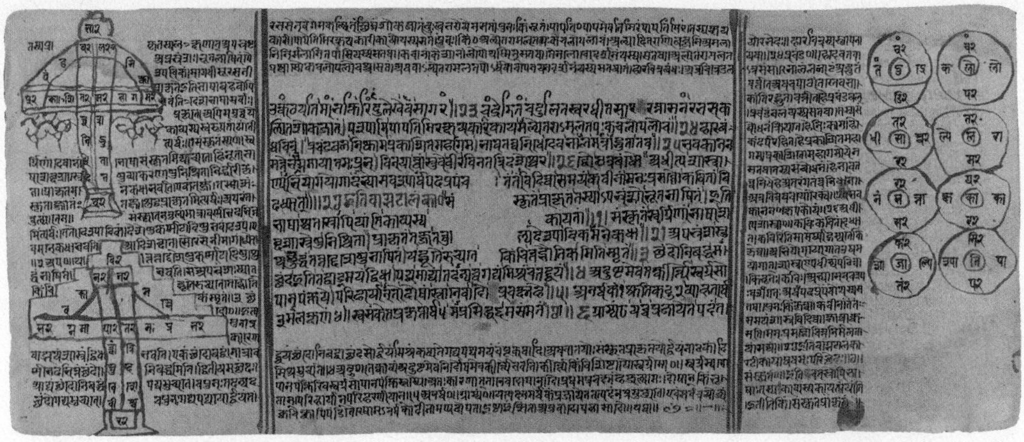

Plate IV: Artistic forms of writing (2)

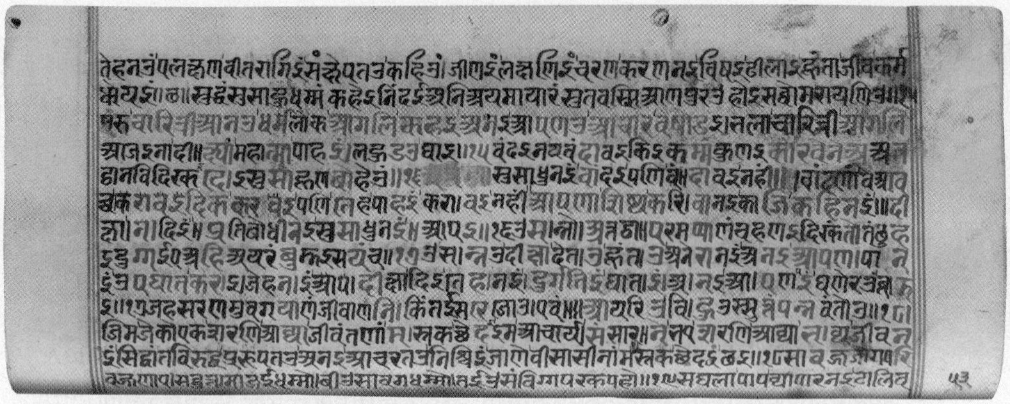

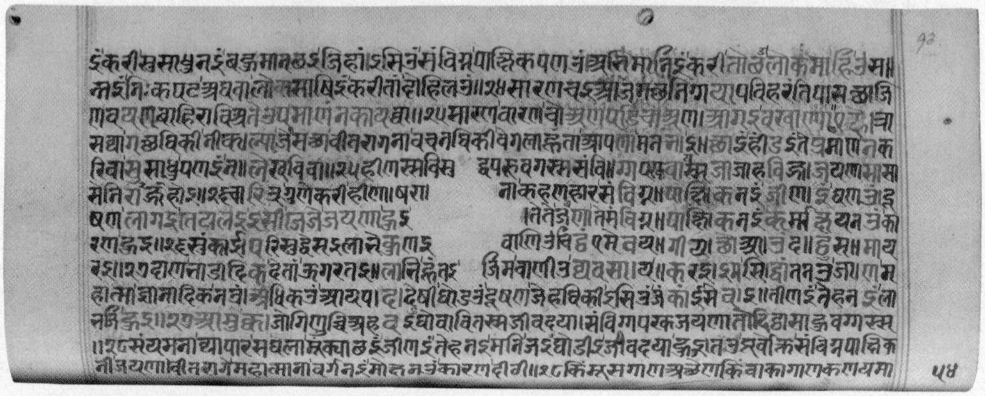

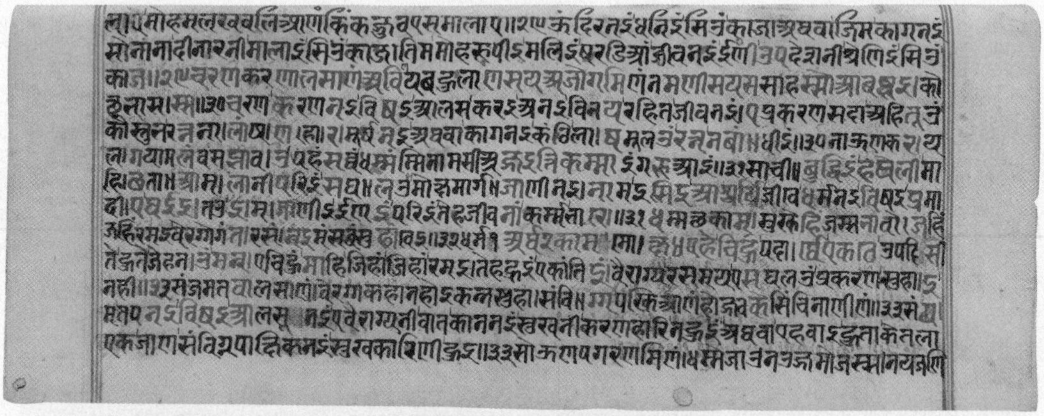

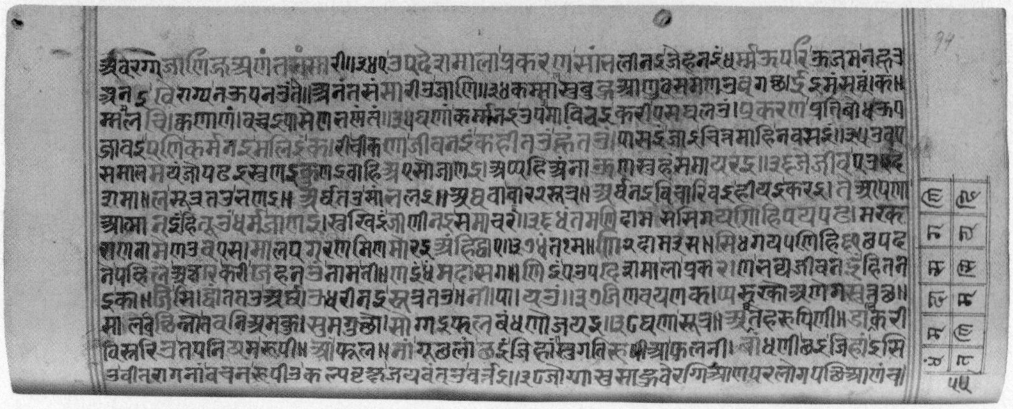

Plate V: Vignettes inlaid in the text

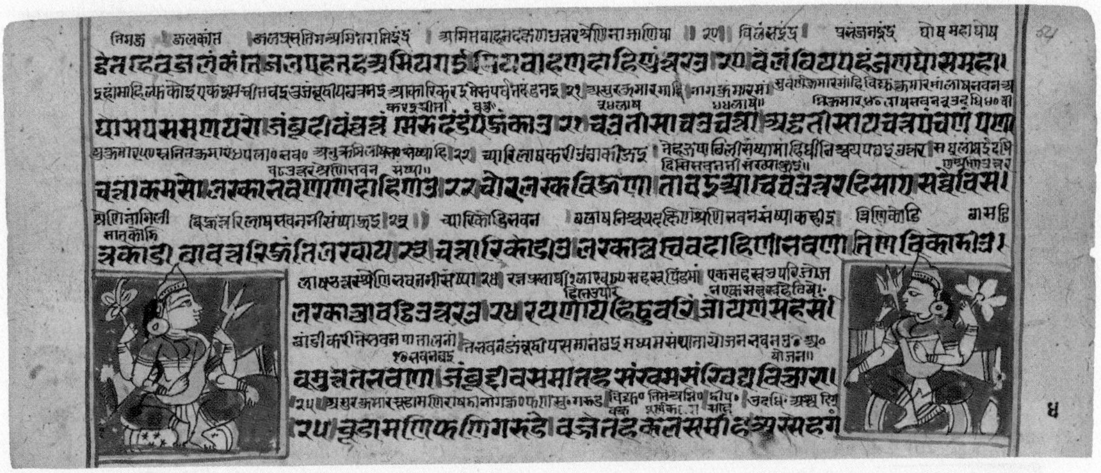

Plate VI: Jain manuscripts in scripts other than Devanāgarī

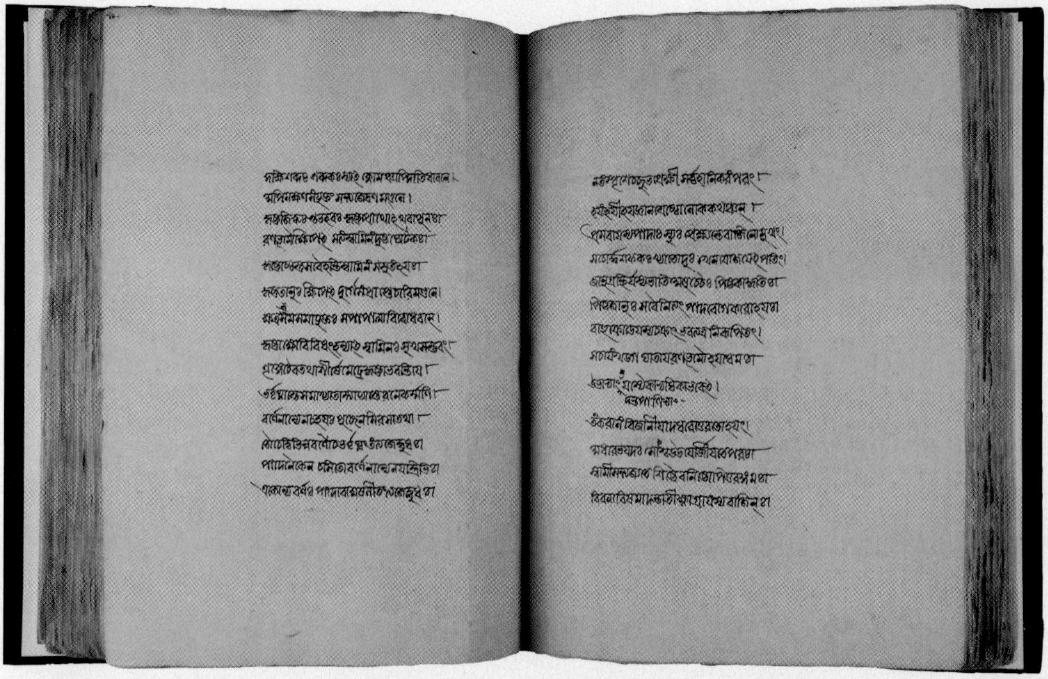

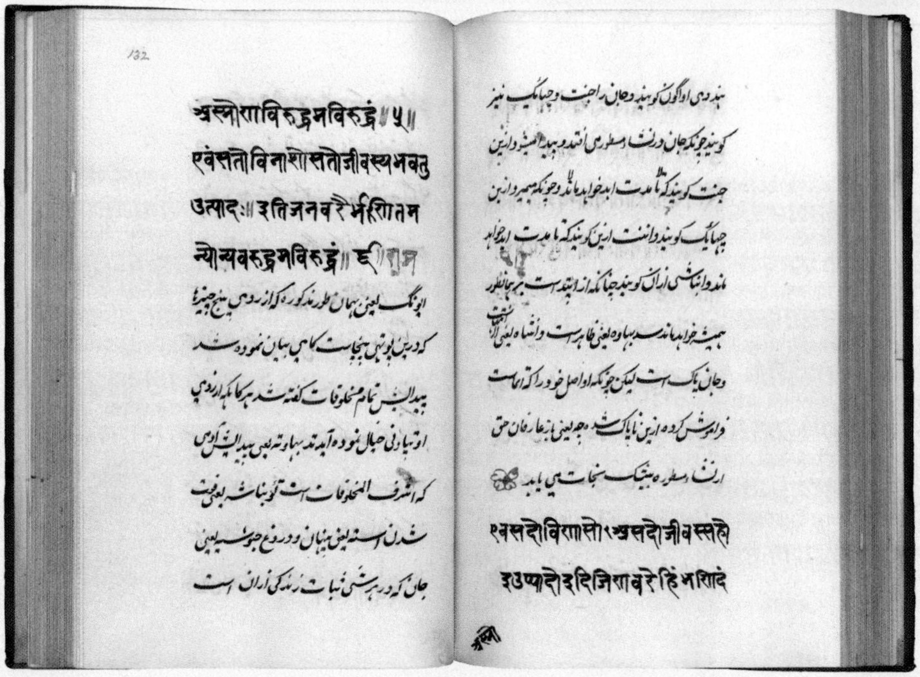

Plate VII: The two oldest Jain manuscripts in the British Library

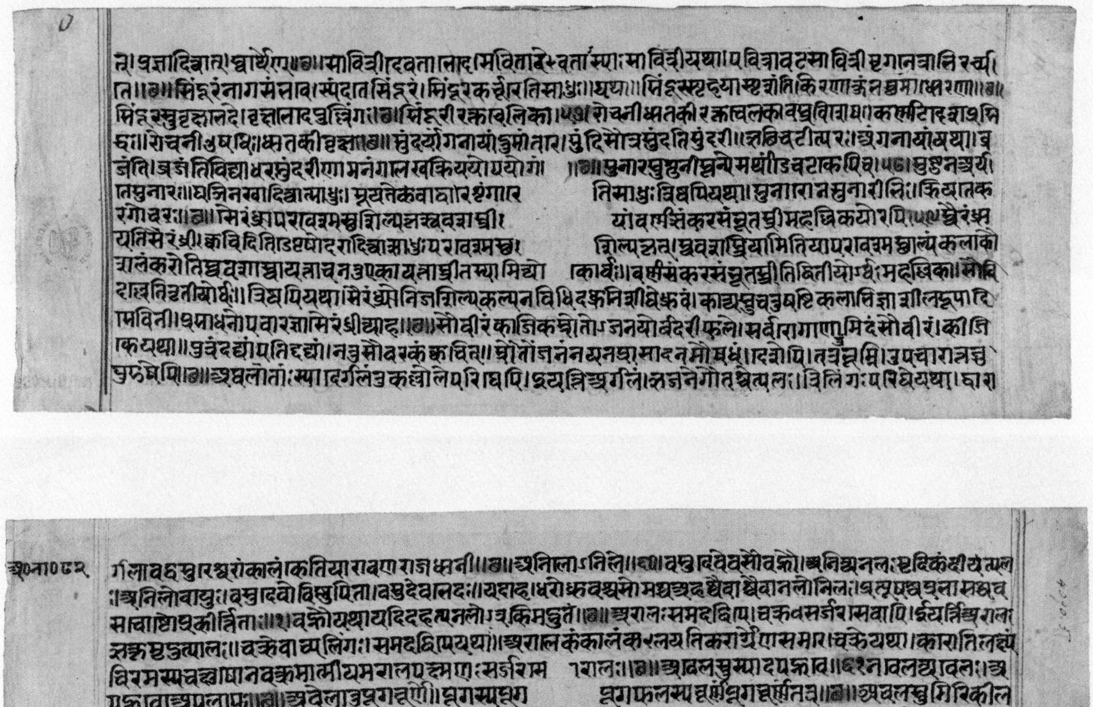

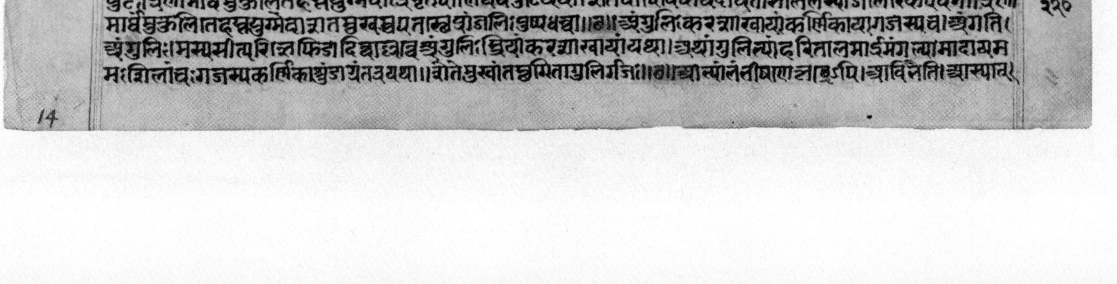

Plate VIII: Kalpasūtra leaves

Plate IX: Instances of Scribal Remarks

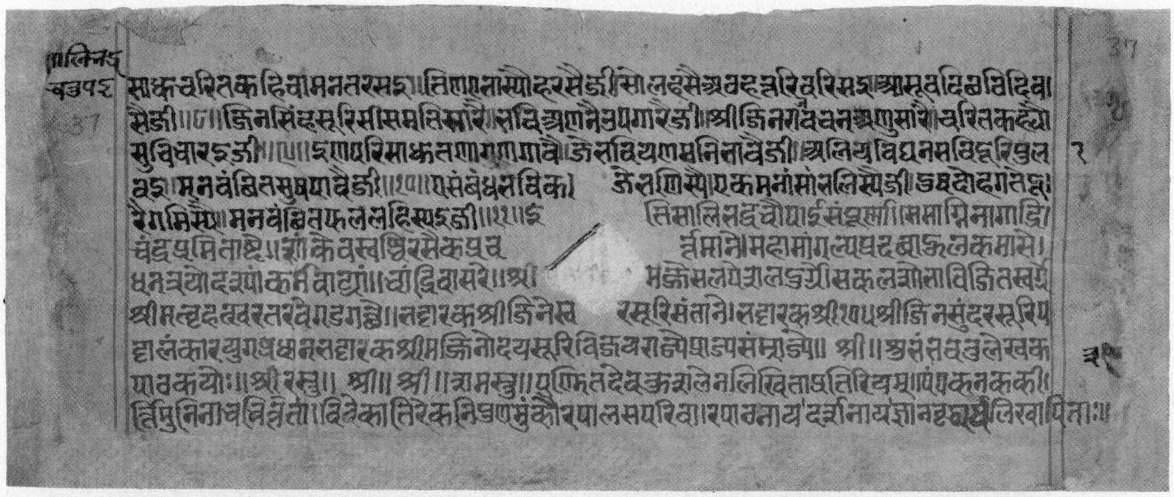

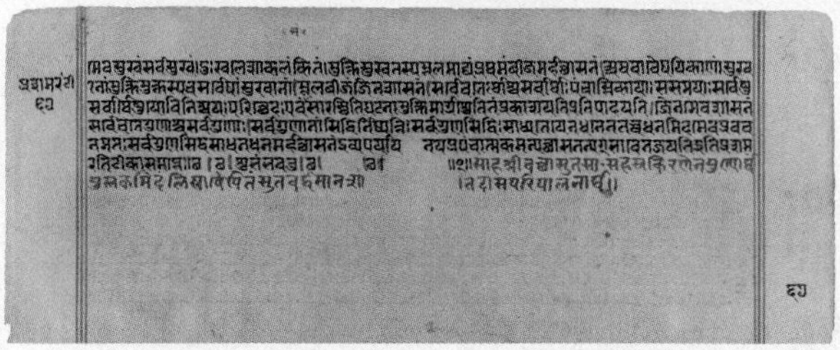

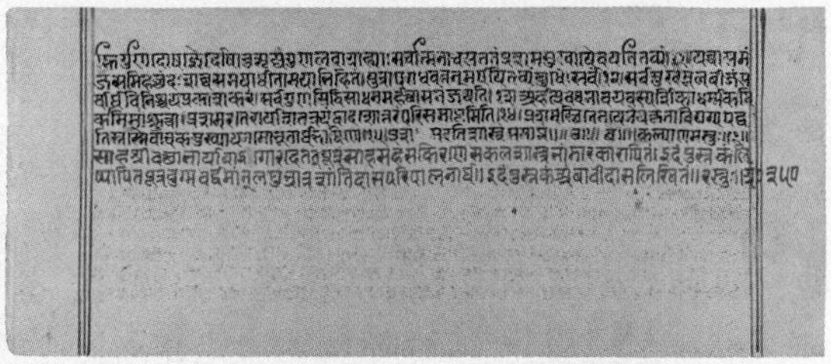

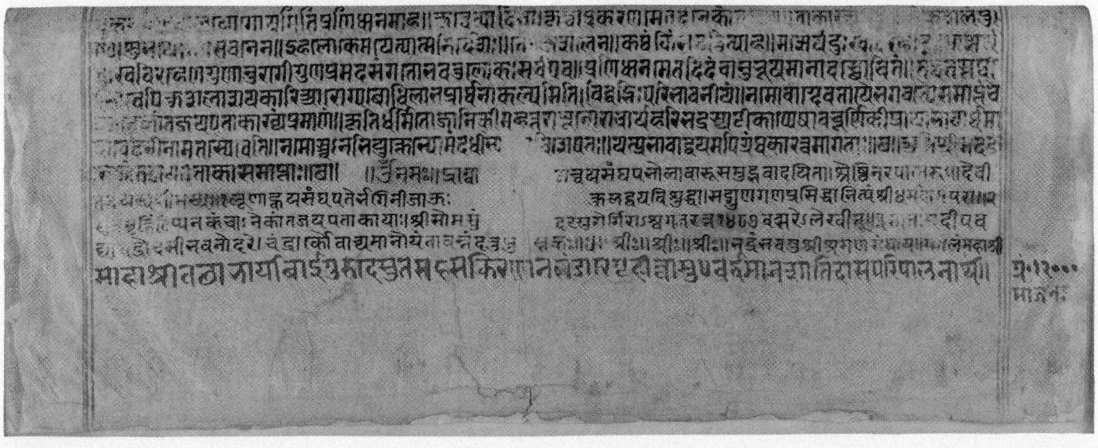

Plate X: Formats of manuscripts and commentaries (1)

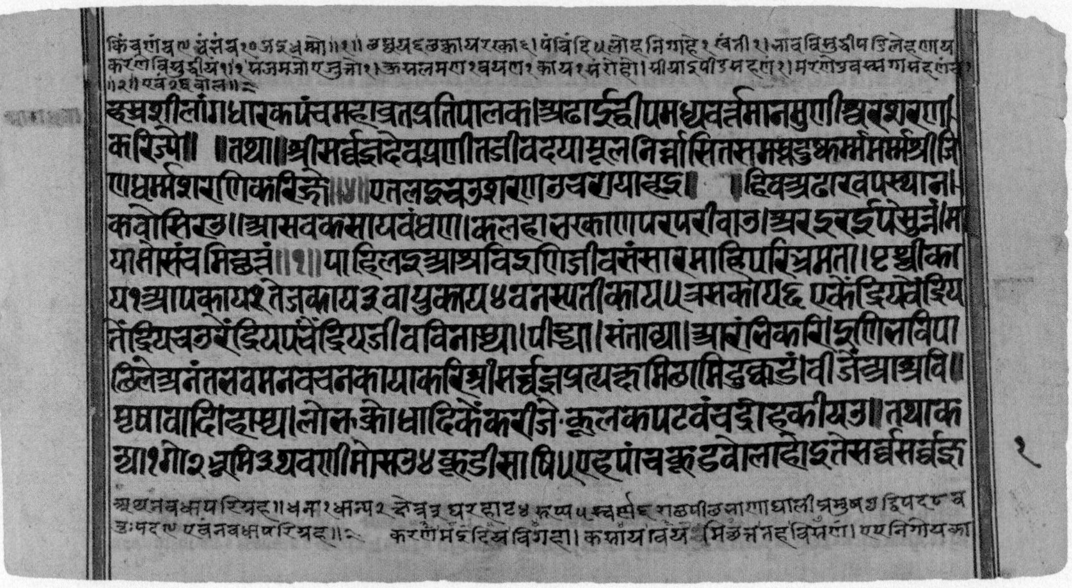

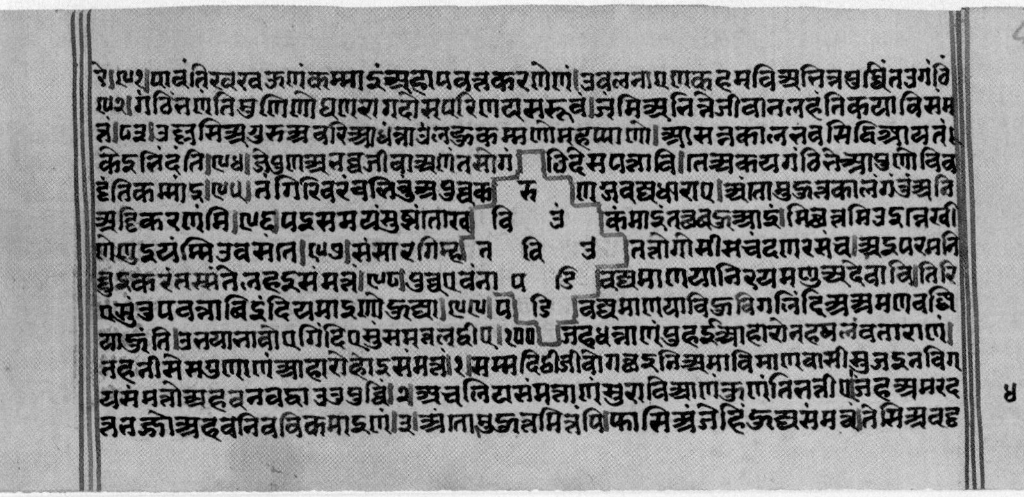

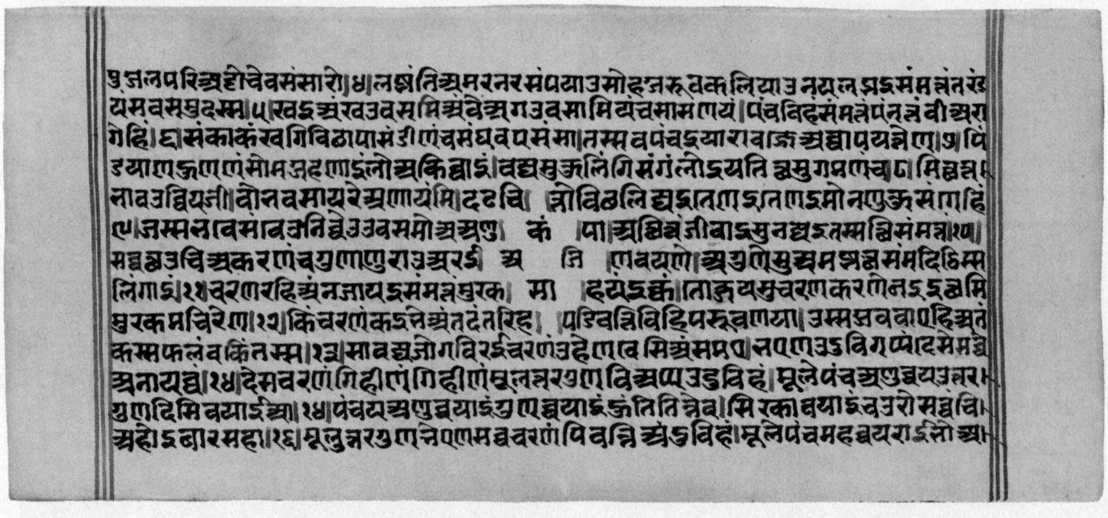

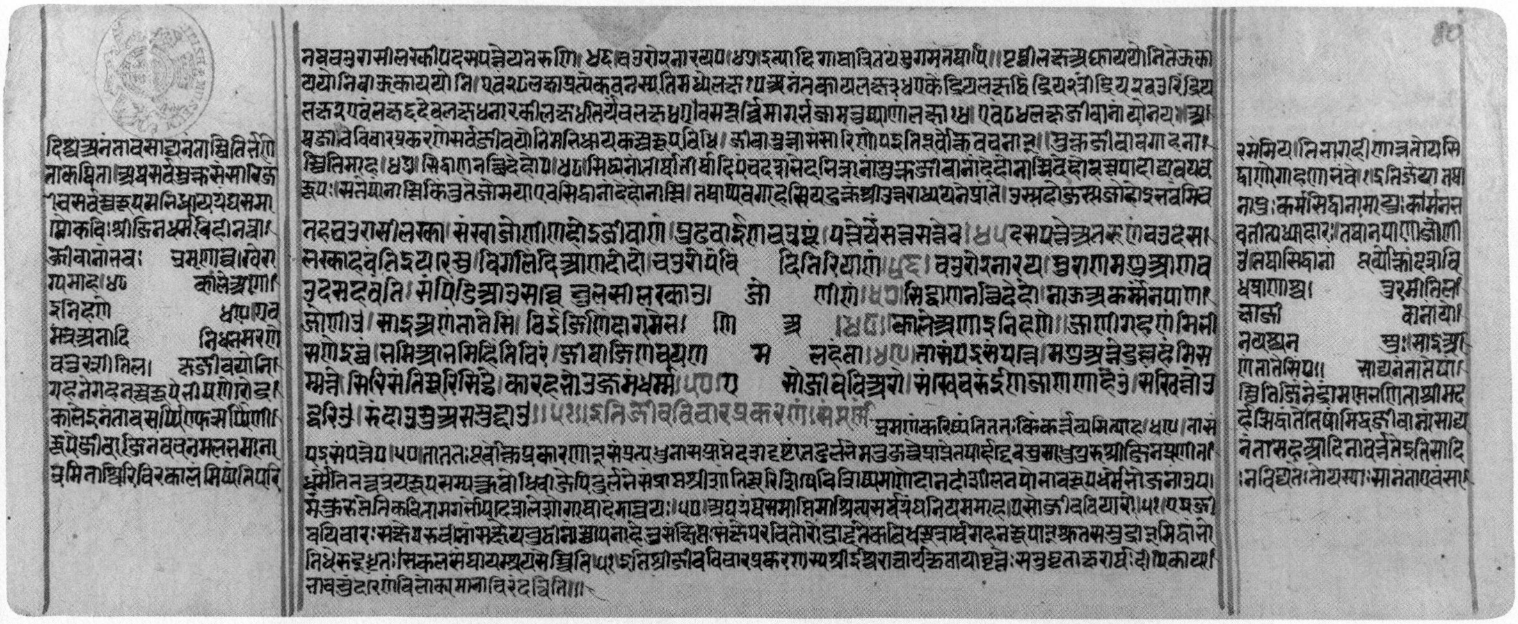

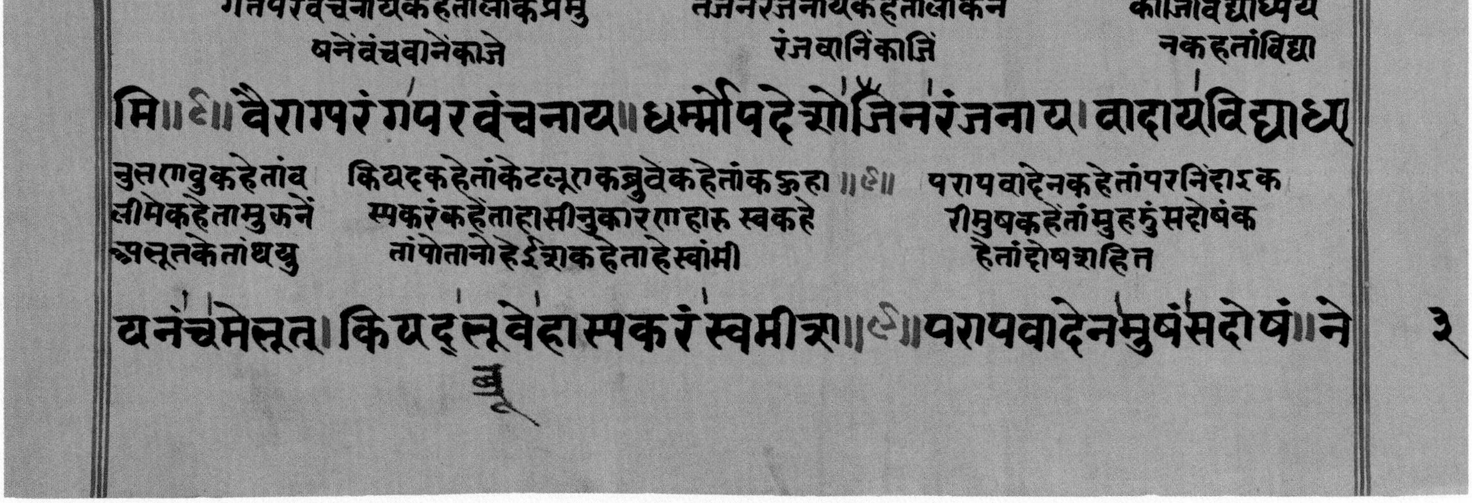

Plate XII: Variety of texts illustrated, religious symbols (1)

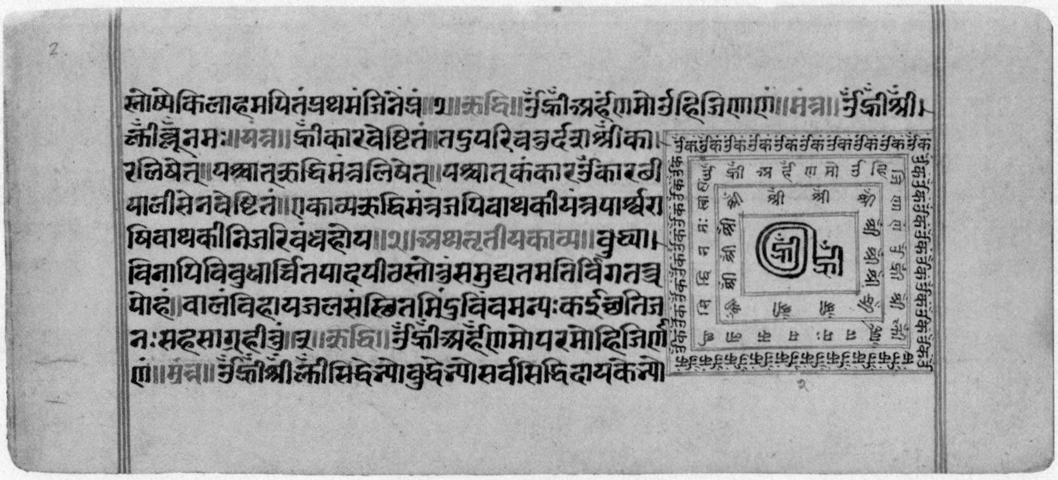

Plate XIII: Variety of texts illustrated, religious symbols (2)

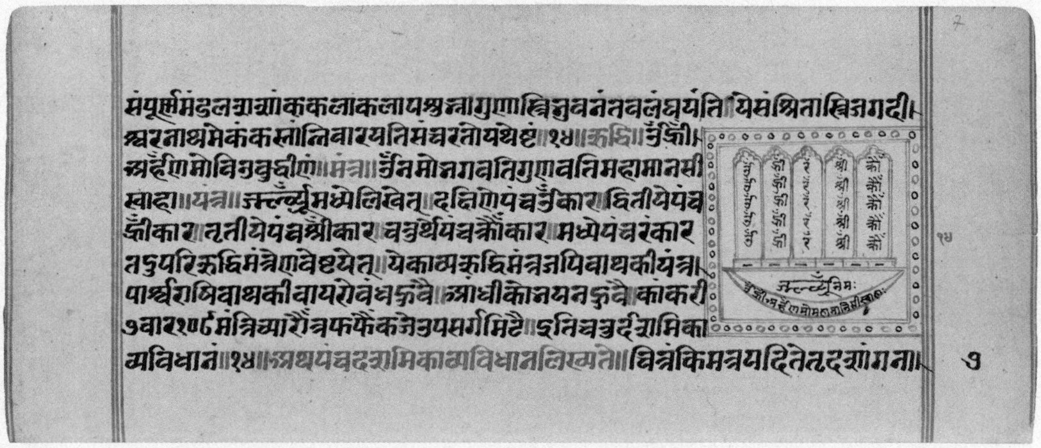

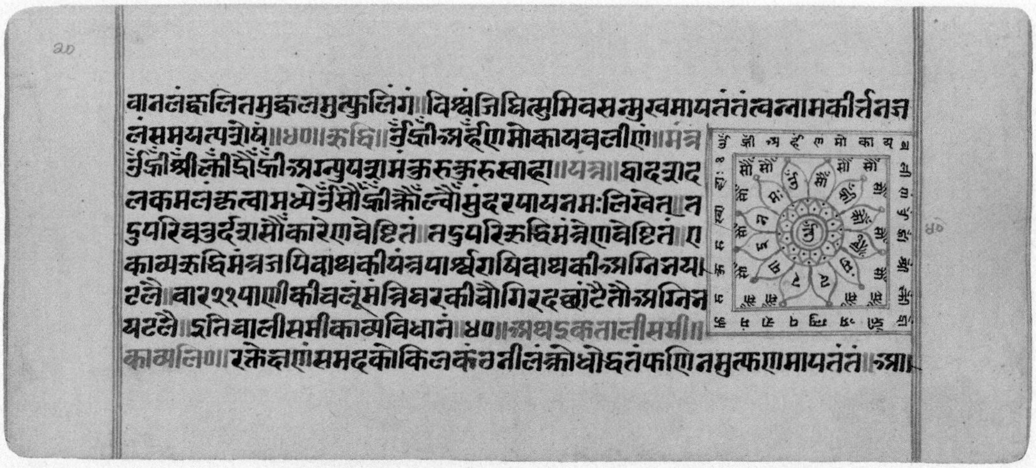

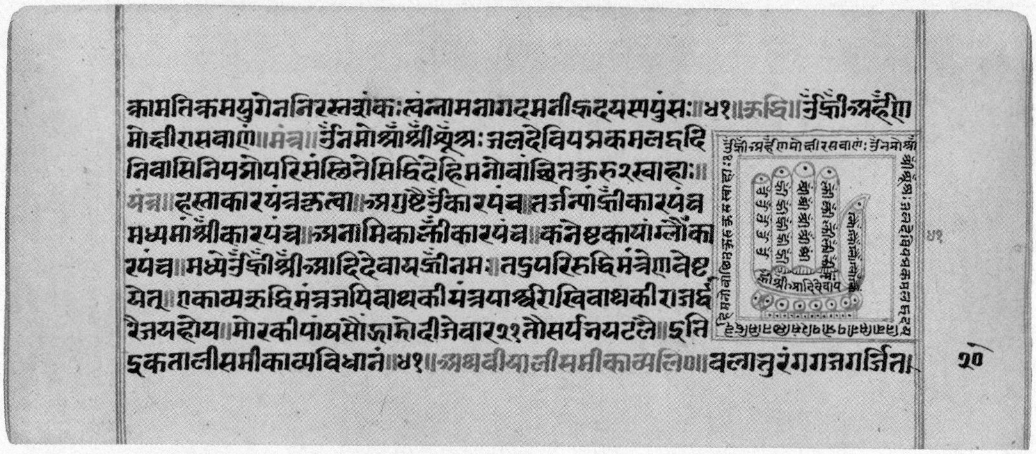

Plate XIV: Variety of texts illustrated, religious symbols (3)

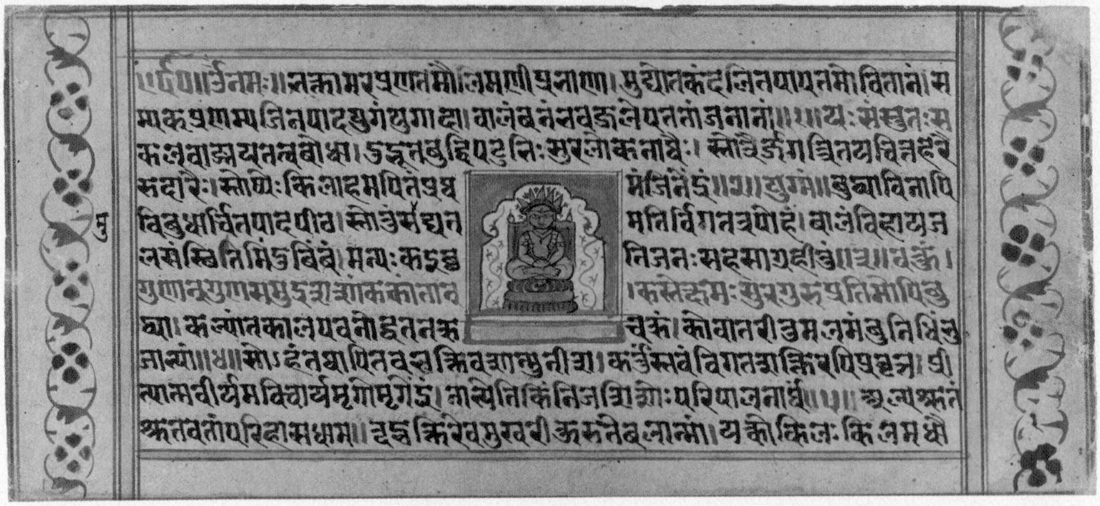

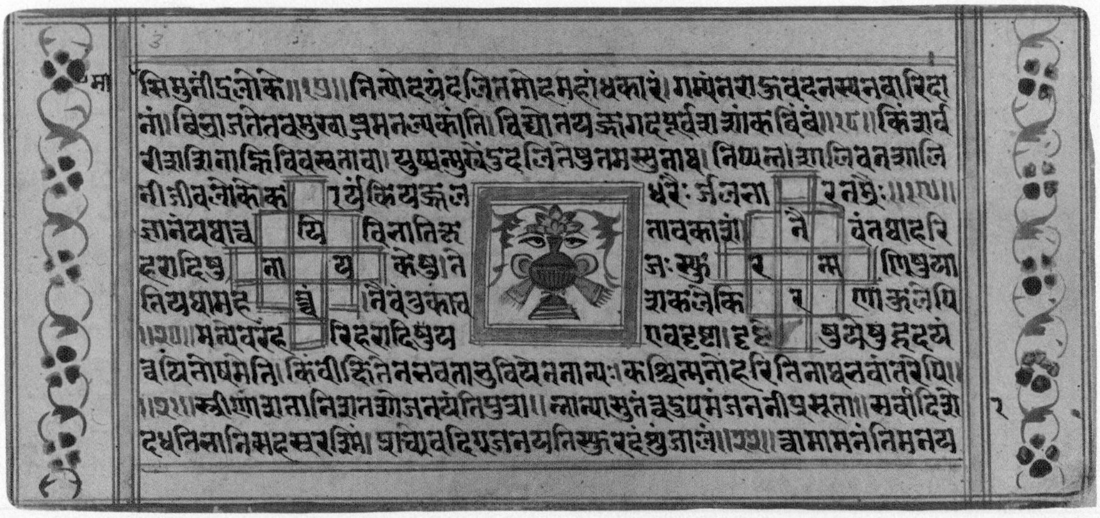

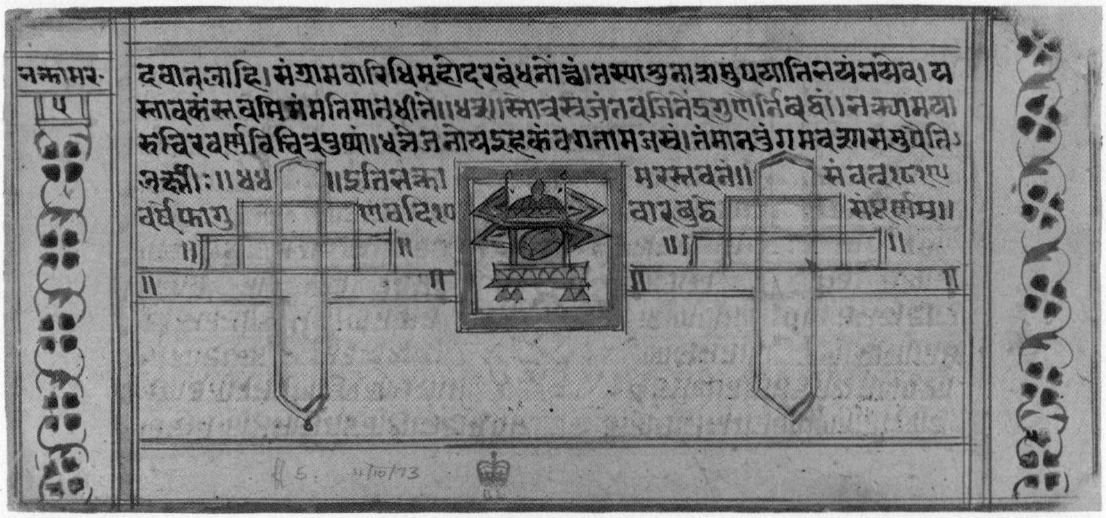

Plate XV: Variety of texts illustrated, religious symbols (4)

Plate XVI: Variety of texts illustrated, religious symbols (5)

Acknowledgements

Government of India
Ministry of Tourism and Culture
On the occasion of 2600th Birth Anniversary of Tirthankara Mahavira

Patron-in-Chief
Hon. Shri Atal Behari Vajpayee
Former Prime Minister of India

Honorary Patron
Dr. L.M. Singhvi
Eminent Jurist, distinguished Parliamentarian and member of Rajyasabha,
Former High Commissioner of India to the United Kingdom

Institutional Donors & Contributors

All India S.S. Jain Conference	Mumbai
Anderson Shaw	London
Anopchand Shah Charitable Trust	Kolkata
Babu Amichand Panalal Adishwar Temple Charitable Trust	Mumbai
Bhagwan Mahavir Memorial Samiti	New Delhi
Bharatvarshiya Digambar Jain Shrut Samvardhini Mahasabha	New Delhi
The British Museum	London
Champaklal Abhechand Doshi Charitable Trust	Kolkata
Chandaria Foundation	London
Dashrathmal Singhvi Memorial Trust	New Delhi
Dipchand Gardi Charitable Trust	Mumbai
Dr. C.J. Desai and Jaswantiben Desai Foundation	Kolkata
G.N. Damani Charitable Trust	Chennai
Enkay (I) Rubber Co. Pvt. Ltd.	New Delhi
Hasmukhlal Shantilal & Co	Mumbai
Hirachand Sayarchand Nahar Trust	Chennai
Jain Academy	Kolkata
Jain Jagruti Centre	Kolkata
Jain Jagruti Centre	Mumbai
Jain Samaj	Manchester
JAINA (Federation of Jain Associations In North America)	USA
Jaybhikhkhu Sahitya Trust	Ahmedabad
Khetshi Nathoobhai Trust	London
Kiran Trust	Ahmedabad
Lalbhai Dalpatbhai Charity Trust	Ahmedabad
Lalbhai Dalpatbhai Smarak Trust	Ahmedabad
Lathia Rubber Manufacturing Co. Ltd.	Mumbai
Leherchand Uttamchand Trust	Mumbai
Madhubani Education Foundation	Mumbai
Mahavir Trust	London
Malini Kishore Sanghvi Foundation	Mumbai
Navnat Vanik Association of the United Kingdom	London
Oshwal Association of the United Kingdom	London
Oswal Charities	Jamnagar
Prakash Pushpa Dugar Foundation	Chennai

Rajath Leasing & Finance Ltd.	Rajkot
Rajmal Rikhavchand Mehta Charitable Trust	Mumbai
Rambo Cane (I) Pvt. Ltd.	Rajkot
Sahu Jain Trust	New Delhi
Santek Foundation	New Delhi
Seth Chunilal Narbheram Memorial Trust	Mumbai
Seth Damjibhai Laxmichand Jain Dharma Sthanak	Mumbai
Sethia Foundation	London
Shah Chandulal Kasturchand Charitable Trust	Mumbai
Sherwood Agencies	Manchester
Sheth Anandji Kalyanji Pedhi	Ahmedabad
Sheth Jivandas Godidas Shankheshwar Paraswanathji Jain Derasar Trust	Ahmedabad
Shethani Mohinabai Trust	Ahmedabad
Shree G.B.V.S Jain Mahasangh	Mumbai
Shree Raj Saubhag Satsang Mandal	Sayla
Shree Saurashtra Dasa Shrimali Jain Bhojanalaya	Mumbai
Shree Saurashtra Dasa Shrimali Seva Samaj	Mumbai
Shree Saurashtra Dasa Shrimali Seva Sangh	Mumbai
Shree V.S. Jain Shravak Sangh	Mumbai
Shrenik Charity Trust	Ahmedabad
Shrimad Rajchandra Kendra	Dharampur
Singhvee Charitable Trust	Chennai
Smt. Aruna Manharlal Charitable Trust	Mumbai
Swetambar Murtipujak Jain Boarding	Ahmedabad
U.N. Mehta Charitable Trust	Ahmedabad
Victoria & Albert Museum	London
Vinubhai U. Shah Charitable Trust	Mumbai

Individual Donors & Contributors

Ratilal Premchand Chandaria

Chairman - Chandaria Group of Companies, Institute of Jainology
Trustee of International Sacred Literature Trust and
Former Chairman of the Board of Trustees of the Oshwal Association of the United Kingdom

Dipchand Savraj Gardi

Barrister, philanthropist, Trustee of the Institute of Jainology
President of All India Jain Shwetamber Conference, Bhagwan Mahavir Memorial Samiti

Sahu Ashok Kumar Jain [1934-1999]

Chairman - Bennet Coleman & Co. Ltd. and Times Group of Companies
Working President Bhagwan Mahavir Memorial Samiti

Sahu Ramesh Chandra Jain [1925-2004]

Executive Director – Times Group of Companies and President of All India Digambar Jain Parishad

Shrenik Kasturbhai

Industrialist, philanthropist, educationalist and former Chairman of Anandji Kalyanji Pedhi

U.N. Mehta [1924-1998]

Philanthropist, industrialist and founder of Torrent Group of Companies,

U.N. Mehta Institute of Cardiology & Research Centre

Arvind Panalal [1918-2002]

Philanthropist and Managing Trustee of Shri Sankheshwar, Bhoyani, Gandhar and Kareda Parshwanath Tirths

Pravin Punjani [1929-2004]

Chartered Accountant, Chairman of Jain Academy Rajkot and Jain Social Group International Federation, Trustee of the Institute of Jainology

Manharlal Chunilal Shah

Chairman - Ruby Mills Ltd, Conwest Jain Clinic Group of Hospitals, Kikabhai Premchand Trust Settlement No. XI, Damji Laxmichand Jain Dharmada Sthanak

Somchand Devchand Shah [1932-2002]

Philanthropist, an eminent member of the Oshwal Community in Kenya and Coordinator of the Institute of Jainology

Dr Nigel Allan	London
Pratap Bhogilal	Mumbai
Prof Dr Madame Colette Caillat	Paris
Kapoorchand Chandaria	Mumbai
Keshavlal Chandaria (Ord. of Ont.)	Toronto
Dr Manu Chandaria OBE	Nairobi
Nyal Chandaria	London
Chinilal Harakhchand Chajjed	Chennai
S. Padamchand Sureshkumar Chajjed	Chennai
Kirit C. Daftary Texas	USA
Sharayu Daftary	Mumbai
Rameshchandra N. Damani	Chennai
Dr Marilyn Deegan	London
Vilas & Rati Dhanani	London
Harshad Doshi	Kolkata
N.J. Doshi	Singapore
Dr Sarayu Doshi	Mumbai
Kailashmull Dugar	Chennai
Dr Gillian Evison	Oxford
Dharmendra Kumar Gandhi	Mumbai
Dr S.L. Gandhi	Jaipur
Amratlal Golawala	Mumbai
Chimanlal Gosalia	Mumbai
Dr John Guy	London
Indu Jain	New Delhi
Dr M.P. Jain	New Delhi
Dr N.P. Jain	Indore
N. Sugalchand Jain	Chennai
Pradip Jain	Mumbai
Rajkumar Jain	New Delhi
Sanjay Jain	Delhi
Chamanlal Kamani	Nairobi
Rekha H. Kapadia	Mumbai
Sharad & Subhash Khara	Kolkata
Kamalkumar Kothari	Jaipur
Shivubhai Lathia	Mumbai
Rajendra Lodha	Kolkata
Jeetendra B. Mehta	London
Kirtilal C. Mehta	Mumbai
Dr Mahendra Mehta	Toronto
Paresh Mehta	London

Shardaben U.N. Mehta	Ahmedabad
Anil Mutha	Mumbai
Prakash Patalia	London
Vipul M. Rupani	Mumbai
Dr Tansukh Salgia	Cleveland
C.N. Sanghvi	Mumbai
Kishore Sanghvi	Mumbai
Nirmal Sethia	London
Anant M.P. Shah	London
Bharat Shah F.C.C.A.	London
Chandramani Gulabchand Virpar Shah	London
Hiralal Chandulal Shah	Mumbai
Khetshi Nathoobhai Shah Family	London
Mahendra H.N. Shah	London
Maniben M.P. Shah	London
Mansukhlal Z. Shah	London
Dr Manubhai M. Shah	London
Pankaj Nathalal Shah	London
Rajnikant Lakhamshi Shah	London
Rohit & Bhavna Shah	Mumbai
Vijay Shantilal Shah	Antwerp
M. Shantilal	Chennai
Chandulal G. Sheth	London
Manubhai Sheth	Bhavnagar
Dr Deborah Swallow	London
Manmohan Tamboli	Bhavnagar
Vinodrai Udani	London
Hasmukh & Satish Vora	London

Institute Of Jainology Coordination Team

Nemu Chandaria, OBE
Dr Kumarpal Desai, Padmashri
Pragna Desai
Jayant U. Doshi
Mahesh Khetshi Gosrani
Arti Jain
Kalpesh Joshi
Dr Vinod Kapashi
Bipin Mehta
Jaysukh Shantilal Mehta
H.C. Parekh
Dr Harshad Nandlal Sanghrajka
Dr Mehool Harshad Sanghrajka
Kantilal Devraj Shah
Ramniklal Jivraj Shah
Ratilal Devchand Shah
Usha Hasmukh Shah

Foreword

Pujya Muniraj Shri Jambuvijayaji Maharaj

It gives me great pleasure to offer this foreword for the Catalogue of Jain Manuscripts being published by the Institute of Jainology, jointly with The British Library. It is commendable to note that the Institute is dedicated to the noble cause of raising awareness of Jainism worldwide through the channels of Art, Culture and Education.

The British Library and other institutions hold rich collections of Jain manuscripts that are well preserved. However, this was not generally known and, despite some existing lists and catalogues, there was no analytical record of the full contents.

Whilst the institutions took great care to preserve the manuscripts it was not possible for such information to be collected and published owing to the scarcity of Jain scholars interested in such a work.

The Catalogue being published contains information from 1,083 manuscripts contained in 1,425 entries and is an exceptionally inspiring and joyous event. The manuscripts are from the collections of The British Library, the Victoria and Albert Museum and The British Museum

In this day and age, even in India, the work of researching and cataloguing manuscripts is extremely difficult and rarely undertaken. It is therefore all the more to be appreciated that such arduous work is undertaken in foreign countries.

When the collections came to light, Jain scholars had to be employed from India to travel to Britain where they undertook in-depth research of each manuscript and generated catalogue entries.

The Institute of Jainology made all arrangements for the scholars to live, travel and work in comfort. For accepting this challenge and publishing this catalogue, the Trustees of the Institute and all those involved as workers, supporters and well-wishers deserve the heartiest congratulations.

Catalogues of manuscripts are of the utmost significance because even with the availability of a printed publication, the importance of the original material never diminishes. Important scriptures have been printed and published with many inaccuracies and such defects can only be verified by comparison with the original palm-leaf or paper manuscript.

As books get re-published, such inaccuracies continue to be propagated in new generations and over a period of time the accurate rendering of the text disappears. Therefore this Catalogue will be indispensable for the scholar.

The publication of this Catalogue brings to light the rich collection of Jain manuscripts that exists in Britain. Such collections contain rare and important texts of Jainism and this catalogue will offer a wealth of scriptural knowledge.

On the occasion of Jñāna Pañcami [a day for respecting knowledge] ritual worship of scriptural texts, with pomp and procession at considerable expense, is undertaken by many organizations across the Country. Whilst it has its own importance the first essential is to bring out the knowledge contained in the texts.

About 25 years ago Prof. Chandrabhal Tripathi met me when he was working in Germany on the catalogue of the Jain manuscripts kept in Strasbourg (France). He started the project at the British Library in 1993, but unfortunately he passed away before the work could be completed. Prof. Nalini Balbir, a scholar of Sanskrit and Jainism at the University of Paris, took over the task assisted by the scholar-couple, Dr. Kanubhai and Dr. Kalpanaben Sheth, from Ahmedabad, India. Together they completed the work in the excellent form which is in your hands now.

The importance of this work is confirmed by the fact that the British organizations have preserved their collection so well and the British Government has offered a grant to digitise selected manuscripts for wider dissemination of their contents.

On this occasion, it is inspiring to review the status of such collections in India.

The genealogical team of Pujya Kantivijayaji Maharaj, Pujya Chaturvijayaji Maharaj and Pujya Punyavijayji Maharaj sorted out the collection in Patan, India, and organized it. Pujya Punyavijayji, known as Āgamprabhākar (the rising sun of scriptural knowledge) organized the collections at Jaisalmer in

Rajasthan and many other locations. The existence of invaluable texts came to light as a result of his work. It is likely that there exist collections of Jain manuscripts in the cities and villages of Rajasthan, Gujarat and other states of India; projects should be undertaken to catalogue these. Unless attended to in time, this ancestral heritage will disappear.

The Institute of Jainology is working to expand and extend this project to many other collections in Britain. I recommend that Jain Institutions in India and abroad should co-operate with the Institute of Jainology to extend their magnificent work to other countries of the world.

I offer my blessings and sincere best wishes for the success of the efforts being made by the Institute of Jainology in India and in Britain.

Jaina Muni Jambuvijaya

Khambhat, 3rd December, 2005. [Pujya Jambuvijayaji Maharaj]

Chairman's Foreword

Jainism is a living, thriving and evolving religion, with a considerable community established in the UK as witnessed by temples in London and Leicester. Its influence in the modern world has spread out of all proportion to the number of its followers, through Rajachandra to Mahatma Gandhi and Martin Luther King. Its lessons of *satyagraha* - adherence to truth - and *ahimsa* – non-violence – have become ever more relevant in a world where man's inhumanity to man confronts us daily.

The British Library is proud to hold one of the most important collections of Jain manuscripts in the West and delighted to publish this magnificent catalogue. It embodies over twelve years of research by four of the leading scholars in the field. It is first and foremost a tribute to Professor Candrabhal Tripathi, who started work on the catalogue in 1994 and had made several visits to the Library compiling entries and checking readings before his untimely death in 1996. The Library was fortunate indeed that one of Professor Tripathi's most gifted collaborators, Professor Nalini Balbir, was able to complete the task, ably assisted by Dr Kanubai Sheth and his wife Dr Kalpana Sheth from Ahmedabad.

The compilation and publication of this catalogue would not have been possible without the tremendous support and generosity of the Institute of Jainology. The Library is particularly grateful that the UK Jain community made it possible for the Drs Sheth to make several long visits to the Library to supplement Professor Tripathi's work. We must also express our particular thanks to Mr Nemu Chandaria for his steadfast encouragement and dedication to this project.

It is hoped that this catalogue will bring to a far wider public the treasures of a great religious legacy and stimulate greater study of them both from within the Jain community itself and beyond.

John Eatwell

Chairman

The British Library Board

Authors' Acknowledgements

The present publication would not have been possible without the financial and material support of the following institutions.

In 2003 part of the Hirayama Prize from the Académie des Inscriptions et Belles-Lettres (Paris) was granted to Nalini Balbir for this project. The research group 'Langues, Textes, Histoire et Civilisation du Monde Indien' (Lacmi, University of Paris-3/CNRS) and, from 2005, the umr 7528 'Mondes iranien et indien', partly subsidised her trips to England and India.

In London and Ahmedabad, the Institute of Jainology deserves our heartiest thanks for the full and manifold commitment of its dynamic team to the project. Among many other things, they supported the work of Dr Kanhaiyalal V. Sheth and Dr Kalpana K. Sheth. Manish Modi of hindi Granth Karyalay Mumbai, was kind enough to see the book through the press.

The contribution of The British Library has been equally invaluable. We express our thanks to Mr Graham W. Shaw, Head of Asia/Pacific & Africa Collections. Mr Michael O'Keefe, Head of South Asia Collections, took personal interest in the project. The staff's competence, kindness, cheerfulness and eagerness to help were a constant encouragement. Mr Vince Harrison, Mrs Dipali Ghosh and Mrs Nalini Persad have to be mentioned. They were our main interlocutors during the time we worked in the private carrels or the so pleasant and well organized reading room of the Oriental and India Office Collections (now APAC).

The map was prepared by Mrs Kimberly Kowal, Curator of Digital Mapping. The International Dunhuang Project, directed by Dr Susan Whitfield, kindly agreed to prepare digital images of Jain manuscripts. The work was done with great care by Mr Jonathan Jackson. Mr Burkhard Quessel, Curator, Tibetan Collections, generously offered his help and time to prepare the final copy.

At the Victoria and Albert Museum we express our thanks to the staff of the South Asian Department: Dr Deborah Swallow, Dr John Guy and Dr Nicholas Barnard, Curator. Dr Barnard, especially, always found time to organize our visits to the Museum and to allow us to examine the Jain material. At the British Museum, we express our thanks to Dr Michael Willis, Curator of the Ancient Indian and Himalayan Collections, Department of Asia. Members of these two institutions made our access to their collections very easy.

Authors' preface

The publication of a catalogue of manuscripts such as this is the culmination of an adventure that involves several persons, from the collectors to the curators to the author(s). In the present case, the adventure became a joint venture.

The idea of preparing a catalogue of the Jain manuscripts at the British Library came jointly from the Institute of Jainology represented by its dynamic Deputy Chairman of the Board of Trustees, Mr Nemubhai Chandaria OBE, and from Candrabhāl Bh. Tripāṭhī who had just retired from the post he had occupied for many years as a Professor of Indology at the Free University of Berlin (Germany). This project, which brought together two natives of Gujarat, started in 1994. No better person than Professor Tripāṭhī could be found to achieve this work: since his years as a student in Göttingen in the 1950s under the supervision of the pioneer German scholar Ernst Waldschmidt (1897-1985) who was so closely associated with the study of the Sanskrit manuscripts discovered in Central Asia, followed by a few years at the University of Köln where he was in charge of cataloguing Sanskrit manuscripts in Germany, C.B. Tripāṭhī had acquired an unequalled experience in the field of codicology. This culminated in the magisterial publication of the *Catalogue of the Jaina Manuscripts at Strasbourg* (Leiden: Brill, Indologia Berolinensis, 1975) his DLitt. thesis.

From 1994 up to the end of 1995, Professor Tripāṭhī enthusiastically embarked on the project, staying in Greater London at his relatives' house three or four times a year, and spending from morning to evening at the British Library (which was not yet located in its splendid new premises), taking notes on the manuscripts on his laptop and actively continuing the work once he was back in Berlin. I had been lucky enough to work with Professor Tripāṭhī, both in Paris and in Berlin, since 1980. The last time I met him was in January 1996 when I was in Berlin for a few days. A heart patient, he had been ill earlier, but this time round he really felt that his days were numbered. It was all the sadder as he was about to settle in a new flat to live near one of his daughters Maya after bearing a lot of difficulties over the last few years. He was extremely keen on finishing the catalogue he had started work on with such energy and dedication. But he somehow knew it would remain an unfulfilled dream and made me promise that I would do everything possible to complete the work. Even though I did not wish to believe that his feelings would come true so soon, my promise was given with due consideration. In the month of February he was hospitalized. When, on my return from India, on 4 March, I wanted to talk with him on the phone, I learnt from his daughter that he was in a critical state, and, a few hours later, that he was no more.

As had been decided much earlier with Professor Tripāṭhī, I could have as many books from his library as I wished, part of the rest was to be kept in the Indological Institute of the Free University (Berlin) and another part sent to the Institute of Jainology (London). Following the promise I had made, I also took with me all the disks and notes that were relevant to the catalogue. This was to form the basis of the present work. For about two years after Professor Tripāṭhī's unfortunate and untimely death, the project remained at a standstill. One of the main difficulties impeding the completion of the work was that Prof. Tripāṭhī had not had sufficient time to take notes on all the manuscripts which were to be included, and that I, as a professor in Paris, could not spare enough time to work for long consecutive periods at the British Library and other London institutions. The Institute of Jainology, through its Deputy Chairman, Mr Nemu Chandaria, then considered employing a scholar from India to collaborate in the work. The search for a competent scholar was not so easy, until the bright idea to call to London Dr Kanubhai Sheth, a Senior officer who had been the head of the Department of Manuscripts in the L.D. Institute of Indology in Ahmedabad for many years, who was now retired and willing to do the work. There could be no better choice, for it brought together an extremely coherent team of persons who already knew each other for more than 15 years and were happy to work together. Thus, in summer 1999, Dr Kanubhai Sheth and his wife, Dr Kalpana K. Sheth, who had also had a good training in Sanskrit and Prakrit under the guidance of Professor H.C. Bhayani and had in the meantime completed her PhD, came for the first time to London and worked energetically at the British Library for several months. This was made possible thanks to the good offices of the Institute of Jainology, in London as well as in Ahmedabad where Dr Kumarpal Desai is in charge. The Sheths again stayed in London in 2000 and 2001.

This is how the present Catalogue, which was started by one author, finally ended with four.

In the course of time, the scope of the Catalogue and the number of entries to be included increased, for it was decided to describe not only the Jain manuscripts belonging to the British Library as such (the so-called Oriental Collections), but also those belonging to the India Office Library. This seemed justified considering the fact that both institutions are now rejoined in the British Library in its new premises at St Pancras. Although some of the manuscripts had already been included in earlier catalogues, it was agreed to catalogue these anew so as to present a comprehensive record of the London collections, based on the standards and the guidelines adopted in C.B. Tripāṭhī's *Catalogue of the Jaina Manuscripts at Strasbourg*, which has been our (unattainable) ideal.

Due to various unavoidable commitments in Paris, the completion of the present book has been delayed more than had been expected and wished by all parties. Thus we should first express our thanks to the Institute of Jainology, and its impatient Deputy Chairman, Mr Nemu Chandaria, for his patience. Although he was quite understandably worried and unsatisfied by promises that the end was approaching, especially when he had to face the Trustees of the Institute, he finally accepted our arguments and tried to keep his faith in the project and its contributors alive in spite of the delays. The same holds true for the authorities of the British Library, and especially for Michael O'Keefe, who was our direct contact there. He tried to accept that the work was progressing and to believe that it would be finished one day. The constant help offered by these two institutions has been acknowledged above.

We all wish to express our sincere thanks to the following Indian institutions and to their directors: Dr Balaji, Director of Mahavir Jain Aradhana Kendra, Koba, to the L.D. Institute of Indology, Ahmedabad, where Dr K.V. Sheth worked for so long, and where Nalini Balbir had been warmly welcomed for the last twenty-five years. Various persons in charge at different levels in this Institute should be mentioned in this context: the late Mr U. Kapadia, Dr J.B. Shah, the present Director, Professor N.M. Kansara, as well as Mr K. Wankad, the Librarian. Conversations with Pandit Rupendra Kumar Pagaria on one work or the other of the collection were always rewarding and stimulating. Several Jain monks and nuns with whom we had the opportunity of discussing in various Upashrays deserve a special word of gratitude: Acharya Shri Shilachandravijayaji Maharaj, Acharyashri Padmasagar and Muni Ajayasagar are among them. It also goes without saying that the memory of late Pandit D.D. Malvania (1910-2000) and late Professor H.C. Bhayani (1917-2000) will always be kept alive by all the authors of this Catalogue who benefitted from their immense knowledge, kindness and generosity. The work of Professor K. Bruhn (Berlin) and Professor P.S. Jaini (Berkeley) was a constant source of inspiration.

Each one of us would also like to express gratitude to institutions and individuals who provided help in various ways. Dr Kanubhai V. Sheth and Dr Kalpana K. Sheth are thankful to the B.J. Institute of Learning which gave them free access to its Library. Nalini Balbir is thankful to the librarians (Institut d'Études Indiennes du Collège de France and Société Asiatique) who did their best to grant access to their collections.

Several institutions and people also helped us in particular cases, by communicating valuable material. Their help is acknowledged in the pages of the present Catalogue. However, we would like to mention Dr Ch. Werba (University of Vienna, Austria) and Dr U. Podzeit, Curator of the Library for South Asian, Tibetan and Buddhist Studies of the same university who provided us with useful material, Professor S.R. Sarma (University of Aligarh) who was consulted on a mathematical manuscript of the collection, and Dr Fausto Freschi (Udine) who put at our disposal the temporary catalogue of manuscripts belonging to the collection of L.P. Tessitori, and provided photocopies of rare publications from Italy. Prof Dr. A. Wezler (University of Hamburg) was kind enough to send the original notebooks of Ernst Leumann which were useful to our work. Although the Jain manuscripts of the Wellcome Trust will be the object of a separate publication and are in the course of being researched, we would not like to postpone our thanks to Dr Nigel Allan, former Curator of Oriental MSS & Printed Books at the Wellcome Library.

We are thankful to those who have shown a friendly interest in our long labour, Dr Jean-Pierre Osier, Professor Dr Georges-Jean Pinault (École Pratique des Hautes Études, Paris).

A few persons encouraged us or inspired us by their presence and experience. Professor Dr Mrs Colette Caillat (Académie des Inscriptions et Belles-Lettres) and Dr Peter Skilling (Fragile Palm Leaves, Bangkok) are the foremost among them.

N.B.

4 March 2006.

Bibliography

Previous lists or catalogues of the British Library Jain manuscripts

Bendall C., *Catalogue of the Sanskrit Manuscripts in the British Museum*, London, 1902

Blumhardt J.F., *Catalogue of the Marathi, Gujarati, Bengali, Assamese, Oriya, Pushtu and Sindhi Manuscripts in the Library of the British Museum*, London, 1905 [Nos. 1-36, pp. 1-19; No. 56, pp. 34-36; = Blumhardt (BM)]

Blumhardt J.F., *Catalogue of the Hindi, Panjabi and Hindustani Manuscripts in the Library of the British Museum* (Part 1-2), London, 1899 [Nos. 2-7, pp. 1-5; BMH]

Blumhardt J.F., *Catalogue of the Gujarati and Rajasthani Manuscripts in the India Office Library.* Revised and enlarged by Alfred Master, Oxford: Oxford University Press, 1954 [= Blumhardt]

Brough J., *Draft Catalogue of Sanskrit and Prakrit Manuscripts in the British Museum*, [1947; not published; incomplete]

Bühler G., 'Two Lists of Sanskrit MSS. together with some remarks on my connexion with the Search for Sanskrit MSS.', *Zeitschrift der Deutschen Morgenländischen Gesellschaft* 42 (1888), pp. 530-559

Department of Oriental Manuscripts and Printed Books. Select manuscript acquisitions January 1970 to June 1973. This covers the more important acquisitions since the last list published in the *British Museum Quarterly,* xxxvi (1972), pp. 59-60: *British Library Journal* 1,1 (1975), pp. 99-104 — Recent Acquisitions. Department of Oriental Manuscripts and Printed Books [Manuscript Acquisitions, 1974]: *British Library Journal* 5,1 (1979), pp. 76-79 — Recent Acquisitions ... Manuscript Acquisitions, 1975: *British Library Journal* 6,1 (1980), pp. 77-85 — Recent Acquisitions ... Manuscript Acquisitions, 1976: *British Library Journal* 9,1 (1983), pp. 76-81

Ghosh D., *A Handlist of Hindi MSS. in the Oriental Collections after Blumhardt's Catalogue of 1899.* Compiled by. (B.L.: ORC HIN MSS 2)

Jacobi H., 'Liste der Indischen Handschriften in Besitze des Prof. H. Jacobi', *Zeitschrift der Deutschen Morgenländischen Gesellschaft* 33 (1879), pp. 693-697 [The collection also contained manuscripts of general Sanskrit Literature copied by Jaina scribes, now numbered Or. 5195-5254, which are described by C. Bendall in *Catalogue of Sanskrit Manuscripts in the British Museum,* 1902]

Keith A.B., *Catalogue of the Sanskrit [and Prakrit] Manuscripts in the Library of the India Office.* Vol. 2 *Brahmanical and Jaina Manuscripts.* In two parts, London, 1887-1935 [= I.O. Cat.]

Leumann E., 'Liste von transcribirten Abschriften und Auszügen aus der Jaina-Literatur', *Zeitschrift der Deutschen Morgenländischen Gesellschaft* 47 (1893), pp. 308-315

Losty J.P., *A Catalogue of Sanskrit and Prakrit Manuscripts in the British Museum,* Vol. II, V+70 pages, typescript (B.L.: ORC SAN MSS 2)

Losty J.P., 'Some Illustrated Jain Manuscripts', *British Library Journal* 1,2 (1975), pp. 145-162

Marrison G.E. (Assistant Keeper), *Department of Oriental Printed Books and Manuscripts, British Museum. Jain Manuscripts.* Temporary List [3rd June 1969], 9 pages, typescript (B.L.: ORC SAN MSS 3)

Other catalogues of manuscripts, lists, praśastis

Ahmedabad = *Catalogue of Sanskrit and Prakrit Manuscripts in the L.D. Institute of Indology, Ahmedabad,* Ahmedabad: Volumes 1-4, 1963-68 (L.D. Series 2, 5, 15, 20) by Muni Punyavijaya — Volumes 5 and 6, 2003 (L.D. Series 137, 138), General editor J.B. Shah

Ahmedabad, Guj. = *Catalogue of Gujarati Manuscripts* compiled by Muni Puṇyavijaya, edited by V. Vora, Ahmedabad: L.D. Institute of Indology 1978 (L.D. Series 71)

Berlin: see Schubring and Weber

Bhandarkar R.G., *Report* .... 1879-80, 1881-82, 1882-83, 1883-84, 1884-87, 1887-91 [see Janert, *Annotated Bibliography* Nos. 272-273 for details]

Bharatiya Vidya Bhavan = *Descriptive Catalogue of Manuscripts in Bharatiya Vidya Bhavan's Library*, Bombay, 400007. Compiled by M.R. Warnekar, Bombay, 1985. [Seen only by K.V. Sheth and K.K. Sheth].

B.J. Institute Museum = *A Descriptive Catalogue of Sanskrit and Prakrit Manuscripts of B.J. Institute Museum* by Bharati K. Shelat, Vibhuti V. Bhatt. B.J. Institute of Learning and Research, Ahmedabad, 1986 [Seen only by K.V. Sheth and K.K. Sheth]

Bombay = H.D. Velankar, *A Descriptive Catalogue of Saṁskṛta and Prākṛta Manuscripts in the Library of the Bombay Branch of the Royal Asiatic Society,* Parts 1-4, Bombay, 1925-30. Second ed. by V.M. Kulkarni and Devangana Desai. Bombay, 1998 (one volume containing the original three volumes: 1. Technical Literature, 1926; 2. Hindu Literature, 1928; 3. Jain and Vernacular Literature, 1930; with an important number of colour or black and white illustrations)

Calcutta: see Mitra

Cambay: see Punyavijaya

Cambridge University Library: preliminary list in Bendall C., *A Journey of Literary and Archaeological Research in Nepal and Northern India during the Winter of 1884-5,* Cambridge University Press, 1886

Catalogus Catalogorum. An Alphabetical Register of Sanskrit Works and Authors. By Th. Aufrecht. Parts 1-3, Leipzig, 1891-1903

Dalal C.D., *A Catalogue of Manuscripts in the Jain Bhandars at Jesalmere,* Baroda, 1923 (Gaekwad's Oriental Series 21)

Dalal C.D., *A descriptive Catalogue of Manuscripts in the Jain Bhandars at Pattan.* Compiled from the notes of the late C.D. Dalal with introduction, indices and appendices by L.Bh. Gandhi. Baroda: Oriental Institute. Vol. 1: Palm-leaf Mss., 1937 (Gaekwad's Oriental Series 76)

Delhi Jina Grantha Ratnāvalī (Catalogue of Sanskrit, Prakrit & Apabhraṁsa Manuscripts of Digambara Jain Saraswati Bhandar, Naya Mandir, Dharmapura, Delhi) by Kundan Lal Jain, Delhi: Bharatiya Jnanpith Publication, 1981 (Jnanpith Murtidevi Jain Granthamala: English No. 9)

Florence = P.E. Pavolini, 'I manoscritti Indiani della Biblioteca Nazionale Centrale di Firenze' (non compresi nel Catalogo dell'Aufrecht): *Giornale della Società Asiatica Italiana* 20 (1907), pp. 63-157

Friedlander = *A Descriptive Catalogue of the Hindi Manuscripts in the Library of the Wellcome Institute for the History of Medicine* by Peter Friedlander, London: The Wellcome Institute for the History of Medicine, 1996

Jaina Siddhant Bhawana Granthavali. Catalogue of Sanskrit, Prakrit, Apabhramsha & Hindi Manuscripts of Sri Devakumar Jain Oriental Library, Arrah. Introduction by Dr. Gokulchandra Jain. Editor: Rishabhacandra Jain, Arrah: Sri Jaina Siddhant Bhawan Publication, 1987, 2 vols.

Jambuvijaya Muni (ed.), *A Catalogue of Manuscripts in Jaisalmer Jain Bhandaras / Jaisalmer ke Prācīn Jain Granthabhaṇḍāroṁ kī sūcī,* Delhi, 2000

Janert K.L., *An Annotated Bibliography of the Catalogues of Indian Manuscripts,* Part 1. Wiesbaden: F. Steiner, 1965 [An indispensable guide]

JGK = M.D. Desai, *Jaina Gūrjar Kavio.* Descriptive catalogue of Jain poets and their works in Gujarati Language. Edition used: revised by Jayant Kothari, Bombay, Shri Mahavir Jain Vidyalay. Vol. 1

[V.S. 12th to 16th century], 1986; vol. 2 [17th century, Part I], 1987; vol. 3 [17th century, Part II], 1987; vol. 4 [18th century, Part I], 1988; vol. 5 [18th century, Part II], 1988; vol. 6 [V.S. 19th & 20th centuries together with a list of works by non-Jaina poets found in Jain bhandaras], 1989; vol. 7 [Alphabetical indexes of the names of authors, works, persons, casts & lineages, places etc. and chronological index of works mentioned in Vol. I to VI], 1991; vol. 8 [Alphabetical list of Deshis - verse-lines of popular songs cited as exemplars in Medieval Gujarati Jain poems and a dictionary of the names of personages of Jain tales, 1997]; vol. 9 [Succession list of Heads (Acharyas) of various sections of Jain Sect and dynasties of Gujarat], 1997 [Reference to the volume and page]

Jinavijaya Muni, *Jaina Pustaka Praśasti Saṁgraha.* Part I, Bombay, 1943 (Singhi Jain Series 1). [Śvetāmbara material]

Jinavijaya Muni, *A Catalogue of Sanskrit and Prakrit Manuscripts in the Rajasthan Oriental Research Institute, Jodhpur,* Jodhpur: Rajasthan Oriental Research Institute, 1963-

Johrapurkar V.S., *Bhaṭṭāraka Saṁpradāya* [In Hindi]. Sholapur, 1958 (Jīvarāj Jaina Granthamālā 8). [Very important repertory of praśastis and scribal remarks in Digambar manuscripts providing a lot of precious information on the Digambara tradition, especially of Northern, Western and Central India]

Karnatak = Pt. K. Bhujabali Śāstrī, *Kannaḍa-prāntīya tāḍapatrīya granthasūcī,* Kāśī, 1948 (Mūrtidevī Series, Sanskrit 2)

Kasliwal K.C., *Praśasti-saṁgraha*, Jaipur, 1950 [Digambara material]

Kielhorn F., [Lists and Reports] 1869-70, 1877-78, 1879-80, 1880-81, 1881-82 [see Janert, *Annotated Bibliography* Nos. 270, 271 and 273 for details]

Koba = *Kailāsa Śrutasāgara Granthasūcī. Descriptive Catalogue of Jain Manuscripts / Descriptive Catalogue of Manuscripts Preserved in Devarddhigaṇi Kṣamāśramaṇa Hastaprata Bhāṇḍāgāra, Acharya Shri Kailasagarsuri Gyanmandir* under the auspices of Shri Mahavir Jain Aradhana Kendra, Koba Tirth. Section - I. Manuscripts' Catalogue, Class - I. Jain Literature. Shri Mahavir Jain Aradhana Kendra, Koba Tirth, Gandhinagar: Vol. 1, 2003; vol. 2, 2004; vol. 3 [includes index of titles], 2004

Mitra R., *Notices of Sanskrit MSS.* [deposited in the Library of the Asiatic Society of Bengal, Calcutta, or in other collections], vols 1-11, 1871-1895

Mukhtar J., *Jaina Grantha Praśasti Saṁgraha,* Part 1, Sarasava, 1954. [Digambara material]

NCC = *New Catalogus Catalogorum*, ed. R. Raghavan et alii, Madras, 1949-

Oxford: A.B. Keith, *Catalogue of Prākrit Manuscripts in the Bodleian Library* with a Preface by E.W.B. Nicholson, Oxford, 1911 — A.B. Keith, A Catalogue of the Sanskrit and Prākrit MSS. in the Indian Institute Library, Oxford, Oxford, 1903

Paris = J. Filliozat, État des manuscrits de la collection Émile Senart: J*ournal Asiatique* (1936), pp. 127-143

Patan: see Dalal for palm-leaf manuscripts; *Catalogue of the Manuscripts of Pāṭaṇa Jain Bhaṇḍāra,* Part: I, II (Detailed catalogue of 20035 paper Mss. preserved in the Hemacandrācārya Jain Jñānamandir at Pāṭaṇa (N. Gujarat). Compiler: Late Muni Śri Puṇyavijayajī; Editor: Muni Jambuvijayajī, Assisted: Muni Dharmacandravijayajī; Part III (The Alphabetical index of all the 20035 paper Mss. preserved ... Pāṭaṇa: (Detailed Catalogue of 3206 paper Mss. preserved in the Bhābhāpāḍā Bhaṇḍāra at Patana ... with the Alphabetical index of all these Mss.), Ahmedabad: Sharadaben Chimanbhai Educational Research Centre, 1991

Peterson P., [Six Reports]: *Report of Operations in Search of Sanskrit Mss. in the Bombay Circle,* Deccan College, Bombay-London, 1883-1899 [see Janert, Annotated Bibliography No. 274 for details]

Pingree = Pingree D., Census of the Exact Sciences in Sanskrit. Series A. Vol. 1, Philadelphia, 1970; 2, 1971; 3, 1976; 4, 1981; 5, 1994

Pingree 2004 = *Catalogue of Jyotiṣa Manuscripts in the Wellcome Library. Sanskrit Astral and Mathematical Literature,* Leiden, Boston: Brill, 2004 (Sir Henry Wellcome Asian Studies vol. 2)

Poleman = H.I. Poleman, *A Census of Indic Manuscripts in the U.S. and Canada,* New Haven, Conn., 1938 (American Oriental Series 12)

Praśastis: see Jinavijaya; Kasliwal; Mukhtar; Shah

Pune: BhORI = *Descriptive Catalogue of the Government Collections of Manuscripts deposited at the Bhandarkar Oriental Research Institute,* Poona, 1916-. [Volumes published are vol. 1, 2.1, 9.1, 9.2, 12, 13.1, 13.2, 13.3, 14, 16.1. The other volumes relate to *Jaina Literature and Philosophy* and are by H.R. Kapadia: 17.1a, 1935 [Āgamika literature] — 17.2a, 1936 [Āgamika literature (with palaeographical appendices)] — 17.3a, 1940 [Āgamika literature] — 17.4a-c, 1948 [Āgamika literature, Miscellaneous, Ritualistic works, Suppl.] — 17.5, 1954 [Āgamika literature, 10 Appendices + Indices to vols 1-4] — 18.1, 1952 [Logic, Metaphysics, etc.] — 19.1, 1957 [Hymnology, Śvetāmbara works] — 19.1.2, 1962 [Hymnology, Śvetāmbara & Digambara works along with Appendices I-X] — 19.2.1, 1967 [Narratives, Śvetāmbara works] — 19.2.2, 1977 [Narratives, Śvetāmbara works] — 19.2.3, 1987 [Narratives, Śvetāmbara works] — 19.2,4, 1988 [Narratives, Digambara]

Punyavijaya Muni, *Catalogue of Palm-leaf Mss. in the Śāntinātha Jaina Bhaṇḍāra.* Cambay, Baroda: Oriental Institute, vol. 1, 1961 (Gaekwad's Oriental Series 135), vol. 2, 1966 (GOS 149)

Rajasthan = K.C. Kasliwal, *Āmera śāstra bhaṇḍāra, Jayapura, kī grantha sūcī.* Jaipur, 1949; continuation in K.C. Kasliwal (and Anūpacanda Nyāyatīrtha), Rājasthāna ke jaina śāstra bhaṇḍāroṁ kī granthasūcī, Jaipur, Śrī Digambara Jain atiśaya ksetra śrīMahāvīrjī. Vol. 2, 1954; vol. 3, 1957; vol. 4, 1962; vol. 5, 1972

Schubring = W. Schubring, *Die Jaina-Handschriften der Preussischen Staatsbibliothek.* Neuerwerbungen seit 1891. Unter der redaktionellen Mitarbeit von Günther Weibgen, Leipzig: Harrassowitz, 1944

Shah A.M., *Praśastisaṁgraha,* Ahmedabad, 1937 [Śvetāmbara material]

Strasbourg = C.B. Tripāṭhī, *Catalogue of the Jaina Manuscripts at Strasbourg,* Leiden: Brill (Indologia Berolinensis 4), 1975

Tod = L.D. Barnett, 'Catalogue of the Tod Collection of Indian Manuscripts in the Possession of the Royal Asiatic Society', *Journal of the Royal Asiatic Society* (1940), Part II, April, pp. 129-178

Udine = 'Fondo Tessitori', Vincenzo Joppi Civic Library [Preliminary list; full catalogue in project by Nalini Balbir, publication planned by the Società Indologica Luigi Pio Tessitori; the collection is fully digitised and available on twelve CDs]

Velankar = H.D. Velankar, *Jinaratnakośa.* An Alphabetical Register of Jain Works and Authors. Vol. 1, Poona, Bhandarkar Oriental Research Institute, 1944 — See also Bombay

Vienna: Bühler = G. Bühler, 'Ueber eine kürzlich für die Wiener Universität erworbene Sammlung von Sanskrit- und Prakrit-Handschriften', *Sitzungsberichte der phil. hist. Klasse der Akademie der Wissenschaften in Wien* 99 (1892), pp. 563-579 [About 75 Jain manuscripts. Minimal information about each one: title - author - number of fols. - date if any. Identification often vague in the case of commentaries: 'mit Commentar'- no extract of text; hence '?' in the heading 'References' of our Catalogue for uncertain cases]

Vienna: Podzeit = U. Podzeit, *Die Handschriften an der Universitätsbibliothek Wien.* Zusammengestellt und mit Indizes und Appendizes versehen, Wien, 1988 [A few Jain manuscripts collected by E. Hultzsch und A. Führer. Precise material description but extracts not always sufficient for identification. A concordance for Bühler's collection is appended (p. 192), but the collection is not described]

Weber = A. Weber, *Verzeichniss der Sanskrit- / Sanskrit- und Prākṛt-Handschriften der Königlichen Bibliothek zu Berlin.* Berlin. Vol. 2,1, 1886; 2,2, 1888; 2,3, 1892

Wellcome Institute: Allan N. (ed.), *Pearls of the Orient, Asian Treasures from the Wellcome Library,* London: The Wellcome Trust, 2003 — See Friedlander

Other main sources (in alphabetical order)

(Publications such as editions and translations of individual texts are listed in the section 'References' of the present Catalogue under the relevant entry. They do not appear here).

Abhidhāna-Rājendra-Kośa, Vols 1-7, Ratlam, 1913-1934

Alphen J. van, *Steps to Liberation:* 2500 Years of Jain Art and Religion, Antwerp, 2000

Alsdorf L., *Kleine Schriften,* ed. A. Wezler, Wiesbaden, 1974

Arberry A.J., *The Library of the India Office*: a historical sketch, London, 1938

Balbir Nalini, 'Sur les traces de deux bibliothèques familiales jaina du Gujerat (XVe-XVIIe siècles', *Anamorphoses. Mélanges en l'honneur de Jacques Dumarçay.* Paris: Les Indes Savantes, 2006

Bhayani H.C. (ed.), *Madhyakālīn Gujarātī Kathākośa* (Treasury of Medieval Gujarati Tales and Narratives), Gandhinagar: Gujarat Sahitya Akademi, vol. 1, 1991; vol. 2 (with the collaboration of Kanubhai Sheth and Vasantaray Dave), 2000

Bühler G., *Indian Palaeography,* Calcutta, 1962 (English translation of Indische Palaeographie. Strassburg, 1896)

Caillat C. & Ravi Kumar, *Jain Cosmology*. English rendering by [K.]R. Norman, Delhi, 1981; new edition Ravi Kumar Publisher, Artemisia Ltd. Hong Kong, Bookwise (India), 2004

Coomaraswamy Ananda K., *Essays on Jaina Art.* Edited, with an Introduction by Richard J. Cohen, Indira Gandhi National Centre for the Arts, New Delhi - Manohar, 2003

Cort J.E., 'The Jain Knowledge Warehouses: Libraries in Traditional India', *Journal of the American Oriental Society* 115 (1995), pp. 77-87

Cort J.E., *Jains in the World: Ideology and Religious Values in India,* New York: Oxford University Press, 2001

Cort J.E., 'The Intellectual Formation of a Jain Monk: A Svetāmbara Monastic Curriculum', *Journal of Indian Philosophy* 29 (2001), pp. 327-349

Cort J.E., 'How Jains Know What They Know: A Lay Jain Curriculum', *Jambū-Jyoti* (Munivara Jambūvijaya Festschrift), ed. M.A. Dhaky, J.B. Shah, Ahmedabad, 2004, pp. 399-413

Darshanavijaya Muni, *Śrī Paṭṭāvalī-samuccaya,* Viramgam, 1933

Deo S.B., *History of Jaina Monachism,* Poona, 1956

Desai M.D., *Bhānucandra Caritra by his pupil Gaṇi Siddhicandra Upādhyāya.* Critically edited in the original Sanskrit from a single rare Ms. with elaborate introduction, summary, appendices etc. by M.D. Desai, Ahmedabad - Calcutta, 1931 (Singhi Jain Series 15) [important for Jain teachers of Akbar and Jahangir period]

Desai M.D.: see JGK (previous section) and below under Kothari

Doshi Saryu, *Masterpieces of Jain Painting,* Marg. Bombay, 1985

Dundas P., *The Jains.* Routledge, London & New York, 2002

Esdaile A., *The British Museum Library a short history and survey*, London, 1945

Flügel P., 'Protestantische und Post-Protestantische Jaina-Reformbewegungen. Zur Geschichte und Organisation der Sthānakavāsī I', *Berliner Indologische Studien* 13-14 (2000), pp. 37-103

Folkert K.W., *Scripture and Community. Collected Essays on the Jains.* Ed. J. Cort, Atlanta, 1993

Géhin P. (sous la direction de), *Lire le manuscrit médiéval. Observer et décrire,* Paris: Armand Colin, 2005

von Glasenapp H., *Der Jainismus,* Berlin, 1925 — English translation by S.D. Shrotri: Jainism: An Indian Religion of Salvation, Delhi: Motilal Banarsidass, 1999

von Glasenapp H., D*octrine of Karman in Jain Philosophy,* Varanasi: P.V. Research Institute Series 60, 1942 (second reprint edition, 1991)

Guérinot A.-A., *Essai de bibliographie jaina,* Paris, 1906

Guérinot A.-A., *Répertoire d'épigraphie jaina*, Paris, 1908

Harris P.R., *A History of the British Museum Library 1753-1973*, London: The British Library, 1998

Hoernle A.F.R., 'The Paṭṭāvalī or List of Pontiffs of the Upakeśa-Gachchha', *Indian Antiquary* 20 (1891), pp. 233-242.

Hoernle A.F.R., 'Two Pattavalis of the Sarasvati Gachchha of the Digambara Jains', *Indian Antiquary* 20 (October 1891), pp. 341-361

Hoernle A.F.R., 'Three further Pattavalis of the Digambaras', *Indian Antiquary* 21 (March 1892), pp. 57-84

Jacobi H., *Jaina Sūtras.* Oxford, 1895 (Sacred Books of the East, vol. 22 & 45)

Jain Jagdishcandra C., *History and Development of Prakrit Literature,* Delhi: Manohar, 2004

Jain Sagarmal & Kumar Vijay, *Sthānakvāsī Jain Paramparā kā Itihāsa,* Varanasi, 2003 (Parshvanath Vidyapith Granthamala 140)

Jain Uttam, *Jaina Sects and Schools,* Delhi, 1978

Jaina Sāhitya kā Bṛhad Itihāsa. Editors: D.D. Malvania & Mohan Lal Mehta. 7 vols, Varanasi, 1966-1981 (= JSBI)

Jainastotrasandohe (Prācīna-stotra-saṁgraha) prathamo bhāgaḥ, ed. Caturvijaya Muni, with English foreword by K.V. Abhyankar, Ahmedabad: Sarabhai Nawab, 1932 [rich collection of Jain hymns in Sanskrit and Prakrit, with introduction in Sanskrit and very useful sixty pages index of incipit of hymns published in various other collections]

Jaina Vrata-Tap [in Gujarati], ed. Padmashri Dr. Sarayu Vinod Doshi, Mumbai: Navabharat Sahitya Mandir, 2002

Jaini P.S., *The Jaina Path of Purification,* Delhi: Motilal Banarsidass, 1979; revised edition, 1998

Jaini P.S., *Collected Papers on Jaina Studies,* Delhi: Motilal Banarsidass, 2000

Jñānāñjali, pūjya muni śrī Punyavijayajī abhivādana grantha, Baroda, 1969 (Khaṇḍa I: 41 Gujarati articles; II: 13 Hindi and Sanskrit articles, III: abhivādana)

Kalyanavijayagani Pandit, *Śrī Paṭṭāvalī-parāga-saṁgraha*, Jalore, 1966

Kapadia H.R., *A History of the Canonical Literature of the Jainas,* Surat, 1941; reprinted Ahmedabad, 2000 (Shree Shwetambar Murtipujak Jain Boarding Series 17)

Kapadia H.R., 'Foliation of Jaina Mss. and Letter-Numerals', *Annals of the Bhandarkar Oriental Research Institute* 18,2 (1937), pp. 171-186

Kapadia H.R., 'The Jaina Manuscripts', *Journal of the University of Bombay* 7,2 (September 1938), pp. 2-30

Kapadia H.R., 'Outlines of Palaeography (with special reference to Jaina Palaeographical data and their evaluation)', *The Journal of the University of Bombay,* 6, 6 (May 1938), pp. 87-110

Kasliwal K.C., *Jaina Grantha Bhandars in Rajasthan*, Jaipur, 1967

Kelting M.W., *Singing to the Jinas: Jain Laywomen, Maṇḍal Singing and the Negotiations of Jain Devotion,* New York, 2001

Kirfel W., *Die Kosmographie der Inder: Nach Quellen dargestellt,* Bonn-Leipzig, 1920; reprint Hildesheim, 1967

Klatt J., *Specimen of a Literary-Bibliographical Jaina Onomasticon,* Leipzig, 1892

Klatt J., 'The Sāmāchāri-Śatakam of Samayasundara and Paṭṭāvalīs of the Anchala Gachchha and other Gachchhas', *Indian Antiquary* 23 (1894), pp. 169-183

Kochar Harivamsh, *Apabhraṁśa Sāhitya* [in Hindi], Delhi: Bhāratī Sāhitya Mandir [1956]

Kothari J. (ed.), *Prācīna Madhyakālīna Sāhityasaṁgraha* (Mohanlāl Dalīcand Deśāī sampādit laghukṛti saṁgraha), Ahmedabad, 2001 (L.D. Series 127)

Kothari J., *Madhyakālin Gujarātī Śabdakośa,* Ahmedabad, 1995

Leumann E., *Übersicht über die Āvaśyaka-Literatur,* Hamburg, 1934 — English translation by Dr G. Baumann, introduction by Nalini Balbir, Ahmedabad: L.D. Institute of Indology, 2006 (in the press)

Leumann E., *Kleine Schriften,* ed. Nalini Balbir, Stuttgart: F. Steiner, 1998

Leumann E.: see Plutat B.

Lienhard S., *A History of Classical Poetry, Sanskrit - Pali - Prakrit,* Wiesbaden: Otto Harrassowitz, 1984 (A History of Indian Literature edited by Jan Gonda, volume III fascicle 1)

Losty J.P., *The Art of the Book in India,* London: The British Library, 1982

Majumdar R.C. (ed.), *The History and Culture of the Indian People,* Bombay: Bharatiya Vidya Bhavan, vol. VI The Delhi Sultanate (1300-1526 A.D.), 2nd edition, 1967; vol. VII The Mughal Empire (1526-1707 A.D.)

Marrison G.E., 'The British Museum, the British Library and South Asian Studies', *South Asian Library Group Newsletter,* 41 (January 1994), pp. 3-9

Nawab S.M., *Jaina Paintings,* vols I-II, Ahmedabad, 1985

Norman Brown W., *A Descriptive and Illustrated Catalogue of Miniature Paintings of the Jaina Kalpasūtra as Executed in the Early Western Indian Style,* Washington, 1934

Malvania D.D., *Jainism: Some Essays,* Jaipur: Prakrit Bharati Academy, 1986

Meulenbeld G. J., *History of Indian Medical Literature,* Groningen: Egbert Forsten, 1999-2002

MHRA Style Guide. A handbook for authors, editors, and writers of theses, London: Modern Humanities Research Association, 2002

Oxford Dictionary of National Biography, Oxford University Press, 2004-2005

Pal P., *The Peaceful Liberators:* Jain Art from India, Los Angeles, 1994

'Pārśva', *Ancalagaccha Digdarśan,* Mumbai: Shri Mulunda Ancalagaccha Jain Samaj, 1968 [in Gujarati]

Paṭṭāvalī and history of the gacchas: see Darshanavijaya; Flügel; Guérinot; JGK vol. 9 (previous section); Hoernle; Jain Uttam; Jain and Kumar; Johrapurkar (previous section); Kalyanavijaya; Klatt; 'Pārśva'; Shivaprasad; Tripuṭi Mahārāj

Pingree D., Jyotiḥśāstra. *Astral and Mathematical Literature,* Wiesbaden: Otto Harrassowitz, 1981

Plutat B., *Catalogue of the Papers of Ernst Leumann in the Institute for the Culture and History of Indian and Tibet, University of Hamburg.* Compiled by, Stuttgart: Franz Steiner Verlag, 1998 (Alt- und Neu-Indische Studien herausgegeben vom Institut für Kultur und Geschichte Indiens und Tibets an der Universität Hamburg 49)

Prakrit Literature: see Jain J.C.

Punyavijaya Muni, *Jñānāñjali, pūjya muni śrī Puṇyavijayajī abhivādana granthamālā,* Baroda, 1969

Premi Nāthurām, *Jain sāhitya aur itihāsa,* Bombay, 1956

Sajjhāyādi saṁgraha, vols. 1-4, ed. Nagindas Kevaldas Shah Patadivala, Ahmedabad, V.S. 2047

Sandesara B.J., *Literary Circle of Mahāmātya Vastupāla,* Bombay, 1953 (Singhi Jain Series 33). [Important for information on authors from Gujarat belonging to the 12th-13th centuries]

Scharfe H., *Indian Grammatical Literature,* Wiesbaden: Otto Harrassowitz, 1977

Schubring W., *Die Lehre der Jainas. Nach den Quellen dargestellt,* Berlin, Leipzig, 1935 — English translation: The Doctrine of the Jainas, Delhi: Motilal Banarsidass, 2000 (2nd revised edition)

Schubring W., *Kleine Schriften,* ed. K. Bruhn, Wiesbaden, 1977

Shah Natubhai, *Jainism. The World of Conquerors,* 2 vols., Sussex Academy Press, 1998.

Shah U.P., *Treasures of Jaina Bhaṇḍāras,* Ahmedabad, 1978

Shivaprasad, *Tapāgacch kā itihās.* Vol. 1, part 1, Varanasi, 2000

Shivaprasad, *Acalgacch kā itihās,* Varanasi, 2001

Skærvø P.O., *Khotanese Manuscripts from Chinese Turkestan in the British Library. A Complete Catalogue with Texts and Translations,* London: The British Library, 2002 (Corpus Inscriptionum Iranicarum Part II, vol. V, Texts VI)

Sutton S.C., *A Guide to the India Office Library,* London, 1952

Tessitori, *Studi Giainici* (introduction by Nalini Balbir), Udine, 2000

Tripuṭī Mahārāj, *Jaina Paramparā no itihāsa.* 3 parts, Ahmedabad, 1952, 1960, 1964

Upadhye A.N., *Papers,* Mysore, 1983

Weber, A., 'Über die heiligen Schriften der Jainas', *Indische Studien* vol. 16, pp. 1-90; vol. 17, pp. 211-479

Wiles R., 'The Works of Kundakunda: An Annotated Listing of Editions, Translations and Studies', in *Vasantagauravam. Essays in Jainism.* Felicitating Professor M.D. Vasantha Raj of Mysore On the Occasion of his Seventy-fifth Birthday. Ed. by Jayandra Soni, Mumbai: Vakils Feffer and Simons, 2001, pp. *183-224*

Wiles R., *The "Śvetāmbara Canon". A descriptive listing of text editions, commentaries, studies and indexes.* Draft version, Canberra, Australia, April 1997

Wiley Kristi L., *Historical Dictionary of Jainism.* The Scarecrow Press, Inc. Lanham, Maryland, Toronto, Oxford, 2004

Williams R., Jaina Yoga. *A Survey of the Medieval Śrāvakācāras*, London, 1963; reprint: Delhi: Motilal Banarsidass, 1983

Winternitz M., *A History of Indian Literature,* vol. II Buddhist Literature and Jaina Literature, University of Calcutta, 1933 (other volumes are mentioned occasionally).

Abbreviations

A	obverse of a folio
Ap.	Apabhraṁśa
B	reverse of a folio
B.L.	British Library
BhORI	Bhandarkar Oriental Research Institute, Pune
Cat. No.	Serial Number of the entry in the present Catalogue
CE	Common Era
fol(s)	folio(s)
Guj.	Gujarati
H.	Hindi
I.O.	India Office
JGK	Jain Gūrjar Kavio, see Bibliography
ka°	Guj. kahatāṁ, kahetāṁ 'when saying ...' (quotation of the main text, the mūla, in a commentary)
L.D.I.	L.D. Institute of Indology, Ahmedabad
MEF	Modern European Foliation
ms(s).	manuscript(s)
No(s.)	number(s)
Or.	Oriental Collections
Pkt.	Prakrit
Skt.	Sanskrit
vs(s)	verse(s)
V.S.	Vikram Saṁvat (substract 56/57 to get the year in the Common Era)

Symbols

*	after a consonant refers to the use of the virāma (relatively rare in manuscripts)
≡, \\	separation or equivalence in the case of glosses
( )	indicates corrected or supplemented akṣaras in case of clear errors
< >	indicates clearly supefluous akṣaras in the manuscript
§O	the way to represent the 'bhale' sign, or auspicious symbol found at the beginning of several Jain manuscripts
☒	the way to represent the cha, a symbol found at the end of manuscripts
///	at the beginning or at the end of a text indicates that what precedes or what follows is lost
+	indicates a lost, damaged or illegible akṣara
x	indicates a lost, damaged or illegible digit
etc.	indicates the end of a quotation in a text that continues
...	indicates omitted passages
(?)	indicates an uncertain reading
☞	refers to a digital image available on the accompanying CD

Introduction

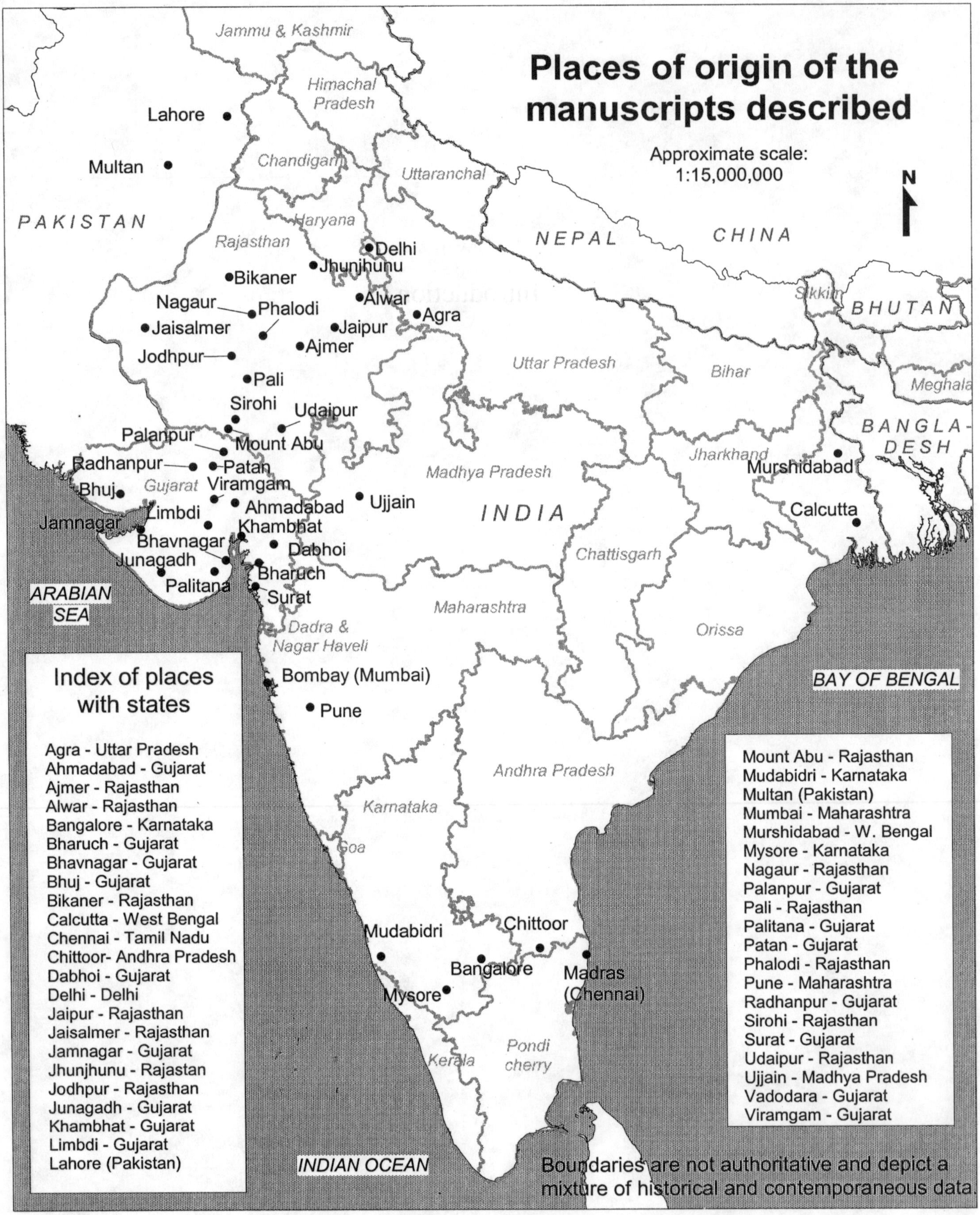

Places of origin of the manuscripts described
Approximate scale: 1:15,000,000
N
Jammu & Kashmir
Himachal Pradesh
Chandigarh
Uttaranchal
Haryana
Rajasthan
PAKISTAN
NEPAL
CHINA
Sikkim
BHUTAN
Meghala
Uttar Pradesh
Bihar
Jharkhand
BANGLA-DESH
Madhya Pradesh
INDIA
Chattisgarh
Maharashtra
Orissa
Gujarat
Dadra & Nagar Haveli
Goa
Karnataka
Andhra Pradesh
Kerala
Pondi cherry
ARABIAN SEA
BAY OF BENGAL
INDIAN OCEAN
Lahore
Multan
Delhi
Jhunjhunu
Bikaner
Alwar
Agra
Nagaur
Phalodi
Jaisalmer
Jaipur
Ajmer
Jodhpur
Pali
Sirohi
Udaipur
Palanpur
Mount Abu
Radhanpur
Patan
Bhuj
Viramgam
Limbdi
Ahmadabad
Ujjain
Jamnagar
Khambhat
Bhavnagar
Dabhoi
Junagadh
Bharuch
Palitana
Surat
Murshidabad
Calcutta
Bombay (Mumbai)
Pune
Mudabidri
Chittoor
Bangalore
Madras (Chennai)
Mysore
Index of places with states
Agra - Uttar Pradesh
Ahmadabad - Gujarat
Ajmer - Rajasthan
Alwar - Rajasthan
Bangalore - Karnataka
Bharuch - Gujarat
Bhavnagar - Gujarat
Bhuj - Gujarat
Bikaner - Rajasthan
Calcutta - West Bengal
Chennai - Tamil Nadu
Chittoor- Andhra Pradesh
Dabhoi - Gujarat
Delhi - Delhi
Jaipur - Rajasthan
Jaisalmer - Rajasthan
Jamnagar - Gujarat
Jhunjhunu - Rajastan
Jodhpur - Rajasthan
Junagadh - Gujarat
Khambhat - Gujarat
Limbdi - Gujarat
Lahore (Pakistan)
Mount Abu - Rajasthan
Mudabidri - Karnataka
Multan (Pakistan)
Mumbai - Maharashtra
Murshidabad - W. Bengal
Mysore - Karnataka
Nagaur - Rajasthan
Palanpur - Gujarat
Pali - Rajasthan
Palitana - Gujarat
Patan - Gujarat
Phalodi - Rajasthan
Pune - Maharashtra
Radhanpur - Gujarat
Sirohi - Rajasthan
Surat - Gujarat
Udaipur - Rajasthan
Ujjain - Madhya Pradesh
Vadodara - Gujarat
Viramgam - Gujarat
Boundaries are not authoritative and depict a mixture of historical and contemporaneous data.

Prolegomenon: On the term 'Jain Manuscript'

The concept of a 'Jain manuscript' for cataloguing purposes is open to several differing interpretations. Four alternative definitions of the term were proposed by H.R. Kapadia (1894-1979), whose name is familiar to anyone interested in codicology, especially in Jain manuscripts. For he is among the main ones to have paved the way by his outstanding articles (see Bibliography) and by his catalogues of the manuscript collections deposited at the Bhandarkar Oriental Research Institute (Pune). His definitions, which were cited by C.B. Tripāṭhī in the Catalogue of the Jaina Manuscripts at Strasbourg (1975, p. 17), are repeated here:

'(1) Whatever is written in the form of a Manuscript by a Jaina is a Jaina Ms.

(2) Whatever Manuscript is written in Jaina Nāgarī characters is a Jaina Ms.

(3) Any Jaina work sacred or even secular written in the form of a Manuscript by a Jaina or a non-Jaina is styled a Jaina Ms.

(4) Any Manuscript that is in possession of a Jaina individual or body is a Jaina Ms.'[1]

In our catalogue, 'Jain manuscript' is used primarily in the third sense. This means that we describe both religious and dogmatical works (whether canonical or non-canonical), narrative works, hymns, ritualistic works, genealogies, etc. but also works belonging to the śāstric disciplines written by Jain authors, such as grammars, lexicons, treatises of metrics, poetics, astrology, mathematics or medicine, as well as commentaries on non-Jain works written by Jain authors. The British Library collections include interesting manuscripts belonging to these categories in a significant proportion. This feature distinguishes these collections from other European collections (except the Berlin collections described by A. Weber), where they are not numerous. Thus it would have been a drawback to leave them aside. This fact needs to be mentioned at the outset since such works are not always considered to be within the scope of catalogues of Jain manuscripts and are sometimes described separately.

In the present catalogue, the script (definition 2) and the ownership (definition 4) are not accepted as sufficient criteria by themselves. Thus a manuscript written in Jaina Nāgarī is not described if it is not a Jain work. Otherwise there would be no limits, since works such as the Bhagavad Gītā have been written in this variety of script. The scribe (definition 1) is a more delicate criterion. Since non-Jain works written by Jain scribes are not numerous in the London collections, they have been included in the catalogue. They provide interesting evidence of the circulation of pan-Indian works and of their relevance to a wide scholarly community, independently of their religious affiliation. A striking instance of this phenomenon is a manuscript of the Līlāvatī, the famous mathematical treatise by Bhāskarācārya, copied by a prominent Śvetāmbara monk belonging to the Ancalagaccha. In the case of 'composite manuscripts' (see below), we follow the method adopted by C.B. Tripāṭhī in his earlier catalogue (p. 17): they 'are classified as Jaina Manuscripts even if they contain one or more non-Jaina works (along with Jaina works'.

I. Collections, users, catalogues

The overwhelming majority of manuscripts described in the present catalogue belong to the British Library. Two much smaller groups belong to the British Museum, and to the Victoria and Albert Museum.

The British Library as we know it today is the result of a complicated history, which is best summarized in the following lines:

'On April 1982 the India Office Library was united with its former rival, protagonist and supplicant, the British Museum Library, which from July 1973 had become part of the newly constituted British Library. Then at the beginning of 1991, the collections of the Department of Oriental Manuscripts and Printed Books, already under the same management as the I.O. Library and Records and renamed the Oriental Collections, were moved to the same building as those of the former India Office and have now become the Oriental and India Office collections of the British Library'.[2]

When these lines were written, the collections were housed in Blackfriars Road. Since 1998 they have been housed in the new British Library complex at 96, Euston Road.

The Jain manuscripts today at Euston Road have a complicated history. They have different origins and originally belonged to two distinct institutions. Considering its size, range of material, and state of preservation, this collection, taken as a whole, constitutes one of the most significant, and in some ways the most significant, collection of such manuscripts outside India. It numbers 1 057 manuscripts, of which 494 are from Oriental Collections (shelfmark 'Or.', 'Add.', etc.) and 563 from the India Office Library

[1] 'The Jaina Manuscripts', *Journal of the University of Bombay* 7,2 (1938), p. 4.

[2] Ilse Sternberg, 'The British Museum Library and the India Office', *British Library Journal* 17,2 (1991), p. 162.

(shelfmark 'I.O. San.', etc.). The first Jain manuscript entered the library before 1753 and belongs to the founding collections of the British Museum. The last one to enter was acquired in December 2005, after a gap of about twenty years since the last acquisition. The Jain holdings of the India Office Library were collected in the 19th century and the beginning of the 20th century. Only one large purchase was made afterwards (the so-called 'Jambuvijaya collection').

The collection was not put together systematically over these two hundred and twenty-three years. In the main it is the result of acquisitions made by the library from individual collectors based in England, through the action of British agents posted in India, or through Indian agents and even, apparently, directly from Jain monks. As will be seen, two prominent non-British Indologists, namely the Austrian Georg Bühler and the German Hermann Jacobi, also contributed in a very important manner to the growth of Jain manuscripts in the library, testifying to the high esteem they had for the London library as a centre of knowledge for the West, and transcending national interests.

The India Office collections

The Colebrooke collection (1819)[1]

Henry Thomas Colebrooke (1765-1837) had gone to Bengal as a 'writer' in 1782 and was in the service of the East India Company for thirty years. His role as an administrator, mainly based in Calcutta, and as a pioneer in many branches of Indian studies (history, religion, Sanskrit, natural history) is well known and justly admired.[2] He was seen as a successor to William Jones and became the president of the Asiatic Society of Bengal. His manuscript collection amounting to a total of 2749 items, which is the 'backbone of the (India Office) Library's Sanskrit resources',[3] was officially presented to the Library via the East India Company through a letter written to the Court of Directors on 15 April 1819.[4] The generous offer was gladly accepted and the collection identified as the 'Colebrooke collection'. Colebrooke's bust, made in 1820 by Chantrey, stands today at the entrance of the India Office room on the third floor of the Euston Road building reminding readers of the immense services rendered by this pioneering Indologist.

Colebrooke's interest also extended to the Jains, as is evidenced primarily from his 'Observations on the Sect of Jains' (1807), at a time when the independence of Jainism as a religion distinct from both Buddhism and Hinduism started to be seen but was not fully recognized. In this perspective gathering information from living sources and collecting Jain books was a bold undertaking and could serve to establish the Jain identity.[5] The beginning of Colebrooke's contribution on the Jains is worth quoting and remembering:

> 'The information collected by Major Mackenzie, concerning a religious sect hitherto so imperfectly known as that of the Jainas, and which has been even confounded with one more numerous and more widely spread (the sect of Buddha), may furnish the ground of further researches, from which an exact knowledge of the tenets and practice of a remarkable order of people may be ultimately expected. What Major Mackenzie has communicated to the Society, comes from a most authentic source; the declarations of two principal priests of the Jainas themselves. It is supported by similar information, procured from a like source, by Dr. Buchanan, during his journey in Mysore, in the year following the reduction of Seringapatam. Having the permission of Dr. Buchanan to use the extracts, which I had his leave to make from the journal kept by him during that journey, I have inserted ... the information received by him from priests of the Jaina sect. *I am enabled to corroborate both statements, from conversation with Jaina priests, and from books in my possession, written by authors of the Jaina persuasion. Some of those volumes were procured for me at Benares; others were obtained from the present Jagat Set, at Murshidābād, who, having*

---

[1] In each case we give the year of acquisition of the manuscripts by the institution. We follow the chronological order.

[2] See R. Gombrich's article in the *Oxford Dictionary of National Biography*, Oxford University Press 2004-2005, which makes use of *The life of H.T. Colebrooke* written by the latter's son T.E. Colebrooke (1873).

[3] A.J. Arberry, *The Library of the India Office. A Historical Sketch,* London, 1938, p. 89.

[4] Cf. *The Life of H.T. Colebrooke* by his son Sir T.E. Colebrooke, London, 1873, pp. 326-328. The letter is reproduced; a short list communicated by Reinhold Rost to T.E. Colebrooke indicating the broad topics and the number of manuscripts for each appears on p. 327 n. 1. There is no heading 'Jain mss.'. They are probably included in the heading 'Mss. of all kinds'.

[5] See also R. Gombrich's clear statement in his contribution to the *Oxford Dictionary of National Biography*: '(Colebrooke's) 'Observation on the sect of the Jains' (1807) was the first significant contribution ever made by a non-Indian to knowledge of that religion; it is based on original Prakrit texts. Unlike his predecessors, he clearly distinguished Jainism from Buddhism, and speculated intelligently, albeit incorrectly, on the relation between them'.

changed his religion, to adopt the worship of Vishnu, forwarded to me, at my request, such books of his former faith as were yet within his reach'.[1]

Thus Colebrooke's Jain manuscripts are not from Western India, as the majority of the Jain manuscripts preserved in Europe, but from Northern and Eastern India, more precisely from Bengal where Murshidabad, a town to the north of Calcutta, is located. In the main part of his contribution, Colebrooke proceeds to the analysis of historico-mythological information connected with Jainism on the basis of two works, the *Kalpasūtra* and Hemacandra's *Abhidhānacintāmaṇi*. A lithographed edition of the latter was prepared under the supervision of Colebrooke and published in Calcutta as early as 1807.[2] The *Kalpasūtra* and the *Abhidhāna°* share a common feature. Indeed, both provide data about the existence of twenty-four Jinas (and other mythological categories, see also I.O. San. 1530 C, D and F, Cat. Nos. 1172, 1179, 1173), their identity and the nature of a Jina, thus showing that Jainism has its own independent tradition different from both Buddhism and Hinduism. Later in the same contribution, Colebrooke gives a presentation of Jain cosmology, again on the basis of standard Jain works on the subject: 'The *Sangrahaṇīratna* and *Lokanāb-sūtra* [i.e. *Lokanāli*], both in Prākrit, are the authorities here used.'[3] Colebrooke's approach is significant for its direct recourse to fundamental works on the tradition, and it distinguishes his undertaking from those of Mackenzie or Buchanan, who handed down information as it was communicated to them by informants and pandits who had read the books for them. Jain manuscripts are far from being a negligible portion of what Colebrooke collected. They include an important selection of canonical and non-canonical Sanskrit and Prakrit works, as well as an interesting set of texts written in Gujarati. One of these (I.O. San. 1638) is a manuscript of the *Kalpasūtra* dated V.S. 1614, which served as the basis of Colebrooke's contribution mentioned above: 'The most ancient copy in my possession and the oldest one which I have seen, is dated in 1614 Saṁvat: it is nearly 250 years old'.[4] Another is the manuscript of the Sangrahaṇī-ratna also used by him and mentioned above (I.O. San. 1553B). We are fortunate to have a list, albeit incomplete, of Jain manuscripts which belonged to Colebrooke in the form of a folio present in the India Office Library collection: the manuscript I.O. San. 1530 (E) contains twenty-

---

[1] Italics ours. Quoted from 'Observations on the Sect of Jains' in *Asiatic Researches* vol. 9, pp. 287-322, Calcutta, 1807 (London ed. 1809), reprinted in *Miscellaneous Essays by H.T. Colebrooke* (With the Life of the Author. By his son, Sir T.E. Colebrooke, in 3 volumes), vol. 2, pp. 171ff. — Jagat Seth is mentioned another time in Colebrooke's works: 'The representative of the great family of Jagat-śeṭh, who with many of his kindred was converted some years ago from the Jaina to the orthodox faith', p. 404 in 'On the philosophy of the Hindus. Part V. On Indian Sectaries', repr. in *Miscellaneous Essays* vol. 2 (originally publ. in *Transactions of the Royal Asiatic Society* I, pp. 549-579). For the extraordinary story of Jagat Seths 'the Rothschilds of India', a family from Rajputana transplanted to Patna in the 17th century, see *The House of Jagatseth*, compiled by Late Mr. J.H. Little, B.A. (originally published in *Bengal Past & Present. Journal of the Calcutta Historical Society* vol. XX, Serials No. 39-40, January-June 1920, pp. 111-200 & vol. XXII, Serials No. 43-44, Jan.-June 1921; collected in one volume at the British Library [shelfmark: V 6710] and reprinted in Calcutta, 1967). The member of the family mentioned by Colebrooke is Harakh Chand (died in 1814): '(he) was the first of the family who abandoned the Jain religion and joined the sect of the Vaishnavs. He was childless and being extremely anxious to have a son he faithfully followed all the ceremonies enjoined by the Jain religion in such a case but with no result. At length a member of the Vaishnav sect advised him to propitiate Vishnu. He did so and obtained his desire. (...) He and his successors have been respected as much as before by the members, of their old religion. In fact it is doubtful whether the members of this family ever renounced entirely their Jain religion' (Little, part 2, pp. 104-105).

[2] The bibliographical details are given in the form of three Sanskrit verses on the title page:

sânekārthanāmamālâtmakaḥ koṣa-varaḥ śubhaḥ
Hemacandra-praṇītâbhidhānacintāmaṇir maṇiḥ ||*1*||
nagare Kalikattâkhye Kolavrūk-sāhâvajñayā
śrīVidyākaramiśreṇa kṛta-sūcī-samanvitaḥ ||2||
Veda-rttv-aṣṭa-kalānātha-saṁmite Vikramâbdake
mudrâkṣareṇa vipreṇa Vāvūrāmeṇa lekhitaḥ ||*3*

The date is indicated by a chronogram in verse 2. As announced here, the book contains two of Hemacandra's lexicons, the *Abhidhānacintāmaṇi* (pp. 1-120) and the *Anekārthasaṁgraha* (pp. 1-140), preceded by an index (pp. 1-96) prepared by Vidyākaramiśra and followed by Corrigenda (pp. 1-4+1). I consulted the copy kept at the Bibliothèque Nationale de France, Paris, Département des manuscrits orientaux (shelfmark: Sanscrit 1049), purchased at Mirzapur, 16 Oct. 1816.

[3] P. 198 note 2 in the reprint.

[4] P. 193 note 4 in the reprint of 'Observations on the Sect of the Jains'.

seven titles accompanied by the number of pages in twenty-two cases, which correspond to manuscripts actually available (see facsimile p. 54; Cat. No. 1187 for concordances).

Colebrooke's Jain manuscripts have already been described in the *Catalogue of the Sanskrit and Prakrit Manuscripts of the India Office* (vol. 2) by A.B. Keith and in the *Catalogue of the Gujarati and Rajasthani Manuscripts in the India Office Library* by J.F. Blumhardt, (revised and enlarged by A. Master, Oxford University Press, 1954). Many of the Gujarati manuscripts were therefore known to M.D. Desai, the author of *Jain Gūrjar Kavio*, and substantial extracts have been quoted by him.

The Mackenzie collection (1822 ?)
Colonel Colin Mackenzie (1753-1821) is mainly known as a collector of Oriental manuscripts and coins (Indian and Persian) and of material relating to the antiquities of South India.[1] He joined the East India Company as an army engineer in 1782 and was posted to Madras. From there he undertook missions throughout South India. He played an important part in military action against Tipu Sultan (1790-1792), and was promoted Colonel in 1819. As Surveyor General to the Government of India he was later posted in Calcutta.[2] He cannot be considered an Indologist *stricto sensu* and he himself recognized his ignorance of Indian languages, but he was surrounded by Indian pandits or scholars who informed him about topics of interest. He built up and trained a personal retinue which included a young Brahmin named Boria (Kavelli Venkata Boria).[3] South Indian culture was not so widely known at that time. As stated by Col. Mackenzie himself: 'It is also proper to notice that in the course of these investigations, and notwithstanding the embarrassments of this work, the first lights were thrown on the history of the country below the Ghats, which have been since enlarged by materials constantly increasing; and confirming the information acquired in the upper country. Among various interesting subjects may be mentioned, 1. The discovery of the *Jain* religion and philosophy and its distinction from that of the *Boudh.*'[4]Indeed, Col. Mackenzie's *Account of the Jains* 'collected from a priest of this sect, at Mudgeri: translated by Cavelly Boria, Brāhmen, for Major C. Mackenzie, including 'Notices of the Jains' received from Cārukīrti Ācārya, at Belligola, in Mysore and 'Historical and Legendary Account of Belligola communicated by the High Priest at that station'[5] is one of the earliest available documents containing information about Southern Indian Jainism and the Digambara tradition as viewed by adepts of the faith at a time when this tradition was hardly known outside narrow circles.[6]

The Jain manuscripts collected by Col. Mackenzie are predominantly palm-leaf manuscripts from South India, mainly from Karnatak where the principal seats of the Digambara community are located (Shravana Belgola, Moodbidri, Humcha, etc.). Wilson's catalogue devotes a specific section to the list and description of the contents of these items, which number 44.[7] They include a few important Sanskrit works in old Kannada script (e.g. Jinasena's *Ādipurāṇa* and Guṇabhadra's *Uttarapurāṇa,* Nos. 1-2) or in Grantha (*Tattvārthasūtra-vyākhyāna*, No. 24) beside a majority of Digambara works in old Kannada (*Purāṇas*, *Kathās*, dogmatical treatises, ritual texts, etc.) or even Tamil. There are also a few paper manuscripts from Northern India in Devanāgarī script which are recorded in the section 'Jain literature' (No. 15 p. 373 *Kalpasūtra* = I.O. San. 2691) or in other sections (Geography, No. 1 p. 169 *Trailokyadīpikā* = I.O. San.

[1] For the 'chequered history' of this collection cf. David M. Blake, 'Colin Mackenzie: Collector Extraordinary', *British Library Journal* 17,2 (1991), pp. 128-150.

[2] For Col. Mackenzie's biography see, for instance, pp. vii-xviii in H.H. Wilson, *The Mackenzie Collection: A Descriptive Catalogue of the Oriental Manuscripts and Other Articles illustrative of the literature, history, statistics and antiquities of the South of India,* Calcutta, 1828; Oxford *Dictionary of National Biography*, Oxford University Press, 2004-2005 (article by P.G. Robb).

[3] Nicholas B. Dirks, 'Colonial Histories and Native Informants: Biography of an Archive' in *Orientalism and the Postcolonial Predicament. Perspectives on South Asia,* ed. by Carol A. Breckenridge and Peter van der Veer, Philadelphia, 1993, pp. 279-314 is a stimulating discussion of this aspect of Mackenzie's activity.

[4] Quoted in H.H. Wilson's introduction to *The Mackenzie Collection: A Descriptive Catalogue* ... Calcutta, 1828, p. 7.

[5] Calcutta, 1809 (*Asiatick Researches*, vol. IX, pp. 244-286).

[6] For recent views on Digambara versus Śvetāmbara and other oppositions see also M. Banks, 'Defining Division: An Historical Overview of Jain Social Organization', *Modern Asian Studies* 20,3 (1986), pp. 447-460.

[7] Op. cit., pp. 176-188.

2583; Mahratta books No. 1 p. 363 *Ādipurāṇa;* Hindi books No. 12 p. 372 *Śrīpālacaritra* = I.O. San. 2728 (A)[1].

The Mackenzie collection underwent many adventures and transfers in the 19th century.[2] At present, the situation is as follows. His collections of Indian manuscripts in classical languages are deposited in the India Office Library, whereas manuscripts in modern languages 'were returned to India in 1828 and are now preserved in Madras'.[3] This explains why items from this collection number so few in the present catalogue, which is not concerned with manuscripts in Kannada and Tamil, except for a few commentaries on Sanskrit or Prakrit texts. Most of Mackenzie's manuscripts are included in Keith's *Catalogue of Sanskrit and Prakrit Manuscripts* where the notices are marked at the end as 'Col. Mackenzie'.

The Burnell collection (1870, 1882)

Arthur Coke Burnell (1840-1882), the co-author of the famous *Hobson-Jobson*, who became a specialist in southern Indian languages and literature, went to India at the age of twenty as a member of the Indian Civil Service and spent most of his time in South India (Madras, Tanjore).[4]His vast and valuable collection of Sanskrit manuscripts was presented to the India Office Library in 1870. Another portion of his collection was acquired by purchase in 1882.[5] Not only did he collect manuscripts, but he also made enormous and pioneering contributions to the cataloguing of collections. This is illustrated by his widely acclaimed *Classified Index to the Sanskrit MSS in the Palace at Tanjore* (1880).

It is not surprising that the Jain manuscripts from Burnell's collection kept in the India Office Library mostly represent the Digambara tradition, which is more prevalent in the southern region of the subcontinent from which they come. Three items (Burnell 229, 354-356 and 235) are from Tamil Nadu and are written in Grantha script. In one (Burnell 235) the original Sanskrit text is accompanied by a Tamil commentary. The other items (Burnell 245, 246-247, 381, 417, 430, 433) are from Karnatak. Manuscripts written on indigenous material (palm-leaf) are only two in number (Burnell 229 and 235). 'Burnell 235' could have well been copied for Burnell, for it is reported to date about 1850 CE. The others are copies of original manuscripts, probably ordered by Burnell and written between 1865 and 1871-72, during his stay in the region. The support is European paper (with a watermark), bound in book form. One (Burnell 245) is in Devanāgarī, the rest are in Kannada script or in Grantha (Burnell 354-356). Several of the Kannada items are transcripts from Moodbidri manuscripts written by the same hand, as is evidenced by accompanying notes. The absence of any specific number makes the identification of the relevant original manuscript impossible or tentative, although a collation with the catalogue of the Moodbidri palm-leaf manuscripts in Kannada script which has since been published is theoretically possible.[6] We are unable to judge the value of the modern copies made for Burnell, but the idea to have such copies made was certainly a commendable initiative. The Moodbidri temple libraries were not easily accessible, and the possibility of acquiring original manuscripts from these well-guarded libraries was unthinkable. The works represented in the Burnell collection are works by Kundakunda and philosophical treatises by Digambara authors in Prakrit and Sanskrit. Since manuscripts of Digambara works are comparatively few in the India Office Library and the British Library as a whole, as well as in European libraries (the only notable exception being the Strasbourg collection built up by E. Leumann), and since Digambara manuscripts from South India are even rarer, the Burnell items have considerable importance. They correspond to books which the Digambaras considered central to their faith at that time (see Buchanan's list below).

---

[1] These three mss. are found in the India Office collections. But the corresponding entries of the I.O. Catalogue for the first two do not mention Mackenzie as having been their owner.

[2] See introduction to Wilson's book p. xvff.

[3] A.J. Arberry, *The Library of the India Office: A Historical Sketch,* London, 1938, p. 76.

[4] For more biographical information see *Oxford Dictionary of National Biography*, Oxford University Press 2004-2005 (article by Stanley Lane-Poole, rev. J.B. Katz).

[5] Cf. A.J. Arberry, *The Library of the India Office: A Historical Sketch,* London, 1938, p. 92.

[6] *Kannad Prantiya Tadapatriya Grantha Soochi* [A descriptive Catalogue of Bhandaras of Jain Matha, Jain Siddhant Bhavan, Siddhant Basadi etc. of Moodbidri, Jain Matha of Karakal, and Adinatha Grantha-Bhandar of Aliyoor etc.], ed. Vidyabhooshan Pandit K. Bhujabali Shastri, Moodbidri, Kashi, 1948 (Jnana-Pitha Moortidevi Jain Granthamala, Sanskrit Grantha No. 2). See the relevant entries of our catalogue for individual references.

The Bühler collection (1888)

Georg Bühler (1837-1898), a pioneer in Indian studies, spent a large part of his life in India, until he became professor of Sanskrit at Vienna University in summer 1881. While in India, he was employed by the Government of Bombay and sent to various places in order to search for and acquire manuscripts. During his numerous and official tours he observed, especially in Western India, that libraries often kept large numbers of copies of the same text, and that manuscripts were on occasions destroyed if considered redundant. Thus, with the permission of the authorities, he informed European scholars of the situation, inviting them to enrich their own university libraries. This was how the Berlin Royal Library bought its rich collection of Indian manuscripts, at the instigation of Albrecht Weber, how the Cambridge University Library was able to acquire a set of the Jain Āgamas and other works.[1] This is how Bühler later acquired a collection of Jain manuscripts for the University Library in Vienna where he was to work.[2] Besides, Bühler also built his own collection, thus fulfilling a long-standing desire:

> When twenty five years ago I landed in India, no idea had a greater charm for me than the hope to acquire a collection of unpublished Sanskrit works which might enable me to solve at least some of the numerous difficult problems which Sanskrit philology and Indian history then offered and, I may add, still offer.[3]

Given the breadth of his interests and culture, the collection covers a wide range of subjects and areas of literature, as can be seen from the list Bühler himself established:

> The first of the two subjoined Lists is that of my private collection which I have lately [1888] presented to the India Office Library. Its contents, 193 modern transcripts made for my use and 128 old MSS., were collected between the years 1863 and 1888, the by far greater number of the acquisitions falling in the period between May 1863 and October 1866.[4]

Each item is described briefly, with a precious indication of the area of provenance as well as statement whether it is a new copy made for Bühler himself or an old one. The list is not as long as it might have been since Bühler had presented some manuscripts from his own collection to various libraries (Berlin Royal Library, University Library at Göttingen, and India Office Library).

The Jain manuscripts in Bühler's collection can be divided into two categories. The first includes manuscripts 'which I purchased for myself between 1873 and 1880, ... fifteen in number'.[5]In Bühler's list, they are followed by the word 'Gujarât'. However, if one counts all the manuscripts labelled in this way, there are seventeen, of which some represent strictly Jain works (Nos. 280, 281, 282, 283, 284, 287, 288, 290, 293, 303) whereas others are works by Jain authors on general subjects (Nos. 119 and 113 on poetics, Nos. 272-273 on Sāmudrika, 275 Āyatatva) and two are non-Jain (No. 79 Setubandha, 81 Kādambarī). The second category, the items of which are labelled 'N.C.' in Bühler's list, refer to new copies: 'From 1872 I employed at intervals professional writers and Pandits ... who copied for me the numbers ... marked N.C. Surat, N.C. Ahmedabad ... The Sanskrit MSS. of this class were transcribed partly from originals belonging to Government and partly from such which I borrowed from private libraries'.[6] As for strictly Jain works, except for one item (No. 308) belonging to the Digambara tradition, they all come from Śvetāmbara milieux and testify to the collector's interest in the history of Mediaeval India in its various aspects (e.g. *Gurvāvalīs, Prabandha*-literature, etc.). Several of them formed the basis for Bühler's work on this topic, as can be seen from his *Life of Hemacandrācārya* (originally published in German in 1889) or his monographs on Arisiṁha's *Sukṛtasaṁkīrtana* and Sarvāṇanda's *Jagaḍūcarita*.[7] Although Jain

---

[1] For details on Bühler's way of working see 'Two Lists of Sanskrit MSS. together with some remarks on my connexion with the Search for Sanskrit MSS.', *ZDMG* 42 (1888), p. 530ff.

[2] 'Über eine kürzlich für die Wiener Universität erworbene Sammlung von Sanskrit- und Prakrit-Handschriften': *Sitzungsberichte der philologisch-historische Klasse der Akademie der Wissenschaften in Wien*, Vol. 99, Wien, 1882, pp. 563-579. There is no extensive and detailed catalogue of these items, since their description has deliberately not been included in Utz Podzeit, *Die Indischen Handschriften an der Universitätsbibliothek Wien*, Zusammengestellt mit Indizes und Appendizes versehen, Wien, 1988. However, they are listed in the indexes and there is a table of concordance between Bühler's number and the shelfmark.

[3] 'Two lists' p. 530.

[4] 'Two lists' p. 530; on Bühler's letter to R. Rost, then librarian at the India Office, and the conditions he set for the donation, see Arberry p. 93.

[5] Bühler in *ZDMG* 42 (1888), p. 533.

[6] Bühler p. 532. The origin of each copy is indicated in the notes to the respective entries.

doctrine as such is not a main focus, the presence of a copy of the *Niśīthasūtra* is to be noted, all the more since the Chedasūtras are rarely represented in collections of Jain manuscripts preserved outside India.

Bühler's manuscripts have already been described in Keith's *Catalogue of Sanskrit and Prakrit Manuscripts of the India Office*.

The Aufrecht collection (1904)

Theodor Aufrecht (1821-1907) started his indological career in Germany, but from 1852 until 1875, when he was appointed professor in Bonn, his name became associated with England, first as an assistant of Max Müller for the edition of the Ṛgveda, and then as a professor at the University of Edinburgh (1861). In the meantime, Aufrecht had been appointed to the Bodleian Library, Oxford, where he catalogued Sanskrit manuscripts (2 vols, 1859-1864). He also catalogued Sanskrit manuscripts in the library of Trinity College, Cambridge, and later manuscripts in the libraries of Florence, Leipzig and Munich. This great work culminated in the *Catalogus Catalogorum* (3 vols, 1891-1903) in which all Sanskrit manuscripts known to date are mentioned. Buddhist and Jain manuscripts, however, are not included.

Aufrecht's collection of Sanskrit manuscripts was painstakingly built up over the years. It 'consists ... partly of Sanskrit MSS., in most cases copied by Professor Aufrecht himself from originals in Europe or India, but including a few copies made, or procured from India, by friends (e.g. Professor Kuhn, Professor Bühler, Professor Kielhorn, and Dr. Stein) or otherwise obtained, and a few originals acquired by gift or purchase; partly of glossaries or word-indices; partly of *pratīka*-indices, i.e. arrangements of initial words, of verses, *mantras*, or *sūtras*.'[1] The bulk consists of works belonging to Vedic and Brahmanical Sanskrit literature. Documents connected with Jain literature are three in number, and thus constitute an extremely small minority: No. 53 consists of three volumes containing materials for an edition of Guṇavinayagaṇi's commentary on Trivikrama's *Damayantīkathā* based on an Oxford manuscript; No. 86 (I-II) is a copy by Aufrecht himself of an Oxford manuscript of Padmasundara's *Pārśvanātha-mahākāvya* and No. 87 is a copy by Aufrecht of an Oxford manuscript of the *Ratnakośa*. Further details are available in the article by F.W. Thomas referred to above. They are also described in the present catalogue.

Smaller collections in the India Office Library

Two manuscripts (I.O. San. 372B, 1561D) belonged to SIR WILLIAM JONES (1746-1794), founder of the Asiatick Society of Bengal and the journal *Asiatick Researches* in the pages of which the English pioneers of Indology expressed their views and published reports and surveys on Indological subjects. Jones is celebrated for his translation of Kālidāsa's *Śakuntalā* (1789) and his *Ordinances of Menu*. The two Jain manuscripts are unremarkable: side-products of the insatiable curiosity of a man who inspired his contemporaries to uncover the beauties of Sanskrit and its literature, in conformity with pre-romantic sensibilities.

Three Jain manuscripts (I.O. San. 2341, 2363, 2470) come from FRANCIS BUCHANAN (1762-1829), later known as Buchanan Hamilton when he added his mother's name.[2] Buchanan was a medical officer in the service of the East India Company.[3] He arrived in India in 1794 and left in 1815 after having been posted mainly in Bengal, where he served as a surgeon, and later was appointed Superintendent of the Botanical Gardens. His work as a botanist made him famous. He published several reports and accounts dealing with Eastern India.[4] But he also travelled in Nepal and South India. The latter tour gave birth to *A Journey from Madras through the countries of Mysore, Canara and Malabar* (London, 1807; 2nd ed. Madras, 1870). A

---

[7] For exact references see the notes to the relevant entries of the present Catalogue.

[1] F.W. Thomas, 'The Aufrecht Collection', *JRAS* 1908, p. 1029.

[2] See *Oxford Dictionary of National Biography*, Oxford University Press 2004-2005 (article by Katherine Prior, with updated bibliography).

[3] See Arberry p. 79 (extremely brief); *The Dictionary of National Biography* founded in 1882 by George Smith, ed. by Sir Leslie Stephen and Sir Sidney Lee. From the Earliest Times to 1900. Published since 1917 by the Oxford University Press, vol. 3, p. 186; M. Vicziany, 'Imperialism, Botany and Statistics in Early Nineteenth Century India: The Surveys of Francis Buchanan (1762-1829)', *Modern Asian Studies* 20,4 (1986), pp. 625-660.

[4] For instance, *An Account of the District of Bhagalpur in 1810-11; An Account of the Districts of Bihar and Patna in 1811-1812; The History, Antiquities, Topography and Statistics of Eastern India*, collected by Montgomery Martin, 3 vols., London, 1838.

man of wide interests, he could not ignore the Jains, on whom he wrote two contributions:[1] 'Particulars of the Jains', *Asiatick Researches* (Calcutta), 9, 1807, pp. 279-286 is in fact an extract from the journal of his travels in Karnataḳ, included in a larger contribution by Colonel Mackenzie. It starts as follows: 'Having invited Pandita Āchārya Swāmī, the Guru of the Jains, to visit me, he came, attended by his most intelligent disciples, and gave me the following account of his sect'. His second contribution 'On the Srawacs or Jains', *Transactions of the Royal Asiatic Society of Great Britain and Northern Ireland (London)*, 1, 1827, pp. 531-540, published after he had come back to England, is based on information gathered during his stay in Eastern India. It is the confrontation of this information with that gathered earlier from South India that led Buchanan to realize that the Jains he met in the South were Digambaras.[2]

The India Office manuscripts that Buchanan collected seem to come from Eastern India, rather than South India, and are all in Devanāgarī script. Two of them are Digambara narrative works: the Yaśodharacarita (I.O. San. 2363) and the Ādipurāṇa (I.O. San. 2470). No direct reference is made to the manuscripts themselves in any of Buchanan's articles. However, the works are mentioned among those which form the list of the sacred books of the Digambara Jains included in Buchanan's contribution 'On the Srawacs':

> This sect has twenty-four books called Purânas, as mentioned in my account of Mysore. The names of these books are: *Ādi* P. or *Chakradhar P., Ajit P., Sambhava P., Abhinandana P., Sanmati P., Padma Prabhava P., Samparsa P., Chandra Prabhava P., Saubodhinathiya P., Saitalnathiya P., Sriyangsanathiya P., Vasupujya P., Bimalnathiya P., Ananta-nathiya P., Dharma nathiya P., Santinathiya P., Kunthunathiya P., Armallanathiya P., Munisabratanathiya P., Naminathiya P., Nemnathiya P., Parsanathiya P., Mahavira P.* and *Uttara P.* These books, so far as I can learn, give an account of the twenty-four Tīrthancaras or lawgivers of the sect; the first twenty-three giving each an account of one such person, while the Uttara Purāna gives an account of the whole.
>
> The sect of the *Digambara*, in performing its ceremonies, is said to be guided by books called *Siddhânta*, which form its code of *agam* (rituals). The books are *Trailokyasâra, Gômatasâra, Pungjaraj, Trailokyadîpak, Kshâpanasâra, Siddhântasâra, Tribhangisâra,* and *Shatpawar.* [...] Besides these books, the *Digambaras* have other books, called *Charitras*, composed by inferior personages. These are *Yasodhar C., Srîpal C., Hanumat C., Sîtâ C., Bhadrabahû C., Jambuwswâmî C.* and *Pradyumna C.*[3]

Such a list is rare in accounts of that time. It is all the more interesting since it is likely to have been faithfully transmitted from oral informers. As such it gives an idea of what the 'living Canon' of the Digambaras was considered to be by Digambara authorities themselves. Only two of the works mentioned in the list are represented in Buchanan's own collection. But the popularity of all of them could explain why some of them are among the Digambara manuscripts which were acquired by other European collectors, such as Burnell or Col. Mackenzie (if one considers the London libraries only).

The third Jain manuscript belonging to Buchanan (I.O. San. 2341) is of Śvetāmbara affiliation. The Śvetāmbara scriptures do not seem to have interested him as much as those of the Digambaras. No relevant information is found in any of his two articles. However, Buchanan was in direct contact with members of the Śvetāmbara Jain community: 'I had several interviews [with two priests at Bihār], and they were abundantly communicative, the chief of them being a man of considerable learning'. Other information came from a Vaishnava Brahman who had been employed to teach Sanskrit to Jain monks, 'which gave him an opportunity of reading their books and knowing their customs'.[4]

John Leyden (1775-1811),[5] a famous poet, patron of Sir Walter Scott and a leading personality of his time, learnt several Oriental languages and was tempted by Africa, but he finally obtained the post of assistant surgeon at Madras where he arrived in August 1803. He was in charge of the Madras General Hospital. In 1805, he accompanied the commissioners on a tour of the Mysore provinces. While recovering from illness in November of the same year, he studied Sanskrit. He was a friend of William Erskine (see below), who greatly admired him, and he also helped Col. Mackenzie. Leaving India for a few years, he returned in

---

[1] For an assessment of Buchanan's (and others') views on the Jains see M. Banks, 'Defining Division: An Historical Overview of Jain Social Organization', *Modern Asian Studies* 20,3 (1986), pp. 447-460.

[2] Buchanan's other contributions on Jainism include epigraphical and iconographical work: e.g., 'Description of Temples of the Jainas in South Bihar and Bhagalpur', *TRAS* 1 (1827), pp. 523-527 (Nawādā, Bhagalpur, Chāmpānagara, Caburpur).

[3] 'On Srawacs', *TRAS*, p. 533.

[4] Both quotations in 'On the Srawacs or Jains', TRAS, p. 531.

[5] Source: *Oxford Dictionary of National Biography,* 2004-2005, by T.W. Bayne, rev. Richard Maxwell.

1806 and settled at Calcutta where he worked as a judge and also pursued various academic interests. One Jain manuscript which has been identified as coming from him was certainly acquired in Bengal during this period of his life: it is an incomplete manuscript of the *Kalpasūtra* (I.O. San. 2879A) written in Bengali characters. Another interesting specimen stamped as belonging to his library (also containing a stamp of the Frenchman Claude Martin) is bound in the format of a European book and contains the commentaries in Hindi by Hemarāja (17th century) on two Digambara treatises (*Pancāstikāya* by Kundakunda and Nemicandra's *Karmakāṇḍa*, I.O. San. 2909). Prakrit was one of the numerous languages which excited J. Leyden's unbounded curiosity. Doubtless it would prove rewarding to have a closer look at his papers which are kept in the Department of Manuscripts at the British Library.[1]

A significant group of Jain manuscripts of some interest bears the stamp or the note GAIKAWAR (I.O. San. 1399, 2112B, 2126A, 2201, 2354, 2468C, 2525D, 2527A-F, 2539F, 2642, 2646B). This refers to Ananda Rao, Gaekwar of Baroda (?-1819) who presented a total of 506 Indian manuscripts to the India Office in 1809.

DR. JOHN TAYLOR (died 1821) was the owner of two Jain manuscripts (I.O. San. 1992 and 1954). He entered the Bombay service, was appointed assistant surgeon on 26 March 1809, and was promoted to the rank of surgeon in 1821. A member of the Asiatic Society of Bombay and the Literary Society of Bombay, he was the author of several translations from Sanskrit.[2] A total of 296 manuscripts from his estate was bequeathed to the India Office in 1821.

The name of JAMES A. BURGESS (1832-1916),[3] one of the most efficient Directors of the Archaeological Survey of India in the British period, is associated with a manuscript of Haṁsaratna's *Śatrunjaya-māhātmyollekha* (I.O. San. 3266), and hence with one of the subjects, Shatrunjaya/ Palitana, for which J. Burgess is best known to all Jainologists and amateurs of Jain architecture through his monumental and pioneering monograph The *Temples of Śatruñjaya, the celebrated Jaina Place of Pilgrimage, near Pālitāṇā in Kāṭhiāwāḍ,* photographed by Sykes and Dwyer; with historical and descriptive introduction by J. Burgess, Bombay, 1869 (reprinted Gandhinagar, 1976). His long-standing interest in Shatrunjaya expressed itself in various articles.[4]

Four Jain manuscripts come from ARTHUR MASON TIPPETTS JACKSON (1866-1909) and are part of a total collection of 95 manuscripts presented in 1912 to the India Office.[5] One of them, a Kalpasūtra (I.O. San. 3600) is said to be 'from Kitas from Pandit Mansukhlal'. Two others (I.O. San. 2606 and 3610) are also canonical works. The remaining manuscript (I.O. San. 3614) is in fact a group of fragmentary manuscripts. Although collecting Jain material was not a priority of this Englishman, who held a number of administrative posts in India, he had studied Sanskrit before he left England and was well-known for his mastery of Indian languages. He published several articles or studies.[6] However, his name is first connected with the post of Senior Collector in Nasik, and the agitated political context of a Brahmanic rebellion against the British, which led to his assassination on the 21st December 1909, on the eve of his departure to Bombay for a further promotion. He was murdered by a youth called Kanhere, in protest against V.D. Savarkar's brother having been sentenced to transportation for life to the Andamans jail.[7]

---

[1]See, for instance, Add. 26,589 'Grammar of the Prakrit language', or Add. 26,591 which includes 'a vocabulary of Prakrit'.

[2] *Oxford Dictionary of National Biography.*

[3] Regrettably, there is no article about him in the Oxford Dictionary of National Biography.

[4] See for instance the English translation of A. Weber's *Śatrunjaya-māhātmya* in *Indian Antiquary* 30 (1901). Burgess also translated into English G. Bühler's *Über die indische Sekte der Jainas,* London, 1903.

[5] See *Oxford Dictionary of National Biography,* Oxford University Press 2004-2005 (article by Anita McConnell).

[6] A.M.T. Jackson was, for instance, co-author of *Folk Lore Notes,* vol. I, Gujarat; vol. II, Konkan, Bombay: British India Press, 1914-1915 (reprinted Gurgaon: Vintage Books, 1989).

[7] The increasingly controversial place of this freedom fighter and leader in India today, his use of violence, and his revival as a hero under the influence of the Hindu Nationalists have brought the name of A.M.T. Jackson to the foreground once more (see documents on the Web).

Finally, a number of manuscript purchases are neither identified as having belonged to any specific collection nor connected with any specific owner. They are marked in the *Catalogue of Sanskrit and Prakrit Manuscripts at the India Office* II simply with the date of accession: 'April 25, 1900', '1906', 'Oct. 9, 1914', 'July 22, 1915', 'Jan. 5, 1916', 'April 6, 1920' or with '?'.

The survey given above is not meant to artificially emphasize the quality of all the Jain manuscripts which entered the India Office collections. Rather, it intends to show that during these years the India Office was considered by a range of people, whether scholars of Jainism or collectors without special focus on Jainism, as one of the best destinations for manuscripts, whether through donation or sale.

The 'Jambuvijaya-collection' (1952?)

The conditions of the accession of this collection, which contains 197 items, remain rather mysterious. Beside the original folio numbers, all these manuscripts have a modern European foliation written in pencil by an unknown hand in a continous sequence independent of the individual manuscripts. Some also bear a title or the name of a literary category in roman script. However, they were never examined properly until they were shown to Professor C.B. Tripāṭhī in 1994. At that time, the manuscripts did not even have a library number. In brief, the collection was not officially registered as a part of any institution. However, it is said that it was donated in 1952.[1] The folios were placed in Indian style paper covers, presumably as they were when they were acquired. The most recent dated manuscript in the collection goes back to V.S. 1965 (= 1908). The identity of 'Jambuvijaya', who, for some obscure reason, has lent his name to the collection (albeit not written anywhere) is also unknown.

In 2000 a collective official number (Or. 15633) was given to the whole group. A shelfmark of the type 'Or.' normally indicates a manuscript of the Oriental Collections (i.e. British Museum/Library). This is an exception to the rule, because the number was ascribed much later than the time of acquisition, when the India Office as such no longer existed. In September 2001, the paper covers were removed and replaced by blue hard covers, in which the leaves are placed. Unlike most paper manuscripts kept in the British Library, these are not bound. The side of each manuscript has a label of the type 'Or 15633 Jambu 1', where the last number refers to the serial number of the manuscript (1 to 197). Tripāṭhī's identifications, titles, etc., handwritten with pencil, are visible. Given the above-mentioned circumstances, there was no handwritten list of the manuscripts in any register of the Library. Thus the list given in the present catalogue is the first one.

Whatever the circumstances of the acquisition of this collection, it was certainly worthwhile. Apart from a number of Prakrit and Sanskrit works, it includes a large number of Gujarati texts, especially hymns. This feature, which would not be remarkable if the collection were housed in an Indian library, is distinctive since the collection is housed in the West. To our knowledge, no Western library (outside Great Britain at least) can boast of such an important ensemble of texts of this type. Neither the German nor the French libraries have so many Gujarati Jain manuscripts. The collection is typically one which focuses on Jain basic teachings (*Karmagrantha*-manuscripts), short treatises or tracts which are well-known to all monks and commonly taught to them during their curriculum (Bhāṣyatraya and other works relating to the necessary duties, *Navapada, Jīvavicāra, Vicārasattriṁsikā*, etc.), or devotional hymns.[2] Hence it is representative of what some call 'living Jainism'. It also fills some lacunae of the other collections kept in the British Library. A noticeable fact is that it includes rather recent manuscripts, some of them copied as late as the beginning of the 20th century (V.S. 1965).

The origin of the collection will probably never be known. However the tools of codicology give some clues and show that the bulk of these manuscripts formed a coherent group. Firstly, several manuscripts use the same type of paper, fairly modern in appearance, yellowish, with similar margins and even the same type of handwriting. This is evident at first glance to anyone who sees several manuscripts of the collection at a stretch. A careful examination of all the Scribal Remarks taken together is even more informative.[3] All the manuscripts were copied in Gujarat, as is evidenced by the names of all the places mentioned (Ahmedabad, Palitana, Patan, Radhanpur). In several cases, two or more manuscripts are

[1] See the fascicle *India Office Library and Records: Guide to the Sanskrit and Prākrit collections,* 197 Blackfriars Road, London SE1 8NG, p. 1: '48 Prakrit (and one Sanskrit) manuscripts in the Jambuvijaya Collection donated in 1952'. This number is much less than reality.

[2] For the use of some of these works see J.E. Cort, 'The intellectual formation of a Jain monk: A Śvetāmbara monastic curriculum', *Journal of Indian Philosophy* 29 (2001), pp. 327-349 (useful, but with mistakes in some of the details).

interrelated. They were copied for the same reader: 5(1), 5(7) and 5(11) are meant for the use of the same laywoman; the nun called Sūryaśrī (Sanskrit form), or Sūrajasarī (vernacular form) is the recipient of several manuscripts which have all been copied around the same years (3, V.S. 1888; 40, V.S. 1889; 16 and 121, V.S. 1890, both also copied by the same scribe; 175, V.S. 1893; and perhaps 164, V.S. 1913). The nun Sobhāgyaśrī, disciple of the nun Vivekaśrī, is the recipient of two manuscripts (18, V.S. 1957 and 2, V.S. 1960) and the nun Candanaśrī is the recipient of three manuscripts (9, 147, 148) as well as of two others which were caused to be written by the same laywoman (65 and 197). One Ānandalakṣmī, probably the same person, is mentioned twice (39 and 77), whereas two other cases are perhaps more uncertain (Jheṁnībāī in 88 and 153; Beṁnākora-bā in 102(2) and 155). The names of the same scribes also recur in different manuscripts, along with other supportive evidence which makes the observation either accurate or at least most probable: Vivekavijayagaṇi (63 and 71), Muni Tejavijaya (30 and 177, both written at Patan), Dave Vajerāṁma Vanamālī (155 copied in V.S. 1904 and 171 copied in V.S. 1908), Bhojaka Ujama Narabherāṁma (55, 127, 152, all copied in V.S. 1956), Nāṁnacandajī (153 copied in V.S. 1941, 141, 150 and 154, copied in V.S. 1942, probably 163 copied in V.S. 1936 and perhaps 108, no date), Jeṭhālāla (18 and 149, both works related and copied in V.S. 1957), Lālavijaya (122, written in V.S. 1911 with more detailed genealogy and 164, written in V.S. 1913) and perhaps Motivijaya (3, V.S. 1888 and 30, V.S. 1878). These elements indicate that the so-called 'Jambuvijaya collection' is indeed an ensemble of manuscripts having a similar origin.

The Oriental Collections

The foundation collections of the British Museum, which was established in 1753, were made of manuscripts which were in European hands before this date. They are the Cotton manuscripts, the Harley manuscripts and the Sloane manuscripts, three remarkable figures of collectors typical of the 18th century. At a time when Jainism was far from being an object of study or even of curiosity, one would not expect that these collections would include a great number of Jain manuscripts. Nevertheless, a rather valuable item has found a place among the 7660 manuscripts which make the Harleian collection, as has another fragmentary item among the 4100 manuscripts of the Sloane collection.

The Harleian Jain manuscript: 'Harley 415' (1753)

The so-called 'Harleian manuscripts' of the British Library are a portion of the great library formed by Robert Harley (1661-1724) and his son Edward Harley (1689-1741), first and second Earls of Oxford, in the first forty years of the 18th century. Hence they are among the oldest preserved in this institution. The 'omnivorous collecting'[1] of these two gentlemen led them to buy from everywhere in all languages and build a specially rich collection for English manuscripts, manuscripts of the Classics (especially Greek) and heraldry. Oriental manuscripts (Hebraic, Chinese and Japanese) were not neglected by the Harleys and seemed to have been acquired 'casually, as appendages to collections great in other respects'.[2]

Jain literature is represented by a single manuscript, 'Harley 415', bound in European style, which includes 25 different short texts. All of them are good examples of the various forms of medieval Jain literature in Gujarati: hymns to the Jinas or to the main places of pilgrimage, verse-narratives, didactic poems on the main principles of Jainism. It is interesting to read how the contents of this manuscript were described, at a time when not much was known about Sanskrit literature, and even less about anything Jain. Three pages precede the beginning of the text itself.

---

[3] They are available in the following manuscripts: No. 2, 3, 5(1), 5(7), 5(11), 8(3), 9, 11, 12, 13(4), 16, 17, 18, 21, 22, 23(3), 24, 25, 28, 30, 33, 34, 36, 39, 40(1), 50(3), 53, 55, 56, 58(2), 60, 62, 63, 64, 65, 69, 70(3), 71, 73, 75, 77, 82, 88(2), 89(2), 91, 94, 96, 99, 102(1), 102(2), 104, 108, 121, 122, 124, 127, 129, 131, 132, 133, 134, 140, 141, 142, 148, 149, 150, 151, 152, 153, 154, 155, 157, 159, 160, 162, 163, 164, 166, 169, 170, 171, 172, 174, 175, 177, 179, 184, 185(10), 197. — For the exploitation of Scribal Remarks and their relationship to the origins of a collection, see, for instance, F. Déroche et alii, *Manuel de codicologie des manuscrits en écriture arabe,* Paris: Bibliothèque Nationale de France, 2000, pp. 372ff.

[1] A. Esdaile, *The British Museum Library a short history and survey,* London, 1946, p. 237. The British Library Journal 15, 2, Autumn 1989 is partly devoted to the Harleys but contains no information directly relevant to our purpose.

[2] *Treasures of the British Library* compiled by Nicolas Barker and the Curatorial Staff of the British Library: The British Library, 1988, p. 142.

On the page numbered '1*', are two successive notes:

'— East Indian writing in the hande, paper, and language of Suratt or Bannian'.

'— D.D. Josuah Best, Clerke of the Trinitie House in Radcliffe.

I suppose this Booke to be the SHASTER mentioned by Mr Lord in his Introduction, or a part of it, which contains the grounds of their Religion, and is their writen word, as so is our Bible'.

On the page numbered '2*', one reads:

'The following testimony in the precinct of Dr. Cartwright Esq. of Chelster and Nathaniel Johnston M. owner of this booke written about July 1677.

One Hassan Pergi & Liogogan Indians of Surat told me that this booke was writt in the Brahmine Language and comes from Dew in the sanganian country in the Moguls country but they are pyrats and robbers who take ships that go and come to Surat. The Brahmins are the priests.'

The page numbered '3*' consists of an attached slip:

'A Book in the Brahma or Hanscreet language (some call it Sanscroot) which is a Fortune-book about lucky and unlucky days and whether a Nativity on such or such days shall be Fortunate or unfortunate etc. It wants the first leave, which was cut out before ever you received it'.

Except for the line 'East Indian...', the three other accounts of the manuscript, given by different persons, are taken into account or repeated in the official catalogue of the Harleian collection: *Manuscripts in the Harleian Collection. A Catalogue of the Harleian Manuscripts in the British Museum. With Indexes of Persons, Places and Matters,* Vol. I. London, 1808.[1] The entry corresponding to the Jain manuscript is found on p. 236:

'An Oriental Book, given by Doctor George Hickes, of which several accounts are given. The first [i.e. the one by D.D. Josuah Best] I omit as unlikely. The second, is written by Dr. Nathaniel Johnston, thus, about July, 1644? [followed by: 'One Hassan', etc., see above]. The third Account seems to have been written by the late Dr. Thomas Hide of Oxford, and I believe is right [followed by 'A Book in the Brahma', etc., see above].

We know for certain that this is not the case. The language of the texts contained in the manuscript is not Sanskrit, but Gujarati. They have nothing to do with a 'Fortune-book'. The only factual information we can retain is the geographical origin of the document: Surat or Diu, and the fact that it never had the first folio. Indeed, the first two pages are missing. We also learn that the manuscript was not acquired directly by Robert Harley, but was presented to him by George Hickes, 'the great Restorer of Northern Learning', a man who never ceased to buy manuscripts and stands among those who offered some to the Harleys.[2] Comparing the date of copying of the manuscript (V.S. 1673 = 1616 A.D.) and the date ascribed to Nathaniel Johnston's description shows that it must have been bought only about thirty years after it had been written. It is probably the first Jain manuscript to have entered any non-Indian library. Moreover, it is a good specimen of what a Jain composite manuscript can be, i.e. a manuscript originally meant to contain different texts written by the same scribe. The amount of 25 is fairly large. In fact, Harley 415 is the largest composite manuscript in the British Library collection of Jain manuscripts. Although it was impossible for those who acquired it to realise its value, it should be stated that it is a document of a good standard, and a very significant collection of poems for use in daily Jain devotion.

The Sloane Jain manuscript: 'Sloane 4090' (1753)

Hans Sloane (1660-1753), a contemporary of Newton, was a scientist trained in medicine. He was known 'as a collector of curiosities, the founder of the British Museum, and Lord of the Manor of Chelsea'.[3] He was also a considerable botanist and natural historian. His immense collection was purchased from his executors in 1753. But the bulk of his library was incorporated into the British Library without any distinctive mark, except for a flyer accompanying the document.[4] The single Jain manuscript belonging to the Sloane collection identifiable as such is a single folio of a lexicographical work, namely Hemacandra's

[1] The author of the catalogue is Humphrey Wanley, who died in 1726, after having reached the entry 2407 of the collection. He had started the catalogue in 1708. He classified the manuscripts according to the sequence they had in Harley's library.

[2] *A Catalogue of the Harleian Manuscripts*, vol. I, Preface p. 5.

[3] M. Ultee, 'Sir Hans Sloane, Scientist', *British Library Journal* 14,1 (1988), p. 3.

[4] See M.A.E. Nickson, 'Hans Sloane, book collector and cataloguer, 1682-1698', *British Library Journal* 14, 1 (1988), pp. 52-89.

Anekārthasaṁgraha with a commentary. It is contained in a binding of large size made of red leather along with various other manuscripts and titled 'Manuscript Bibliotheca Slovaeiana'.

Thus the Harley and the Sloane Jain manuscripts are two curiosa which found their way to the British Library by chance. They are isolated traces of the vast range of their owner's intellectual interests.

One had to wait until the second half of the 19th century to see a significant number of Jain manuscripts enter the Oriental Collections, according to three patterns: isolated acquisitions, small collections of Jain manuscripts within broader collections of Oriental manuscripts, and specifically Jain oriented collections. During this period, two individuals were successively in charge of Oriental manuscripts: Charles Rieu was the keeper of Oriental manuscripts within the Department of Manuscripts, from 1867 to 1891. In 1892 when a specific Department of Oriental Printed Books and Manuscripts was set up, he was succeeded by Robert Kennaway Douglas who was active up to 1907.[1] A grant of £. 1000 per year was given for the purchase of Oriental books and manuscripts.

The Erskine collection (1865; Add. 26362 and foll.)

William Erskine (1773-1852), who was trained in the field of law, stayed in India from 1804 to 1823. First appointed Recorder of Bombay, he later became Clerk of the Court of Small Causes and Master in Equity. He took an active part in the founding of the Literary Society of Bombay, of which he was Vice President. A famous Persian scholar, he translated the autobiography of Baber (published in London in 1826), thus completing the work started by his friend John Leyden (for whom see above), and wrote *The History of India under the first two sovereigns of the House of Timur, Baber and Humayuns* (published in 1854). His collection of Oriental manuscripts amounts to 436 volumes in Arabic, Persian (195), Turkish, Sindhi, Sanskrit, Prakrit, Marathi and Hindi. It was purchased by the British Museum in 1865 from his son, Claude Erskine.[2] Indeed, a note written on the first page of the Jain manuscripts indicates that they were bought in February 1865 from his son C.J. Erskine.[3] Erskine's group of Indian manuscripts are marked Add. 26.337 to Add. 26.662. It might well be that some of them had been collected or purchased by Claudius James (1821-1893), who was born in Bombay, worked there for several years, was the first director of public instruction in Western India, and was also a scholar. The Jain manuscripts (Add. 26.362 to 26.519) come from Western India, the area where Erskine worked. Prakrit and Sanskrit works are in a minority. The focus of this group is Gujarati works. When a manuscript of a canonical text is available, it is always accompanied by a Gujarati commentary (*ṭabo, bālāvabodha*). Hardly any manuscript of the Prakrit *mūla* alone is found in this collection. Other categories include commentaries on non-canonical texts, hymns or texts connected with worship.

Three palm-leaf manuscripts from Western India (1876; Or. 1385A, 1385B and 1386)

The origin of this acquisition is unknown. The three manuscripts appear in the Register as having entered the library in 1876. They make a coherent unit for they revolve around the same text belonging to the corpus of the Śvetāmbara canon, namely the *Jītakalpa*, of which they provide the *sūtra* (Or. 1385A), the *cūrṇi* (Or. 1385B) and a commentary on the *cūrṇi* (the *Bṛhaccūrṇivyākhyā*, Or. 1386). Or. 1385B is dated saṁvat 1258 = 1201 CE, and is thus the oldest Jain manuscript in the British Library. These three items are a rarity worthy of notice. In the first place, they are palm-leaf manuscripts from Western India, which are considered extremely precious and valuable. Such manuscripts are found in the old libraries of Cambay and Patan (Gujarat), or Jaisalmer. But, to my knowledge, the number having entered any library outside India is extremely limited. A noteworthy exception is provided by a composite palm-leaf manuscript of 220 leaves belonging to F. Kielhorn's collection available in Göttingen University Library which contains, among other texts, portions of the *Vyavahāra-cūrṇi*.[4] In the second place, the texts they transmit belong to the so-called *Chedasūtras* (like the Göttingen palm-leaf manuscript!), or books of discipline devoted to

[1] On the birth of the Oriental Department see P.R. Harris, *A History of the British Museum Library* 1753-1973, London, The British Library, 1998, pp. 408-409, and p. 757 for the list of Keepers.

[2] The information about Erskine is taken from the *Catalogue of the Persian Manuscripts in the British Museum* by Charles Rieu, vol. III, London, 1883, p. XIXff.; see also *Oxford Dictionary of National Biography*, Oxford University Press, 2004-2005 (article by Katherine Prior).

[3] The source of C. Bendall's information, giving the date of acquisition as 1868 (Bendall 1902, p. vi), is not known.

[4] See below the comparative chart of Jain manuscripts in Europe for references.

rules of monastic behaviour, a group of canonical texts, copies of which are comparatively rare. Within this group itself the Jītakalpa is even less copied than its companions.

The Ratnavijaya collection (1879; Or. 2094-2156)

The collection is named after Ratnavijayasūri, a Jain monk from Ahmedabad who is supposed to have been the original owner of the manuscripts. However, nothing is known about his precise identity, date and whereabouts. The first page of each item of the collection has a note written in a European hand which says 'Bought of Bhagavandas Kevaldas 1879'. At the end of each item a note written in pencil by the then Librarian gives the number of folios counted followed by 'March 1880 GJG', thus giving the date when the manuscripts were officially recorded. Bhagavandas Kevaldas (1850-1900) was a native of Sigrampur, near Surat in South Gujarat. He was in the service of G. Bühler, P. Peterson and R. Bhandarkar and worked as an agent who helped in the acquisition of Indian manuscripts.[1] He also helped scholars interested in the acquisition of Jain manuscripts, such as E. Leumann (Strassburg University Library) or C. Bendall (see below) and was one of the key persons in the process which led to the entry of Indian manuscripts into Indian and Western libraries at the end of the 19th century. The initials 'GJG' probably refer to the staff-member of the British Museum who checked the manuscripts, but his identity could not be traced.

All the manuscripts of this collection are bound in a dark blue leather binding. In case of thin manuscripts, several of them have been bound together. As a whole, this collection can be qualified as excellent considering the variety of texts it includes as well as the quality of the individual items. It has nothing much to offer as far as the basic canonical groups (Angas, Upāngas, Chedasūtras, Mūlasūtras and Prakīrṇakas) are concerned. But it comprises an interesting group of polemic works, a good variety of dogmatic treatises, representatives of Karma literature, hymns (with commentaries) and narratives. Prakrit and Sanskrit are the prevalent languages of these manuscripts, except for some commentaries which are written in Gujarati, but original Gujarati works are not among the highlights of this collection. If one is in search of totally unpublished Jain works or rarities which are unrecorded so far, even in a comprehensive catalogue such as H.D. Velankar's *Jinaratnakośa*, or not represented outside India, Ratnavijaya's collection provides some interesting cases (e.g. Dharmasāgara's works, *Śrāddhavidhi-viniścaya,* the *Dhanarāja-Prabodhamālā*, etc.). This is obviously a learned collection which was meant for a scholar, whether a Jain monk or a Western scholar, or a person who was intent on carefully preserving precious or rare testimonies of the Jain literary heritage.

Only the part of the collection relating to *śāstras* such as grammar, lexicography, metrics, astrology (Or. 2139+) has been described in C. Bendall, *Catalogue of the Sanskrit Manuscripts in the British Museum* (London, 1902). Some of the manuscripts of Jain religious and dogmatic works have been consulted and described in the form of unpublished notes by Ernst Leumann (see below). Most are described for the first time in the present catalogue.

The Bendall collection (1886; Or. 3347-3354)

Cecil Bendall (1856-1906) stands among those whose role was significant in building up a library of Sanskrit manuscripts at the British Museum as well as in cataloguing the material. A pupil of E.B. Cowell, whose teaching inspired Bendall's devotion to Sanskrit, he was appointed Assistant in the care of the Museum's Indian collections in May 1883 and worked in the Museum until his retirement in 1898. His *Catalogue of the Sanskrit Manuscripts in the British Museum* (London, British Museum, 1902) stands out among reference works and will be frequently referred to in the present Catalogue since it includes a good number of notices on Jain manuscripts pertaining to śāstric disciplines (grammar, lexicography, etc.) from Jacobi's, Erskine's and Ratnavijaya's collections. Bendall was also Professor of Sanskrit, first at University College, London (1885-1903) and later at Cambridge University (1903-1906).[2]

As a collector, Bendall's main interest focused on Buddhist Sanskrit manuscripts and other antiquities from Nepal. During his academic career, he had the opportunity to travel in India and Nepal in search of material on two occasions. The first tour took place from 22nd October 1884 to 1st May 1885, while the second tour in the winter 1898 was shorter. The two reports written by Bendall provide precious

[1] See E. Leumann, *Unvergessene, gestorben in den Jahren 1891-1908. Lebensdaten, Bilder und Beileidbriefe,* Straßburg i. E. 1900, p. 23 (with a photograph).

[2] See obituary notice by E.J. Rapson in *JRAS* 1906, pp. 527-533 and *Oxford Dictionary of National Biography,* Oxford University Press, 2004-2005 (article by W.B. Owen, rev. R.S. Simpson).

information on the manifold aspects of his activity during these trips: *A Journey of Literary and Archaeological Research in Nepal and Northern India during the Winter of 1884-5* (Cambridge University Press, 1886, xii-100 p.) and 'Outline-Report on a Tour in Northern India in the Winter 1898-9' (*The Cambridge University Reporter* of 5 December 1899, p. 263; extract in JRAS 1900, pp. 162-164).[1] In both cases, Nepal 'formed the chief goal of [his] journey'.[2] However, his port of disembarkation and embarkation was Bombay, which meant that Bendall had to pass through India on his way to Nepal. Moreover, the travels were made at a time when Indian traders or go-betweens knew of the European scholars' interest in all types of manuscripts, especially Jain. Bendall was no exception and had an opportunity to meet the relevant sources during his two trips. During his first tour, he had contacts with the Jain community in Benares and had access to the library of the temple at Rāmghāṭ which did not seem to have been visited by any European before him. 'The Maṇḍalācārya kindly had a transcript made, for my use, of his list of MSS., adding a promise to allow copies to be taken'.[3] This list is published as an Appendix to the report.[4] A copy of a Digambara *Kathākośa* (one of the few Digambara manuscripts of this collection) was sent to England. On his way back, during the same tour, Bendall visited various towns of Rajasthan (Jaipur, Udaipur, Chittor) and paid special attention to the Jain temples of the village of Aṛ (Ahaṛ, three kilometers to the east of Udaipur)[5]before reaching Bombay where, he writes,

> [he] met by appointment Pandit Bhagvān Dās, who has long been the energetic agent of the Bombay Government for the collection of Sanskrit MSS. By a minute of this Government the agent is allowed to sell duplicates of works in the Government collections for the use of certain institutions in this country, of which our University Library is one.[6]

This Bhagvān Dās is the same Bhagavandas Kevaldas who provided the Ratnavijaya collection mentioned above. During the second tour, in 1898, Bendall again met the Indian agent, and visited other Jain sites: 'I landed at Bombay on 23 November 1898, and commenced search for MSS. by conferring with Bhagvān Dās of Surat. I next visited, chiefly for architectural study, Ahmadabad and Mount Abu. At Jeypore the Digambara Jain pandit, Cimanlāl, not only gave me a full list of his valuable MS. library, from which copies can be made, but also presented me with several MSS. I further succeeded in obtaining some Digambara MSS. through my old friends amongst the brahmans of the city.'[7]

This resulted in a fairly important collection of Jain manuscripts amounting to about 212 items as can be seen from the 'Classified list of MSS. personally collected'[8] and from the 'Rough list of MSS. purchased at Bombay'.[9] To those should perhaps be added other manuscripts (especially Digambara) not found in these lists. The majority of them are kept in the Library of Cambridge University, where Bendall taught from 1903 to 1906, and still await proper cataloguing and description. They do not seem to have been touched by scholars, except by Ernst Leumann who used some of them for his own work and whose posthumous papers include notices on a few items.[10] From this collection a group of ten items (Or. 3347 A, B, C, 3348 A, B, 3349 A, B, 3350, 3351, and 3354) entered the British Museum Library in 1886.[11] But why this lot

[1] See also, for instance, I. Sternberg, 'The British Museum Library and the India Office': *British Library Journal* 17 (1991), p. 157ff.

[2] 'Outline-Report' p. 263.

[3] *A Journey of literary and archaeological research* p. 24.

[4] *A Journey* pp. 88-91.

[5] *A Journey* p. 32. For more details on the history and antiquities of Ahar see for instance K.C. Jain, *Ancient Cities and Towns of Rajasthan,* Delhi, Varanasi, Patna: Motilal Banarsidass 1972, pp. 219-224.

[6] *A Journey* p. 34.

[7] 'Outline-Report' p. 263.

[8] *A Journey* pp. 46-48 (the rest of the list includes Indian manuscripts belonging to other categories than Jain literature).

[9] Op. cit. pp. 49-51 for Jain manuscripts.

[10] Notebook Nos. 47, 49, 49/1, 51, 94, 196 109, 124 (references from B. Plutat, *Catalogue of the Papers of Ernst Leumann,* Stuttgart, 1998. See also Leumann, *Übersicht über die Āvaśyaka Literatur*).

[11] The note found in Leumann's note-book 112 about Or. 3347 'A copy brought from India by Bendall in 1899', viz. during his second tour, is contradicted by the handwritten registers of the Library where the date of entry of this manuscript into the Library is given as 1886. — Or. 3352 and 3353 which also come from Bendall's collection and

was selected and separated from the rest of the collection is unknown. Its components are described in the present catalogue for the first time.

The Miles collection (1891, Or. 4530-4533; 1911, Or. 7619-7623)

The notes written on the Jain manuscripts ('Presented by S.B. Miles') indicate that Miles here means Colonel Samuel Barrett Miles (1838-1914).[1] He was born as the son of a General in the Military Service of the East India Company.[2] In 1857, after an education at Harrow, he joined the 7th Regiment of the Bombay Native Infantry and spent the next nine years at various stations in India. Between 1866 and 1885, he was outside India, mainly as Political Agent and Consul in Muscat or temporary Resident in Baghdad. In 1885, he was appointed Political Agent in the Indian North West Province and Oudh. After a year in the Gulf, he came back to India in 1887 and was promoted Colonel and Political Resident until his retirement at the end of 1893. He then returned to England, and died of illness on 28 August 1914. He travelled much in Iraq and is considered a pioneer as far as the Gulf countries are concerned. His book *The Countries and Tribes of the Persian Gulf* (London, 1919; new ed. 1994, Garner Publishing) is a major contribution. Several references to 'Banian merchants', some of whom emigrated from Cutch, are found there. Col. Miles made donations of several Sanskrit manuscripts (see C. Bendall, *Catalogue of the Sanskrit Manuscripts in the British Museum.* London, 1902, p. v). Jain manuscripts are a very small minority. A first group (Or. 4530-4533) was presented by Col. Miles on November 20, 1891. A second group (Or. 7619-7623) was presented on December 9, 1911. They were probably not selected on purpose, for the interests of their owner were of a different nature, but they do not tarnish the collection in the least.

Hermann Jacobi's collection (1897; Or. 5115-5194, 5255-5258 and I.O. San. 3177)

Hermann Jacobi (1850-1937) stands among the most important German Indologists who made himself a name in various fields, such as Rāmāyaṇa studies, poetics, etc.[3] He was a pioneer in the field of Jaina studies, having demonstrated definitively in 1879 that Jainism was distinct from Buddhism from the earliest times. In the present context, he distinguishes himself from the collectors previously mentioned by the fact that the manuscripts he collected with discrimination were the raw material which he partly used himself for several critical editions of texts not published earlier outside India.

In winter 1873-1874, H. Jacobi joined G. Bühler on his tour in search for manuscripts in Rājputānā and assisted him in his mission of collecting and copying.[4] They visited Jodhpur, Jaisalmer and Bikaner. The bulk of Jacobi's collection seems to have come from the latter place. Bühler explains how he acquired it: '[H. Jacobi] acquired also at Bikaner, while on a tour with me a good collection of Jaina books, a list of which has been published in this Journal [*ZDMG]* vol. 33, p. 693. He very courteously asked for my permission, which I readily gave, as I was unable to take more than a small fraction of the heaps of MSS. which the Bikaner Dalâls brought every day to our tents'.[5] Jacobi's own list of the manuscripts in his possession was published a few years after: 'Liste der indischen Handschriften im Besitze des Prof. H.

entered the Library at the same date are non-Jain manuscripts (respectively a commentary on the *Meghadūta* in Kashmiri nāgarī and a commentary on the *Tattvacintāmaṇi* in Bengali script).

[1] No article in the *Oxford Dictionary of National Biography* 2004-2005.

[2] Hence a different person from Lieut. Colonel William Miles (1780-1860) who was posted in Western India and had some interest in the Jains, as is shown by his contribution 'On the Jains of Gujerat and Mârwâr', Communicated by the Bombay Branch of the Royal Asiatic Society. Read 7th of January 1832. Published in *Transactions of the Royal Asiatic Society* 3 (1835), pp. 335-371.

[3] For a convenient and detailed overview of Jacobi's work see L. Renou, 'Hermann Jacobi (1850-1937)': *Journal Asiatique* 230 (1938), pp. 129-143 (reprinted in Choix d'études indiennes, Paris: EFEO 1997, pp. 803-817).

[4] See, for instance, Bühler's letter of 29 January 1874 (published in *Indian Antiquary* March 1874, p. 89 and 'Dr. Bühler on the celebrated Bhaṇḍâr of Sanskrit Mss. at Jessalmir' in *Indian Antiquary* March 1875, p. 83) where reference is made to Jacobi's assistance in copying the ms. of Bilhaṇa's *Vikramānkacarita* kept in Jaisalmer and later on edited by Bühler (see *The Vikramânkadevacharita. A Life of Ḱing Vikramâditya-Tribhuvana Malla of Kalyāṇa* composed by his Vidyâpati Bilhaṇa. Edited with an Introduction by G. Bühler. Bombay, 1875). In the introduction (p. 46), Bühler writes: 'As soon as I recognised the importance of the MSS., I resolved to copy it out myself. My time at Jesalmîr was limited. But with the help of my companion Dr. H. Jacobi of Bonn, who kindly lent me his assistance during my whole tour in Rajputana, the task was accomplished in about seven days. He copied Sargas V. VI, XIV-XVII and XVIII.1-74, while the rest fell to my share. We then revised our copy together'.

[5] G. Bühler, 'Two Lists of Sanskrit MSS.', *ZDMG* 42 (1888), p. 535.

Jacobi in Münster i. W.', *ZDMG* 33, 1874, pp. 693-697. Although this list includes non-Jain works, Jain works form the most part of it: 79 entries corresponding to 87 manuscripts.

The Jain manuscripts of Jacobi's collection formed the basis of his work in Jainism in the period from 1876 to 1895 and were decisive in his successful attempt to assert the independent position of Jainism.[1] They were used for his editions, translations or analyses, either as the main documents or as subsidiary aids which were occasionally consulted by him, in the following cases:

1876 Edition and translation of *Bhaktāmara-* and *Kalyāṇamandira-stotra*
1878 Edition and translation of the *Śobhanastuti*
1879 Edition of the *Kalpasūtra*
1880 Edition and translation of the *Kālakācārya-kathānaka*
1882 Edition of the *Ācārāngasūtra*
1883 First edition of Hemacandra's *Pariśiṣṭaparvan*
1884 Translation of the *Ācārānga-* and the *Kalpa-sūtra*
1886 Edition of Prakrit stories found in Devendra's commentary on the *Uttarādhyayana* (under the title *Ausgewählte Erzählungen in Māhārāṣṭrī*)
1895 Translation of the *Uttarādhyayana* and the *Sūtrakṛtānga*.

References to these documents always appear in the form 'a manuscript in my possession' (without any number). Relevant bibliographical information along with Jacobi's observation on the condition or the value of individual manuscripts used by him will be found in the notes of the respective entries in the present catalogue.

Jacobi's collection of Jain manuscripts was bought by the then British Museum on 14 June 1897, as is testified by a handwritten note systematically found on a blank page placed before the beginning of the text itself: 'Bought of Dr. H. Jacobi 14 June 1897' followed by a stamp of the British Museum. Why Jacobi sold his private collection, and the circumstances of the purchase, are not known.[2] The initiative for this purchase seems to have come from Robert Kennaway Douglas, the then Keeper of Oriental manuscripts, who had them bought for £. 200 from Berlin.[3]What is clear is that the purchase was unanimously and highly praised by all those who had some interest in increasing the collections of the British Museum: '[Douglas] described these as the most important collection of Indian manuscripts ever purchased by the Museum' (Harris 1998: 409)'.[4] The manuscripts were serially numbered according to their place in the Jain literary classifications (see below) and properly bound. Some of them contain handwritten notes (in pencil) from Jacobi's hand.

The Jain portion is a systematic collection of Canonical texts which includes the various categories subsumed under the term 'Canonical': Angas (Or. 5115-5134), Upāngas (Or. 5135-5146), Prakīrṇaka (Or. 5147), Chedasūtra (Or; 5148), Kalpasūtra (Or. 5149-5152), Nandisūtra (Or. 5153), Anuyogadvārasūtra (Or. 5154-5155), and Mūlasūtras (Or. 5156-5163). The categories are not complete: strangely enough, no manuscript of the *Samavāyānga* (the 4th Anga) is available. The fact that it does not appear in Jacobi's own list suggests that it was never procured by him. All other Angas are represented at least by one

[1] For the second period of his work on Jain literature, H. Jacobi used manuscripts kept in the Indian libraries, especially during the visit he made to Ahmedabad in 1914 (1905: edition of Pradyumna's *Samarādityasaṁkṣepa;* 1914: edition of Siddharṣi's *Upamitibhavaprapancakathā;* 1918: edition of Dhaṇavāla's *Bhavisattakahā;* 1921: edition and translation of Haribhadra's *Sanatkumāracarita* in Apabhraṁśa).

[2] Jacobi's archive in Bonn was destroyed during the Second World War. Nothing remains, as Prof. C. Vogel confirmed: 'Jacobi's correspondence, comprising more than 1600 letters, post-cards, etc. from at least 260 different scholars, was deposited after his death in the Bonn University Library (shelfmark: S 2507 to S. 2513), whereas it was completely destroyed towards the end of the Second World War. So your questions will unfortunately have to remain unanswered' (letter dated November 20, 2003).

[3] Harris 1998: 409.

[4] See also A. Esdaile, *The British Museum Library: A short history and survey,* London, 1945, p. 312: 'and in recent times has been acquired the splendid series of 143 MSS formed in Rajputana by Dr. H. Jacobi and for the most part bearing on Jainism'; C. Bendall (*Catalogue*, 1902, p. VI) mentions 'the series of MSS. (Or. 5115-5258) which form the finest individual collection of Indian MSS. on the shelves of the British Museum'.

manuscript (either of the Prakrit *mūla* alone or of the Prakrit text along with a commentary of one type or the other); only one work belonging to the Prakīrṇakas is to be found. The Chedasūtras are represented by several specimens of the *Kalpasūtra*; the presence of one *Bṛhatkalpasūtra* is noticeable, for copies of strictly disciplinary texts are not so easily accessible and not numerous. The European official collectors knew this and therefore normally did not make them available to Western libraries.[1]

On the other hand, Jacobi's collection includes sets of Sanskrit and Prakrit hymns (*Bhaktāmara-stotra, Kalyāṇamandira*, etc.) forming the so-called *Navasmaraṇa* or *Saptasmaraṇa* which are in use in daily Jain liturgy as performed both by monks and lay people (Or. 5190-5192). This is a testimony of the scholar's interest in the living tradition of Jainism and the varieties of its literary tradition. In between comes an important group of Sanskrit and Prakrit treatises pertaining to ethics, dogmatics, etc. (Or. 5164 and foll., as well as Or. 5255-5258). Narrative works are comparatively few. This collection was obviously formed with clear objectives and a desire to get all that was important for a comprehensive knowledge of classical and contemporary Śvetāmbara Jainism, its doctrine as well as its practice.

Apart from these specifically Jain manuscripts, which are described for the first time in our Catalogue, Jacobi's collection also comprises manuscripts of 'Jain authors on general subjects and copies by Jain scribes of Brahmanical works' which were included in Bendall's *Catalogue of the Sanskrit manuscripts in the British Museum* (London, 1902) and defined as being 'amongst the most interesting MSS. now described' (p. vi). Those which correspond to our definition of a 'Jain' manuscript have been included again in the present catalogue and described according to the same standards as the other entries, i.e. with extracts given for each item and up to date bibliographical information. They pertain to all important Indian *śāstric* disciplines to which the Jains have contributed significantly: grammar, lexicography, philosophy and astronomy (Or. 5196ff.).

Beside the main collection, sold to the British Museum, there is the isolated case of one manuscript in Jacobi's collection which was deposited in the India Office Library (I.O. San. 3177). It is a lavishly illustrated and decorated *Kalpasūtra* manuscript written in silver letters and containing an interesting *praśasti*. The donation was made at the instigation of G. Bühler: 'When I saw [Jacobi's] MSS. in Europe, I found among them an illustrated copy of the Kalpasūtra which, I thought, should have gone to the Govt. collection. At my suggestion he presented it afterwards to the India Office Library and thus kindly rectified an oversight of mine.'[2] This must have taken place after 1883, since the edition of the *Kālakācārya-kathā* published in 1883 by Ernst Leumann, for which Jacobi's manuscript of the work was used, mentions that it was still in the German scholar's possession.[3]

Finally, three manuscripts which belonged to Jacobi and are mentioned by him in his own list, never reached London with the rest of the collection.

The generosity of Hermann Jacobi, who in his time was the international doyen of Jaina studies, consulted by all scholars desirous to work in the field, probably accounts for the absence of the manuscript of Haribhadra's *Saddarśana-samuccaya* with a commentary. The reason is that Jacobi had put it at the disposal of the Italian scholar F.L. Pullé (1880-1934) who was preparing an edition of Haribhadra's work and its commentary. The intricate details of the fate of this document, which is probably still somewhere in an Italian public or private library, are narrated under the relevant catalogue entry (Cat. No. 672), although the corresponding manuscript is virtual and has no shelfmark.

The fate of two manuscripts containing the *Vipākasūtra* (the 11th Anga), one the mūla only and the other one the mūla along with the *Pradeśavivarana*,[4] is even more mysterious. They were never part of the lot sold to the then British Museum, as is shown by the fact that the numbering is continuous from the tenth Anga to the first Upānga, without any gap.[5] If they were given on loan or presented to any scholar, his identity has not been traced. The only European scholar who was interested in the *Vipākasūtra* was

[1] See, for instance, Bühler's remark in 'Two lists': 'The Piṇḍaniryukti and the Pañchakalpa, the few obtainable MSS. of which I kept for the Govt-Collection' (n. 2 p. 534).

[2] G. Bühler, 'Two lists of Sanskrit MSS.': *ZDMG* 42 (1888), p. 536.

[3] E. Leumann, Kleine Schriften, p. 1 ('am Ende eines sehr guten Kalpasūtra-Manuscriptes im Besitze von Prof. Jacobi').

[4] *ZDMG* 33 (1879), p. 694.

Ambroglio Ballini, who prepared a critical edition and an Italian translation of the work. But he did not use any of Jacobi's manuscripts for this task (see the Remark appended to Cat. No. 60 for bibliographical details).

Other individual sources in the 19th-20th centuries

During his years in England and before he was called to join the Boston Museum of Fine Arts in 1917, Ananda Kentish Coomaraswamy (1877-1947) sold a few Jain manuscripts to British institutions.[1] He had probably collected them from India, during one of the three visits he made there between 1909 and 1913, when he started to get Jain objects reserving them for further investigations (see below). They represent relatively minor pieces, compared to the bulk of what formed Coomaraswamy's private collection and later became part of the Boston Museum of Fine Arts. They seem to have been distributed according to their contents. The Victoria and Albert Museum acquired two folios of a *Kalpasūtra* manuscript in March 1914 (see below). One Prakrit text, a manuscript of the *Prākṛtachandaḥkośa* (Or. 8061), was acquired by the British Museum in June of the same year; the Gujarati manuscripts (MSS. Guj. x) were acquired by the India Office Library; their description is accompanied by the label 'Coomaraswamy' in Blumhardt's catalogue.

Recent acquisitions (Or. 13343 and following; 1970s-1980)

Jain manuscripts have continued to come to the British Library in recent decades (1970s). They do not represent a unitary collection but are generally of a rather good quality or include works which were not previously available in the Library. They are listed and briefly described in the handwritten accession-lists available in the reading room of the Library and published in various issues of the *British Library Journal*: 1, 1, 1975, p. 101, pp. 103-104 (selective list of manuscripts acquired between January 1970 and June 1973); 5, 1, 1979, pp. 76-79 (manuscripts acquired in 1974); 6, 1, 1980, pp. 78-83 (acquisitions of 1975); 9, 1, 1983, pp. 76ff. (acquisitions of 1976). All the manuscripts of this group are carefully protected by additional paper or glass, whenever necessary. The last page has a pencil written note of the type 'JPL [= Jeremiah P. Losty], date, number [of folios as counted by JPL]'. The acquisitions show a particular but not exclusive interest in illustrated manuscripts (especially for the period 1970-1973), some of which have been described by Dr. J.P. Losty: 'Some illustrated Jain Manuscripts' in *British Library Journal* 1, 2, 1975, pp. 145-152, about Or. 13362, 13475, 13476, 13454 [and Or. 2116 (C)]. These acquisitions have enriched the collection of Jain Prakrit or Sanskrit works accompanied by Gujarati commentaries. The provenance of this part of the collection is obviously not uniform since it is the result of purchases made over the years. However, there are exceptional cases where codicology can point to a common source: e.g. Or. 13598, 13599 and 13600 which have exactly the same Scribal Remark and were copied by the same scribe at the same place (Bhuj).

One of the most recently acquired manuscripts, probably around 1980, is a fragmentary specimen of Indravāmadeva's *Trailokyadīpikā* (Or. 15892: Cat. No. 1221), a Digambara work on Jain cosmology. This is an aesthetically interesting item, neatly written and illustrated, of an unusually large size. However, the text is incomplete. The origin of this manuscript is intriguing. It was acquired from an auction sale (see details in the relevant entry), but originally belonged to the collection of Sir Thomas Phillipps (1792-1872), a bibliophile, whose life's main business was the collection of rare manuscripts of all ages, countries, languages and subjects'.[2] He worked in the tradition of the great founders of the British Library, Sir Robert Cotton and Sir Robert Harley who, as he writes, were the examples he always kept in view. His purchases were made at sales in Europe only. They resulted in a collection of about sixty thousand items, including some four or five hundred volumes of Oriental manuscripts.

---

[5] The *Praśnayvyākaraṇa* with Abhayadevasūri's comm. (the 10th Anga) is numbered Or. 5134. It is followed by Or. 5135 and Or. 5136, two manuscripts of the *Aupapātika*. Had the *Vipākasūtra* been there, it would have stood in between.

[1] For more details see *Oxford Dictionary of National Biography,* Oxford University Press 2004-2005 (article by G.R. Seaman); Roger William Lipsey, *Coomaraswamy. His Life and Work,* Princeton University Press, 1977 (Bollingen Series 89); introduction to A.K.C., *Selected Letters,* Delhi: Indira Gandhi National Centre for the Arts, 2003, pp. xixff.

[2] The *Dictionary of National Biography* ed. by Sir Leslie Stephen and Sir Sidney Lee, vol. 15, Oxford University Press, 1917, p. 1078.

A remarkable recent acquisition: an invitation scroll from Sirohi

In the autumn of 2005 Sam Fogg in London offered a wide variety of Jain illustrated items which are described in *The Coloured Cosmos: Jain Painting* 1450-1850 (freely available on www.samfogg.com). The British Library was able to enrich its important collections by the acquisition of an invitation scroll on paper. To our knowledge, this is the only instance of such a document to be kept in a public institution in Europe. The formal letter (*vijñaptipatra*) was sent in V.S. 1801 (= A.D. 1744) by the Kharataragaccha community from Sirohi in order to invite the leader Jiṇabhaktisūri who was residing at Radhanpur to spend the rainy-season in Sirohi (Cat. No. 1425).

Appendix: Two Jain manuscripts from Général Claude Martin's library

The India Office and Oriental Collections hold two Jain manuscripts which can be considered as curiosities. I.O. San. 2909 contains the Hindi commentary by Hemarāja (17th century) on Kundakunda's *Pancāstikāya* and the Hindi commentary by the same author on Nemicandra's *Karmakāṇḍa*. Add. 25,022 contains a Persian commentary by Dilārām on the same two works. The first comes from the collection of John Leyden; the second was bought by the British Museum. Both of them however originally belonged to Claude Martin's library. The name of the French General (1735-1800) is mentioned on the last page of I.O. San. 2909; at the end of the first commentary of Add. 25,022, Dilārām states explicitly that he wrote this commentary at the command of Claude Martin and completed it in 1796. A French native from Lyon, Claude Martin had been so much disappointed 'by his country's wavering policies that he settled in Lucknow for the rest of his life and became a Major-General in the Bengal army'.[1] He acquired a remarkable fluency in Persian and built an immense oriental library, which contained more than five hundred and seven titles and was sold in public auctions from 1801 to 1805. Not much is known about its exact contents.[2] The presence of these two Digambara works with their Persian and Hindi commentaries is historically significant and testifies to the vast curiosity of the French polymath:

> 'Martin's religious beliefs, expressed in his will, blend with Enlightenment deist thinking, acknowledging a Supreme Being but discounting organized religion ... He still sought out the true path of religion, endeavouring 'to learn the religion of other nations and sects, that I might be a proper judge for myself'.[3]

Indeed, the two Digambara treatises can serve such a purpose, through their analysis of mechanisms at work in the world and the soul.

Jain manuscripts of the British Museum and the Victoria and Albert Museum

The Jain manuscripts kept in what is today the British Museum make up only a small lot. As can be expected, their value as art objects was the reason for their purchase or inclusion in the collections, and, the case arising, for their preservation in the British Museum. Had they been considered as 'ordinary manuscripts', they would have been united with the rest and would have gone to the British Library when it was constituted in 1973. At that time the agreement on the transfer of materials specified that manuscripts would go to the Department of Oriental Printed Books and Manuscripts, whereas albums and single pages would remain with the Department of Oriental Antiquities. The items described in the present catalogue are a few illustrated pages of the *Kalpasūtra* and a metal *yantra* of Digambara origin. This object (OA 1880-4057) has been selected as one of the nine items representing Jainism in COMPASS (COllections Multimedia Public AccesS System on the Web).

The same holds true for the Victoria and Albert Museum. The number of relevant items however is larger and shows a wider variety. A preliminary printed list with very brief descriptions is available in *Art of India. Paintings and Drawings in the Victoria & Albert Museum. Catalogue & Microfiche Guide (*Emmett Publishing, 1992), section 'Western India', pp. 8-10. There are a few cosmological paintings, scattered illustrated folios of the *Kalpasūtra*, a continuous manuscript of the same with 38 illustrations, an illustrated manuscript of the *Uttarādhyayanasūtra*, some illustrated folios of cosmological works and some

[1] J.-M. Lafont p. 29 in *Indika. Essays in Indo-French Relations*, 1630-1976, Delhi: Manohar, 2000.

[2] For this question see Lafont, Indika p. 106 and n. 164 referring to S.C. Hill, *The Life of Claude Martin*, Calcutta, 1901, pp. 111-122 and R. Llewellyn-Jones, *A Very Ingenious Man. Claude Martin in Early Colonial India, Delhi,* OUP, 1992, chap. V, 'The Polymath', pp. 119-154; J.-M. Lafont, 'The French in Lucknow' in *Lucknow. Memories of a City,* Delhi, 1997, pp. 67-82.

[3] R. Llewellyn-Jones, *A Man of Enlightenment in Eighteenth-century India. The Letters of Claude Martin, 1766-1800,* edited and introduced by, New Delhi: Permanent Black, 2003, p. 9.

miscellaneous objects. The accession list shows that most items were bought directly in England, from famous owners and art-specialists such as A.K. Coomaraswamy (letter dated 11.3.1914, '39 Brookfield, West Hill, Highgate N' for IM 161-1914 and IM 161A-1914) or Robert Skelton (IS 83-1963 and IS 84-1963), or less famous individuals (Cat. Nos. 107, 165). A few illustrated pages are permanently exhibited in the Nehru Gallery. Some items were shown to the public during the 1995 exhibition *Peaceful Liberators*. Consequently, several items have been reproduced in various publications (see references under the individual entries).

Users of the collections

In short, the Jain manuscripts of the India Office and of the Oriental Collections belong to two groups: those which were bought or collected by British administrators or employees who were not scholars in the first place, although some of them became quasi-indologists and developed a genuine interest in the Jains (Mackenzie, Buchanan), and those who collected manuscripts with a definite purpose because Jainism was one of their fields of research (Bühler, Jacobi). The latter often used their own manuscripts for their own work. Besides, there are several Jain manuscripts both of the India Office and the Oriental Collections of the then British Museum which were used for editions or studies by Indologists of the 19th century and the first thirty years of the 20th century. These manuscripts have a significant place in the development of their research; these scholars deserve a special mention, which will be the topic of this section (see also Alphabetical index p 43).

The help provided by the librarians of the two institutions, especially to those who could not come to England, was instrumental in the growth of a research based on original documents and was gladly acknowledged by the scholars of the past. Three names are often mentioned in this context and deserve a few words, for many things could not have been done without them.

1) Reinhold Rost (1822-1896), a German born in Eisenberg, near Jena (Sax-Altenberg), who had been attracted by Oriental studies at an early age, 'came at once to England, the great storehouse of Sanskrit MSS.'[1] He was Secretary to the Royal Asiatic Society from 1864 to 1869, and was then appointed Librarian to the India Office. His personal publications are not numerous, but significant. It is however the prominent part he played in the spreading of knowledge thanks to the functions he had at the India Office that really earned him public recognition.

> 'Dr. Rost will long be remembered as Librarian to the India Office. If he left it to others to catalogue and edit the MSS., this was not through incapacity for either task. Though primarily a Sanskritist, he had to consider the claims of Arabic and Persian, of Pāli, Burmese, and Sinhalese, of Tibetan and Malay, and of countless vernaculars. (...). In brief, Dr. Rost elected to turn himself into an Oriental encyclopaedia, which no one ever consulted in vain. Through his initiative MSS. were lent freely to foreign scholars; and it is hardly too much to say that on the Continent he was regarded as a steward of Oriental knowledge to whom everyone might appeal without hesitating for assistance and advice. This feeling was strongly expressed in a testimonial presented to him in 1892, when it was rumoured that he was to be retired compulsorily from his post. Frenchmen joined with Germans to testifying to the kindness and impartiality which he had always displayed towards fellow-students'.[2]

Scholars who had recourse to him for obtaining Jain manuscripts gladly acknowledged the librarian's help.[3]

2) Frederick William Thomas (1867-1956),[4] a famous Indologist and Tibetologist, was appointed assistant librarian of the India Office under C.H. Tawney in 1898. He held the post of main Librarian of the India

[1] Obituary Notice published in the *Journal of the Royal Asiatic Society* 1896, p. 367 (source of the information given here); see also *Oxford Dictionary of National Biography,* Oxford University Press 2004-2005 (article by A.N. Wollaston, rev. J.B. Katz).

[2] Quoted from the Obituary notice in *JRAS* 1896, p. 368.

[3] E. Leumann: see *Unvergessene, gestorben in den Jahren 1891-1908. Lebensdate, Bilder und Beileidbriefe,* Strassburg, 1909, p. 17: 'Dr. Reinhold Rost, hochverdienter und gastfreier Bibliothekar des India Office zu London'; P.P. Pavolini: cf. 'Il compendio dei cinque elementi', *Giornale della Societa Asiatica Italiana* 14 (1901) p. 4: '... la copia che dal ms. 2909 dell' India Office io trassi a Londra nel settembre del 1892, avendo ottenuto in prestito detto ms. dalla liberale condiscendenza del tanto compianto R. Rost'; A.C. Burnell, 'A Letter to Dr. Rost, On Sanskrit MSS. procured by him in South India' in *Transactions of the German Oriental Society* 22 (1868), p. 326.

[4] See *Oxford Dictionary of National Biography,* Oxford University Press, 2004-2005 (article by A.J. Arberry, rev. J.B. Katz).

Office, having succeeded Tawney, from 1903 to 1927, before he was elected Boden Professor of Sanskrit at Oxford from 1927 to 1937. The work he accomplished in arranging printed books and manuscripts at the India Office was a matter of admiration for all. Beside dealing with all the Tibetan documents from Tunhuang, he was also an authority of Jainism.[1] His works in this field include the edition and annotation of Jagmandarlal Jaini's *Outlines of Jainism* (1916), an introduction to the English translation of Kundakunda's *Pravacanasāra* with Amṛtacandra's commentary by B. Faddegon (1935), and the authoritative English translation of Hemacandra's *Anyayogavyavaccheda-dvātriṁśikā* with Malliṣeṇa's *Syādvādamanjarī* under the title *The flower-spray of the quodammodo doctrine*, which was published after his death in 1956 through the good offices of Edward Conze, to whom the translation was actually dictated (Deutsche Akademie der Wissenschaften Berlin; Indian reprint, 1968). F.W. Thomas's interest in this field encouraged him to help all scholars who needed to get Jain manuscripts[2]

3) Lionel David Barnett (1871-1960) joined the staff of the British Museum as assistant keeper in the department of Oriental Printed Books and Manuscripts in 1899. From 1908 to 1936 he was keeper of this department, succeeding Sir Robert Douglas to the post.[3] His erudition as an orientalist was tremendous. His contribution both to the acquisition of printed books and manuscripts in the British Museum and to bibliography are highly significant. Like F.W. Thomas and C. Bendall, L.D. Barnett was also a recognized Indologist. From 1906 to 1917 he was professor of Sanskrit at University College, London. In common with F.W. Thomas, Barnett had a special interest in Jainism and Prakrit as shown by a large number of reviews of German, French and Indian publications on Jainism and his introduction to *The first principles of the Jain Philosophy* (compiled and published by Hīrāchand Līlādhar Jhaverī. 61 p., London, 1910).[4] Last but not least, Barnett translated from Prakrit into English two books of the Jain Āgamas: the *Antagaḍa-dasāo* (7th Anga) and the *Aṇuttarovavāiya-dasāo* (8th Anga), published in 1907 (London; reprint Varanasi, 1973). For the *Antagaḍa-dasāo* Barnett did not include the original text, but had to 'constitute a provisional text' (Introduction p. x). The original text of the eighth Anga, however, is included as an appendix to the translation. Among the materials used for both are four manuscripts from the then British Museum: Or. 2100 (Ratnavijaya collection) and Or. 5129 (Jacobi collection) on the one hand, and Or. 5130 and Or. 5131 on the other. Barnett was thus a scholar-librarian whose help is readily acknowledged, among many others by A.K. Coomaraswamy.[5]

Ernst Leumann

Ernst Leumann (1859-1931) was a Swiss(-German) Indologist who taught in Strassburg[6] and who is well known to all specialists of Jainism. He managed to acquire systematically an extremely important collection of Jain manuscripts (Sanskrit, Prakrit, Śvetāmbara and Digambara) for the University Library. It is no surprise to read his name in connection with the Jain manuscripts at the India Office Library and the then British Museum. Although he did not take any part in collecting or donating manuscripts to these institutions, he was one of the rare persons to realize their usefulness as a whole, as he did with other collections in Europe, whether Berlin, Vienna or Florence, not to speak of manuscripts kept in India which he got sent to him on loan. Curiosity, or even avidity, for new documents was one of his characteristics. Thus the publication of the list of Jacobi's manuscripts (see above) aroused his, as did the presence of the Ratnavijayasūri collection in the British Museum. This collection was acquired in 1879-1880; the first notes taken by Leumann date back to 1883.

---

[1] For some information see the Obituary by L.D. Barnett in *Journal of the Royal Asiatic Society* 1957, pp. 142-143.

[2] See Kirfel, preface to *Die Kosmographie der Inder,* Bonn, Leipzig, 1920; L.P. Tessitori, in *Studi Giainici,* Udine, 2000, p. 67; A. Ballini, Rivista degli Studi Orientali 4, 1912, p. 1006, etc.

[3] See *Oxford Dictionary of National Biography*, Oxford University Press 2004-2005 (article by A.S. Fulton, rev. J.B. Katz).

[4] See for more details the 'Bibliography of the Published Writings of Dr. L.D. Barnett' compiled by Edith M. White, *Bulletin of the School of Oriental and African Studies* 12, 3-4 (1948), pp. 497-523.

[5] *Catalogue of the Indian Collections in the Museum of Fine Arts,* Boston, Part IV Jaina Paintings and Manuscripts (1924), introduction (summary of the story of Śālibhadra based on the original Sanskrit text of Dharma Kumāra from a manuscript in the British Museum, 'kindly communicated by Dr. L.D. Barnett'; see Cat. No. 746).

[6] The town was known as Strassburg between 1871 and 1919, as it was part of the German territory.

Leumann made several visits to England, and the libraries in London, Oxford and Cambridge. He noted extracts of manuscripts in 1883 and 1888. Later on, seizing the opportunity given by the Congress of Orientalists which took place in London in 1892, Ernst Leumann spent the autumn of that year in England, consulting the London manuscripts, but also those kept in Cambridge (Bendall collection) and Oxford. The London manuscripts used by Leumann were the Prakrit and Sanskrit ones kept at the India Office Library, the Ratnavijayasūri collection, and manuscripts belonging to H. Jacobi, before and after they were presented to the British Museum. Probably because they were isolated items not belonging to any special collection and had not been catalogued, the palm-leaf manuscripts of the *Jītakalpa-sūtra, -cūrṇi* and *-bṛhadvyākhyā* (Or. 1385 and 1386), acquired by the British Museum in 1876, remained unknown to him although the study of this corpus counts among his pioneering works. Had he seen them, even after the publication of his monograph in 1892, he would certainly have recorded their existence.

The three manuscripts of the *Aupapātika-sūtra* belonging to H. Jacobi (Or. 5135, 5136 and 5137) and one manuscript of the *Kālakācārya-kathā* also from the same source (I.O. San. 3177) were used by E. Leumann for his editions of these works published in 1883. But for all other London manuscripts which he used, the reader has to refer to unpublished extracts or lists found in a number of his notebooks kept in the Institut für Kultur und Geschichte Indiens und Tibets (University of Hamburg). Fortunately, Leumann himself published two lists which help the reader to locate the notebooks where particular manuscripts have been listed or copied: 'Liste von transcribirten Abschriften und Auszügen vorwiegend aus der Jaina-Literatur' (*ZDMG* 45, 1891, pp. 454-464, notebooks 1-90) and 'Liste von transcribirten Abschriften und Auszügen aus der Jaina-Litteratur' (*ZDMG* 47, 1893, pp. 308-315, notebooks 91ff.). The second list was meant by its author as a substitute for a full catalogue:

> 'Die in London verbrachten Herbstferien haben meine Sammlung wieder sehr bereichert. Namentlich ist ein Ueberblick über die Jaina-Handschriften des British Museum gewonnen worden, der schon immerein Desiderium unserer Forschung war. Da so bald kein Catalog zu jenen Schätzen erscheinen wird, dürften die folgenden Zeilen zur vorläufigen Orientirung willkomen sein' (p. 308).[1]

The two lists have recently been reprinted in the *Catalogue of the Papers of Ernst Leumann in the Institute for the Culture and History of India and Tibet, University of Hamburg* compiled by Mrs. Birte Plutat,[2] which also provides an invaluable detailed list and analysis of all the notebooks. Leumann's interest was not to catalogue manuscripts for the sake of cataloguing. Manuscripts were almost the only available source of information about certain texts or groups of texts (e.g. the so-called *Āvaśyaka*-literature) which were crucial in Leumann's holistic conception of the description of Jain literature. It would be out of place here to give a full list of Leumann's notebooks dealing with all the London manuscripts. In the case of notebooks dealing with an individual manuscript, the reader is referred to the notes about the relevant manuscript in the present catalogue for more information. Here we give only a brief description of the main notebooks which have a more general relevance.

No. 113 'Gesammtliste der Jaina MSS. des Brit. Mus. unter Ausschluss der wenigen canonischen'. Notebook perhaps given by the Library ('Oriental' in red printed on each page). Black binding, blue paper, 6 p., 12,5 x 10,5 cms. Alphabetical list of titles and shelfmark written in pencil. In ink are added the number of folios (occasionally) and the mention 'Exc.' (= Excerpt) or 'Orig. Extr.' which mean that extracts of the given manuscript are available in other notebooks (for instance No. 60). Manuscripts of the Ratnavijayasūri collection (Or. 2102ff.), of the Bendall collection (Or. 3348 etc.) and of the Erskine collection ('Add.'), Harley manuscript ('Harley 415') are listed.

No. 60 'Vom Jahre 1883: Excerpte aus Manuscripten des Brit. Mus. und aus dem Druck Prakaraṇa-ratnākara vol. III & IV'. Notebook. Green binding. Pages are numbered in different ways. The first part contains notes on manuscripts of the Ratnavijayasūri collection. The *Prakaraṇaratnākara,* vols. III-IV, which forms the other part, is a series of Jain treatises which had been recently published in India at a time when rather few published editions were generally available, hence, probably, Leumann's interest in these volumes.

[1] 'The autumn holidays spent in London have again increased my collection in a large extent. More precisely, it has led to an overview on the Jain manuscripts of the British Museum, which was always since long a desideratum for our research. *Since it is unlikely that a catalogue of these treasures will appear in a near future* [italics ours], the following lines could be wellcome as a general orientation'.

[2] Stuttgart, Franz Steiner Verlag, 1998: *Alt- und Neu-Indische Studien* 49.

No. 111 'Londoner Excerpte vom Herbst 1892. Quart-Collectivheft'. Notebook. Black binding. Pages are unnumbered. 17 x 21,7 cms. The first page is an 'Alphabetische Liste der Londoner Excerpte vom Herbst 1892'. Each page contains some notes on the description or/and on the text of an individual manuscript. Besides manuscripts of the British Museum (Ratnavijayasūri and Bendall collection), those of the Royal Asiatic Society (Tod collection) and of the Cambridge collection are described. See the relevant entries of the present catalogue for further information.

No. 112 'Londoner Excerpte von Herbst 1892. Octav-Collectivheft'. Notebook. Black binding. Pages are unnumbered. 12 x 17,4 cms. Same method as in No. 111. Includes British Museum as well as Royal Asiatic Society and Cambridge collections. See the relevant entries of the present catalogue for further information.

Ananda Kentish Coomaraswamy

Not only did Coomaraswamy sell a few Jain items to British institutions; he also drew from their material for his own studies on Jain art. His founding role in the establishment of Indian art as a full-fledged subject and the work he did to awaken Western minds to the beauty of Indian art did not initially take in Jain art. The specialized nature of this field seems to have been recognized by him in the course of time. Although his appreciation of Jain art and the achievements of Jain artists was initially not very high, as has been recently recalled by R. Cohen,[1] Coomaraswamy soon became more interested, seeing the curiosity of Western scholars, especially Germans, for the Jain tradition in the beginning of the 20th century. Thus A.K.C., as he was commonly known, bought several Jain illustrated manuscripts which added to his private collection. He was the author of practically the first contribution to Jain art (exception made of Hüttemann's *Miniaturen zum Jinacaritra,* Baessler Archiv, 1913). This was 'Notes on Jaina Art' published in 1914, when A.K.C. was still living in England. This contribution centres around the Life of Mahāvīra and other Jinas, around the story of Kālaka and, more secondarily, around Jain cosmology. Hence it chiefly concerns manuscripts of the *Kalpasūtra* and the *Kālakācārya-kathā*, the illustrations of which are described at length and reproduced, but also the *Uttarādhyayana* and the *Laghukṣetra-samāsa*. The material used is divided between *Kalpasūtra* manuscripts belonging to the author (labelled as 'C.A.' to 'C.F.A') and manuscripts from the India Office or the British Museum collections, namely I.O. San. 3177 and Or. 5149 (*Kalpasūtra* manuscripts from Jacobi's collection), Or. 5257 (manuscript of the *Uttarādhyayana* from Jacobi's collection) and Add. 26.374 (manuscript of the *Laghukṣetrasamāsa*), the value of which is shown by this pioneering study.[2]

Other famous users

A *nāmamālā* of other scholars who had recourse to one or several Jain manuscripts kept in the India Office and Oriental Collections can easily be woven. It would include the names of R.A. Hoernle (ed. of the *Uvāsagadasāo*), E. Windisch (ed. of Hemacandra's *Yogaśāstra*), P.A. Pavolini (*Pancāstikāya*), and L.P. Tessitori (published or unpublished editions of several texts and manuscripts used for their linguistic data). Johannes Klatt (1852-?), who used several of H. Jacobi's manuscripts for his unfortunately unfinished *Specimen of a Literary-Bibliographical Jaina-Onomasticon* (Leipzig, 1892) and Paul Goldschmidt (1850-1877), who transcribed a few Jain manuscripts belonging to the India Office, also deserve a special mention. The Notes to the relevant entries provide the necessary details.

[1] See the introduction by Richard J. Cohen to Ananda K. Coomaraswamy, *Essays on Jaina Art,* Delhi: Indira Gandhi National Centre for the Arts / Manohar, 2003 for a general assessment and quotations. (Unfortunately this extremely useful book lacks a simple biography or chronology of A.K.C. and does not clearly indicate the first date of publication of the various contributions collected in the volume).

[2] A.K.C., 'Notes on Jaina Art', pp. 81ff. (page numbering as in the reprint of Essays on Jaina Art).

Manuscripts and scholars: alphabetical index

(Restricted to manuscripts used for a description or an edition; references are to the Catalogue numbers)

Balbir N. 651, 920
Ballini A. See Remark following 60
Barnett L.D. 41, 50, 51, (746)
Bender E. 749
Bühler G. 760, 762, 765, 767a-767b
Colebrooke 333
Coomaraswamy A.K. 96, 98, 164, 316, 708, 746
Dave T.N. 527
Goldschmidt P. 117, 125, 130
Hertel J. 850; see Schmidt
Hoernle R. 36
Jacobi H. 1, 2, 3, 8, 9, 96, 98, 115, 132, 171, 172, 703, 708, 878, 879, 880, 887, 908, 912, 914
Kirfel W. 316, 333, 1220
Kosambi D.D. 1300
Laber J. 1291
Leumann E. 61, 62, 63, 201, 253, 268, 650, 651, 707, 863
Losty J.P. 165, 178, 327, 337
Norman K.R. 215, 217
Parikh V.G. 683
Pavolini P.E. 1200
Pullé F.L. 672
(Reuter J.N. 515)
Schmidt R. & Hertel J. 1228
Tawney C.H. 755, 756, 776
Tessitori L.P. 525, 559, 579, 585
Vogel C. 1360
Weber A. 855
Williams R. 723
Windisch E. 548
Zachariae Th. 1353

Recapitulative table

The Jain manuscripts at the British Library today

Collection	Year	Number of mss.
Founding collections (B.L.)	1753	2 (Harley & Sloane)
Colebrooke (I.O.)[1]	Presented 1819	86
Col. Mackenzie (I.O.)	Purchased 1822	21
W. Erskine (B.L.)	1865	62
Burnell (I.O.)	Presented 1870, purchased 1882	13
Palm-leaf mss. from Western India	1876	3
Bühler (I.O.)	Presented 1888	43
Other collections, Skt. & Pkt. (I.O.)[2]	various dates	184
Bhagavandas Kevaldas/Ratnavijaya (B.L.)	1879	163
Bendall (B.L.)	1886	11
Miles (B.L.)	1891, 1911	13
Jacobi (B.L.)	1897	109
Guj., Raj. or Hindi mss. (I.O.)	? 1914	21
Jambuvijaya (I.O.)	1950s	195 (197)[3]
Additional groups of unknown origin (B.L.)	?	17 (13+4)
Recent acquisitions	1970s	113 (including one from Phillipps)
	2005	1 (Invitation scroll)
		TOTAL: 1057

Based on our own count and on the following sources: A.B. Keith, *Catalogue of the Sanskrit and Prakrit Manuscripts in the Library of the India Office.* vol. 2 *Brahmanical and Jaina Manuscripts* (in two parts). London, 1935. — J.F. Blumhardt, *Catalogue of the Gujarati & Rajasthani Manuscripts in the India Office Library.* Oxford University Press, 1954. — India Office Library and Records. *Guide to the Sanskrit and Prākrit Collections* (fascicle, n.d.). — J.P. Losty and M.J.C. O'Keefe, *Sanskrit and Prakrit collections in the British Library,* n.d. — *Department of Oriental Printed Books and Manuscripts, British Museum, Jain Manuscripts.* Typed unpublished document kept in the reading room of the India Office & Oriental collections prepared by John Brough. — J.F. Blumhardt, *Catalogue of the Marathi, Gujarati, Bengali, Assamese, Oriya, Pushtu, and Sindhi Manuscripts in the Library of the British Museum.* British Museum, 1905. — C. Bendall, *Catalogue of the Sanskrit Manuscripts in the British Museum.* London, 1902. — For recent acquisitions see articles in the *British Library Journal* 1 (1975); 5,1 (1979); 6,1 (1980); 9,1 (1983)

[1] Considered separately in this list, although not belonging to the so-called 'special collections' (e.g., Bühler, Burnell, Mackenzie) in the I.O. Catalogue.

[2] Th. Aufrecht, F. Buchanan, A.K. Coomaraswamy, Gaikawar, A.M.T. Jackson, J. Leyden, J. Taylor.

[3] Officially there are 197 items, but Nos. 191 and 194 are not available.

— For individual lists prepared by the owners themselves (e.g. Jacobi) see the relevant section of the Introduction, above.

British Museum & Victoria and Albert Museum

British Museum	20th century	8 (including one yantra, copper plate)
Victoria and Albert Museum	20th century	18

Comparative table: Towards an Inventory of Jain Manuscripts in Europe

As conceived by C.B. Tripāṭhī, the present Catalogue was to form one important component in a much larger visionary project which would include, over the years, a complete survey of all Jain manuscripts in Europe. He used to call it 'IJME' (Inventory of Jain Manuscripts in Europe). Whether enough minds and hands will one day be found to fulfil such a goal remains to be seen. Our comparative table is a modest preliminary and does not intend to cover the whole of Europe exhaustively. We had to take into account practical reasons: size of the collections, availability of descriptive material at hand.

To enrich the comparison here are some approximate statistical figures regarding the number of Jain manuscripts in the Western world outside Europe in the narrow sense of the word:

United States of America

Total number of Jaina manuscripts c. 415. (based on a rough survey of the various sections of A Census of Indic Manuscripts in the United States and Canada, compiled by H.I. Poleman, New Haven: American Oriental Society, 1938). See Introduction p. xiii:

> 'These American manuscripts are especially rich in Jain texts, the bulk of which are found at Harvard. It can be readily ascertained by glancing through this list and M.B. Emeneau's A Union List of Printed Indic Texts and Translations in American Libraries that even among the canonical Jain works the manuscript collection contains items not found in any American library in printed form'.

The total number of Indian manuscripts listed in this compilation reaches between 7500 to 8000.

Russia: St. Petersburg, Asiatic Museum & Russian National Library.

About 150 Jain manuscripts (according to the hand-written list kindly communicated by Professor A. Vigasin, Moscow).

Note: The six published volumes of the Catalogue of the manuscripts kept at the L.D. Institute of Indology in Ahmedabad contain a total of 21,197 entries (vol. 1-3: 7611; vol. 4: 1369 + 1042; vol. 5: 6108, vol. 6: 5067). More than 80 to 90% correspond to Jain works. There are still more to be catalogued.

Library	Years of acquisition by the collector	Number of mss.	Number of entries or texts
Tod Collection, Royal Asiatic Society	1799-1823	53	ca. 70
Kielhorn collection, Göttingen University Library[1]	1866-1881	14	27
Berlin, Königliche Bibliothek	1873-1878 (+ 1886-89), official letter dated 30 June 1873: 'It appears to His Excellency the Governor in Council to be no objection to Dr. Bühler's supplying the Royal Library of Berlin with copies of such sacred writings of the Jainas as have already been collected for Government' (in Weber, vol. 2.3, p. VIII)	259 (out of a total of 901 described in vol. 2, cf. vol. 2.3, p. V)	328 (259 + 69 śāstric works)
Oxford, Indian Institute (Sir Monier Monier-Williams)	'procured in 1877-1878 through the agency of Prof. Georg Bühler' (p. 1)	39	39

[1] This is the only 'small' German collection surveyed for this table. Isolated Jain manuscripts of more or less importance are found in some of the pubished volumes of the series Verzeichnis der Orientalischen Handschriften in Deutschland. Indische Handschriften: vol. II,1 (Marburg), II,2 (Göttingen), II,5; II,7 (Munich); II,8; II,9; II,12.

Remarks	Catalogue
A little more than one third of the full collection which has 171 mss.; Jain mss. from Western India, a few Canonical texts with or without comm., works of doctrine and cosmology, Old Gujarati works (narratives, hymns, etc.). To be added to the 53: two Sanskrit classics written by Jain scribes (No. 15 and 38)	Descriptive list by L.D.Barnett, 'Catalogue of the Tod Collection of Indian Manuscripts of the Royal Asiatic Society', JRAS 1940, Part II, April, pp. 129-178.
9 mss. out of the total are grammatical or lexicographical works by Hemacandra (Śabdānuśāsana, with comm., Lingānuśāsana, Abhidhānacintāmaṇi); noteworthy are one illustrated Kalpasūtra (with 15 miniatures), a fragmentary collection or Prakīrṇakas, and, above all, a palm-leaf composite ms. (220 leaves) containing portions of the Vyavahāracūrṇi ('Sanskrit 239', cf. 'Nachtrag', pp. 117-119).	R. Fick, 'Kielhorns Handschriften-Sammlung. Verzeichnis der aus Franz Kielhorns Nachlass 1908 der Göttinger Universitäts-Bibliothek überwiesenen Sanskrit-Handschriften', Nachrichten von der Gesellschaft der Wissenschaften zu Göttingen aus dem Jahre 1930, pp. 65-94; 'Nachtrag', Nachrichten ..., 1941, 4, pp. 115-119.
Understandable emphasis on the Siddhānta (160 entries) in view of the time: the Jain 'canon' was not known in the West; Weber's contribution to its knowledge was tremendous. As he himself writes, the contribution 'Über die heiligen Schriften der Jainas' (publ. in Indische Studien vol. 16 & 17, 1883-84) was a kind of commentary to the catalogue of the canonical mss. (Verz. 2.2). The Berlin coll. contains copies of the 45 Āgamas (2 lacunae only) and includes copies of some bhāṣyas and cūrṇis. The rest is divided into the following sections: 1. Dogmatics and religious discipline (36 mss.); 2. Stava & Stotra (9); 3. Legendary works (21); 4. Didactic lit. (33). In these sections there are also a few Digambara works.[2]	Weber, Verzeichnis 2.1, 1886 (Śāstric disciplines); 2.2, 1888 (Siddhānta), 2.3, 1892 (other Jain works + additions).
Emphasis on canonical literature (23 entries) with comm. in Sanskrit. Only two comm. in Guj.; moreover, Āvaśyaka literature (4 items), cosmology (4), dogmatics (2), narrative literature (3), hymns (3). Only one representative of Dig. literature (Raviṣeṇa's Padmacarita).	A.B. Keith, A Catalogue of the Sanskrit and Prākrit MSS. in the Indian Institute Library Oxford, Oxford, 1903.

[2] Compare A. Parpola: 'His second major field was Jainism, on which he started publishing pioneering and fundamental works in 1858. A catalyst to tremendous further achievements was the arrival to the Royal Library of Berlin of a collection of 259 Jaina manuscripts in 1873 and 1878, sent from India by Georg Bühler. This resulted in new large volumes of manuscript catalogues almost amounting to text editions (1886-1892), and a first detailed account of the extensive Jaina literature (1883-1884). Although the study of Prakrit had been initiated already by Weber's teacher Christian Lassen ..., the Jaina studies of Weber and his monumental edition of Hāla's Sattasaī (1881) ... put it on an altogether new level', p. 194 of 'Publications of the Great Indologist Fr. Albert Weber' in Studia Orientalia published by the Finnish Oriental Society 97, 2003 (Remota Relata. Essays on the History of Oriental Studies in Honour of Harry Halén).

Library	Years of acquisition by the collector	Number of mss.	Number of entries or texts
Bühler collection Vienna University Library	1881-1882, Gujarat (procured through Bhagavandas Kevaldas, who encouraged Bühler to bring some mss. to Europe)	74	74
Oxford, Bodleian Library	1884-85, mss. obtained by the German scholar E. Hultzsch (1857-1927) and purchased by the Bodleian in 1897; a few items from Wilson, Mill or Walker.	ca. 135	ca. 148 (two composite mss.)
Cambridge University Library, Bendall collection	1884-5 (help of Bhagavandas Kevaldas)	70 (Rajputana) + 140 (Bombay)	± 220
Florence, Bibliotheca Nazionale Centrale	1885-86 around Bombay & Surat, mainly by A. de Gubernatis	ca. 295	ca. 350

Remarks	Catalogue
30 mss. of the Āgamas in the strict sense; the rest: non-canonical works on dharma and karma (21 mss.); hymns (10 mss.); narrative lit. (9 mss.); other (4 mss.). Mostly in Pkt. & Skt. Few in Guj.	G. Bühler, 'Ueber eine kürzlich für die Wiener Universität erworbene Sammlung von Sanskrit- und Prakrit-Handschriften', SPAW 1892, pp. 563ff. (list); U. Podzeit, Die Indische Handschriften an der Universitätsbibliothek Wien, Wien: Selbstverlag, 1988 (includes the description of mss. from the Bühler coll. as well as other items acquired from other sources).
All major literary categories are represented: canonical literature, Āvaśyaka texts, cosmology, dogmatics, narrative literature, hymns. Languages: Pkt. and Pkt.; Guj. isolated. Dig. tradition represented by 10 works. One instance of a Dig. work with a Persian comm. (Wilson 261, Skt. Cat. No. 1371).	Nos. 1334-1418 in M. Winternitz, A.B. Keith, Catalogue of Sanskrit MSS. in the Bodleian Library, vol. 2, Oxford, 1905; A.B. Keith, Catalogue of the Prākrit Manuscripts in the Bodleian Library, Oxford, 1911 (16 entries are common to the two catalogues).
Certainly an interesting collection which would deserve a full cataloguing (planned for the near future): 'I could have wished ... that [my notes] could have been fuller and more comprehensive. But I trust that the MSS. may be properly catalogued, along with the valuable collection of Jain MSS. acquired by the University some years ago' (A Journey p. 39). Indeed, it includes some valuable and rather rare items.	Lists with brief notes on some mss. in C. Bendall, A Journey of Literary and Archaeological Research in Nepal and Northern India during the winter of 1884-5, Cambridge, 1886, pp. 46-48 and 49-51.
65 mss. from the Siddhānta (among which the Piṇḍa-niryukti and the Niśītha-cūrṇi are noteworthy); the rest belongs to the 'extra-siddhānta': Dogmatics and religious literature (60 mss.); hymns (30); narrative lit. (50); belles-lettres & śāstric disciplines (ca. 30). Several mss. used by the Italian indologist L.P. Tessitori for eds. or linguistic data.	Belles-lettres & śāstric disciplines: cf. Florentine Sanskrit Manuscripts examined by Dr. Th. Aufrecht, Leipzig, 1892; for the Jain mss. proper cf. F.L. Pullé, 'The Florentine Jaina Mss.'. Prefatory remarks by Prof. Leumann; idem, 'Les mss. de l'extra-siddhânta (gainas) de la Bibliothèque Nationale Centrale de Florence'; idem, 'I manoscritti indiani della Biblioteca Nazionale Centrale di Firenze', GSAI 20, 1907, 65 pages (brief description & index); 'Catalogo dei MSS indiani appartenenti alla Biblioteca Nazionale Centrale di Firenze non compresi nei Cataloghi dell' Aufrecht e del Pavolini' (hand-written doc., communicated by F. Freschi), includes 3 Jain works.

Library	Years of acquisition by the collector	Number of mss.	Number of entries or texts
Strasbourg Bibliothèque Nationale et Universitaire (E. Leumann)	1891ff.; mss. purchased for the Strasbourg University Library through Bhagavandas Kevaldas for Śvet. literature from Western India and through Brahmasūri and his son Jinadāsa of Śravaṇa Belgola for the Dig. works.	193	336
Berlin Preussische Staatsbibliothek	between 1892 and 1944	770	1127
Paris, collection Émile Senart. [Also ca. 15 isolated items in Cabaton, Catalogue sommaire des manuscrits sanscrits et pālis, Paris, 1907 and 1912 (strictly Jain works + grammars, lexicons)]	around 1897-98	266 (+ 55 non- Jain)	ca. 281

Remarks	Catalogue
Coll. systematically started by E. Leumann: 'Leumann's main interest was the Āvaśyaka literature in its widest sense, including not only Śvetāmbara but also Digambara texts. He also collected Jaina Manuscripts not connected with the Āv. literature and had some of these copied. See for instance the Manuscripts (= modern copies) of the Vasudevahiṇḍi and of the Aṅgavidyā. As far as Digambara Manuscripts are concerned, the Strasbourg collection is richer than any other Jaina collection outside India' (Tripāṭhī 1975 p. 13). Significant number of mss. of early Śvetāmbara commentaries (niryuktis, bhāṣyas); Dig. mss. also from Karnatak including rare works.	Tripāṭhī 1975.
Overwhelming coll. of Śvetāmbara texts (1003) against Digambara (124); 322 independent texts (i.e. not commentaries) in languages other than Skt. or Pkt., i.e. Gujarati or Hindi. The importance of these languages and of the literature they represent for the history of the living religion was emphasized by Schubring (1944 p. VI).	Schubring 1944.
Mostly Skt. & Pkt. texts; Guj. works in minority. One illustrated Kalpasūtra ms. dated 1493 A.D. (described by Nalini Balbir in Bull. d'Etudes Indiennes 2, 1984).[1] Ca. 85 dated mss., between 1424 and 1898 A.D. (majority from the 18th cent.); include some modern copies. Dig. literature also represented. Nothing really remarkable, but a few mss copied at a date rather close to the date of composition (e.g. com. on Uttarādhy. by Bhāvavijayagaṇi; Munisundara's Gurvāvalī; Udayavīra's Pārśvanāthac.). Average selection of canonical, philosophical, dogmatical, cosmological works, narrative literature, hymns, ritualistic works; a few grammars and lexicons. A ms. of the Aṅgacūliyā.	J. Filliozat, 'État des manuscrits de la collection Émile Senart', Journal Asiatique 1936, 17 pages.

[1] There are also a few illustrated Kalpasūtra pages which are kept in the Musée Guimet (Paris) and have not hithertoo been described. They will be dealt with by Nalini Balbir in the near future.

Library	Years of acquisition by the collector	Number of mss.	Number of entries or texts
Tessitori Collection ('Fondo Tessitori') Vincenzo Joppi Civic Library, Udine (Italy)	between 1914 and 1916 in Jaipur and Jodhpur; donated to the Civic Library by Tessitori's family in 1923	215	374
London, Wellcome Institute	between 1911 and 1939	?[2]	?

[2] The Jain collections of the Wellcome Institute, which are being catalogued by Dr K.V. Sheth and K.K. Sheth, and are more difficult to count because of the fragmentary condition of many manuscripts. Hence no total number, even tentative, is given here.

Remarks	Catalogue
Contents comparable to the Jambuvijaya collection of London: Śvetāmbara works; mss. from Western India (mainly from Jodhpur and Bikaner areas); Prakrit texts represented by only a few current treatises (Uttarādhyayana, Daśavaikālika, Jīvavicāra, Karmagranthas, cosmological works); an overwhelming coll. of narrative poems and religious hymns in Old Gujarati or Rajasthani (in accordance with Tessitori's main interest for this stage of Indo-Aryan languages); about a dozen of non-Jain mss.	Provisional catalogue (to be revised and completed) put at Nalini Balbir's disposal by Dr. Fausto Freschi, President, Società Indologica L.P. Tessitori (Udine).
21 entries in the section 'Jainism' (Wujastyk, Handlist vol. I), Sanskrit & Prakrit works; 228 entries in the section 'Jain literature' (Friedlander), overwhelming majority of texts in Guj.; a few illustrations from Kalpasūtra mss. in Pearls of the Orient; for Jyotiṣa mss., cf. Pingree.	D. Wujastyk, A Handlist of Sanskrit and Prakrit Manuscripts, Volume I (1985); Volume II (1998); P. Friedlander, A Descriptive Catalogue of the Hindi Manuscripts, The Wellcome Institute, 1996 ('Hindi' is here a broad and somewhat inaccurate desgination which in fact often means Gujarati or Rajasthani); D. Pingree, Catalogue of Jyotiṣa Manuscripts in the Wellcome Library, Sanskrit Astral and Mathematical Literature, Brill, 2004; Pearls of the Orient, Asian Treasures from the Wellcome Library, ed. by Nigel Allan, The Wellcome Trust, 2003 (pp. 87ff.).

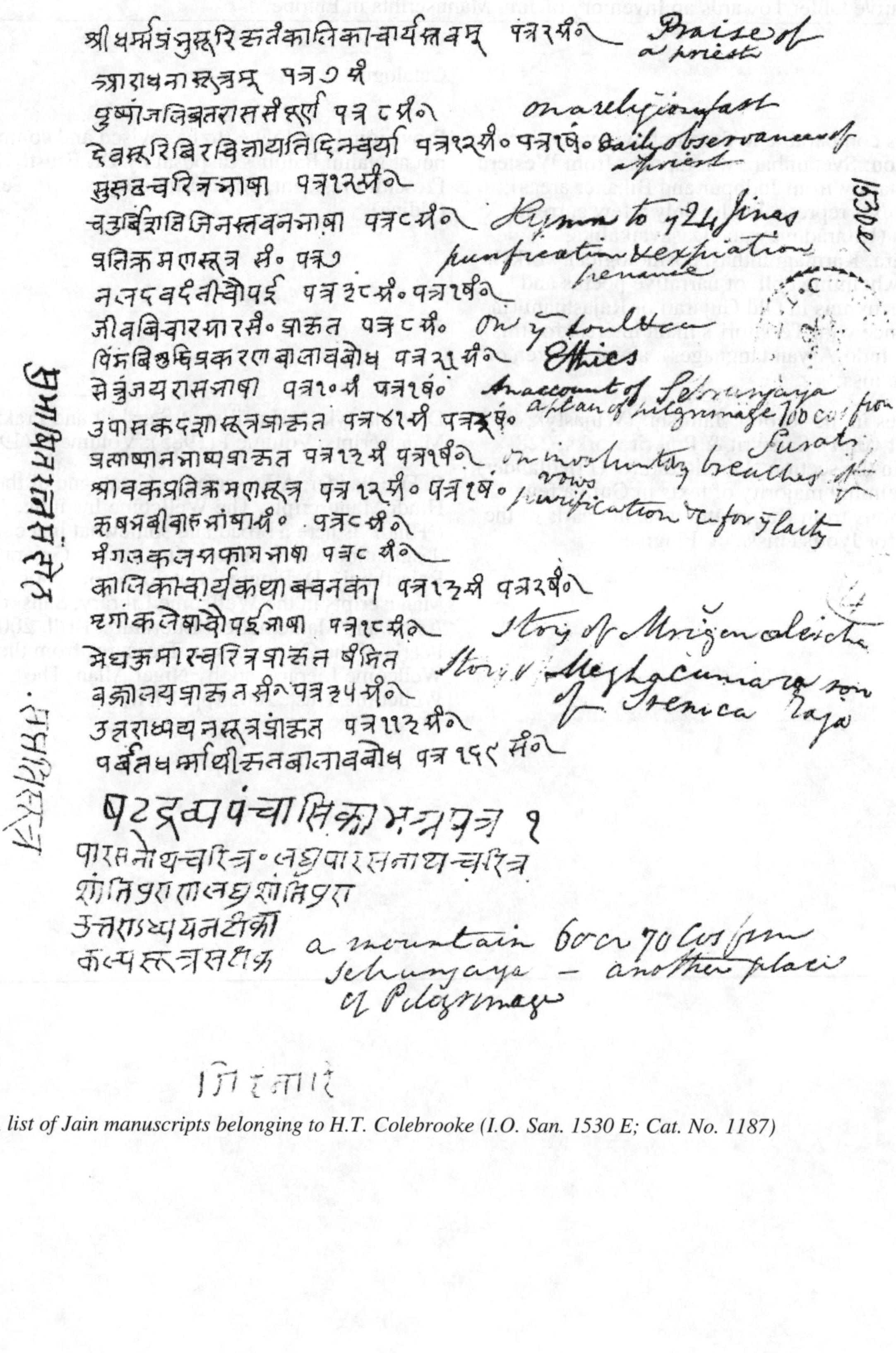

A list of Jain manuscripts belonging to H.T. Colebrooke (I.O. San. 1530 E; Cat. No. 1187)

II. The manuscripts - The present catalogue

Organization of the catalogue - List of entries

The vast quantity of material available in the India Office and Oriental collections has affected the organization of the catalogue and its division into sections and sub-sections. Details of these sections and sub-sections are to be found in the extensive 'Classified list of entries' which should be used as a *vademecum* to the present Catalogue. Moreover, additional details are given, wherever necessary, in preliminary remarks to the sections. Even if all catalogues of Jain manuscripts have common divisions, i.e. Śvetāmbara versus Digambara, canonical literature versus non-canonical, Angas versus Upāngas, etc., each catalogue has its own particular approach obviously derived from the manuscripts it has to describe. We have tried to evolve new categories or headings so as to emphasise the interest of the available material both for the scholars and for the Jains in connection with their faith and practice (e.g. 'Hymns to local images of Tīrthaṁkaras', 'Vrata literature', etc.). The broad sectarian division between Śvetāmbara and Digambara has seemed relevant. Although Section II dealing with Digambara literature is much shorter than Section I Śvetāmbara literature, it is better that it exists on its own because it has a specificity and a unity. Section III *Belles-lettres* and Śāstric disciplines, on the other hand, transcends sectarian divisions.

For a given work the arrangement is made according to the following principles: the commentaries follow the work commented upon (*mūla*), commentaries in Sanskrit come before commentaries in Gujarati, and an incomplete or fragmentary text follows a complete text.

Structure and contents of an entry

In principle, one entry corresponds to one text. In the case of a composite manuscript (see below), there are as many entries as the number of texts it contains: e.g. Harley 415 contains 25 texts, i.e. 25 entries located at their proper places according to the contents of the catalogue as described in the table of contents or the list of entries.

There are two different *numberings* for each entry: on the left side is the Catalogue Number in the sequence adopted for the present catalogue; on the right side is the shelfmark *exactly* as it should be mentioned by anyone wishing to order the manuscript in the Library. Within brackets an indication is given about the collection to which it belongs (e.g. Bühler, Jacobi, Bendall, etc.) or any other relevant information.

Then come a few lines about the *material description* of the manuscript. In case one shelfmark or one binding corresponds to different manuscripts, we write MANUSCRIPT A (B, C, etc.) before the description. This capital letter has not been included in the shelfmark for it is generally not a part of it. In the case of composite manuscripts containing two texts or more, the material description is to be found in the section 'Description of composite manuscripts' (p.112) where their individual descriptions are gathered.

The information given in this part of the entry concerns:

- the paper.
- the foliation. OFN = Original Folio Numbering refers to the figures written by the scribe of the manuscript, whatever they are; MEF = Modern European Folio Numbering, if any, refers to the figures written by (European) librarians or by scholars who read the text.
- measurements of the manuscript in centimetres. See below 'Size of the manuscript'
- types of margins, designs, ornamentation, use of red pigment, etc.
- other relevant information depending on individual cases.
- type of script.
- condition of the manuscript: good/reasonable/poor. The proportion of manuscripts in a good condition is rather high in the present collections.

- indication about the date: No date/dated: V.S. followed by the year.

The *heading* contains the following elements:

- If required, an indication of the type 'TEXT 1', in case the manuscript has more than one.
- Title of the work. In case the manuscript itself does not give any title, it is supplied when identifiable and indicated within square brackets. In cases of unidentifiable fragments or incomplete texts, a label has been supplied tentatively. Very rarely, we had no other choice than to write 'Unidentified'.
- Language of the work.
- Author of the work.
- If required, generic name of the commentary (Avacūrṇi, Ṭabo, Bālāvabodha, etc.) and, if available, proper name of the commentary (*Sukhabodhā*, etc.). The language of the commentary is indicated if it is not obvious (Avacūrṇi implies Sanskrit, Ṭabo means Gujarati).
- Author of the commentary.
- Extent of the text, in case it is incomplete or fragmentary.

The *quotations* are in two parts. In case some words or elements are omitted, they are indicated by '...':

1) Beginning of the text (and the commentary), with auspicious symbols (generally the *bhale* symbol, rendered as '||§O||', the syllable *arhaṁ*), initial homage, etc.[1]

2) 2) End of the text (and the commentary) includes final verses or sentences of the work itself. They are followed by two elements: the Colophon, a phrase of the form *iti* ... giving the title of the work and indicating its end, and the Scribal Remark of a more or less elaborate form (see below). The author's or commentator's *praśasti* containing his spiritual genealogy is often detailed, but is not regularly found.

When the information necessary for the author's identification is found insufficient in the final part of the text, but is found in the chapter-colophons, we also quote at least one of them.

As will be seen, the lengths of the quotations vary considerably. In case of extremely well-known texts which have a long publication history (e.g. *Ācārāṅga-sūtra*, *Kalpa-sūtra*), a short extract is sufficient. In case of rare texts which are not found in a lot of manuscripts, especially outside India, or in case of texts difficult to identify, longer extracts have been supplied.

The section called 'References' contains the following information in the following sequence:

— References to previous cataloguing of the manuscript in question in the following form:

I.O. Cat. II for Sanskrit and Prakrit manuscripts of the India Office Library;

Blumhardt for Gujarati and Rajasthani manuscripts of the India Office;

Blumhardt (BM) for Gujarati manuscripts of the British Museum;

Blumhardt (BMH) for Hindi manuscripts of the British Museum;

Bendall for Sanskrit manuscripts of the British Museum (concerns only Section III '*Belles-lettres* and śāstric disciplines').

It can happen that 'I.O. Cat. II' and 'Blumhardt' are mentioned for one and the same manuscript if it includes both a Sanskrit or Prakrit text and a Gujarati commentary, for language was the main criterion of

[1] For a discussion of the auspicious symbol found at the beginning of manuscripts from Gujarat and Rajasthan which is called *bhale*, meaning perhaps 'be blessed' see Gouriswar Bhattacharya, 'The *bhale* symbol of the Jainas' in *Berliner Indologische Studien* 8 (1995), pp. 201-228 (with illustrations): it is not specific to Jain manuscripts and should be equated with *siddham*.

these earlier catalogues. We have used these catalogues very freely and in different ways, depending on the manuscript concerned. Quotations have been abridged whenever the identity of a work, which was hardly known at the time the I.O. Cat. was compiled, has now become clear due to the expanding material made available from all sources. For the manuscripts written in Grantha and Kannada script we have relied entirely upon the quotations as appearing in the I.O. Cat.

— References to comprehensive catalogues listing manuscripts from various sources: Velankar (*Jinaratnakośa*) is the basic work of the type for Jain manuscripts. An indication is given about the general situation of manuscripts of the text in question, especially if they do not seem to be numerous or available outside India. Another extremely precious reference work is D. Pingree's *Census of the Exact Sciences in Sanskrit*, which is of use here for mathematics, astronomy and cosmology. When this book is referred to, only references to manuscripts in collections outside India are detailed (below) and an attempt is made to provide general characteristics about the manuscripts of the text in question (datation, origin, etc.).

— References to other manuscripts of the same text found in other collections, whether in London (Royal Asiatic Society: Tod; Wellcome Institute: Friedlander's catalogue) or elsewhere in Europe and India. But the reader should bear in mind that our aim could not be to provide a *Census* of each and every available manuscript of a given text, a task which is clearly out of hand. We have tried to indicate as many references as possible for comparatively rare works, so that one is able to estimate the real diffusion of a given text. In other cases, the references are not fully systematic.

The non-Indian collections which have been surveyed, partly or fully, are the following:

- Berlin (Weber and Schubring)
- Florence (Pavolini's catalogue)
- Paris (Senart collection)
- Strasbourg (Tripāṭhī's catalogue)
- Udine (Tessitori's collection)
- United States (Poleman's catalogue)
- Vienna (Bühler's list and Podzeit's catalogue).

The information is precise and reliable when full catalogues are available (Berlin, Strasbourg, Vienna: Podzeit) or when the manuscripts could be seen directly, either through the original (Paris) or through published CD-ROMS of the collection (Udine). It can only be indicative and should be checked when the available lists do not give sufficient identification about the precise nature of a text or a commentary (Florence, Vienna: Bühler). A question-mark indicates a case of doubt.

The Indian collections which have been surveyed, partly or fully, are the following:

- Ahmedabad (L.D. Institute)
- Koba
- Pune (Bhandarkar Oriental Research Institute).
- Rajasthan (Jaipur libraries) for the Digambara section.

We generally confine ourselves to references pertaining to manuscripts of the same text or commentary as the one considered. Only in cases where the identification is problematic do we extend the scope of these references. On the other hand, their scope has been considerably restricted in the case of canonical literature in the strict sense of the term, for which there would be no point to list large numbers of manuscripts which are not of great value. We know that the best manuscripts are palm-leaf manuscripts and that they have been used by the Indian editors of the Jaina Āgama Series or other collections.

As far as possible, references to at least one published edition have been given. But we are fully aware that some published works may have escaped our notice. All Jain scholars know that there is no end to Jain series of publications ('Granthamālās'), some of them short-lived, which are very useful but are not always easily available on the market or in libraries. This part of the work has been especially painstaking for the numerous short Gujarati hymns, stories, *rāsas* and *sajjhāyas*, which are difficult to trace. A reference to JGK (= M.D. Desai, *Jain Gūrjar Kavio*), an indispensable tool, should be of some help for the interested reader.

The section called 'Notes' is meant to throw light on the manuscript as an object as well as on the text it represents.

First, we always try to give indications as to whether a particular manuscript has been used for an edition by a given scholar. As a matter of fact, several of the India Office Library manuscripts were used or referred to in *editiones principes* of several Jain works by scholars from all over Europe, at a time when this library provided an easily accessible source. The Englishman C.H. Tawney, the Germans E. Windisch or W. Kirfel, the Italian L.P. Tessitori and others would not have known about works of their interest without these manuscripts. The part played in this process by enlightened librarians who were also prominent scholars has been recalled above.

Indications about the distribution of the chapters of a given work in a given manuscript are supplied as far as possible. This is not always an easy task, for the chapter colophons may be absent, very difficult to trace, or irregularly written.

Further notes concern the author of the text, his religious affiliation, his spiritual lineage, his other works and his date and the work itself. When the title is not obvious, when the text is not widely known or when our readings have convinced us that the available histories of literature give insufficient details about the general contents and purport, we try to supply the relevant information.

Finally, where relevant, comes a section called 'Illustrations'. We do not intend to study the illustrations from the point of view of art-history, but to give sufficient information for the identification. When labels in Sanskrit, Gujarati (or mixed language) accompany the pictures, we give their original texts.

Whenever necessary, we have introduced a preliminary remark (in italics) before describing a group of connected texts. This is a practical device to collect at one place information which would have been either scattered or repeated, or to warn the reader about some specific problems (e.g. *Navatattva*, *Sambodhasaptatikā*, etc.).

The Manuscripts

Material

The vast majority of the manuscripts described in the present catalogue are on *paper*. There are two varieties. The first, prevalent here, is of Indian manufacture and is hand-made. No attempt could be made here to undertake chemical analyses of the material. The paper differs considerably both in appearance and in touch, going from white or pale yellow to almost dark brown, from extremely thin, brittle texture, to rather thick and rough material state. The second variety is the machine-made modern paper of European origin bearing a water-mark, exclusively in the case of modern copies specially commissioned (e.g. in Burnell's or Bühler's collection). European paper then goes with European format (bookform and not *pothī*).

The *palm-leaf* manuscripts (from the Burnell and Mackenzie collections) are not especially remarkable, since they hail from South India (Karnatak and Tamilnad), where this is the most commonly used material. However, the presence of three palm-leaf manuscripts from the North (Or. 1385A, 1385B, 1386, **Cat. Nos. 158-161**), more precisely from Western India, acquired by the British Museum at a rather early date (1876) needs a special mention for at least four reasons. First, palm-leaf manuscripts not coming from the South are extremely rare in non-Indian libraries, and even in Western India, outside the famous *bhaṇḍārs* such as Jaisalmer, Cambay, Patan and Ahmedabad. Outside India, even such a wisely made collection as the

Strasbourg University Library built up by E. Leumann has only two,[1] whereas no such manuscript is available in the Berlin collections, for instance. Second, one of the British Library manuscripts is dated (Or. 1385B, dated V.S. 1258 = 1201 CE). Third, all three are representatives of the so-called *Chedasūtras* (disciplinary texts), a class of works which is not among the most common outside India. Fourth, they are all manuscripts of the *Jītakalpa*-group, which is even rarer among the *Chedasūtras*.

The few items using other materials than paper or palm-leaf are not always manuscripts in the strict sense of the word. They are cosmological paintings on *cloth*, with labels or detailed explanatory text, or objects on *wood* or *metal* (*yantra*).

Format

The vast majority of the manuscripts described in the present catalogue are in the *pothī* format, i.e. the traditional format of Indian manuscripts where the length is greater than the width. *Pothī* is a Neo-Indian word (especially used in Gujarati), derived from Skt. *pustikā*. This format originated with palm-leaf and was continued when paper came in use. It is subject to many adjustments, depending on the contents of the works. Most commonly, the text is written continuously. But there are other possible formats when the basic text (*mūla*) is accompanied by a commentary. In one notable case (**Cat. No. 331**), the text is entirely written on one side, and the commentary on the other side. But the common formats in such cases are what is known as *tripāṭha* and *pancapāṭha*. They have the obvious advantage of keeping the text and the commentary separate and are particularly welcome in the case of discursive and lengthy commentaries which are more than word-to-word glosses. In the *tripāṭha* format, the *mūla* is written in the centre, generally in bigger script, whereas the commentary is written above and below the central part, in smaller script. Examples are I.O. San. 1350, Bühler 290, Or. 2112 (C), Or. 2120 (F), Or. 2128 (B), Or. 2131 (D), Or. 2132 (A), Or. 2133 (G), Or. 5169, Or. 5236, Or. 13789. The term *tripāṭha* is normally used when the three parts which form the page are clearly distinguished, but there are also ambiguous cases where the spatial limits have not been defined and where the text and commentary overlap to some extent. In the *pancapāṭha* format, there are two additional parts on the left and on the right of the page which are reserved for the commentary. Instances are I.O. San. 1561 (C), Or. 2105 (F), Or. 2105 (G), Or. 2106 (B,1), Or. 2107 (A), Or. 2113 (A), Or. 2120 (F), Or. 2132 (B), Or. 2132 (H), Or. 2133 (H), Or. 2134 (A), Or. 5182, Or. 13543, etc. In such cases the margins are extremely narrow or almost absent, and it is not rare that, if the corners of the pages are slightly damaged or torn, some parts of the text may be lost. In the *pancapāṭha* format, the sequence of reading is as follows: upper part - right part - left part - lower part. In texts accompanied by Gujarati commentaries of the type *bālāvabodha* or *ṭabo*, which are generally meant to explain the wording and give Gujarati equivalents to the Prakrit or Sanskrit words, a common format is the so-called interlinear commentary. Good examples in the present collections are Or. 13603, Or. 13606, Or. 13604, Or. 15633/172. The *mūla* is written in normal or large script, and a wide space is reserved in between the lines for writing the commentary. The commentary is written in smaller script, often exactly below the corresponding words of the *mūla*. The literal gloss uses some stereotyped devices, for instance the abbreviation *ka*° = Guj. *kahetāṁ*, equivalent in its use to Skt. *iti*, in the sense 'X *ka*°' followed by the explanation: 'By saying '[word of the *mūla*] he means ...'. Thus, the glosses are presented in the form of small compartments, which may or not be separated by vertical lines in order to make things easier and clearer. In several cases, these compartments are enhanced by decorative patterns of aesthetic value.

The pages of Jain *pothīs* are traditionally left unbound and are either placed between two wooden covers or cloth-covers (often beautiful objects ornamented with auspicious signs), or, in modern times, wrapped in paper, where indications about the title, the date and the foliation may have been written by the librarian. In most cases, and in all cases as far as the Jain manuscripts of the Oriental collections are concerned, the pages have not been kept loose. The manuscripts have been leather bound or cloth bound by the librarians in charge. The following situations are met with:

- One manuscript in one binding with one shelfmark = one entry in the present catalogue.

- Two or more manuscripts in one binding with different shelfmarks = two or more entries.

[1] See C.B. Tripāṭhī, *Catalogue of the Jain Manuscripts at Strasbourg*, p. 23, n. 1 (Nandi-sūtra and Nandi-cūrṇi).

- Two or more manuscripts in one binding with one shelfmark = as many entries as the number of manuscripts, the individual manuscript being referred to by capital letters, e.g. Or. 2098, MANUSCRIPT A ... N. These groupings are modern and do not tell us anything about the history of the texts or the way of writing. Sometimes these groupings are systematic so that manuscripts of the same text are bound together (e.g. Or. 2098: three manuscripts of the Praśamarati; Or. 2114, A, B, and C: three manuscripts of the Upadeśamālā, with different commentaries, etc.), but sometimes they are purely occasional or pratical (manuscripts of a similar size are bound together but have no connection whatsoever in terms of contents).

These are rather simple situations when one manuscript contains only one text. But there are also several cases where one manuscript (whether or not individually bound) contains two texts or more, i.e. where the same material object contains two or more texts following each other and written by the same hand. This is what is known as a 'composite manuscript', e.g.

Or. 15633/133, TEXT 1 > one entry

... Or. 15633/133, TEXT 2 > one entry .... Or. 15633/133, TEXT 8 > one entry.

This situation is significant for the history of texts or the groupings as conceived by Indian scribes and can provide information about the principles of consistency: e.g. Gujarati narratives and hymns grouped together, different works on Karman put together as to form a set of five or six Karmagranthas, two Prakīrṇakas connected by their contents written in continuation, etc. In such cases, there are different ways to present the description of the manuscript as a whole. The Strasbourg Catalogue gives the material description under the first entry and gives the list of the other texts with cross-references. This method becomes rather unpractical when the composite manuscripts are numerous, when the texts they include are mostly more than two and when the relevant entries may be located in sections of the catalogue which are wide apart. Therefore we have adopted a different method. A separate list of such manuscripts has been established in the section 'Description of composite manuscripts or codices' (p. 112), which gives both the material description of the manuscript and its contents. Thus one can see at a glance which texts have been put together and why. In the catalogue itself, the sentence 'Contains x texts' and the indication 'TEXT 1', 'TEXT 2', etc. mean that one has to consult this list in order to get information on the material aspect of the manuscript and on its components.

In the India Office and Oriental collections there are also several instances of the so-called *guṭakā* format comparable to a codex. A *guṭakā* has a format comparable to a western pocket-book or note-book. It may have originally been bound, but in most cases the folded sheets are placed inside a cover without binding. A *guṭakā* is generally made of several individual texts, which may have something in common (e.g. Or. 13221 is a collection of basic texts or hymns common among Digambara circles). They can be written all by the same hand, or by different hands (e.g. the interesting and complicated case of I.O. San. 3400). If they are written by several hands, they can be called collective manuscripts. The object is one, but it can be ornamented in different ways in different places (different margins, different types of blank space in the middle, etc.). A table of contents prepared by some users of the manuscript may occasionally be included. In most cases of this type, there are on the one hand full-fledged texts which have been copied neatly and properly, as any other manuscript, and, on the other hand, some sorts of notes in cursive script (accounts, recipes) which are rather meant for personal use than for others to read. The analysis of such manuscripts is problematic. They are dealt with in the section 'Description of composite manuscripts and codices'. Some of their very brief and hardly legible components are analysed in this Appendix but are not described in a specific entry in the present catalogue.

Script

The vast majority of manuscripts described in the present catalogue come from North India or, more specifically, Western India (contemporary Rajasthan and Gujarat). Thus the script predominantly used is the so-called *Jaina nāgarī*.[1] The variety called *pṛṣṭhamātrā* where the long vowels (*e*, *o*) and the

[1] See, for instance, H.R. Kapadia, 'Outlines of Palaeography (with special reference to Jaina Palaeographical data and their evaluation)', *The Journal of the University of Bombay* vol. 6,6 (1938), especially pp. 98ff.; idem, Appendix to the

diphthongs (*ai*, *au*) are noted with vertical strokes placed before and/or after the consonants is widely used, especially in manuscripts written in Sanskrit or Prakrit. However, it is difficult to define its use chronologically, for even rather recent manuscripts may resort to it too. The 'modern' way of noting these vowels and diphthongs is also in use, and there are several cases where both methods come side by side in the same manuscript.

There is no calligraphy in the strict sense of the word in Jaina nāgarī. However, the levels of carefulness in the script vary considerably. Very cursive (and rather untidy) script is normally characteristic of stray personal notes found in the *guṭakās* (see above) or in small pieces of texts written by a later hand in order to fill the blank space in a page, after a perfectly carefully written text. On the other hand, extremely neat, legible script is a common feature of the *Kalpasūtra* manuscripts, and is to be connected with the special religious value ascribed to this book in the Jain tradition. An interesting case of official careful script in this style is also provided by a manuscript of Hemacandra's *Yogaśāstra* (I.O. San. 3386).

Grantha script is found in a few manuscripts coming from South India (e.g. I.O. San. 3545), while *Kannada* script is used in the manuscripts of Digambara texts collected by Mackenzie or Burnell.

An unusual case is provided by a commentary on two Digambara works written in *Persian* language and script (Add. 25022).

Language

The languages represented in majority in the texts described in our Catalogue are Sanskrit (Skt.) and Prakrit (Pkt.). The latter abbreviation refers to all varieties of Prakrit illustrated by our corpus: Ardhamāgadhī in the Śvetāmbara canon, Jaina Śaurasenī in what the Digambaras consider as their canon (Kundakunda's works) and Jaina Māhārāṣṭrī widely used in the textbooks (*prakaraṇas*) and in narrative works. The label 'Guj.' refers to all stages of Gujarati, whether older or more recent, as used in manuscripts dating back to the end of the 19th century.

Other languages are in a minority: Apabhraṁśa (Ap.) is extremely rare. Hindi and Rajasthani, sometimes very difficult to distinguish from each other, sometimes even hard to distinguish from Gujarati, are found in a few commentaries or poems of the Digambara section. In many cases the postpositions are the only sign of a difference between Gujarati (*no, nī, nuṁ*), Rajasthani (*ro, rī*) and Hindi (*kā, kī*). Kannada and Tamil, also attested in a restricted number of texts of the corpus, are the languages of a few commentaries on Digambara Sanskrit works. — See preceding paragraph for an isolated instance of Persian as the language of two commentaries on a Digambara work.

The co-existence of Sanskrit, Prakrit and vernacular languages in the same manuscript and the same text is a source of difficulties for any consistent transliteration. As for nasals, we are *generally* following Leumann's and Schubring's habit (*n* and not *ṅ* or *ñ*). In the transitional stages of language the boundary between Sanskrit/Prakrit and the vernaculars is not clear. This affects the notion of compound, and the use of hyphens in transliteration. We hope our inconsistencies are of minimal consequence. The coexistence of several levels of language also accounts for the high proportion of nasalized syllables found everywhere (e.g. *Vardhamāṁna*, *Gaṁṇeśa*, *dāṁna*, etc.).

Foliation

As a rule, the original foliation by the scribe is written in the lower right-hand corner of the verso of each folios. Thus it has not been mentioned in the individual descriptions. We have given an indication only in cases where the foliation is also written a second time in the left-hand corner of the verso (often along with a marginal full or abbreviated title). This original foliation is called by us OFN, and is to be distinguished from MEF. The latter refers to the continuous page numbering in Arabic figures written in pencil by the librarians, and probably meant for the binders or other users not conversant with Indian figures. OFN and MEF do not coincide when original folios are missing but this lack has not been taken into account by the European user, or when different manuscripts have been bound together, e.g.

Catalogue of the Manuscripts deposited at the Bhandarkar Oriental Research Institute.

Or. 2140

A	OFN: 1-9	MEF: 1-9
B	OFN: 1-10	MEF: 10-19
C	OFN: 1-11	MEF: 20-30
D	OFN: 1-19	MEF: 31-50
E	OFN: 1-5	MEF: 51-55
F	OFN: 1-6	MEF: 56-61

In an extremely vast majority of manuscripts, the foliation is written with numbers (*ankapallī*).[1] These folio numbers are liable to be ornamented in various ways, being surrounded by red floral motifs, blue lines, etc. to make them more conspicuous (e.g. I.O. San. 2126 A., I.O. San. 3379, Or. 2126 A, Or. 13618, Or. 13620, Or. 15633/28, Or. 15633/142, Or. 15633/180). The scribe may insert extra folios for charts, drawings, or other reasons, which are not numbered continuously, but numbered as 'N dvi', 'N tr', etc. This does not necessarily point to a later date for these folios. They have a status similar to plates in modern books.

The present catalogue has two instances of manuscripts using letter-numerals (*akṣarapallī*). One is a palm-leaf manuscript from Western India (Or. 1385). The other is even more remarkable because it is a paper manuscript (Or. 13455). In this system, which is not very common in paper manuscripts but has been used at least up to the 16th century, 'each of the numbers from 1 to 10 has a separate representation, and that similar is the case for numbers such as 20, 30, 40, 50, 60, 70, 80, 90, and for 100, 200, 300 and 400'.[2] In both our manuscripts, both numbers and letter-numerals are used simultaneously.

Size of folios

We give the length and breadth in centimetres: 1) the measurements of the full page, 2) the measurements of the script-area. In the *pothī* format, derived from palm-leaves, the length is greater than the breadth. The average size of the paper manuscripts in our collections is 25 x 10 cm. The smallest representatives measure 16,4 x 9 cm. (MSS. Guj. 6) and 13 x 8,4 cm. (Add. 26,455 AP: **Cat. No. 780**). There are exceptions, of paper manuscripts which have a rather important length and an extremely short breadth, after the pattern of palm-leaf manuscripts. In the *guṭakā* format, the breadth is normally greater than the length.

We also give the number of lines per page. This is an average figure, for in many manuscripts there is a small variation from page to page. In *tripātha* and *pancapātha* manuscripts, the number of lines is difficult to assess precisely, since some pages may include only the commentary and not the *mūla*.

We have followed the principle adopted by Tripāṭhī in the Strasbourg Catalogue (p. 29) and have not indicated the number of *akṣaras* per line, although it is done in Indian catalogues (beside Kapadia and Bhujabali śāstri, see catalogues of the manuscripts kept in the L.D. Institute of Indology, Ahmedabad). To quote Tripāṭhī's statement: 'The number varies considerably even in otherwise well executed Manuscripts. Therefore the average number is of no use'.

Illustrated manuscripts

Illustrated Jain manuscripts are found in almost all the collections described in the present catalogue. There has been regrettable tendency in recent decades for illustrated manuscripts to be split up for

[1] See Tripāṭhī, *Catalogue* p. 24 (with references).

[2] H.R. Kapadia, 'Foliation of Jaina Manuscripts and Letter-Numerals': *Annals of the Bhandarkar Oriental Research Institute* 18,2 (1937) p. 178; idem, Appendix in the Catalogue of the mss. deposited at the Bhandarkar Oriental Research Institute. See Notes on Or. 13455 (**Cat. No. 106**), for the specific system used in this manuscript and Appendix to vol. II of the present Catalogue.

commercial gain and come on the market in the form of separate leaves. This is why so many isolated *Kalpasūtra*-leaves are available, without the full text to which they belong. The same holds true for illustrated pages of the cosmological manuscripts which have come in fashion and have wrongly been connected with Tantric art by some *amateurs*.

The illustrated Jain manuscripts kept in the India Office and Oriental collections are all carefully preserved. Either the illustration is protected from external contact by a tissue or the leaves are preserved in glass frames and special boxes with compartments (e.g. Or. 13341). The same careful conditions of preservation are true for the holdings of the British Museum and the Victoria & Albert Museum. Many of the illustrated Jain leaves in the India Office and Oriental collections have been photographed by the British Library, so that a good lot of slides is available at hand. Some have been already studied from the art historical viewpoint by J.P. Losty (see *British Library Journal* 1,2, 1975). In the present catalogue, no such attempt has been made. However, a brief description of all individual illustrations has been given, along with a transcript of the label, when available.

A number of manuscripts contain only one picture, generally of a Jina, of the goddess Sarasvatī, etc. This single illustration appears as a kind of developed auspicious motif which certainly enhances the value of the object for the believer.

Beside, most illustrated manuscripts are connected with well-known narrative cycles or specific works (see Appendix 5). Among them manuscripts of the *Kalpasūtra* stand in the first place, which is no surprise given the extremely wide popularity of this Prakrit work, its numerous commentaries, the famous legends handed down about the lives of the Jinas and the essential part the telling of these legends plays during Paryuṣaṇa. Manuscripts of the story of Kālaka, which is often appended to the *Kalpasūtra*, are also important. Next come the cosmological works, which are extremely well represented in the present collections, both as texts accompanied with illustrations and cosmological paintings (on cloth). Two lavishly illustrated manuscripts of the *Uttarādhyayana* deserve a special mention. For all these, standard publications containing a wide selection of reproductions are available and pave the way.[1] Beside such manuscripts, belonging to the Canonical scriptures at large, there are some manuscripts illustrating various narratives which are equally worth mentioning. Paintings connected with the *Śrīpālarāsa*, the *Śālibhadra-caupaī* or the *Ḍholā-Marū* are generally well-known and have been reproduced in various standard publications. This does not diminish in the least the artistic value of the London illustrations, which are mostly of high quality. There is at least one remarkable case of an illustrated legend which has not yet given birth to any comprehensive study, viz. the *Ādityavāra-kathā* (Or. 14290). This Digambara *vratakathā* would require a book like A.N. Upadhye's *Sugandhadaśamī-kathā*, in which the different versions would be analysed and accompanied by illustrations. Given its quality, the British Library manuscript could well play a role in such an undertaking.

Apart from illustrated manuscripts in the strict sense of the term, a number of manuscripts are elaborately decorated in different ways, especially by the presence of an initial and/or a final folio having *citrapṛṣṭhikās*, decorated page with multicoloured floral motifs occupying the full page (see the full list in Appendix 5).

There are also other ways to make a manuscript stand out in appeareance, e.g. by enhancing the folio-numbering (see above) or simply using red ink (for *daṇḍas*, numbers, margins). The free area in the centre of the folios, which is a remnant of the string-hole of the palm-leaf manuscripts,[2] is a suitable place for various types of ornamentation. If it is kept blank, it can be devised as a square, a rectangle or a lozenge. But it can be filled with *akṣaras* of the text arranged in sophisticated ways (e.g. Or. 2137B) or decorated with ornamental motifs (*svastikas*, etc.). One exceptional case of a manuscript where *akṣaras* are arranged and spread along four folios so as to make a sequence in which the scribe's name is to be recognised

[1] See W. Norman Brown, *The Story of Kālaka: Texts, History, Legends and Miniature Paintings of the Śvetāmbara Jain Hagiographical Work The Kālakācāryakathā*, Washington, 1933; *A Descriptive and Illustrated Catalogue of Miniature Paintings of the Jaina Kalpasūtra as Executed in the Early Western Style*, Washington, 1934; *Manuscript Illustrations of the Uttarādhyayana Sūtra Reproduced and Described*, New Haven, 1941; C. Caillat - Ravi Kumar, *The Jain Cosmology*, Paris, 1981; new ed. Delhi, 2004, and Indian publications by Sarabhai Nawab, Ahmedabad.

[2] See for more details, Tripāṭhī, *Catalogue* p. 25.

should be noticed, as it is generally rare even in Indian collections (Or. 2114B: see Notes on **Cat. No. 527**). The margins, which are kept empty for glosses, or filled with them, may have ornamental drawings (Or. 2119 A, Or. 2136 A, Or. 13481), or, more often, red disks (the regular pattern being one disk on the rectos and three on the versos). Coloured folios are occasionally met with in the present collections: the manuscript I.O. San. 1377 (*Kalpasūtra*) is a remarkable, although not quite exceptional, case of silver and gold background, whereas Or. 13623A is an interesting instance of a manuscript using folios of different colours.

Scribal Remark

We use this term as it was used in Tripāṭhī's *Catalogue of the Jaina Manuscripts at Strasbourg* in order to designate the more or less elaborate text written by the scribe at the end of a manuscript (which he calls *pustaka, prati, parata*). In Jain manuscripts, such remarks are often rich in contents and would deserve to be studied more carefully. Our Appendix 1 'Selected Scribal Remarks' is an attempt towards this goal. We summarize here the type of information this kind of document can provide and how we have dealt with it in the present Catalogue.

Language

In most cases, the language of the Scribal Remarks *is meant* to be Sanskrit, even when the text copied is not in Sanskrit. The Scribal Remark is a *genre* with its stereotypes and formulaic style. It has been handled by all types of scribes, whose primary language could not have been Sanskrit at the time when they worked, but was one of the vernaculars (Hindi, Rajasthani, Gujarati). The knowledge of Sanskrit necessary to write *astu*, *śubhaṁ bhavatu*, plus a date or the names of a few people, needs not be very important. On the other hand, the style of the Scribal Remarks is a combination of Sanskrit phraseology and of vernacular syntax. This is shown in the status of compounds, which are often loose and loosely connected to the rest of the sentence. They are a problem which is difficult to solve in a fully satisfactory manner when coming to roman transcription. In short, behind the language of the Scribal Remarks the evolution of Sanskrit and its being influenced by the vernaculars can be seen.

Prakrit as the language of a Scribal Remark is met with in a single (problematic) case (**Cat. No. 42**).

Scribal Remarks are normally written in the third person singular. However, first person Scribal Remarks are represented by three instances: **Cat. Nos. 15** (short verse-composition), **773** (*ahaṁ*) and **1316** (*likhitaṁ mayā*).

Date

In the case of undated manuscripts, we write 'No date', and no attempt is made to estimate the age, unless some indication of another type (proper names, for instance) make a plausible dating possible. When indicated, the date is normally mentioned in the Scribal Remark and is indicated in the headings of the descriptions as 'Dated: V.S. NNNN'. A list of the dated manuscripts in the present collections is found in Appendix 2. The era used predominantly is the Vikrama era, for which *saṁvata* and a wide range of graphic and phonetic variants of the word are met with.[1] When the date in the Śaka (*śāka*) era is given, it mostly appears along with the date in the Vikrama era. This can be a precious way of checking the correctness of a date in case of a problematic reading.[2] It cannot be ruled out in some cases that the Śaka era (and not the Vikrama era), which is common in Western India, is the one referred to by the date given, although it is not specified (see Appendix 1, 'Interconnected manuscripts', p. 155). Whenever necessary, various other means have been resorted to in order to assess the authenticity of a doubtful date or confirm it; such cases are discussed in the Notes. The Vīra Era, which is commonly used in printed books of the Jains, never appears in the manuscripts, and is probably of recent usage. When the date of the manuscript

[1] See Tripāṭhī, *Catalogue* p. 28.

[2] For an interesting example of a Digambara Jain manuscript (from North India) copied in the 17th century where the year is indicated in the Vikrama era, in the Śaka era and in the sixty-year cycle of Jupiter see Berlin: Schubring No. 207.

includes the day of the week and the day of the fortnight, we tried to check it with the help of the 'Pancanga' programme (version 3.13) evolved by the Japanese scholars Michio Yano and M. Fushima (http://www.kyoto-su.ac.jp/~yanom/pancanga). This tool has now replaced Swamikannu Pillai's *Indian Ephemeris*. However, there are numerous problematic cases (some of which also puzzled M. Yano himself, when he was consulted). Therefore, we finally gave up the task of finding out the equivalents of Indian dates.

Years of copying are mostly given in numbers. However, chronograms are also sporadically used by scribes, and even more often by authors of the works in order to indicate the date of composition, especially when these works are written in verse. A full list of the chronograms available in the manuscripts of our collections is given in Appendix 4. This system, which is well attested in Indian manuscripts and inscriptions, expresses numbers by words (*bhūta-saṁkhyā*) which normally have to be read from right to left (*ankānāṁ vāmato gatiḥ*). Lists of words used for specific numbers have been recorded by various authors.[1] Generally speaking, Jain manuscripts use the same numerical conventions as the other Indians, viz. 'moon' for 1, 'qualities' (*guṇa*) for 3, 'ocean' for 4, 'tastes' (*rasa*) for 6, etc., even when they refer to non-Jain mythology. The reason is partly that this system took birth in the field of mathematics.[2] However, there are some cases where the words used are marked from the doctrinal point of view and refer to items or concepts of Jainism exclusively, such as *leśyā* for 6, *śāsana-jananī* for 8, 'Pūrvas' or *guṇasthāna* for 14, *saṁyama* for 17 and *jinâtiśaya* for 34, to take instances from the present corpus only.[3] Chronograms can be as problematic as numbers since some of the words used are polysemic or can have different meanings subject to different interpretations, especially if they are not followed by the number expressed in digits which can act as a means to counter-check: see, for instance, the discussion about the date of Ratnakāra's commentary on the *Jīvavicāra* (**Cat. No. 486**) or the interpretation of *viśva* as 13 or 14 in the date of Bhāvadevasūri's *Pārśvanāthacaritra*.[4] Mixed systems are also available, viz. chronograms *cum* number in words (e.g. *bāṇâṣṭa-darśanêndu* = 1685, Or. 11745; *tri-catuṣ-tithi* = 15 4 3, Or. 2114B), and combination of orders (e.g. *sattara saṁvata vahni locana* = 17 2 3, Or. 15633/26(2)), reverse order, attested elsewhere, although more seldom (*viśva-nanda-ṛṣi* = 14 9 7, Bühler 300), or unusual order (*yugma vyomêndu pancabhiḥ* = 1 5 0 2, I.O. San. 1358). An illustrated manuscript of the *Śālibhadra-caupaī* (**Cat. No. 747**) is a sophisticated instance: the date is given both in the Vikrama Era and in the Śāka Era, twice with a chronogram.

The oldest dated manuscript of the present catalogue is a palm-leaf manuscript dated V.S. 1258, the oldest paper manuscripts go back to the 13th-14th centuries and the most recent one dates back to the beginning of the 20th century (V.S. 1970-71; see Appendix 3).

Names for the month and for the day of the week vary in their orthographic and phonetic forms,[5] for the language of the Scribal Remarks is generally mixed, Sanskrit *cum* Hindi/ Rajasthani/ Gujarati, as can be seen from the variety of postpositions used (*kā, ro, no*). Use of synonymic designations for the month and for the day of the week also contributes to the variety (e.g. *arka-vāra* for 'Sunday' in Or. 3349B, not recorded by Tripāṭhī). Among the less common terms are *kuja-vāra* 'Tuesday' (the day of the one who is born from the earth, i.e. Mars, **Cat. No. 1414**) or *jña-vāsara* 'Tuesday' or 'Wednesday' since *jña* can mean Mars or Mercury (**Cat. No. 535**). Occasionally, the indication that the day coincided with a special religious moment is supplied (e.g. *Maunaikādaśī*, **Cat. No. 1415**; *Dīvālī*, **Cat. No. 37**). The lunar calendar,

---

[1] See G. Bühler, *Indian Palaeography*, Calcutta, 1962, pp. 127-129. D.C. Sircar, *Indian Epigraphy*. Delhi, 1965, pp. 230-233; P.V. Kane, *History of Dharmaśāstra* V, 1, Poona, 1958, pp. 701-703. All these references are mentioned in R. Salomon, *Indian Epigraphy*. Oxford: Oxford University Press, 1998, p. 173.

[2] See also the list given as Appendix 1 (pp. 1-10) in Mahāvīrācārya's *Gaṇitasāra-saṁgraha*, ed. L.C. Jain. Sholapur, 1963 (Jīvarāja Jain Granthamālā 12).

[3] For Jain manuscripts see for instance Pune: BhORI 17.5, Appendix VIa and 19.1, Appendix VIa.

[4] For an interesting discussion of a problematic chronogram and its solutions see W.H. Maurer, 'The Jaina Commentator Sumativijaya: his date and place of literary activity': *Brahmavidyā, Adyar Library Bulletin* 25, 1-4, 1961 Jubilee Volume, pp. 371-379.

[5] See Appendix 4 'Terms of Indian Chronometry' in Tripāṭhī, *Catalogue* p. 382, for a convenient list.

used throughout, implies reference to the bright or the dark fortnight. Both are designated by the standard expressions: *śukla, sudi, sita* and *kṛṣṇa, vadi, asita*. The concept of 'day' is expressed by *tithi*, *dina*, more rarely, by *karmavāṭī*, a term apparently restricted to Jain circles which has been misunderstood (see Appendix 1 about **Cat. No. 747**), once by *tārīka* (**Cat. No. 736**) in a manuscript where the language has features of Hindustani. Some scribes go into further details. They mention the season (**Cat. No. 1265**), the time of the day (afternoon, **Cat. No. 854**; junction of the day, **Cat. No. 1389**; third watch, **Cat. No. 15**). Astronomical specifications concern the *muhūrtta*, the *nakṣatra*, or the astral conjunction (e.g. **Cat. No. 102**).

Geographical information

Indication about the place where the manuscript was copied also appears in the Scribal Remarks (Index 5 for the full list). It is obviously precious for it may provide information about important Jain routes, centres or pilgrimage-places which were visited by the scribes. However, it does not appear systematically. Instead of dealing with this point in the notes to the relevant entries, it has been decided to gather all the relevant information in the Index. A look at this Index shows the following features. Not surprisingly, most Jain manuscripts catalogued here were copied in Western India, i.e. what corresponds to the modern states of Gujarat and Rajasthan where Śvetāmbara Jains mainly live. The cities of Patan and Ahmedabad prevail but a rather large variety of important commercial centres, *tīrthas*, or small villages where the Jain monks spent the rainy season, taking this opportunity to copy a text, are also mentioned. A few manuscripts (mainly from the India Office Library) originate from what is now Punjab and testify to a glorious history of cities such as Multan or Lahore, especially in Akbar's time. Interestingly, a few manuscripts (dating back to the 18th century and coming from Colebrooke) were copied in what is now Murshidabad (Bengal) and in the smaller neighbouring cities of Ajīmaganja and Mahīmāpura, testifying to the growing importance of these Jain sites of Bengal developed by Jain Marwari communities who settled there. The family of Jagatseth (see footnote 4) is a prominent representative of a family who came from Rajputana to Eastern India and settled there for centuries. Their patronage was an incentive to many Osval families who also established themselves in neighbouring places. Jain temples were built as a consequence of these settlements.[1]

Older place-names co-exist with modern names (e.g. Satyapura / Sācora, Rājanagara / Ahmadavāda, etc.) and orthographic variants are numerous. In many cases they are obvious and do not affect the identification, but in other cases they are problematic and can give rise to ambiguity.

The traditional formula 'copied through the grace of the Jina so and so' is normally an indirect reference to a local image of a given Jina and may help to identify precisely the temple or *upāśraya* in the town or the village where the manuscript was copied.

Religious and social information

The Scribal Remarks are invaluable sources of information about names and social status. They exhibit various patterns of writing: non-Jain professional scribes letting go their devotion to their own god at the end of a Jain manuscript (e.g. *kāyastha*, **Cat. No. 571**: Hanumān!), laypeople (*śrāvaka, śrāvikā*) writing for other laypeople, or for mendicants, monks writing for laypeople (e.g, for a couple, **Cat. No. 527**), monks writing for monks, monks writing for nuns (**Cat. Nos. 185, 479**), nuns writing for nuns (**Cat. No. 250**) or for laywomen, teacher composing and pupil writing (**Cat. Nos. 663, 721**), non-Jain writing non-Jain texts for a non-Jain (**Cat. No. 239**, probably). In two cases (**Cat. Nos. 116** and **316**) the monk specifies that he wrote the manuscript during the rainy season. The Jain layfollowers are mostly, as expected, of a merchant background. Some of them were probably prominent businessmen. However, no indication is given about the kind of business concerned. The social status of these individuals is defined by the abbreviations *vya*° (for *vyavahārin, vyavahārika*), and quite often *sā*° (for *sāha* < *sādhu*, compare the common proper name 'Shah'). This term is difficult to translate: it refers probably as much to an occupation as to a social status of prestige (compare French 'notable', 'Sieur'). In the most interesting cases, a full joint family can be involved in the sponsoring of a specific manuscript (see the instances collected in Appendix 1; and also

[1] Cf. J.H. Little, *The House of Jagatseth* (quoted earlier) for more details.

Cat. No. 654). The genealogy supplied in such Scribal Remarks is part of the prestige which extends to the whole family or even the community. Several important male donors have the title *sanghapa* or *sanghapati*, which by itself means that these individuals spent a lot of their wealth for religious activities going beyond their own circle.

The manuscript copied is mostly meant for a specific person, either the copyist himself if he is not a scribe by profession but a layfollower or somebody else, or a small group of persons to read (*paṭhanârthaṁ*; *vācanârthaṁ*, cf. Guj. *vāṁcvuṁ* 'to read'). The desire to perform a meritorious action is the first motivation adduced (*puṇyârthaṁ*). Here again, it can be directed towards oneself, or towards somebody else (e.g. *X-śreyo 'rthaṁ*). In this case, the question of transfer of merit arises, but is not easy to decide. The desire 'to eliminate the obscuring knowledge karmans' is considered typical of Digambara manuscripts of Western India (**Cat. No. 1211**). But reference to the general elimination of karman, expected from copying or from giving a manuscript, is found throughout (**Cat. Nos. 53, 69, 308**). Beside explicit religious motivation, what could be called scholarly motivations are also occasionally present. They are clear in the case of the family of Sahasakiraṇa and his sons, Vardhamāna and Śāntidāsa (the ancestor of Kasturbhai Lalbhai) who are enlightened book collectors of the 16th-17th centuries (see Appendix 1 p.156). On a smaller scale, collection-*praśasti*s are evidence that a given manuscript was copied or offered with the aim to enrich knowledge, and to build up a collection (**Cat. Nos. 199, 202, 557, 1395**). The library numbers, which are found at the end of several manuscripts (e.g. **Cat. No. 507**) could give a clue to the organization of individual collections, but they are extremely difficult to interprete once the manuscripts are scattered far from their orignal place.

In the Śvetāmbara manuscripts of our collections, the religious orders which are most frequently met with are those belonging to the Mūrtipūjak tradition: the Kharataragaccha, the Tapāgaccha, and much less frequently, the Ancalagaccha. The Āgamagaccha and the Pūrṇimāgaccha are far behind. The place of the Sthānakvāsis is much more difficult to appreciate. Although the word Sthānakvāsin never appears, there are some Sthānakvāsī and Lonkāgaccha lineages hidden in our collections. The designation *ṛṣi* which occurs frequently seems to refer predominantly to Jain monks of these groups (**Cat. Nos. 77, 274**, etc.).

The manuscripts often changed hands. In several cases the original name of a monk has been fully or partly erased with the help of yellow pigment in order to be simply removed or to be replaced by other names. They were acquired, for money (see example in Appendix 1), taken and given (**Cat. No. 464**), offered or transfered (*vihārita, vihārāpita*, **Cat. Nos. 23, 171**), and collected (see above). The new owner was keen on adding his own name from his hand and stating his ownership (e.g. **Cat. No. 177**).

Several manuscripts dating from the Mughal period mention the names of the Mughal emperors Akbar, Jahangir and Shah Jahan in connection with important Jain leaders of the time such as Jinacandrasūri of the Kharataragaccha (**Cat. No. 84**).

Although there are several illustrated manuscripts in the collections, only one of them supplies information about the artist, who was a monk! (**Cat. No. 747**). In some cases, the layout of the manuscript shows that it was meant to be illustrated but for some reason was not (**Or. 6832**). This is shown by blank spaces reserved for illustrations.

Scribal maxims

This expression was first coined by C.B. Tripāṭhī in the *Catalogue of the Jaina Manuscripts at Strasbourg* (p. 48). It refers to floating verses found within the Scribal Remarks or in place of them. An alphabetical list is given in Appendix 2. Such verses, which are different from general *subhāṣitas* sometimes added after the main text, fulfill different purposes: the scribe describes the toils of copying, the physical pain caused by the work, the unconfortable position which makes his limbs contracted, spoils his eyes, bends his back, etc. (e.g. *bhagna-pṛṣṭhi kaṭi-grīvā*; *vanka-grīvā kaṭi-bhagnā*, *saṁkociaya-kara-caraṇaṁ*). He requests forgiveness for his mistakes and asks the readers to show leniency, for he has copied whatever he has seen (e.g. the extremely common verse *yādṛśaṁ pustakaṁ dṛṣṭvā*) and is not responsible if letters or words are missing. He asks the reader to handle the manuscript carefully and to protect it against damage arising from men or nature (*jalaṁ rakṣe*; *udakânala-caurebhyaḥ*), wishes that the life of the manuscript may last as long as the most steady elements of the world (*yāvat...*), or pronounces a benediction (*sarva-*

mangala-māngalyaṁ). In the present collections, the maximum number of such verses at a stretch is five (Or. 13624). Although larger numbers are met with (e.g. eight scribal maxims in Kapadia BhORI 17.4, pp. 170-171), they are usually fewer (one to three as a rule). These maxims are composed in Prakrit, Sanskrit or Gujarati, or, more often, a mixture of the three, as can be seen easily, for instance, from the orthographic and phonetic variants of the verses *yādṛśaṁ pustakaṁ dṛṣṭvā* and *jalaṁ rakṣe*. Special mention should be made of the verse *jñānavān jñāna-dānena*, which is typical of Digambara manuscripts written in Western India, as rightly noticed by C.B. Tripāṭhī,[1] and of the so-called *jñāna-pūjā-gāthā* in Prakrit found at the end of a *Kalpasūtra* manuscript (**Cat. No. 115**).

Phrases of benediction

They are generally simple statements made to bless the reader, or the reader as well as the scribe. They are formulas, similar to the formulas found at the end of a letter, and do not show any attempt at originality, except, sometimes, in their orthography.

Auspicious syllables

The Scribal Remark generally contains syllables such as *śrī* or *cha*. The origin and the meaning of the latter, always noted as '⊠' in the present catalogue, are rather mysterious and have not been elucidated so far.[2] Sometimes, it appears that series of such syllables, separated or not by *daṇḍas*, were written simply to finish the line (or the page) and avoid blank spaces.

Later additions

The same horror of blank spaces may explain the presence of some later additions by the scribe himself or by a later reader. It can consist of a short indication in cursive writing about the ownership of the manuscript with a library-number. It might also be a stray verse or a small tract, or the beginning of a new text, which could either be written fully or which remained incomplete due to the lack of space. Only in cases where it is really an additional text do we consider it as a separate entry of the catalogue (see Description of composite manuscripts for references). Otherwise, the contents are discussed in the Notes.

[1] *Catalogue* p. 48.

[2] See Tripāṭhī, *Catalogue* p. 48.

Classified list of entries

Note: When ordering a manuscript the indications given within brackets should not be mentioned. A letter within brackets (A, B, etc.) refers to different manuscripts bound under the same cover and having the same shelfmark. A number within brackets (1, 2, etc.) refers to the sequence of texts within a composite manuscript. The abbreviation 'Suppl.' refers to a text added after the main text to which an independent entry has been assigned in the present catalogue.

I. Śvetāmbara literature

[Volume II]

1. The Canonical literature

1.1 Angas

1. Ācārāngasūtra	Or. 5115
2. Ācārāngasūtra with Jinahaṁsa's *Pradīpikā*, frag.	Or. 5116
3. Ācārāngasūtra (1 śr.) with Pārśvacandra's *Ṭabo*	Or. 5117
4. Ācārāngasūtra (1 śr.) with Dharmasiṁhamuni's *Ṭabo*	Or. 13601
5. Ācārāngasūtra with a Guj. comm., frag.	I.O. San. 3301 A
6. Ācārāngasūtra, Gujarati glosses	Mss. Guj. 4
7. Sūtrakṛtānga	Or. 5118
8. Sūtrakṛtānga	Or. 5119
9. Sūtrakṛtānga, with Harṣakula's *Dīpikā*	Or. 5120
10. Sūtrakṛtānga (1 śr.) with Pārśvacandra's *Bālāvabodha*	I.O. San. 3356
11. Sūtrakṛtānga (2 śr.) with Pārśvacandra's *Bālāvabodha*	I.O. San. 3355
12. Sūtrakṛtānga (1 śr.) with a Guj. commentary	Or. 13603
13. Sthānānga	Or. 5121
14. Sthānānga with Abhayadeva's comm.	Or. 2099
15. Sthānāngasūtra with Megharāja's *Dīpikā*	Or. 5122
16. Sthānāngasūtra with a Guj. gloss, frag.	I.O. San. 3301 (C)
17. Sthānāngasūtra, extracts with Guj. glosses	I.O. San. 3392
18. Samavāyāngasūtra with a Guj. Vārttika	Or. 13604
19. Bhagavatīsūtra	Or. 5123 (A)
20. Bhagavatīsūtra	I.O. San. 3352 (A)
21. Bhagavatīsūtra	I.O. San. 2642
22. Bhagavatīsūtra, fragments	Or. 5123 (B)
23. Bhagavatīsūtra with Abhayadeva's comm.	Or. 5124
24. Bhagavatī-sajjhāya by Paṇḍita Mānavijaya	I.O. San. 3614 (O1, O2)
25. Jñātādharmakathānga	I.O. San. 3353
26. Jñātādharmakathānga	Or. 5125
27. Jñātādharmakathānga with Abhayadeva's comm.	Or. 5126
28. Jñātādharmakathānga with Abhayadeva's comm.	Or. 13605
29. Jñātādharmakathāḥ with Kanakasundara's *Ṭabo*	I.O. San. 1532
30. Jñātādharmakathāḥ with a Guj. comm., incomplete	Add. 26,454 (B)
31. Jñātādharmakathāḥ with a Guj. comm., frag.	I.O. San. 1524
32. Jñātā-upanaya-kathāḥ	Or. 2122 (C)

33. Upāsakadaśānga	Or. 5127
34. Upāsakadaśānga	I.O. San. 3610
35. Upāsakadaśāḥ	Or. 5128
36. Upāsakadaśāḥ, incomplete	I.O. San. 1363 (D)
37. Upāsakadaśāḥ with Abhayadeva's comm.	Or. 2100 (A)
38. Upāsakadaśāḥ with Abhayadeva's comm. (1-8)	Or. 2100 (B)
39. Upāsakadaśānga with a Guj. commentary	Or. 13602
40. Daśa-śrāvaka-sajjhāya by Jñānavimala	Or. 15633/10 (1)
41. Antakṛddaśāḥ with sporadic marginal glosses	Or. 2100 (C)
42. Antakṛddaśāḥ	I.O. San. 3358
43. Antakṛddaśāḥ with a brief Skt. comm.	Or. 5129
44. Antakṛddaśāḥ with Abhayadeva's comm.	Or. 5131 (1)
45. Antakṛddaśāḥ with a Guj. comm.	Or. 13740
46. Gajasukumāla-carita by Nannasūri	Or. 16133/4 (2) + 2 (1)
47. Gajasukumāla-carita by Nannasūri, incomplete	I.O. San. 3614 (M)
48. Anuttaropapātikadaśāḥ	I.O. San. 3375
49. Anuttaropapātikadaśāḥ	Bühler 280
50. Anuttaropapātikadaśāḥ with marginal glosses	Or. 5130
51. Anuttaropapātika-daśāḥ with Abhayadeva's comm.	Or. 5131 (2)
52. Anuttaropapātikadaśāḥ with a Guj. comm.	Or. 13598
53. Dhanā-Kākandī-sajjhāya by Jayavijaya	Or. 15633/12 (2)
54. Praśnavyākaraṇānga	Or. 5132
55. Praśnavyākaraṇāni	Or. 5133
56. Praśnavyākaraṇāni with Abhayadeva's comm.	Or. 5134
57. Praśnavyākaraṇāni with a Guj. comm.	Or. 13606
58. Praśnavyākaraṇāni with a Guj. comm., incomplete	Or. 13617
59. Vipākasūtra with Gujarati glosses	I.O. San. 3370
60. Vipākasūtra with a Guj. comm.	Or. 13607

1.2 Upāngas

61. Aupapātikasūtra	Or. 5135
62. Aupapātikasūtra	Or. 5136
63. Aupapātikasūtra with Abhayadeva's comm.	Or. 5137
64. Aupapātikasūtra with Abhayadeva's comm.	Or. 2100 (D)
65. Aupapātikasūtra with Rājacandra's Guj. *Bālāvabodha*	Add. 26,453 (A)
66. Rājapraśnīyasūtra	Or. 5138
67. Rājapraśnīyasūtra	Or. 5139
68. Rājapraśnīyasūtra	I.O. San. 1363 (B)
69. Rājapraśnīyasūtra with Malayagiri's comm.	Or. 5140
70. Rājapraśnīyasūtra with Malayagiri's comm., incomplete	Or. 13784
71. Rājapraśnīyasūtra with the Guj. *Vārttika*	Add. 26,462
72. Rājapraśnīyasūtra with a partial Guj. comm.	I.O. San. 3366
73. Keśi-Pradeśi-vicāra (Guj.)	Add. 26,455 (AI,1)

74. Jīvābhigamasūtra with Malayagiri's comm.	Or. 5141
75. Prajñāpanāsūtra	Add. 26,378
76. Prajñāpanāsūtra	Or. 7619
77. Prajñāpanāsūtra	I.O. San. 3351
78. Prajñāpanāsūtra, incomplete	I.O. San. 3606 (A)
79. Prajñāpanāsūtra with a lacuna	Or. 5142
80. Prajñāpanā-tṛtīya-pada-saṁgrahaṇī with Kulamaṇḍana's comm.	Or. 2122 (B)
81. Prajñāpanā, vs. 131, Malayagiri's comm.	Or. 2120 (E,2)
82. Sūryaprajñapti	I.O. San. 3407
83. Sūryaprajñapti	Or. 5143 (A)
84. Sūryaprajñapti	I.O. San. 3376
85. Sūryaprajñapti	Or. 13608
86. Jambūdvīpaprajñapti	Or. 5144
87. Jambūdvīpaprajñapti with Jīvavijayagaṇi's *Ṭabo*, incomplete	Or. 13609
88. [Janma-mahimā]	I.O. San. 3388
89. Candraprajñapti	Or. 5143 (B)
90. Candraprajñapti	Or. 13551
91. Candraprajñapti with Malayagiri's comm.	I.O. San. 3006
92. Nirayāvalikāsūtra	Or. 5145
93. Nirayāvalikāsūtra	Or. 5146
94. Nirayāvalikāsūtra with marginal glosses	I.O. San. 3369
95. Nirayāvalikāsūtra with a Guj. comm.	Or. 13599

1.3. Chedasūtras

1.3.1. [Dasāo:] Kalpasūtras

1.3.1.1. Complete manuscripts

96. Kalpasūtra	I.O. San. 3177 (1)
97. Kalpasūtra	Or. 13700
98. Kalpasūtra	Or. 5149
99. Kalpasūtra	Or. 11921
100. Kalpasūtra	Or. 12744
101. Kalpasūtra	Or. 13785
102. Kalpasūtra	I.O. San. 1638 (B)
103. Kalpasūtra	I.O. San. 3600 (A)
104. Kalpasūtra	Or. 13959
105. Kalpasūtra	Or. 6832 (B)
106. Kalpasūtra with Skt. glosses, incomplete	Or. 13455
107. Kalpasūtra	IS 46-1959 (V&A)
108. Kalpasūtra with a Skt. comm., incomplete	I.O. San. 2879
109. Kalpasūtra with Jinaprabhasūri's *Saṁdehaviṣauṣadhi*	Or. 5152
110. Kalpasūtra with Sanghavijayagaṇi's *Pradīpikā*	Bühler 281 (A)
111. Kalpasūtra with Sahajakīrti's and Śrīsāra's *Kalpamannjarī*, incomplete	Or. 11745
112. Kalpasūtra with Samayasundara's *Kalpalatā*, with a lacuna	I.O. San. 3348

113. Kalpasūtra with Samayasundara's *Kalpalatā*, incomplete — I.O. San. 2691
114. Kalpa-sūtra with Vinayavijaya's *Subodhikā*, incomplete — Add. 26,379
115. Kalpasūtra with Lakṣmīvallabhagaṇi's *Kalpadruma* — Or. 5151 (1)
116. Kalpasūtra with Lakṣmīvallabhagaṇi's *Kalpadruma* — I.O. San. 1622
117. Kalpasūtra with a Skt. comm. — I.O. San. 1599
118. Kalpasūtra with a Skt. comm., incomplete — Or. 6832 (A)
119. Kalpasūtra with a Skt. and Guj. comm. — I.O. San. 3349
120. Kalpasūtra with Sukhasāgara's *Ṭabo*, incomplete — Add. 26,463
121. Kalpasūtra with Sukhasāgara's *Ṭabo*, incomplete — Add. 26,459 (2)
122. Kalpasūtra with a Guj. comm., incomplete — Or. 13701
123. Kalpasūtra with a Guj. comm. — Or. 13626
124. Kalpasūtra with a Guj. comm., incomplete — Or. 13616
125. Śrāvakadharma-Kalpasūtra (Guj.) — I.O. San. 2727
126. Kalpasūtra nī vācanā (Guj.) — I.O. San. 80
127. Kalpāntarvācya by Guṇaratnasūri — Or. 3349 (C)
128. Kalpāntarvācya by a pupil of Haṁsacandra, incomplete — I.O. San. 867
129. Kalpāntarvācya, anonymous — Or. 13787
130. Kalpāntarvācya with a Guj. comm. by Somavimalasūri, frag. — I.O. San. 2646 (A)
131. Kalpasūtra with a Guj. comm. — I.O. San. 2646 (B)
132. Kalpavṛtti-vācanā — Or. 5150
133. Kalpāntarvācya — I.O. San. 2539 (F)
134. Kalpāntarvācya — Or. 2120 (H)
135. [Kalpāntarvācya] (Guj.), selective — Add. 26,452 (C)
136. Kalpāntarvācya, frag. — Add. 26,454 (G)
137. [Sketches of the lives of five Jinas] — Or. 7623 (B)

1.3.1.2. Isolated illustrated folios

A. British Library

138. Kalpasūtra with an *Avacūrṇi* (23 fols.) — Or. 13341
139. Kalpasūtra (4 fols.) — Or. 13342
140. Kalpasūtra (3 fols.) — Or. 13950 (B, C, D)
141. Kalpasūtra (3 fols.) — Or. 14262

B. Victoria and Albert Museum

142. Kalpasūtra (1 fol.) — IM 161-1914
143. Kalpasūtra (1 fol.) — IM 161 A-1914
144. Kalpasūtra (2 fols.) — IM 6-1931 & IM 7-1931
145. Kalpasūtra (5 fols.) — IM 8-1931, 9-1931, 10A-1931, 11A-1931, 12-1931
146. Kalpasūtra (1 fol.) — IS 83-1963
147. Kalpasūtra (1 fol.) — IS 84-1963

C. British Museum

148. Kalpasūtra (1 fol.)	BM 1959-4-11-05
149. Kalpasūtra (1 fol.)	BM 1948-10-9-0159
150. Kalpasūtra (1 fol.)	BM 1947-7-12-02
151. Kalpasūtra (1 fol.)	BM 1947-7-12-03
152. Kalpasūtra (1 fol.)	BM 1966-10-10-05 (1)
153. Kalpasūtra (1 fol.)	BM 1966-10-10-05 (2)

1.3.2. Specialized Chedasūtras

154. Bṛhatkalpachedasūtra with Skt. glosses	Or. 16133/1
155. Bṛhatkalpasūtra	Or. 5148
156. Niśīthasūtra	Bühler 283
157. Niśīthasūtra with a Guj. comm.	Or. 13600
158. Jītakalpa-sūtra by Jinabhadra	Or. 1385 (A,1)
159. Jītakalpa-cūrṇi by Siddhasena	Or. 1385 (B)
160. Bṛhaccūrṇivyākhyā on the Jītakalpa by Śrīcandrasūri	Or. 1386
161. Sāvayapacchitta	Or. 1385 (A,2)
162. Śrāddha-jītakalpa-sūtra by Dharmaghoṣasūri with a Skt. comm.	Or. 2105 (G)

1.4. Mūlasūtras

1.4.1. Uttarādhyayana

163. Uttarādhyayanasūtra	I.O. San. 1522
164. Uttarādhyayanasūtra	Or. 5257
165. Uttarādhyayanasūtra, with a lacuna	IS 2-1972 (V&A)
166. Uttarādhyayanasūtra (with lacunae)	Or. 5156
167. Uttarādhyayanasūtra, 4th chapter only	I.O. San. 2527 (F)
168. [Uttarādhyayanasūtra] (chap. 30-31, frag.)	I.O. San. 3614 (G)
169. [Uttarādhyayanasūtra], a part of chap. 36	I.O. San. 3614 (H)
170. Uttarādhyayanasūtra with Devendra's *Sukhabodhā*	I.O. San. 354
171. Uttarādhyayanasūtra with Devendra's *Sukhabodhā*	Or. 5158
172. Uttarādhyayanasūtra with Devendra's *Sukhabodhā*	Or. 5157
173. Uttarādhyayanasūtra with Devendra's *Sukhabodhā*	Or. 2096
174. Uttarādhyayanasūtra with Devendra's *Sukhabodhā*, incomplete	Or. 2097
175. Uttarādhyayanasūtra with Devendra's *Sukhabodhā*, frag. of the commentator's praśasti only	I.O. San. 3954 (D)
176. Uttarādhyayanasūtra with Vinayahaṁsa's *Dīpikā*	Or. 2094
177. Uttarādhyayanasūtra with an *Avacūrṇi*	Or. 2095
178. Uttarādhyayanasūtra with an *Avacūrṇi*	Or. 13362
179. Uttarādhyayanasūtra with Skt. and Guj.	Or. 13476

comm.

180. Uttarādhyayanasūtra with a *Dīpikā* — I.O. San. 3165
181. Uttarādhyayanasūtra, *mūla* with Skt. and Guj. glosses — I.O. San. 3367
182. Uttarādhyayanasūtra with a Guj. comm., incomplete — I.O. San. 1015
183. Uttarādhyayanasūtra (frag. of chap. 1) with a Guj. comm. — I.O. San. 3301 (B)
184. Uttarādhyayanasūtra with a Guj. comm., beginning only — Or. 15633/195
185. Uttarādhyayana-sūtra (chap. 2), Guj. exposition, frag. — Add. 26,452 (F)
186. Mahāniyaṇṭhijja [= Utt. chap. 20] with a Guj. comm. — Or. 13790
187. Uttarādhyayanasūtra (chap. 36) with a Guj. comm. — I.O. San. 1558 (C)
188. Uttarādhyayana-kathāḥ rendered from Śāntisūri's *Bṛhadvṛtti* — Or. 5159
189. Uttarādhyayana-svādhyāya (Guj.) by Udayavijaya — Or. 15633/123
190. Keśī-Gautama-adhyayana-sajjhāya (Guj.) by Udayavijaya — Or. 15633/26 (3)
191. Keśi-Gotama-sandhi (Guj.) by Paramānanda — Or. 3347 (C, 13)
192. Keśī-Gautama-sajjhāya (Guj.) by Rūpavijaya — Or. 15633/118

1.4.2. Daśavaikālika

193. Daśavaikālikasūtra — Or. 5161
194. Daśavaikālikasūtra — Or. 5162
195. Daśavaikālikasūtra (adhy. 1-10) — I.O. San. 3374
196. Daśavaikālikasūtra (adhy. 1-10) — Or. 3349 (A)
197. Daśavaikālikasūtra, beginning only — Or. 15633/161
198. Daśavaikālikasūtra with a brief Skt. comm. — I.O. San. 1954
199. Daśavaikālika-sūtra and -niryukti with Haribhadra's *Śiṣyabodhinī* — Or. 2101
200. Daśavaikālika-niryukti-vyākhyā, fragment — I.O. San. 2341 B
201. Daśavaikālikasūtra with Sumatisūri's comm. — Or. 5163
202. Daśavaikālika, with Sumatisūri's comm., fragment — I.O. San. 3954 (B)
203. Daśavaikālikasūtra with an *Avacūri* (Skt., Guj.) — Bühler 282 (1)
204. Daśavaikālikasūtra with a comm. based on Samayasundara's *Śabdārthavṛtti* — Bühler 282A
205. Daśavaikālikasūtra with a Guj. comm. — Or. 4531
206. Daśavaikālikasūtra with a *Bālāvabodha* (Guj.) — Or. 13610
207. Daśavaikālika-sajjhāya (Guj.) by Vṛddhivijaya — Or. 15633/2
208. Daśavaikālika-sajjhāya (Guj.) by Vṛddhivijaya, incomplete — Or. 15633/31

1.5. Nandīsūtra & Anuyogadvāra

209. Nandīsūtra	I.O. San. 3360
210. Nandīsūtra	Or. 5153
211. Anuyogadvārasūtra	I.O. San. 1564d
212. Anuyogadvārasūtra	Or. 5154
213. Anuyogadvārasūtra with Hemacandra maladhārin's comm.	Or. 5155

1.6. Prakīrṇakas

214. Catuḥśaraṇa-prakīrṇaka	Or. 3347 (C,11)
215. Catuḥśaraṇa-prakīrṇaka with a Skt. *Avacūri*	I.O. San. 3391
216. Catuḥśaraṇa-viṣamapada-vivaraṇa	Or. 2105 (E)
217. Catuḥśaraṇa-prakīrṇaka with a Guj. comm.	Add. 26,464 (A)
218. Catuḥśaraṇa with a Guj. comm.	Or. 15633/174
219. Catuḥśaraṇa with a Guj. comm.	Or. 15633/175
220. Bhaktaparijñā-prakīrṇaka	Or. 5147 (1)
221. Saṁstāraka-prakīrṇaka	Or. 5147 (2)
222. Paryantārādhanā by Somasūri	Or. 3347 (C,12)
223. Paryantārādhanā by Somasūri, incomplete	I.O. San. 1561c (3)
224. Paryantārādhanā by Somasūri with a Guj. comm.	Or. 2122 (E,1)

2. Dogmatics and Ethics

2.1. Āvaśyaka literature

225. Āvaśyakaniryukti, with prefixed Therāvali	Or. 13786
226. Āvaśyakaniryukti, with prefixed Therāvalī	Or. 2105 (C)
227. Āvaśyakaniryukti, with prefixed Therāvali	Or. 13550
228. Āvaśyakaniryukti, with prefixed Therāvali	Or. 5160
229. Āvaśyaka-niryukti with Guj. comm. on the Therāvalī	Or. 3347 (B)
230. Āvaśyaka-niryukti with Tilakācārya's *Laghu-vṛtti*	Or. 2102 (B)
231. Āvaśyaka-niryukti with Jñānasāgara's *Avacūri*	Or. 2102 (A)
232. Viśeṣāvaśyakabhāṣya of Jinabhadra with Hemacandra mal.'s comm.	Or. 2103
233. Pākṣikasūtra	Or. 15633/145
234. Pākṣikasūtra	Or. 15633/146
235. Pākṣikasūtra	Or. 16132/10
236. Pākṣikasūtra	Bühler 282 (2)
237. Pākṣikasūtra with an *Avacūrṇi*	I.O. San. 1526 (B)
238. Āvaśyaka-saptatikā by Municandrasūri with Maheśvarācārya's comm.	Or. 2109 (D)
239. Śramaṇasūtra	I.O. San. 3287 (B)
240. Śramaṇasūtra with Guj. comm.	Or. 7621 (A)
241. [Yati]pratikramaṇasūtra with Guj. comm.	I.O. San. 1558 (A)
242. Śrāddhapratikramaṇasūtra with Guj. comm.	Or. 2109 (C)
243. [Ṣaḍāvaśyaka-bālāvabodha]	I.O. San. 1558 (B)
244. Śrāvakapratikramaṇasūtra	I.O. San. 3400 (A)

245. Ṣaḍāvaśyaka-sūtra with Anuṣṭhānavidhi (Vandāruvṛtti)	Or. 2104
246. Ṣaḍāvaśyaka-vyākhyāna by Hitaruci/Udayaruci	Or. 4532
247. Ṣaḍāvaśyaka-bālāvabodha by Hemahaṁsagaṇi	Or. 2105 (B)
248. Ṣaḍāvaśyaka-ṭabo by Tārācanda	Or. 15633/163
249. Ṣaḍāvaśyaka-bālāvabodha	Or. 7620
250. Ṣaḍāvaśyaka-bālāvabodha	Or. 13477
251. Ṣaḍ-āvaśyaka-bālāvabodha by Samayasundara	Or. 5192 (B)
252. Ṣaḍāvaśyaka-bālāvabodha	I.O. San. 3368
253. [Āvaśyaka ritual from the Ancalagaccha]	Or. 2122 (D)
254. Bhāṣya-traya by Devendrasūri	Or. 5194
255. Bhāṣya-traya by Devendrasūri	Or. 15633/155
256. Bhāṣya-traya by Devendrasūri	Or. 15633/154
257. Bhāṣya-traya by Devendrasūri with Somasundara's *Avacūri*	Or. 2105 (D)
258. Bhāṣyatraya by Devendrasūri with a Guj. comm.	Or. 15633/182
259. Caityavandana-bhāṣya by Devendra with a Guj. comm.	Or. 15633/171
260. Panca-namaskāra with a Guj. comm.	Or. 7621 (C)
261. Panca-namaskāra with a Guj. comm., incomplete	Or. 7621 (D)
262. Navakāra-mantra with a Guj. comm.	Or. 15633/185 (1)
263. Navakāra-mūla-mantra (Pkt. and Guj.)	I.O. San. 3606 (B)
264. Navakāra-rāsa	Or. 15633/12 (1)
265. Navakāra-chanda by Kuśalalābha	Or. 15633/38
266. Navakāra-guṇa-varṇana-svādhyāya by Jñānavimala	Or. 15633/133
267. Navakāra-sajjhāya, beg. only	Or. 13642 (10)
268. Caityavandana-bhāṣya by Śāntyācārya	Or. 2109 (B)
269. Caityavandanāvacūri (Skt.), incomplete	I.O. San. 862 (A)
270. Caityavandanasūtra-vṛtti by Haribhadra with Municandra's Panjikā, incomplete	I.O. San. 2527 (C)
271. Jinapratimā-caityavandana-phala by Vinayavijaya	Or. 15633/116
272. Arhad-ādi-kṣāmaṇā	Or. 15633/60
273. Iriyāvahī nā micchā mi dukkaḍaṁ by Meruvijaya	Or. 16133/3 (E)
274. Sāmāyika-pratikramaṇa-vidhi	I.O. San. 1564e
275. Hetugarbha-pratikramaṇa-vidhi by Jayacandrasūri	Or. 5255
276. [Samyaktva]	Or. 15633/37
277. Sādhu-aticāra	Or. 15633/139 (1)
278. [Aticāra formula]	Or. 16133/9 (R)
279. [Aticāra formula]	Or. 16133/5 (B)
280. [Aticāra of the layman's vow]	I.O. San. 3400 (E)
281. [Aticāra formula]	Or. 15633/188

282. Sthāpanā-kalpa by Yaśovijaya	Or. 15633/127
283. Sthāpanā-kalpa by Yaśovijaya	Or. 15633/55
284. Pratyākhyāna nī sajjhāya by Uddyotavijaya	Or. 15633/5 (8)
285. Upadhāna-ḍhāla by Vinayavijaya	Or. 15633/39
286. Saṁthārā-vidhi with Guj. comm.	Add. 26,464 (E)
287. Ārādhanā-vidhi	I.O. San. 1603 (A)
288. Ārādhanā-vidhi	MSS. Guj. 6 (1)
289. Aṇagāra-guṇa or Sādhuvandana	I.O. San. 3614 (I)
290. Aṇagāra-guṇa or Sādhuvandana	I.O. San. 3614 (J)
291. [Unidentified]	Or. 16133/2 (13)

2.2. Works on monastic discipline

292. Panca-nirgranthī by Abhayadevasūri	Or. 2122 (G)
293. Panca-nirgranthī by Abhayadeva with Yaśovijaya's Guj. comm.	Or. 15633/164
294. Yatidinacaryā by Devasūri	I.O. San. 1354 (D)
295. Piṇḍaviśuddhi by Jinavallabha with a *Dīpikā*	Or. 2105 (F)
296. Piṇḍaviśuddhi by Jinavallabhagaṇi with Somasundara's *Bālāvabodha*	I.O. San. 862 (B)
297. Annāya-uncha-kulaka with Ānandavijaya's Skt. comm.	I.O. San. 1530 (J)
298. Saṁvigna-sādhu-sādhvī-sāmācārī-kulaka	Or. 3347 (C,17)
299. Panca-mahāvrata-sajjhāya by Kāntivijaya, incomplete	Or. 16133/5 (A)
300. [Unidentified] by Brahma	Or. 16133/2 (11)
301. [Unidentified] (Guj.)	Or. 16133/5 (D)
302. [Sāmācārī of the Tapāgaccha]	Or. 5165

2.3. Cosmological manuscripts

2.3.1. Texts

303. Kṣetrasamāsa by Jinabhadragaṇi with Malayagiri's *Ṭīkā*	Or. 2118 (C)
304. Kṣetrasamāsa by Jinabhadragaṇi with Malayagiri's *Ṭīkā*, incompl.	I.O. San. 1357
305. Jambūdvīpa-saṁgrahaṇī by Haribhadrasūri with a Skt. *Avacūri*	Or. 2116 (E)
306. Kṣetrasamāsa by Somatilakasūri with Guṇaratna's *Avacūrṇi*	Or. 2118 (D)
307. Kṣetrasamāsa by Somatilakasūri with Guṇaratna's *Avacūrṇi*	Or. 5178
308. Laghu-Kṣetrasamāsa by Ratnaśekharasūri	I.O. San. 3409
309. Laghu-Kṣetrasamāsa by Ratnaśekharasūri	I.O. San. 2126 (A)
310. Laghu-Kṣetrasamāsa by Ratnaśekharasūri	Or. 2117 (A)
311. Laghu-kṣetrasamāsa by Ratnaśekharasūri	Or. 15633/147
312. Laghu-kṣetrasamāsa by Ratnaśekharasūri	Or. 15633/148
313. Laghu-Kṣetrasamāsa by Ratnaśekharasūri with auto-comm.	Or. 2117 (D)
314. Laghu-Kṣetrasamāsa by Ratnaśekharasūri with auto-comm.	Or. 2117 (C)

315. Laghu-Kṣetrasamāsa by Ratnaśekharasūri with Pārśvacandra's *Vivaraṇa* — Or. 2118 (A)
316. Laghu-Kṣetrasamāsa by Ratnaśekhara with Pārśvacandra's *Ṭabo* — Add. 26,374
317. Laghu-Kṣetrasamāsa by R. with Dayāsiṁhagaṇi's comm. — Or. 2118 (B)
318. Laghu-Kṣetrasamāsa by Ratnaśekhara with a Guj. comm. — Or. 15633/170
319. Laghu-Kṣetrasamāsa by Ratnaśekhara with a Guj. comm. — Or. 16132/11
320. Laghu-Kṣetrasamāsa by Ratnaśekharasūri with a Guj. comm. — Or. 2117 (B)
321. Saṁgrahaṇīratna by Śrīcandra — Or. 2116 (B)
322. Saṁgrahaṇīratna by Śrīcandra — Or. 2137 (B,1)
323. Saṁgrahaṇīratna by Śrīcandra — Or. 13549
324. Saṁgrahaṇīratna by Śrīcandra — Or. 13611
325. Saṁgrahaṇīratna by Śrīcandra — I.O. San. 2341 (C)
326. Saṁgrahaṇīratna by Śrīcandra — Or. 13495
327. Saṁgrahaṇīratna by Śrīcandra — Or. 13454
328. Saṁgrahaṇīratna by Śrīcandra with Devabhadra's comm. — Or. 2116 (D)
329. Saṁgrahaṇīratna by Śrīcandra with an *Avacūrṇi* — Or. 2116 (A)
330. Saṁgrahaṇīratna by Śrīcandra with an *Avacūrṇi* — Or. 5191
331. Saṁgrahaṇīratna by Śrīcandra with a Skt. comm. — I.O. San. 3359
332. Saṁgrahaṇīratna by Śrīcandra with a Skt. comm., incomplete — I.O. San. 3954 (F)
333. Saṁgrahaṇīratna by Śrīcandra with a Guj. & Skt. comm. — I.O. San. 1553 (B)
334. Saṁgrahaṇīratna by Śrīcandra with Śivanidhānagaṇi's *Bālāvabodha* — Or. 13613
335. Saṁgrahaṇīratna by Śrīcandra with Śivanidhānagaṇi's *Bālāvabodha* — Or. 13614
336. Saṁgrahaṇīratna by Śrīcandra with Dharmameru's comm. (Guj.) — Or. 13456
337. Saṁgrahaṇīratna by Śrīcandra with a Guj. comm. — Or. 2116 (C)
338. Saṁgrahaṇīratna by Śrīcandra with a Guj. comm. — Or. 13612
339. Saṁgrahaṇīratna by Śrīcandra with a Guj. comm. — IS 35-1971 (V&A)
340. Saṁgrahaṇīratna by Śrīcandra with a Guj. comm., incomplete — Add. 26,365
341. [Fragment of a Ṭabo to a cosmological work] — Add. 26,452 (H)
342. Cauvīsadaṇḍaka by Gajasāra — I.O. San. 3395 (2)
343. Vicāraṣaṭtriṁśikā by Gajasāra — I.O. San. 3389
344. Vicāraṣaṭtriṁśikā by Gajasāra — Or. 15633/153
345. Cauvīsadaṇḍaka by Gajasāra — Or. 15633/149

346. Vicāraṣaṭtriṁśikā by Gajasāra with auto-comm.   Or. 2132 (F)

347. Vicāraṣaṭtriṁśikā by Gajasāra with auto-comm.   Or. 5258

348. Vicāraṣaṭtriṁśikā by Gajasāra with auto-comm.   Or. 5173

349. Vicāraṣaṭtriṁśikā by Gajasāra with a Guj. comm. by a pupil of Yaśassoma   Or. 7621 (B)

350. Vicāraṣaṭtriṁśikā by Gajasāra with a Guj. comm.   Or. 15633/152

351. Covīsadaṇḍaga by Gajasāra with a Guj. comm.   Or. 15633/178

352. Cauvīsadaṇḍaga by Gajasāra with a Guj. comm.   Or. 13618

353. Vicāraṣaṭtriṁśikā by Gajasāra with a Guj. comm.   Or. 13619

354. Vicāraṣaṭtriṁśikā by Gajasāra, incompl., with a Guj. comm.   Or. 15633/179

355. Cauvīsadaṇḍaka by Gajasāra with a Guj. comm.   MSS. Guj. 18

356. Trīsa dvāra   Or. 15633/32

357. Daṇḍaka nāṁ ogaṇatrīsa dvāra based on Gajasāra's Daṇḍaka   Or. 15633/18

358. Gatāgati nā bheda, Guj.   Or. 15633/130

359. [Fragment of a list of 29 dvāras], Guj.   Or. 15633/120

360. Lokanāli-dvātriṁśikā by Dharmaghoṣasūri with a Guj. comm.   Or. 15633/184

361. [Naraka-yātanā-sajjhāya] by Paramakrapāla   Or. 15633/35

362. Bāra ārā nuṁ māna   Or. 15633/44

363. Bāra ārā nuṁ stavana, incomplete   Or. 15633/84

364. Avagāhanā nuṁ māna   Or. 15633/45

365. [Kevali-samudghāta] (Skt.)   Or. 5191

366. Samudghāta-vicāra (Guj.)   MSS. Guj. 6 (3)

2.3.2. Diagrams and illustrations

367. Saṁgrahaṇī-yantra   Or. 13459

368. [Length and dimensions of the cosmic man]   Or. 13974

369. Aḍhāīdvīpa   Or. 13294

370. Aḍhāīdvīpa   Or. 13937

371 [a]. Aḍhāīdvīpa with labels and texts   Add. Or. 1812

371 [b]. Key to Aḍhāī-dvīpa in English   Add. Or. 1813

372. Aḍhāīdvīpa   Add. Or. 1814

373. Aḍhāīdvīpa   Circ. 91-1970 (V&A)

374. The seven armies of the Bhavanavāsins   IS 2-1984 (V&A)

375. Personification of a planet   Circ. 325-1972 (V&A)

376. Personification of a planet   Circ. 326-1972 (V&A)

377. The seven Chakras of the Subtle Body   Circ. 321-1972 (V&A)

2.4. Karma literature
2.4.1. Sets of five or six Karmagranthas

2.4.1.1. Karmavipāka

378. Karmavipāka by Gargarṣi	Or. 2137 (B,2)
379. Karmavipāka by Devendrasūri	Or. 2106 (A,1)
380. Karmavipāka by Devendrasūri	Or. 15633/150 (1)
381. Karmavipāka by Devendrasūri	Or. 15633/151 (1)
382. Karmavipāka by Devendrasūri	Or. 15633/156 (1)
383. Karmavipāka by Devendrasūri	Or. 13552 (1)
384. Karmavipāka by Devendra-sūri	Or. 3347 (C,1)
385. Karmavipāka by Devendrasūri	I.O. San. 1350 (1)
386. Karmavipāka by Devendrasūri with auto-comm.	Or. 5168 (1)
387. Karmavipāka by Devendrasūri with auto-comm., incompl.	I.O. San. 1372 (A)
388. Karma-vipāka by Devendrasūri with Guṇaratna's *Avacūri*	Or. 2106 (D,1)
389. Karmavipāka by Devendrasūri with an *Avacūri*	Or. 2106 (B,1)
390. Karmavipāka by Devendrasūri with an *Avacūri*	Or. 5188 (1)
391. Karmavipāka by Devendrasūri with a Guj. comm.	Or. 2106 (C,1)
392. Karmavipāka by Devendrasūri with a Guj. comm.	Or. 15633/176 (1)

2.4.1.2. Karmastava

393. Karmastava by Jinavallabha	Or. 2137 (B,3)
394. Karmastava-bhāṣya	Or. 2137 (B,4)
395. Karmastava by Devendrasūri	Or. 2106 (A,2)
396. Karmastava by Devendrasūri	Or. 15633/150 (2)
397. Karmastava by Devendrasūri	Or. 15633/151 (2)
398. Karmastava by Devendrasūri	Or. 15633/156 (2)
399. Karmastava by Devendrasūri	Or. 13552 (2)
400. Karmastava by Devendrasūri	I.O. San. 1350 (2)
401. Karmastava by Devendrasūri with auto-comm.	Or. 5168 (2)
402. Karmastava by Devendrasūri with Guṇaratna's *Avacūri*	Or. 2106 (D,2)
403. Karmastava by Devendrasūri with an *Avacūri*	Or. 2106 (B,2)
404. Karmastava by Devendrasūri with an *Avacūri*	Or. 5188 (2)
405. Karmastava by Devendrasūri with an *Avacūri*	Or. 5182 (1)
406. Karmastava by Devendrasūri with a Guj. comm.	Or. 15633/33
407. Karmastava by Devendrasūri with a Guj. comm.	Or. 15633/176 (2)

2.4.1.3. Bandhasvāmitva

408. Bandhasvāmitva	Or. 2137 (B,7)

409. Bandhasvāmitva by Devendrasūri Or. 2106 (A,3)
410. Bandhasvāmitva by Devendrasūri Or. 15633/150 (3)
411. Bandhasvāmitva by Devendrasūri Or. 15633/151 (3)
412. Bandhasvāmitva by Devendrasūri Or. 15633/156 (3)
413. Bandhasvāmitva by Devendrasūri Or. 13552 (3)
414. Bandhasvāmitva by Devendrasūri I.O. San. 1350 (3)
415. Bandhasvāmitva by Devendrasūri with Sādhukīrti's comm. Or. 5182 (2)
416. Bandhasvāmitvaby Devendrasūri with a Skt. comm. Or. 5168 (3)
417. Bandhasvāmitva by Devendrasūri with a Skt. comm. Or. 2106 (B,3)
418. Bandhasvāmitva by Devendrasūri with a Skt. comm. Or. 5188 (3)
419. Bandhasvāmitva by Devendrasūri with Guṇaratna's *Avacūri* Or. 2106 (D,3)
420. Bandhasvāmitva by Devendrasūri with a Guj. comm. Or. 15633/176 (3)
421. Bandhasvāmitva by D. with a Guj. comm., frag. Or. 15633/177 (1)

2.4.1.4. Ṣaḍaśītikā

422. Āgamikavastu-vicāra-prakaraṇa by Jinavallabha Or. 2137 (B,5)
423. Ṣaḍaśīti-laghubhāṣya Or. 2137 (B,6)
424. Ṣaḍaśītikā by Devendrasūri Or. 2106 (A,4)
425. Ṣaḍaśītikā by Devendrasūri Or. 15633/150 (4)
426. Ṣaḍaśītikā by Devendrasūri Or. 15633/151 (4)
427. Ṣaḍaśītikā by Devendrasūri Or. 15633/156 (4)
428. Ṣaḍaśītikā by Devendrasūri Or. 13552 (4)
429. Ṣaḍaśītikā by Devendrasūri Or. 15633/157
430. Ṣaḍaśītikā by Devendrasūri I.O. San. 1350 (4)
431. Ṣaḍaśītikā by Devendrasūri with auto-comm. Or. 5168 (4)
432. Ṣaḍaśītikā by Devendrasūri with Guṇaratna's *Avacūri* Or. 2106 (D,4)
433. Ṣaḍaśītikā by Devendrasūri with an *Avacūri* Or. 2106 (B,4)
434. Ṣaḍaśītikā by Devendrasūri with an *Avacūri* Or. 5188 (4)
435. Ṣaḍaśītikā by Devendra with Dhanavijaya's *Ṭabo* Or. 15633/177 (2)
436. Ṣaḍaśītikā by Devendrasūri with a Guj. comm. Or. 15633/176 (4)

2.4.1.5. Śataka

437. Śataka ascribed to Śivaśarman Or. 2137 (B,8)
438. Śataka-bhāṣya Or. 2137 (B,9)
439. Sārdhaśataka-prakaraṇa by Jinavallabhasūri Or. 2137 (B,10)
440. Sārdha-śataka-bhāṣya Or. 2137 (B,11)
441. Śataka by Devendrasūri Or. 2106 (A,5)
442. Śataka by Devendrasūri Or. 15633/150 (5)
443. Śataka by Devendrasūri Or. 15633/151 (5)

444. Śataka by Devendrasūri Or. 15633/156 (5)
445. Śataka by Devendrasūri Or. 13552 (5)
446. Śataka by Devendrasūri I.O. San. 1350 (5)
447. Śataka by Devendrasūri with auto-comm. Or. 5168 (5)
448. Śataka by Devendrasūri with auto-comm. I.O. San. 1372 (B,1)
449. Śataka by Devendrasūri with Guṇaratna's *Avacūri* Or. 2106 (D,5)
450. Śataka by Devendrasūri with Guṇaratna's *Avacūri* Or. 5188 (5)
451. Śataka by Devendrasūri with an *Avacūri* Or. 2106 (B,5)
452. Śataka by Devendrasūri with a Guj. comm., incomplete Or. 15633/176 (5)
453. Śataka by Devendrasūri with a Guj. comm. Or. 15633/177 (3)
454. Śataka-karmagrantha-sūcīyantra by Sumativardhana Or. 15633/6

2.4.1.6. Saptatikā

455. Saptatikā-bhāṣya by Abhayadeva Or. 2137 (B,14)
456. Saptatikā by Candrarṣi Mahattara Or. 2106 (A,6)
457. Saptatikā by Candrarṣi Mahattara Or. 2137 (B,12)
458. Saptatikā by Candrarṣi Mahattara I.O. San. 1350 (6)
459. Saptatikā by Candrarṣi Mahattara Or. 15633/150 (6)
460. Saptatikā by Candrarṣi Mahattara Or. 15633/151 (6)
461. Saptatikā by Candrarṣi Mahattara Or. 13552 (6)
462. Saptatikā by Candrarṣi Mahattara, frag. Or. 15633/156 (6)
463. Saptatikā by Candrarṣi Mahattara with Malayagiri's comm. I.O. San. 1372 (B,2)
464. Saptatikā by Candrarṣi Mahattara with Guṇaratna's *Avacūri* Or. 2106 (D,6)
465. Saptatikā by Candrarṣi Mahattara with a Guj. comm. I.O. San. 1032
466. Sattarī-sāra Or. 2137 (B,13)
467. [Verses from the Saptatikā and from Malayagiri's comm. on the Saptatikā with a Guj. comm.] Or. 15633/181

2.4.2. Other works on Karman and Guṇasthāna

468. Pancasaṁgraha by Candrarṣi with auto-comm. Or. 2107 (B)
469. Bandhahetūdaya-tribhangī by Harṣakula with Vijayavimala's comm. Or. 2107 (A)
470. Kṣullaka-bhavāvalī-prakaraṇa by Dharmaśekharagaṇi with an *Avacūri* Or. 2122 (H)
471. Aṣṭa-karma-vicāra Or. 15633/129
472. Aṣṭa karama cūraṇa karī by Devavijaya Or. 15633/113 (1)
473. Aṣṭamī-sajjhāya (Guj.) by Vijayasiṁhasūri Or. 16133/9 (E)
474. Aṣṭa-karmaprakṛti-bola-vicāra-stavana by Nagāgaṇi Or. 15633/13 (1)
475. Panca-karmaprakṛti-prathama-sajjhāya and Tṛtīya-karmaprakṛti-sajjhāya by Maṇivijaya Or. 15633/13 (3)-(4)

476. Āṭha karma nī 136 prakṛti	Or. 15633/46
477. Āṭha karma nī ekaso aṭṭhāvana prakṛti	Or. 15633/34
478. Jambū-pṛcchā or Karma-phala by Vīrajī	Or. 15633/30
479. 62 bola (Guj.)	Or. 16132/7
480. Bhāva-prakaraṇa by Vijayavimala with a Guj. comm.	Or. 15633/169
481. Guṇasthāna-kramāroha by Ratnaśekhara with auto-comm.	Or. 5170
482. Cauda-guṇaṭhāṇa nī sajjhāya by Yaśovijya	Or. 15633/43 (2)
483. Guṇa-ṭhāṇā caupaī by Kanakasoma with comm.	MSS. Guj. 9

2.4.3. On time

484. Kāla-saptatikā by Dharmaghoṣasūri	Or. 15633/159
485. Kāla-saptatikā by Dharmaghoṣasūri with a Guj. comm.	Or. 15633/162

2.5. On *jīvas*, *ajīvas* and *ātman*

486. Jīvavicāra by Śāntisūri with Ratnakāravācaka's comm.	Or. 5172
487. Jīvavicāra by Śāntisūri with Bhāvasundara's *Avacūri*	Or. 2112 (E)
488. Jīvavicāra-sūtra by Śāntisūri with a Guj. comm.	Add. 26,464 (C,1)
489. Jīvavicāra by Śāntisūri with a Guj. comm.	Or. 15633/167
490. Jīvavicāra by Śāntisūri with a Guj. comm.	Or. 15633/168
491. Jīvavicāra-sāra by Ugrasenasūri	I.O. San. 1553 (D)
492. [Jīva-dayā], fragment	I.O. San. 3400 (P)
493. Nigoda-ṣaṭtriṁśikā by Abhayadeva with comm.	Or. 13789
494. Alpabahutva-stavana	Or. 15633/144 (2)
495. Alpabahutva-stavana with Skt. comm.	Or. 2132 (H)
496. Cha kāya nī vigata, incomplete	Or. 15633/136
497. [Karaṇāntargata-kiyad-vicāra-bālābodha]	MSS. Guj. 6 (4)
498. Kāya-jīva-gīta by Samayasundara	Add. 26,452 (M,2)
499. Mana-bhamarā-sajjhāya by Memanda	Or. 14064 (B,25)
499[a]. Bhramara-gīta (Guj.) by Māladeva	Or. 16133/2 (16)
500. Dravyaguṇaparyāya no rāsa by Yaśovijaya with a Guj. comm.	Or. 4533
501. Ṣaṭ-dravya-gāthāḥ, 3 vss., with tabular explanations	Or. 15633/108
502. [Leśyā-varṇana] (Guj.)	Or. 15633/14
503. Corāsī lākha jīva-yonī nā prāṇa	Or. 15633/56
504. [Jīva-dravya-]sajjhāya by Maṇicanda	Or. 16132/4
505. Yogasāra	I.O. San. 1564h
506. Ātmānuśāsana (Skt.) by Pārśvanaga	Or. 2121 (F)
507. Ātmabodha-kulaka by Jayaśekhara with a Guj. comm.	Or. 2122 (F)
508. Ātmā ne hita śikṣā sajjhāya by Viśuddhavimala	Or. 15633/1

509. Ātmā ne hita-śikṣā sajjhāya by Viśuddhavimala — Or. 15633/5 (9)
510. Ātmā nī sajjhāya by Udayacandra — Or. 15633/5 (2)
511. Ātmā nī sajjhāya by Udayaratna — Or. 15633/5 (3)
512. Ātmā nī ātmatā — Or. 15633/23 (3)
513. Adhyātma ni thoa (Guj.) by Bhāvaprabhasūri — Or. 16133/9 (D)
514. [Unidentified] (Guj.) — Or. 16133/2 (2)

2.6. Ethics: General teaching
515. Tattvārthasūtra with Bhāṣya — Or. 5174
516. Praśamarati by Umāsvāti vācaka — Or. 2098 (B)
517. Praśamarati by Umāsvāti with a *Ṭīkā* — Or. 2098 (A)
518. Praśamarati by Umāsvāti vācaka with an *Avacūri* — Or. 2098 (C)
519. Upadeśamālā by Dharmadāsagaṇi — Or. 2114 (A)
520. Upadeśamālā by Dharmadāsagaṇi — Or. 13479
521. Upadeśamālā by Dharmadāsagaṇi — Or. 13480
522. Upadeśamālā by Dharmadāsagaṇi — Or. 13553
523. Upadeśamālā by Dharmadāsagaṇi, incomplete — I.O. San. 3293
524. Upadeśamālā by Dh. with a Skt. comm. — I.O. San. 3413
525. Upadeśa-mālā by Dharmadāsagaṇi with Rāmavijaya's comm. — Add. 26,460
526. Upadeśamālā by Dharmadāsagaṇi with an *Avacūri* — Or. 2114 (C)
527. Upadeśamālā by Dharmadāsagaṇi with Nannasūri's Guj. comm. — Or. 2114 (B)
528. Upadeśamālā by Dharmadāsagaṇi with a Guj. comm. — Or. 15633/180
529. Upadeśamālā-kathāḥ (Skt.) — Or. 5164
530. Upadeśataranginī by Ratnamandira-gaṇi — Or. 2115 (B)
531. Upadeśa-ratna-kośa by Padmajineśvarasūri — Or. 3347 (C,14)
532. Upadeśa-sandhi (Ap.) by Hemasāra — Or. 3347 (C,8)
533. Śīlopadeśamālā by Jayavallabha — Or. 3347 (C,16)
534. Śīlopadeśamālā by Jinavallabha with an *Avacūri* — Or. 2113 (A)
535. Śīlopadeśamālā by Jayakīrti with Merusundara's *Bālāvabodha* — Or. 2113 (B)
536. Puṣpamālā by Hemacandra maladhārin — Or. 2115 (A)
537. Puṣpamālā by Hemacandra maladhārin — I.O. San. 2112 (B)
538. Bhavabhāvanā by Hemacandra maladhārin — Or. 5185
539. Dharmaratna-prakaraṇa by Śāntisūri — Or. 15633/158
540. Śrāddha-dina-kṛtya by Devendra — Or. 2120 (I)
541. Pravacanasāroddhāra by Nemicandra — I.O. San. 3354
542. Pravacanasāroddhāra by Nemicandra — Or. 5181
543. Pravacanasāroddhāra by Nemicandra, incomplete — I.O. San. 1610
544. Pravacanasāroddhāra by Nemicandra with Siddhasena's comm., frag. — Or. 2110
545. Āgamasāroddhāra-bālāvabodha (Guj.) by — Or. 2105 (H)

Devacandra(gaṇi)

546. Yogaśāstra by Hemacandra (1-4)	Or. 2119 (A)
547. Yogaśāstra by Hemacandra (1-4)	Or. 2119 (B)
548. Yogaśāstra by Hemacandra (1-4)	I.O. San. 1992
549. Yogaśāstra by Hemacandra (1-4)	I.O. San. 3386
550. Yogaśāstra by Hemacandra (5-12)	Or. 2119 (C)
551. Yogaśāstra by Hemacandra (1, frag.)	I.O. San. 3400 (D,d)
552. Yogaśāstra by Hemacandra (1-4) with a Skt. comm.	Or. 2119 (D)
553. Yogaśāstra by Hemacandra (1-4) with Somasundara's *Bālāvabodha*	Or. 2119 (F)
554. Yogaśāstra by Hemacandra (1-4) with a Guj. comm.	Or. 2119 (E)
555. Yogaśāstra by Hemacandra (1-4) with a Guj. comm.	Or. 5186
556. Śrāddhavidhi-prakaraṇa by Ratnaśekhara-sūri with auto-comm.	Or. 2120 (A)
557. Śrāvakavratabhanga-vicāra with Skt. comm.	Or. 2120 (F)
558. Ādinātha-deśanoddhāra	Or. 3347 (C,6)
559. Ādinātha-deśanoddhāra with a Guj. comm.	I.O. San. 1561c (2)
560. Vardhamāna-deśanā by Rājakīrtigaṇi	Or. 5187
561. Vividha-śāstra-vicāra-subhāṣita-gāthā	I.O. San. 3397
562. [Jīva-dayā jiṇa-dhammo]	Or. 15633/183 (2)

2.7. Tracts on specific topics

563. Navatattva-prakaraṇa	Or. 2112 (A,1)
564. Navatattva-vicāra	Or. 15633/143
565. Navatattva-prakaraṇa, frag.	I.O. San. 3395 (1)
566. Navatattva-vicāra	Or. 15633/141
567. Navatattva	Or. 15633/140
568. Navatattva	Or. 15633/142
569. Navatattva with a Skt. comm.	Or. 5177
570. Navatattva with a Skt. comm.	I.O. San. 1367 (B)
571. Navatattva with a Guj. comm.	I.O. San. 3385
572. Navatattva with a Guj. comm.	Or. 2112 (A,2)
573. Navatattva-vicāra with Pārśvacandra's *Ṭabo*	Add. 26,464 (C,2)
574. Navatattva with a Guj. comm.	I.O. San. 3287 (C)
575. Navatattva-vicāra by Maṇiratna with Jñānavimala's *Bālāvabodha*	Add. 26,452 (A)
576. Navatattva-vicāra-caupaī by a pupil of Bhāvasāgarasūri	Add. 26,461 (4)
577. Navatattva-copāī by Devacandra, incomplete	Or. 15633/135
578. Navatattva-ḍhāla by Mayācanda muni	Or. 15633/40 (1)
579. Vairāgya-śataka with Guṇavinaya's comm.	I.O. San. 1564a
580. Vairāgya-śataka with a Guj. comm.	Or. 2133 (F)
581. Vairāgya-śataka with a Guj. comm.	Or. 13498
582. Vairāgya-sandhi (Ap.) by Ajita/Harṣa	Or. 3347 (C,7)
583. Vairāgya-gīta (Guj.) by Māladeva	Or. 16133/2 (15)
584. Indriyaparājaya-śataka	Or. 3347 (C,5)

585. Indriyaparājaya-śataka with a Guj. comm. I.O. San. 1561c (1)
586. Ṣaṣṭi-śataka by Nemicandra Bhāṇḍagārika with a Skt. comm. Or. 13179
587. Ṣaṣṭi-śataka by Nemicandra Bh. with Guj. glosses I.O. San. 2341 (A)
588. Sambodha-saptatikā by Ratnaśekhara Or. 15633/24
589. Sambodha-saptatikā by Ratnaśekhara Or. 3347 (C,3)
590. Sambodha-saptatikā by Ratnaśekhara Or. 2133 (D)
591. Sambodha-saptatikā by Ratnaśekhara with Amarakīrti's comm. Or. 2133 (C)
592. Sambodha-saptatikā by Ratnaśekhara with a Guj. comm. Or. 15633/183 (1)
593. Vivekamanjarī by Āsaḍa Or. 3347 (C,2)
594. Samyaktva-saptatikā I.O. San. 3379
595. Samyaktva-svarūpa-garbhita-Jinastavana with Guj. comm. MSS. Guj. 6 (2)
596. Samakita nā 67 bola (Guj.) by Yaśovijaya Or. 15633/137
597. Jñānakalā-caupaī by Sumatiranga MSS. Guj. 7
598. Dṛṣṭi-rāgopari sajjhāya by Yaśovijaya Or. 15633/43 (1)
599. Buddhi-rāsa by Śālibhadrasūri I.O. San. 3400 (L,ec)
600. Āvyaprabodha-sajjhāya by Cārudatta vācaka Or. 14064 (B,6)
601. Sikhāmaṇi nī caupāī Harley 415 (16)
602. Śrīsāra-sīkhāmaṇa-rāsa by Saṁvegasundara I.O. San. 3400 (A,aa)
603. Śrāvakavidhi-rāsa by Guṇākarasūri, beg. MSS. Guj. 6 (5)
604. Ātmopadeśa-sajjhāya by a pupil of Vinayaprabha Or. 15633/105 (2)
605. Cāritra-mālā by Lālavijayagaṇi Or. 15633/131
606. [Unidentified] Or. 16133/2 (12)
607. [Kaliyuga-sajjhāya] Or. 16133/5 (G,1)
608. Saṁtoṣa nī sajjhāya by Kaviyaṇa Or. 15633/58 (1)
609. Dvādaśa-bhāvanā (Guj.) by Sakalacandra Add. 26,464 (F)
610. Dvādaśa-bhāvanā-sajjhāya by a pupil of Yaśaḥsoma Or. 15633/36
611. Bāra-bhāvanā-sajjhāya Or. 16133/2 (3)
612. Ekonatriṁśati-bhāvanā I.O. San. 3394 (2)
613. Ekonatriṁśati-bhāvanā with Guj. explanations, frag. Add. 26,452 (I)
614. Ikatīsī bhāvanā (Guj.) MSS. Guj. 15
615. Dhyāna chattīsa (Guj.) by Gurudāsa MSS. Guj. 14 (2)
616. Dvādaśa-kulaka by Jinavallabhasūri with Jinapāla's comm. Or. 5176
617. Śīla-kulaka by Devendrasūri with a Guj. comm. Or. 15633/165
618. Śīla-kulaka by Devendrasūri with a Guj. comm. Or. 15633/166
619. Śīla-sandhi (Ap.) by a pupil of Jayaśekhara Or. 3347 (C,15)
620. Śīla nī nava vāḍa (Guj.) by Udayaratna Or. 15633/20
621. Nava-vāḍī-sajjhāya (Guj.) by Hīrānanda Or. 16133/2 (4)
622. Sīla-gīta (Guj.) by Ajitadevasūri Or. 16133/2 (9)
623. Sīla-gīta (Guj.) Or. 16133/2 (8)

624. [Unidentified] (Guj.) by Puri-kavi (?) — Or. 16133/2 (7)
625. Dāna-śīla-tapo-bhāvanā by Aśoka Muni — I.O. San. 3394 (1)
626. Dāna-śīla-tapa-bhāvanā-gīta (Guj.) by Samayasundara — Or. 13627
627. Upaśamarasa-kulaka (Ap.) — Or. 3347 (C,10)
628. Rātribhojana-sajjhāya by Muni Vasatā — Or. 15633/78
629. Krodha, māna, māyā, lobha nī sajjhāya by Udayaratna — Or. 15633/8 (1)
630. Samakita nī sajjhāya & Māna nī sajjhāya by Udayaratna — Or. 15633/54
631. Āṭha mada sajjhāya (Guj.) by Mānavijaya — Or. 16133/9 (O)
632. Puṇyapāpa-svarūpa-kulaka with a Guj. comm. — Or. 15633/173
633. [Puṇya-prakāśa nuṁ stavana] (Guj.) by Vinayavijaya, frag. — Or. 16133/9 (P)
634. [Puṇya-prakāśa nuṁ stavana] (Guj.) by Vinayavijaya, beg. — Or. 16133/9 (J)
635. Gautama-kulaka with a Guj. comm. — Or. 8060
636. Prastāvikā-gāthā — Or. 16132/5 (2)
637. Guruguṇa-ṣaṭtriṁśikā by Ratnaśekhara with auto-comm. — Or. 2133 (E)
638. Kuguru-pacīsī (Guj.) by Tejapāla — Or. 15633/8 (3)
639. Siddha-pancāśikā by Devendrasūri with an *Avacūrṇi* — Or. 2133 (G)
640. Siddha-pancāśikā by Devendrasūri with an *Avacūrṇi* — Or. 2133 (H)
641. Ekaviṁśati-sthāna-prakaraṇa by Siddhasena — Or. 15633/22
642. Ekaviṁśati-sthānaka by Siddhasena, incomplete — Or. 13629
643. Ekaviṁśati-sthāna-prakaraṇa by Siddhasena with Guj. comm. — I.O. San. 3401
644. Ekaviṁśati-jina-sthānaka by Siddhasena with a Guj. comm. — Or. 15633/172
645. Saptati-śata-sthānaka by Somatilakasūri with a Guj. comm. — Or. 13696
646. Mātā-putra-sambandha-sajjhāya by Kāntivijaya — Or. 15633/51
647. Tamāṣū-sijjhāi (Raj.) by Jasobhadra — Or. 16133/2 (6)

2.8. Polemic works

648. Saṅghapaṭṭaka of Jinavallabha with Sādhukīrti's *Avacūri* — I.O. San. 2527 (A)
649. Sanghapaṭṭaka of Jinavallabha with a Guj. comm. — Add. 26,435 (B)
650. Tattvaprabodha-prakaraṇa by Haribhadra — Or. 2112 (B)
651. Śrāddhavidhi-viniścaya by Harṣabhūṣaṇa — Or. 2120 (B)
652. Śrāddhavidhi-viniścaya by Harṣabhūṣaṇa — Or. 2120 (C,1-2)
653. Dharmatattva-vicāra-huṇḍī — Or. 2120 (D)
654. Dharmatattva-vicāra-huṇḍī — Or. 2120 (E,1)
655. Senapraśna by Śubhavijayagaṇi, incomplete — Or. 16132/12

656. Pravacanaparīkṣā by Dharmasāgara-gaṇi Or. 2109 (A)
657. Pravacanaparīkṣā by Dharmasāgara with auto-comm. Or. 2108
658. Tattvataranginī by Dharmasāgara with auto-comm. Or. 2112 (C)
659. Tattvataranginī by Dharmasāgara with auto-comm. Or. 2112 (D)
660. Gurutattva-pradīpikā by Dharmasāgara with auto-comm. Or. 2121 (C)
661. Gurutattva-pradīpikā by Dharmasāgara, beg. only Or. 2105 (A)
662. Gurutattva-pradīpa Or. 2121 (B)
663. Sūtra-vyākhyāna-vidhi-śataka with a Skt. comm. Or. 2120 (G)
664. Praśnottara or Dharmaratnākara by Śrutasāgara Or. 2136 (B)
665. Īryāpathikā-ṣaṭtriṁśikā by Jayasoma with auto-comm. Or. 13541
666. Siddhāntālāpaka Or. 2137 (A)
667. Ālāpaka Or. 16132/3
668. Nānā-vicāra-ratna-saṁgraha, incomplete Or. 5256
669. [Quotations from various scriptures], incomplete I.O. San. 1530 (G)

3. Philosophy

670. Anekāntajayapatākā by Haribhadra with the auto-comm. *Bṛhadvṛtti* Or. 2111
671. Ṣaḍdarśanasamuccaya by Haribhadra Bühler 306
672. [Ṣaḍdarśanasamuccaya by Haribhadra with Guṇākara's comm. Jacobi's ms. - missing]
673. Ṣaḍdarśanasamuccaya by Haribhadra with a Skt. comm. Bühler 307
674. Sarvajñasiddhiprakaraṇa by Haribhadra Or.2134 (D,4)
675. Pramāṇamīmāṁsā by Hemacandra Or. 2134 (D,1)
676. Pramāṇamīmāṁsā-vṛtti by Hemacandra Or. 2134 (D,2)
677. Anyayogavyavacchedikā by Hemacandra with an *Avacūri* I.O. San. 2527 (D,1-2)
678. Syādvādamanjarī by Malliṣeṇasūri Or. 5193
679. Syādvādamanjarī by Malliṣeṇasūri I.O. San. 1094
680. Vivekavilāsa by Jinadattasūri I.O. San. 3292 (B)
681. Vivekavilāsa by Jinadattasūri Or. 2136 (A)
682. Vivekavilāsa by Jinadattasūri with a Guj. comm. I.O. San. 3400 (A,b)
683. Tarkataranginī by Guṇaratna Or. 5211
684. Pramāṇamanjarī by Śarvadeva, incomplete Add. 26,452 (E)
685. [Citrarūpa-kārya-kāraṇa-bhāva-rahasya] Or. 2121 (D)
686. Niścaya nī sajjhāya by Haṁsabhuvanasūri Or. 15633/5 (6)
687. [Darśana-bheda] Or. 2122 (E,2)

[Volume III]

4. Śvetāmbara narrative literature

4.1. Lives of the Jinas and related works

688. Triṣaṣṭiśalākāpuruṣa-caritra by Hemacandra (I.1-6)	Or. 2123 (A)
689. Triṣaṣṭiśalākāpuruṣa-caritra by Hemacandra (VIII.1-12)	Or. 2123 (B)
690. Triṣaṣṭiśalākāpuruṣa-caritra by Hemacandra (VIII.1-12)	Or. 2123 (C,1)
691. Triṣaṣṭiśalākāpuruṣa-caritra by Hemacandra (VIII.1-12)	Or. 2124
692. Candraprabha-carita by Devendrācārya	I.O. San. 3410
693. Vāsupūjya-carita by Vardhamānasūri	I.O. San. 3411
694. Vimalanātha-carita by Jñānasāgarasūri	Or. 2127
695. Śāntinātha-carita by Ajitaprabhasūri	I.O. San. 1527
696. Śāntinātha-caritra by Bhāvacandra	Or. 3347 (A)
697. Śāntinātha-carita	Or. 2128 (A)
698. Śānti-vṛtta by Munidevasūri, incomplete	I.O. San. 1354 (A)
699. Pārśvanātha-carita by Bhāvadevasūri	I.O. San. 888
700. Pārśvanātha-carita by Bhāvadevasūri	I.O. San. 3361
701. Pārśvanātha-caritra by Udayavīra	Add. 26,362
702. Pārśvanātha-carita by Padmasundarasūri	Aufrecht 86 (I-II)

4.2. Lives of the teachers

703. Pariśiṣṭa-parvan by Hemacandra	Or. 5180
704. Pariśiṣṭa-parvan by Hemacandra	Bühler 293
705. Gautamasvāmi-rāsa by Vinayaprabha	Harley 415 (15)
706. Gotamasvāmī ro rāsa (Raj.) by Vinayabhadra, end	Or. 16133/9 (M)
707. Kālakācārya-kathā by Dharmaprabhasūri	I.O. San. 1530 (B)
708. Kālakācārya-kathānaka by Devacandrasūri	I.O. San. 3177 (2)
709. Kālakācārya-kathā	Or. 13475
710. Kālikācārya-kathā, incomplete	Or. 13950 (A)
711. Kālakācārya-kathā, frag.	BM 1959-4-11-04
712. Kālikācārya-sambandha	Or. 3349 (B)
713. Kālikācārya-sambandha	Or. 5151 (2)
714. Kālikācārya-kathā (Guj.)	I.O. San. 1571 (B)
715. Jambūcarita by Padmasundarasūri with a Guj. comm.	Or. 13615
716. Jambūcarita by P. with a Guj. comm., incompl.	Add. 26,459 (1 and 3)
717. Jambūsvāmī-caupaī by Depāla	Or. 2126 (B)
718. Jambūsvāmī-caupaī by Depāla	I.O. San. 3400 (B,cf)
719. Jambusāmī-sajjhāya	Or. 14064 (B,2)
720. Bhuvanabhānu-kevali-carita by Hemacandra Maladhārin	I.O. San. 3373
721. Bhuvanabhānu-kevali-carita by Hemacandra M. with Tattvahaṁsagaṇi's Guj. comm.	I.O. San. 2354

722. Bhuvanabhānu-kevali-carita with Harikalaśagaṇi's Guj. comm. — Or. 2122 (I)

4.3. Great Jain narrative models

723. Maṇipati-carita by Haribhadra — I.O. San. 3365
724. Maṇipati-carita by Haribhadra with a Guj. gloss — I.O. San. 1354 (B)
725. Samarāditya-saṁkṣepa by Pradyumnasūri — Or. 2130 (A)
726. Yaśodhara-carita by Māṇikyasūri — Or. 13544
727. Yaśodhara-carita by Māṇikyasūri — I.O. San. 3416
728. Mahīpāla-carita by Vīradevagaṇi — I.O. San. 3357
729. Mahīpāla-carita by Vīradevagaṇi — I.O. San. 3362
730. Mahīpāla-carita by Vīradevagaṇi, frag. — I.O. San. 3387
731. Śrīpāla-kathā by Ratnaśekhara — Or. 2126 (A)
732. Śrīpāla-kathā, selection of verses — I.O. San. 3390
733. Sirivālakahā by Ratnaśekhara, incomplete — I.O. San. 3287 (A)
734. Śrīpāla-rāsa by Vinayavijaya and Yaśovijaya — Or. 15633/122
735. Śrīpāla-rāsa by Vinayavijaya and Yaśovijaya — I.O. San. 2728 (A)
736. Śrīpāla-rāsa by Vinayavijaya and Yaśovijaya — MSS. Hin. C 17
737. Śrīpāla-rāsa by V. and Y. with a lacuna, Guj. comm. — Or. 13622
738. Śrīpāla-rāsa by Vinayavijaya and Yaśovijaya, incomplete — Add. 26,363
739. Śrīpāla-rāsa by Vinayavijaya, frag. (1st khaṇḍa) — Or. 16133/5 (E)
740. Śrīpāla-rāsa by vācaka Yaśovijaya, frag. (4th khaṇḍa) — Or. 16133/5 (F)
741. Śrīpāla-rāsa by vācaka Yaśovijaya, frag. (4th khaṇḍa) — Or. 15633/101
742. Śrīpāla-rāsa (Guj.) — MSS. Guj. 12
743. Uttamakumāra-caritra — Or. 2129 (A)
744. Uttama-caritra by Rājakīrti — I.O. San. 3372
745. Dhanya-Śāli-carita or Dānakalpadruma by Jinakīrti — I.O. San. 3412
746. Śālibhadra-carita by Dharmakumāra — Or. 2129 (B)
747. Sālibhadra-caupāī by Matisāra — Or. 13524
748. Sālibhadra-caupāī by Matisāra — I.O. San. 1553 (A)
749. Sālibhadra-caupāī by Matisāra — I.O. San. 2358 (B)
750. Śālibhadra-caupai by Sādhuhaṁsamuni — Harley 415 (25)
751. Sālibhadraji nī sajjhāya by Sahajasundara — Add. 26,452 (M,1)
752. Sālibhadraji nī sajjhāya by Sahajasundara — Or. 14064 (B,5)
753. Dhanya-kathā by Dayāvardhana — Or. 13548 (2)
754. Dhanya-kathā — Or. 2126 (D,2)

4.4. Prabandhas

755. Prabandhacintāmaṇi by Merutunga — Bühler 296
756. Prabandhacintāmaṇi by Merutunga, incomplete — Bühler 297
757. Prabhāvaka-carita by Prabhācandrasūri — Bühler 298
758. Prabhāvaka-carita by Prabhācandrasūri, — Bühler 299

incomplete
759. Prabandhakośa by Rājaśekharasūri Or. 4778
760. Prabandhakośa by Rājaśekharasūri Bühler 294
761. Prabandhakośa by Rājaśekharasūri, incomplete Bühler 295
762. Kumārapāla-caritra by Jinamaṇḍanagaṇi Bühler 286
763. Kumārapāla-caritra-bālāvabodha by Jayasiṁhasūri Bühler 287
764. Vastupāla-caritra by Jinaharṣagaṇi Bühler 300
765. Sukṛtasaṁkīrtana by Arisiṁha Bühler 302
766. Kīrtikaumudī by Someśvara Bühler 64
767 [a]. Jagaḍū-carita by Sarvāṇandasūri Bühler 291
767 [b]. Jagaḍū-carita by Sarvāṇandasūri: a part of Bühler's essay Bühler 325
768. Bhoja-caritra by Rājavallabha I.O. San. 3363
769. Tribhuvana-dīpaka-prabandha (Guj.) by Jayaśekharasūri, incomplete Bühler 292

4.5. Collections of stories
770. Gautamapṛcchā-vivaraṇa by Śrītilaka I.O. San. 3350
771. Gautama-pṛcchā by Śrītilaka, incomplete Or. 11748
772. Antarakathā-saṁgraha by Rājaśekharasūri I.O. San. 3406
773. Samyaktvakaumudī-kathā I.O. San. 3371
774. Samyaktvakaumudī-kathānaka with a Guj./H. comm. I.O. San. 1565
775. Samyaktva-kaumudī with a Guj. comm. Add. 26,367
776. Kathā-kośa I.O. San. 3405
777. Kathā-kośa I.O. San. 3404
778. Kathā-sancaya Or. 5179
779. [Stories from the Ṛṣimaṇḍalastotra] Bühler 303

4.6. On other heroes (mainly in Guj.) (in alphabetical order)
4.6.1. Males
780. Anāthī-sādhu-gīta by Samayasundara, frag. Add. 26,455 (AP)
781. Amarasena-Varasena-caupaī I.O. San. 3399
782. Araṇikamuni-sajjhāya by Rūpavijaya Or. 15633/7
783. Araṇikamuni-sajjhāya Or. 14064 (B,3)
784. Avantisukumāla-ḍhāla by Jinaharṣa Or. 13642 (5)
785. Ārdrakumāra-vivāhalu by Depāla Harley 415 (18)
786. Āṣāḍhabhūti-gīta by a disciple of Śubhavardhana Harley 415 (20)
787. Elāputra-sajjhāya by Labdhivijaya Or. 15633/53
788. Kīrtidhara-Sukośala-sambandha by Māladeva MSS. Guj. 10
789. Gajasiṁharāja-caritra by Namikunjara, incomplete I.O. San. 3400 (B,ca)
790. Gajasiṁha-kumāra-caritra by Namikunjara, incomplete Add. 26,450 (C)
791. Gajasukumāra-sajjhāya by a disciple of Saubhāgyaharṣa Harley 415 (24)

792. Candanarāja-caupaī by Kesara kavi Or. 15289
793. Candanṛpati-rāśa by Mohanavijaya MSS. Guj. 19
794. Rājācanda no rāsa by Mohanavijaya, beginning only Or. 13642 (11)
795. [Campaka-Līlāvatī-kathā] by Paramasāgara, incomplete Add. 26,450 (D)
796. Jayānanda-caritra by Padmavijaya, fragm. Or. 15633/125
797. Thāvaccāputra-gīta by Depāla Harley 415 (23)
798. ŚrīNandiṣeṇamuni-sajjhāya (Guj.) by Jinaharṣa I.O. San. 1564c
799. Nandiṣeṇa-kathā Or. 2126 (D,3)
800. [Naravāhana-Lalitānga and Jinasena-Devasenā stories] I.O. San. 3954 (L)
801. Puṇyasena-caupaī by Muni Dīpa MSS. Raj. 2
802. Purandarakumāra-copāi by Māladeva, incomplete I.O. San. 1561d
803. Prīyamelakatīrtha-prabandha by Samayasundara MSS. Guj. 3
804. [Bharata-Bāhubali-sajjhāya] by Rāmavijaya, incomplete Or. 13642 (8)
805. Mangalakalaśa-rāsa by Mangaladharma I.O. San. 3400 (B,cb)
806. Mangalakalasa-phāga by Kanakasoma I.O. San. 1609B
807. Mangalakalaśa-caupaī by Jīvanasiṁha MSS. Raj. 1
808. Madana-kumāra-kathā, incomplete Or. 14064 (A)
809. Manaka-muni-sajjhāya by Labdhivijaya Or. 14064 (B,18)
810. Mānatungarāja-caritra by Mohanavijaya I.O. San. 2728 (B)
811. Meghakumāra-gīta Harley 415 (21)
812. Ratnacūḍamuni-rāsa by Jinaharṣasūri I.O. San. 1564b
813. Rahanemi-sajjhāya by Rūpavijaya Or. 15633/112
814. Rātribhojana-caupaī by Dharmasamudragaṇi I.O. San. 3400 (B,cc)
815. Rātribhojana-rāsa by Dharmasamudragaṇi I.O. San. 1530 (K)
816. Vidyāvilāsa-kathā I.O. San. 3383
817. Vidyāvilāsa-rāsa by Hīrānandasūri I.O. San. 3400 (B,cd)
818. Vīrāngada-caupaī by Māladeva MSS. Guj. 2 (1)
819. Śivakumāra-gīta Harley 415 (22)
820. Subāhukumāra-sajjhāya Or. 15633/57
821. Suṣadha-caritra by Brahmaśiṣya I.O. San. 1354 (C)
822. Sthulībhadra-bhāsa by Ṛddhivijaya Add. 26,452 (P,2)
823. Haṁsa-Vacharāja-caupaī by Jinodayasūri Or. 13623 (A)
824. Haribalakathā (Skt.) I.O. San. 2543 (B)

4.6.2. Females

825. Anjanasundarī-caupaī by Puṇyasāgara I.O. San. 1564 (C)
826. Ṛṣidattā-rāsa by Jayavantasūri Or. 2122 (A)
827. Ṛṣidattā-mahāsatī-rāsa by Ṛṣimegharāja I.O. San. 1553 (C)
828. Karmarekhā-bhāva nī caritra by Rāmadāsa ṛṣi, incomplete I.O. San. 1609
829. Jayantī-śrāvikā nī guṁhalī by Śubhavīra Or. 15633/77
830. Mṛgānkalekhā-satī-caritra by Vaccha-vācho I.O. San. 3400 (B,ce)

831. Mṛgānkalekhā-satī-caritra by Vaccha-vācho	I.O. San. 1561b
832. Mṛgāvatī-caritra-caupaī by Samayasundara	MSS. Guj. 13
833. Rājimatī-sajjhāya by Somavimala	Or. 15633/4 (2)
834. Rājimatī-sajjhāya by Nārāyaṇa	Or. 14064 (B,21)
835. Nemi-Rājulā-saṁvāda by Amṛtavijaya	Or. 16132/2
836. [Cauka] by Amṛtavijaya, incomplete	Or. 13697 (C)
837. [tuma tajakara Rājula nāra] by Jinadāsa	Or. 15633/187
838. Rukmiṇī-sajjhāya by Rangavijaya	Or. 15633/99
839. Revatījī-sajjhāya by Vallabhamuni	Or. 15633/114
4.7. Pan-Indian heroes and stories	
840. Pāṇḍavacarita by Devaprabhasūri	I.O. San. 3415 (A)
841. [Virāṭa-parva] (Guj.) by Śālisūri, incomplete	Or. 2123 (C,2)
842. Pānca-Pāṇḍava-sajjhāya by Kaviyaṇa	Or. 15633/4 (1)
843. Ḍhālasāgara (Guj.) by Guṇasāgarasūri	Or. 13624
844. Draupadī-copaī by Kanakakīrti vācaka	I.O. San. 1564 (F)
845. Nala-Davadantī-prabandha (Guj.) by Guṇavinaya vācaka	I.O. San. 1564 (I)
846. Nala-Davadantī-kathā by Samayasundara (Guj.)	I.O. San. 1166
847. Sītā-carita	Bühler 301
848. Meghadūta by Merutungasūri	I.O. San. 2525 (D)
849. Pancākhyāna by Viṣṇuśarman with Yaśodhīra's Guj. comm.	I.O. San. 3400 (A,c)
850. Pancākhyāna by Meghavijaya	Bühler 90
851. Śukasaptati by Ratnasundara	Add. 26,519 (1)
852. Śukasaptati-kathā by Ratnasundara (1-3)	Or. 15633/19
853. Vetālapacīsī-rāsa by Devaśīla	Or. 13792
854. Vetālapacīsī by Rājendrasāgara (?)	Bühler 91
855. Vikramāditya-panca-daṇḍa-chattra-prabandha	Add. 26,542 (B)
856. Siṁhāsana-batrīsī by Muni Hīrakalaśa	I.O. San. 1632
857. Siṁhāsana-battīsī by Muni Hīrakalaśa	I.O. San. 1571 (C)
858. Mādhavānala-prabandha by Kuśalalābha Upādhyāya	I.O. San. 1564 K/XX
859. Mādhavānala-prabandha by Kuśalalābha Upādhyāya	Or. 14687 (2)
860. Ḍholā-Māru-copaī by Kuśalalābha Upādhyāya, with a lacuna	Or. 14687 (1)

5. Śvetāmbara Stotra literature

5.1. Basic hymns (Navasmaraṇas, etc.)

861. Vītarāga-stotra by Hemacandra with Prabhānandamuni's comm.	Or. 2131 (I)
862. Saptasmaraṇa	Or. 16132/9
863. Ajita-Śānti-stavana by Nandiṣeṇa with a Skt. comm.	Or. 2132 (A)
864. Ajita-Śānti-stava by Nandiṣeṇa with Sādhukīrti's Guj. comm.	Or. 5192 (A,3)
865. AjitaŚānti-stavana by Nandiṣeṇa with a Guj. comm.	Or. 15633/185 (6)

866. Laghuśānti-stava by Mānadeva with Harṣakīrti's comm. Or. 13543
867. Laghuśānti-stava by Mānadeva with Harṣakīrti's comm. Or. 5192 (A,2)
868. Laghuśānti-stavana with a Guj. comm. Or. 15633/185 (8)
869. Bṛhacchānti-stavana by Mānadeva with Harṣakīrti's comm. Or. 2128 (B)
870. Bṛhacchānti-stavana by Mānadeva with Harṣakīrti's comm. Or. 5192 (A,15)
871. Bṛhacchānti-stotra by Mānadeva with a Guj. comm. Or. 15633/185 (9)
872. Śāntikara-stotra by Munisundarasūri Or. 13697 (B,1)
873. Śāntinātha-stavana by Munisundarasūri Or. 16133/3 (D)
874. Śānti-stavana by Munisundarasūri with a Guj. comm. Or. 15633/185 (3)
875. Ullāsika-stava by Jinavallabhasūri with a Guj. comm. Or. 5192 (A,4)
876. Bhaktāmara-stotra by Mānatunga Or. 13478
877. Bhaktāmara-stotra by Mānatunga I.O. San. 3396
878. Bhaktāmara-stotra by Mānatunga with Śāntisūri's comm. Or. 5183
879. Bhaktāmara-stotra by Mānatunga with Guṇākara's comm. Or. 5184
880. Bhaktāmara-stotra by Mānatunga with Harṣakīrti's comm. Or. 5192 (A,1)
881. Bhaktāmara-stotra by Mānatunga with a comm. Or. 2131 (C)
882. Bhaktāmara-stotra by Mānatunga with a comm. I.O. San. 3364
883. Bhaktāmara-stotra by Mānatunga with a Guj. comm. Add. 26,453 (B)
884. Bhaktāmara-stotra by Mānatunga with a Guj. comm. Or. 13741
885. Bhaktāmara-stotra by Mānatunga with a Guj. comm. Or. 15633/185 (7)
886. Bhaktāmara-stotra by Mānatunga, frag. I.O. San. 3614 (D)
887. Kalyāṇamandira-stotra by Siddhasena divākara with Kanakakuśala's comm. Or. 5169)
888. Kalyāṇamandira-stotra by S. D. with Māṇikyacandra's comm. Or. 2131 (D)
889. Kalyāṇamandira-stotra by S. D. with a Guj. comm. Or. 15633/185 (10)
890. Kalyāṇamandira-bhāṣā Or. 15633/41
891. Bhayahara-stotra Or. 13697 (B,2)
892. Bhayahara-stotra by Mānatunga with a Skt. comm. Or. 2132 (B)
893. Bhayahara-stotra with a Guj. comm. Or. 15633/185 (5)
894. Bhayahara-stavana by Mānatunga with a Guj. comm. Or. 5192 (A,5)
895. Taṁ-jayau-stotra by Jinadattasūri with a Guj. comm. Or. 5192 (A,6)

896. Guru-pāratantrya-stotra (maya-rahiyaṁ) by Jinadattasūri with a Guj. comm. — Or. 5192 (A,7)

897. Siggham-avaharau-stotra by Jinadattasūri with a Guj. comm. — Or. 5192 (A,8)

898. Upasargahara-stotra by Bhadrabāhu with a Skt. comm. — Or. 2132 (C)

899. Pārśvajina-stotra by Bhadrabāhu with a Guj. comm. — Or. 5192 (A,9)

900. Upasargahara-stotra with a Guj. comm. — Or. 15633/185 (2)

901. Jina-stuti with a Skt. comm. — Or. 5192 (A,12)

902. Tijaya-pahutta-stotra by Mānadeva with Harṣakīrti's comm. — Or. 5192 (A,13)

903. Saptatiśata-stavana with a Guj. *Ṭabo* — Or. 15633/185 (4)

904. Pārśvanātha-stuti by Abhayadeva with Skt. comm. — Or. 5192 (A,14)

905. Sādhāraṇajina-stotra by Ratnākara with Kanakakuśala's comm. — Or. 5192 (A,11)

906. Ratnākara-paṁcaviṁśatikā by Ratnākara with a Guj. comm. — Or. 15633/197

907. Śobhana-stutayaḥ by Śobhana Muni — I.O. San. 3382

908. Śobhana-stutayaḥ by Śobhana Muni with a Skt. comm. — Or. 5190

909. Śobhana-stutayaḥ by Śobhana Muni with a Skt. comm. — Or. 2131 (G)

910. Śobhana-stutayaḥ by Śobhana Muni with a Skt. comm. — Or. 2131 (F)

911. Ṛṣimaṇḍala-stotra by Dharmaghoṣasūri — Or. 2132 (E)

912. Ṛṣimaṇḍala-stotra by Dharmaghoṣasūri — Or. 5166

913. Ṛṣimaṇḍala-stotra by Dharmaghoṣasūri — I.O. San. 3400 (M,f)

914. Ṛṣimaṇḍala-stotra by Dharmaghoṣasūri with Padmamandiragaṇi's *Kathārṇava* — Or. 5167

915. Ṛṣimaṇḍala-stotra by Dharmaghoṣasūri with a Skt. comm. — Or. 2132 (D)

916. Jinaśataka by Jambūguru with Samba Kavi's *Panjikā* — Or. 2134 (B)

917. Jinaśataka by Jambūguru with a Skt. comm. — Or. 2134 (A)

918. Jinaśataka by Jambūguru with a Skt. comm. — Or. 2134 (C)

919. Stotrāvalī by Nemiratnagaṇi — Or. 2131 (H)

920. Praśnagarbha-pancaparameṣṭhi-stava with a Skt. comm. — I.O. San. 2527 (E,1)

921. Navagraha-stavana by Jinaprabhasūri with Skt./Guj. comm. — Or. 5192 (A,10)

5.2. The 24 Jinas as a whole

922. Caturviṁśatijina-stava by Jinaprabhasūri with Kanakakuśala's comm. — Or. 5171

923. Jina-stuti (Guj.), incomplete — I.O. San. 3400 (A',gd)

924. Caturviṁśatijina-gīta (Guj.) by Jinarāja — I.O. San. 1530 (H)

925. Caturviṁśatijina-stava (Guj.) by Yaśovijaya — Or. 13623 (B,1)

926. [āja mhārā prabhujī re] (Guj.) by — Or. 15633/102 (1)

Jñānavimala
927. Cauvīsa-tīrthaṁkara-vīnatī (Guj.) Harley 415 (6)
928. Jina-stavana (Guj.) by Rāmavijaya Add. 26,519 (2)
929. Caityavandana-stuti (Guj.) Or. 15633/67 (1)-(2)
930. Tīrthaṁkara-dehamāna-varṇa-stavana (Guj.) by Jñānavimala Or. 15633/50 (2)
931. Tīrthaṁkara-ananta-guṇāḥ (Guj.) Or. 15633/23 (2)
932. Covīsa-jina-parivāra-stavana (Guj.) by Jñānavimala Or. 15633/92
933. Covīsa-jina-parivāra-stavana (Guj.) by Jñānavimala Or. 15633/93
934. Jinaparivāra-stavana (Guj.) by Jñānavimala Or. 16133/3 (F)
935. Tresaṭhisalākā-stavana (Guj.)by Durgadāsa (?) I.O. San. 3614 (K)
936. Tresaṭhisalākā-stavana (Guj.), incomplete I.O. San. 3614 (L)
937. [Unidentified] Or. 16133/2 (14)

5.3. Hymns to each of the 24 Jinas

5.3.1. Ṛṣabhanātha

938. Ṛṣabha-sajjhāya by Mayācandra Or. 14064 (B,8)
939. Ṛṣabha-sajjhāya Or. 14064 (B,13)
940. Ādinātha-abhiṣeka (Ap.) by muni Ratnākara Add. 26,461 (12)
941. Ādinātha-abhiṣeka (Ap.), incomplete Add. 26,461 (1)
942. Ṛṣabha-vivāhalo by Sevaka Add. 26,464 (D)
943. Ṛṣabhadeva-dhavalabandha-vivāhalu by Sevaka Harley 415 (14)
944. Ṛṣabhadeva-dhavalabandha-vivāhalu by Sevaka I.O. San. 1596 (B)
945. Ṛṣabhadeva-dhavalabandha-vivāhalu by Sevaka, incompl. I.O. San. 1530 (A)
946. Ṛṣabhanātha-vivāha by Sevaka, fragment Add. 26,461 (13)
947. Ādinātha-gīta (?) (Guj) Harley 415 (17)
948. 28labdhimaya-Ṛṣabhajina-stavana (Guj.) by Dharmavardhana Or. 15633/98
949. Ṛṣabhajina-stavana (Guj.) Or. 15633/90
950. Ādīśvara-stavana (Guj.) by Lāvaṇyasamaya Add. 26,461 (3)
951. Ṛṣabhajina-stuti (Guj.) by Kṣamāvijaya Or. 15633/70 (2)
952. Ṛṣabhadeva-namaskāra (Guj.) I.O. San. 3400 (L,ed)
953. Ādijina-stavana (Guj.) by Sahajasundara Or. 16133/2 (5)
954. [sudharmā deva loka ...] by Ṛṣabhadāsa Or. 15633/5 (10)
955. Jina-stavana (Guj.) by Guṇasāgara Or. 15633/5 (7)
956. [hamāṁcaḍī] (Guj.) by Vardhamāna paṇḍita Add. 26,461 (9)
957. [merā nehā lagyā] by Ratnavijaya? Or. 15633/192 (2)
958. [prabhāte pankhiḍāṁ bole] by Lakṣmīvijaya Or. 15633/87 (1)
959. Stavana (Raj.) Or. 16133/2 (17)
960. Ṛṣabhānandana-stavana (Guj.) Or. 16133/9 (I)

5.3.2. Śāntinātha

961. Śānti-stavana (Pkt.) by Vimalakevala Or. 2138 (A,2)

962. ŚrīŚāntinātha-stavana (Pkt.) by Āc. Manahara — I.O. San. 3362 (Suppl.)
963. Śāntinātha-stavana (Guj.) by Lakṣmaṇa — Harley 415 (3)
964. Śāntinātha-vīnatī (Guj.) by Sādhuhaṁsa — Harley 415 (5)
965. Śāntijina-stuti (Guj.) by Rūpavijaya — Or. 15633/ 58 (2)
966. Śāntinātha-stavana (Guj.) by Jinacanda — Or. 14064 (B,17)
967. Śāntinātha-vīnatī (Guj.) — Harley 415 (9)
968. Śāntijina-chanda by Guṇasāgara — Or. 15633/75
969. Śāntinātha-stavana (H.) by Rūpacanda — Or. 15633/79 (1)
970. [Śānti jiṇinda avadhārīe] (Guj.) by Ratnavijaya — Or. 15633/192 (1)
971. Śāntinātha-snātra (Guj.) by Jñānavimala — Or. 15633/132
971 [a]. [Śānti sadā sukhadāyī] (Guj.) by Vijayasaubhāgya — Or. 2106 (C, Suppl.)

5.3.3. Neminātha

972. [Neminātha-stavana in six languages with Skt. comm.] — Or. 5171 (Suppl.)
973. [Neminātha-bhramaragītā] (Guj.) by Vinayavijaya — Add. 26,542 (D)
974. Nemajī-sajjhāya (Guj.) by Hira muni — Or. 14064 (B,12)
975. Nemi-Rājimatī-sajjhāya (Guj.) — Or. 14064 (B,23)
976. Nema-Rājimatī-sajjhāya (Guj.) by Padmacandramuni — Or. 16133/2 (10)
977. Neminātha-bāramāsa (Guj.) by Tilakaśekhara — Or. 14064 (B,11)
978. Neminātha-stavana (Guj.) by Hīravijaya — Or. 15633/79 (2)
979. [Neminātha-stavana] (Guj.) — Or. 14064 (B,19)
980. [Nemijinavara-stavana] (Guj.) — Or. 14064 (B,20)
981. Nemīśvara-bhāsa (Guj.) by Ṛddhivijaya — Add. 26,452 (P,1)
982. Neminātha-nava-rasa (Guj.) by Rūpacanda — Or. 15633/29
983. Neminātha-navabhava-rāsa by Māla (Guj.) — MSS. Guj. 8
984. Neminātha-stavana (Guj.) — I.O. San. 3362 (Suppl.)
985. ŚrīNeminātha Reṣatā-chanda (Guj.) by Gurudāsa — MSS. Guj. 14 (1)
986. [Unidentified] (Guj.) — Or. 16133/3 (A)

5.3.4. Pārśvanātha

987. [Pārśvajina-saṁgīta] (Skt.) by Jinakuśalasūri — I.O. San. 3391 (Suppl.)
988. Pārśvanātha-covīsa-daṇḍaka (Guj.) by Dharmasiṁha — Or. 15633/5 (1)
989. Pārśva-jina-stava (Guj.) by Nityalābha — Or. 13642 (7) = (9)
990. Pārśva-dhāmāla by Yaśovijaya — Or. 16132/1
991. [Pārśva-jina-stavana] (Guj.) by Śubhavīra — Or. 15633/193
992. [Pārśva-stavana] (Guj.) by Gurudāsa, fragm. — Or. 16133/4 (1)
993. [Pārśvajina-stavana] (Guj.), incomplete — Or. 14064 (B,24)
994. Pārśvanātha-vinati (Guj.) — Harley 415 (2)
995. Pārśvanātha no vivāhalo (Guj.) by Rangavijaya — Or. 15633/25
996. Pārśva-jina-stavana (Guj.) — Or. 16133/9 (B)

5.3.5. Mahāvīra

997. Mahāvīra-stavana (Skt.) by Jinavallabhasūri with Kṣemasundaragaṇi's comm. — Or. 2131 (E)
998. Vardhamāna-stotra (Skt.) by Jayacandrasūri with a comm. — I.O. San. 2527 (E,2)
999. Vīra-stavana (Guj.) — Or. 15633/128 (2)
1000. Vīrajina-stavana (Guj.) — Or. 15633/97 (2)
1001. Mahāvīra-kalaśa (Skt., Pkt., Ap.) by Jayamangala — Add. 26,461 (2)
1002. Mahāvīra-kalaśa (Guj.) by Jayamangala — Add. 26,461 (14)
1003. Mahāvīra-phāga (Guj.) by Vimalavijaya — Or. 15633/89 (2)
1004. Mahāvīra-nirvāṇa-stavana (Guj.) — Or. 15633/121
1005. Vardhamāna-sattāvīsa-bhava-stavana (Guj.) by Lālavijaya — Or. 15633/124
1006. Mahāvīra-sajjhāya (Guj.) — Or. 14064 (B,10)
1007. Pancakāraṇa-bola-Mahāvīra-stavana (Guj.) — Or. 15633/26 (2)
1008. [Mahāvīra-stavana] (Guj.), incomplete — I.O. San. 3614 (P)
1009. Mahāvīra-stavana (Guj.), incomplete — Or. 16133/2 (18)
1010. [Mahāvīrasvāmī nī janmakuṇḍalī nuṁ stavana] by Śubhavīra — Or. 15633/65
1011. [amalakalpa udyāna māṁ devācī nārī] (Guj.) by Rāmavijaya — Or. 15633/189
1012. [amalakalpa udyāna māṁ devācī nārī] (Guj.) by Rāmavijaya — Or. 15633/52 (1)

5.3.6. Other Jinas among the twenty-four

1013. Ajitanātha-stavana (Guj.) by Cāritravijaya — Or. 15633/10 (2)
1014. Sambhavajina-stavana (Guj.) by Rāmavijaya — Or. 14064 (B,22)
1015. [huṁ to mohyo re Jina] (Guj.) by Nityalābha — Or. 15633/102 (3)
1016. Abhinandanajina-stavana (Guj.) by Mayācanda — Or. 14064 (B,9)
1017. Jinavāṇi-stavana (Guj.) by Uttamavijaya? — Or. 15633/80
1018. Śītalanātha-deva-vinatī (Guj.) by Rājahaṁsa — I.O. San. 3400 (A,a,3)
1019. Kunthujina-stavana (Guj.) by Ānandaghana — Or. 13642 (3) = (6)
1020. Aranātha-stavana (Guj.) by Padmavijaya — Or. 15633/104
1021. Munisuvrata-stavana (Guj.) by Haṁsa(vijaya) — Or. 15633/74

5.4. Hymns to all other Jinas

1022. Satyakī-sambandha by Muni Māla (Guj.) — MSS. Guj. 11
1023. Anāgata-covīsī-vandana (Guj.) by Jñānavimala — Or. 16133/9 (A)
1024. Anāgata-covīsī-vandana (Guj.) by Jñānavimala, incomplete — Or. 15633/190
1025. Caitya-vandana (Guj.) by Kalyāṇavimala — Or. 15633/69
1026. Sīmandharajina-stavana (Guj.) by Siddhavijaya — Or. 16132/6
1027. Sīmandharajina-stavana (Guj.) by Siddhavijaya, beginning — Or. 16133/7 (A)
1028. Sīmandhara-stuti (Pkt.) by Sakalacandra — Or. 15633/144 (1)

1029. Sīmandharajina-stavana (Guj.) by Sakalacandra — Or. 15633/73
1030. Simandhara-jina-stuti (Pkt.) — Or. 15633/105 (1)
1031. Sīmandharasvāmi-stavana (Guj.) by Jñānavimala — Or. 15633/47
1032. Sīmandhara-svāmi-stavana (Guj.) by Haṁsa(vijaya) — Or. 15633/8 (2)
1033. Sīmandharasvāmi-stavana (Guj.) by Śāntisūri — Harley 415 (8)
1034. Śrīmandara-stavana (Guj.) by Jinarāja — Or. 14064 (B,4)
1035. Sujātajina-vasanta (Guj.) by Nyāyasāgara — Or. 15633/89 (1)
1036. Anthology of stavanas by Padmavijaya — Or. 15633/17

5.5. Hymns to goddesses

1037. Sarasvatī-stotra (Skt.) — Or. 15633/64
1038. Kamalā-gīta (Guj.) — Harley 415 (19)

5.6. Hymn to the Scriptures

1039. Pīstālīsa-āgama-stavana (Guj.) by Uttamavijaya — Or. 15633/85

5.7. Hymns to religious teachers

1040. Tīrthapati-bhāsa (Guj.) — Or. 15633/86
1041. Gaṇadharasaṁvāda-stavana (Guj.) by Sakalacandra — Or. 15633/16
1042. Guruvandana-guṁhalī by Giradhara — Or. 15633/91
1043. Guru-bhāsa-phūlaḍāṁ — Or. 15633/97 (1)
1044. [Guru-stavana] (Guj.) — Add. 26,455 (AI,2)
1045. [Unidentified] (Guj.) — Or. 16133/5 (G,2)
1046. [Kuguru°?] (Guj./H.) by Jinadāsa — Or. 13623 (B,3)
1047. Śrīmallarṣi-stavana (Guj.) by Ānandasevaka — Add. 26,450 (C,2)
1048. Hemavimalasūri-stuti (Ap) by his pupil Vimala — Or. 3347 (C,9)
1049. [Rājasāgara-guru-guṁhalī] (Guj.) by Dolatasāgara — Or. 15633/82

5.8. Tīrthas

5.8.1. Śatrunjaya

1050. Śatrunjaya-māhātmya by Dhaneśvarasūri — Or. 5189
1051. Śatrunjaya-māhātmya by Dhaneśvarasūri, incomplete — Or. 2125
1052. Śatrunjaya-māhātmyollekha by Haṁsaratna — Add. 26,375
1053. Śatrunjaya-māhātmyollekha by Haṁsaratna — I.O. San. 3266
1054. Śatrunjaya-sāroddhāra (Guj.) by Nayasundara, incomplete — I.O. San. 1363 (C)
1055. Setruṁja Udhāra by Premavijaya — Or. 2137 (C)
1056. [Śatrunjaya-uddhāra-rāsa] (Guj.), incompl. — Or. 16133/9 (K)
1057. Puṇḍarīkagiri-stotra — Or. 15633/70 (1)
1058. Siddhācala-stavana (Guj.) by Jñānavimala — Or. 15633/87 (2)

1059. Siddhagiri-stavana (Guj.) by Jñānavimala Or. 15633/70 (3)
1060. Siddhagiri-jātrā-phala-stavana (Guj.) by Jñānavimala Or. 16133/9 (L,1)
1061. Śatrunjayagiri-stavana by a pupil of Jñānavimala Or. 15633/106
1062. Siddhagiri-stavana (Guj.) by Udayaratna Or. 16133/9 (F)
1063. Siddhācala-jina-stavana (Guj.) by Kṣamāvijaya Or. 15633/42
1064. Siddhācala-stavana (Guj.) by Siddhivijaya Or. 15633/61
1065. Siddhācala-stavana (Guj.) by Padmavijaya Or. 15633/62
1066. Siddhācala-stavana (Guj.) by Padmavijaya Or. 16133/9 (C)
1067. Siddhagiri nī horī by Rūpacanda Or. 15633/81 (1)
1068. Siddhagiri no vasanta by Dharmacandra Or. 15633/81 (2)
1069. Vimalācalatīrtha-mālā (Guj.) by Amṛtavijaya, fragmentary Or. 16133/8
1070. [Unidentified] (Guj.) Or. 16133/6 (D)

5.8.2. Girnar
1071. Giranāra-tīrthoddhāra-mahimā-prabandha (Guj.) by Nayasundara Add. 26,461 (6)

5.8.3. Mythical places: Aṣṭapada, Siddhaśilā
1072. Aṣṭāpada-stavana (Guj.) by Samaro Harley 415 (12)
1073. Aṣṭāpada-ṛddhivarṇṇana-stavana (Guj.) by Samaro Harley 415 (13)
1074. Siddhaśilā-sajjhāya by Nayavijaya Or. 15633/76
1075. Siddhaśilā-sajjhāya by Nayavijaya Or. 15633/117
1076. Tīrthamālā-stavana (Guj.) frag. Harley 415 (1)

5.9. Hymns to local images of Tīrthaṁkaras
1077. Śatrunjaya-Ādinātha-namaskāra (Guj.) by Haṁsavijaya Or. 15633/115
1078. [Śatrunjaya-Ādinātha-namaskāra] (Guj.) by Haṁsavijaya Or. 15633/96
1079. ŚrīSetrunjaya-maṇḍana Śrīyugādideva-stavana (Guj.) by Nayavimala I.O. San. 1564c (3)
1080. Ādinātha-Śatruṁjaya-maṇḍana-stavana (Guj.) by Lakṣmaṇa Harley 415 (4)
1081. Śatruṁjaya-maṇḍana-śrīĀdinātha-vinatī (Guj.) Harley 415 (11)
1082. Śaṁkheśvara-Pārśvanātha-stotra Or. 15633/40 (2)
1083. Śaṁkheśvara-Pārśvanātha-stavana by Haṁsabhavana Add. 26,461 (8)
1084. Śaṁkhêśvara-Pārśvanātha-chanda by Udayaratna Or. 15633/59
1085. Pratiṣṭhā-kalpa-stavana by Rangavijaya Or. 2132 (G)
1086. Godī-Pārśvanātha-stavana (Guj.) by Lāvaṇyacandra Or. 13642 (2)
1087. Vaṭapadra-maṇḍana-śrīCintāmaṇi-Pārśvanātha-vīnatī (Guj.) Harley 415 (10)

1088. Vadodarā Pārśva-jina-stuti (Guj.) — I.O. San. 3400 (L,db)
1089. Jīrāulā-Pārśvanātha-stavana (Guj.) by Lāvaṇyasamaya — Add. 26,461 (10)
1090. Jīrāulā-Pārśvanātha-vīnatī — Harley 415 (7)
1091. ŚrīPālavīya-Pārśvanātha-stavana (Guj.) — Or. 16133/3 (B)
1092. Nagadraha-svāmī-vinatī by a pupil of Jinaratnasūri — I.O. San. 3400 (A,a,2)
1093. [Keśariyājī-lāvaṇī] (Guj.) by Dīpavijaya — Or. 15633/9
1094. Śreyāṁsa-jina-caitya-sambandha (Guj.) by Bheravacanda — Or. 15633/134
1095. Bhoyaṇī Mallinātha nāṁ ḍhāliyāṁ (Guj.) by Dayāvimala, beg. — Or. 16133/9 (H)
1096. Bhoyaṇī Mallinātha nāṁ ḍhāliyāṁ (Guj.) by Dayāvimala, end — Or. 16133/5 (C)

6. Vrata literature and ritualistic works
6.1. Vrata literature

1097. Comāsī-pāraṇuṁ by Śubhavīra — Or. 15633/119
1098. Ratnaśekharanṛpa-Ratnavatī-kathā / Parva-tithi-vicāra by Dayāvardhana — Or. 13548 (1)
1099. Ratnaśekharanṛpa-Ratnavatī-kathā by D. — Or. 2126 (D,1)
1100. Paryuṣaṇā-parva-stuti by Nayavimala — Or. 15633/49
1101. Paryuṣaṇa-hita-śikṣā-sajjhāya by Jagavallabha — Or. 15633/71
1102. Dīpālikā-kalpa by Jinaprabhasūri — I.O. San. 3402
1103. Dīpālikā-kalpa by Jinaprabhasūri — Bühler 284
1104. Dīpālī-kalpa by Jinasundara — Or. 13788
1105. Dīpālikā-kalpa by Jinasundara with Sukhasāgara's *Ṭabo* — Or. 2133 (A)
1106. Dīpālikā-kalpa by Jinasundara with a Guj. comm. — Bühler 305
1107. Dīpāvalī-kalpa by Jinasundara-sūri with a Guj. comm., incomplete — Add. 26,366
1108. Dīpālī-kalpa by Jinasundara with a Guj. comm. — Or. 2133 (B)
1109. Dīvālī nuṁ stavana by Jñānavimala — Or. 15633/13 (2)
1110. Dīpālikā-kalpa (Guj.) by Guṇaharṣa — Or. 15633/128 (1)
1111. Saubhāgyapancamī-kathā (Jñānapancamī-kathā) by Kanakakuśala — Or. 15633/11
1112. Saubhāgyapancamī-deva-vandana-vidhi (Guj.) by Vijayalakṣmī-sūri — Or. 15633/3
1113. Jñānapancamī-stavana by Jñānavimala — Or. 15633/26 (1)
1114. Pancamī-tapa-mahimā-sajjhāya by Devavijaya — Or. 15633/68 (2)
1115. Jñānapancamī-sajjhāya (Guj.) — Or. 16133/9 (G)
1116. [Unidentified] (Guj.) by Śubhavīra — Or. 16133/9 (L,2)
1117. Igyārasa no tava by Kāntivijaya — Or. 15633/126
1118. [Mauna-ekādaśī-stavana] by Jñānavimala, incomplete — Or. 15633/138
1119. [Mauna-ekādaśī-stavana] by Jñānavimala, — Or. 15633/196

incomplete
1119 [a]. Maunaikādaśī-stuti (Skt.) I.O. San. 2341 (C)
1120. Poṣadaśamī-kathā Or. 2130 (B)
1121. Meru-trayodaśī-kathā Or. 2126 (C)
1122. Rohiṇī-kathā (Guj., Skt.) Or. 2130 (C)
1123. Rohiṇi-tapa-sajjhāya by Vivekavijaya (?) Or. 15633/63
1124. Rohiṇī-tapa-sajjhāya (Guj.) Or. 16133/6 (B)
1125. Rohiṇī-stavana (Guj.) Or. 15633/15
1126. Vāsupūjya-stavana (Guj.), frag. Or. 16133/7 (B)
1127. Aṣṭamī-caityavandana by Kṣamāvijaya Or. 15633/50 (1)
1128. Aṣṭamī-tapa-sajjhāya by Devavijaya Or. 15633/68 (1)
1129. Aṣṭamī-sajjhāya Or. 15633/139 (2)
1130. [Aṣṭamī-tapa-sajjhāya] (Guj.) by Labdhivijaya Or. 16133/9 (N)
1131. Caitrī nī thoya by Labdhivijaya Or. 15633/5 (4)
1132. [Ṛṣabhadeva-vinatī] by Udayaratna Or. 15633/52 (2)
1133. Śrāvanaśuklapancamī nī thoya by Ṛṣabhadāsa Or. 15633/5 (5)
1134. Akṣayanidhitapa-stavana (Guj.) by Padmavijaya Or. 15633/83
1135. Bīja nī sajhāya (Guj.) by Labdhivijaya Or. 16133/9 (Q)
1136. [Bīja nī sajhāya] (Guj.) by Labdhivijaya Or. 16133/6 (C)
1137. Tapaś-caraṇāni I.O. San. 3954 (A)

6.2. Ritualistic works
6.2.1. Siddhacakra, Viṁśatisthānaka
1138. Siddhacakra-stavana (Pkt.) Or. 15633/23 (1)
1139. Siddhacakra-namaskāra (Guj.) by Jñānavimala Or. 15633/28
1140. Siddhacakra-stavana (Guj.) Or. 15633/72
1141. Siddhacakra-pūjā-stavana (Guj.) by Padmavijaya Or. 15633/97 (3)
1142. Navapada-mahimā (Guj.) by Vimalavijaya Or. 15633/113 (2)
1143. Olī nī thoa (Guj.) by Udayaratna Or. 15633/5 (11)
1144. Viṁśatisthānaka-vicārāmṛta-saṁgraha by Jinaharṣa I.O. San. 1358
1145. Viṁśatisthānaka-vicāra (Guj.) by Kṣamāvijaya Or. 15633/66
1146. Viṁśatisthānaka-pūjā-vidhi (Pkt. & Guj.) Or. 15633/160
1147. Viṁśatisthānaka-vidhi Or. 15633/21
1148. [Viṁśatisthānaka] (Guj.) I.O. San. 3400 (R,gc)
1149. Viṁśati-tīrthapada-pūjā (Guj.) by Vijayasaubhāgya Or. 15633/88 (2)

6.2.2. Pūjā
1150. Jina-snātra-vidhi (Skt.) by vādivetāla Śāntisūri Or. 2121 (A)
1151. [Kusumānjali] (Skt., Ap., Guj.) by Bhāna Add. 26,461 (11)
1152. [Snātra-vidhi] (Pkt.) Add. 26,461 (15-17)

1153. Pūjā nī vidhi — Or. 15633/48
1154. Cāmara-pūjā (Guj.) by Kuśalakṣema — Or. 15633/88 (1)
1155. Sattara-bheda-pūjā (Guj.) by Sakalacandra — Or. 15633/27
1156. Bimba-pratiṣṭhā-vidhi — I.O. San. 3400 (L,eb)
1157. Vara-ghoḍā nī ḍhāla by Śubhavīra — Or. 15633/103

6.2.3. Kalpas, mantras, etc.
1158. Bhairava-Padmāvatī-kalpa by Malliṣeṇasūri (Tessitori) — I.O. San. 1952
1159. Ghaṇṭākarṇa — Or. 13623 (B,2)
1160. [Mantra] — I.O. San. 3400 (V, i)
1161. Tantrākhyāla — Or. 13642 (4)
1162. [Catuḥṣaṣṭhī-yoginī] — I.O. San. 3400 (V,h)
1163. Prastāvikā-bāvanī (Guj.), frag. — Or. 16133/10

7. Paṭṭāvalīs
1164. [Paṭṭāvali-saṁgraha] — Or. 7621 (E)
1165 [a]. Gurvāvalīsūtra by Dharmasāgara with auto-comm. — Bühler 290
1165 [b]. [Index of names of persons and places in Bühler 290] — Bühler 290 (A)
1166. [Commentary on Dharmasāgara's Gurvāvalī], incomplete — Bühler 285
1167. Gurvāvalīsūtra with a Guj. comm. — Bühler 288
1168. Paṭṭāvali by Jayavijayagaṇi with Gautama's comm. — Bühler 289
1169. [Tapāgaccha and Lonkāgaccha-paṭṭāvalīs] — Bühler 281 (B)
1170. [Lonkāgaccha-paṭṭāvalī] (Guj.) — Add. 26,452 (N)

8. Varia
8.1. Lists and tables
1171. Tabular presentation of the 24 Jinas — I.O. San. 3384 (B)
1172. [Tabular presentation of the 24 Jinas] — I.O. San. 1530 (C)
1173. [A list of the names of the 24 Jinas] — I.O. San. 1530 (F)
1174. [Three lists of 24 Jinas: past, present, future] — Or. 16133/6 (A)
1175. [Names of the 24 past Jinas], [Names of the 24 future Jinas] — Or. 13623 (B,5-6)
1176. Jina-nāma-yantra — Or. 15633/95
1177. [Nirvāṇas of Tīrthaṁkaras] — I.O. San. 2646 (C)
1178. Caturviṁśati-jina-antarāla — Or. 15633/107
1179. [Information on Jain mythology] — I.O. San. 1530 (D)
1180. Aṣṭa-mahāprātihārya-nāmāni — Or. 15633/50 (3)
1181. Sarva-sūtrādhyayanoddeśa-nirṇaya — Bühler 284 (A)
1182. [Names of the 45 Āgamas and the 14 Pūrvas] — Or. 15633/94
1183. [Āgama-nāmādi] — Or. 15633/110
1184. [Āgama-sūcī] & [Saṁyama-samyaktva-viryādi-bhedāḥ] — Or. 15633/111 (1)
1185. Ogaṇapacāsa bhāṅgā — Or. 15633/109

1186. [Lists of days, months, asterisms, etc.] Or. 15633/100
1187. [A list of Jain mss. of the Colebrooke collection] I.O. San. 1530 (E)

8.2. Objects

1188. Illustrated folio BM 1926-3-16-01
1189. The 14 auspicious dreams Or. 14064 (D)
1190. The 14 auspicious dreams IS 50-1983 (V&A)
1190 [a]. Jain ms. cover (14 dreams) IS 20-1978 (V&A)
1191. Cardboard ms. holder Or. 1385
1192. Cardboard ms. holder Or. 13950
1193. Folding ms. holder Or. 13457 (B)
1194. A mandala representing the 24 Jinas Or. 13472
1195. Jñāna-copaḍa [Game of snakes and ladders] 324-1972 (V&A)
1196. Victory banner IM 89-1936 (V&A)

II. Digambara literature

1. Kundakunda's works

1197. Samayasāra with *Ātmakhyāti* and Kalaśas by Amṛtacandra I.O. San. 3635
1198. Samayasāra with Amaracandra's *Ātmakhyāti*, incomplete I.O. San. 2201
1199. Pancāstikāya with Amṛtacandra's *Tattvadīpikā*, incomplete I.O. San. 1525 (B)
1200. Pancāstikāya with Hemarāja's Hindi comm. I.O. San. 2909 (1)
1201. Pancāstikāya with Dīlārām's Persian commentary Add. 25,022 (2)
1202. Aṣṭaprābhṛta with a comm. in Jaipurī by Jayacanda Burnell 245
1203. Dvādaśānuprekṣā Burnell 433 (3)

2. Dogmatics, ethics, philosophy

1204. Tattvārthādhigama-sūtra Or. 13221 (3)
1205. Tattvārtha-sūtra I.O. San. 3532 (2)
1206. [Tattvārtha-sūtra with Bhāskaranandin's *Sukhabodhā*], incompl. Mackenzie VIII.93
1207. Dravyasaṁgraha by Nemicandra with Brahmadeva's comm. Or. 5175
1208. Dravyasaṁgraha by Nemicandra with Haṁsarāja's *Ṭabo* Or. 13620
1209. Dravyasaṁgraha by Nemicandra with a Rajasthani comm. I.O. San. 3393
1210. Dravyasaṁgraha by N. with a Rajasthani gloss, frag. I.O. San. 3614 (F)
1211. Karmaprakṛti by Nemicandra with Sumatikīrti's comm. Or. 13621
1212. Karmakāṇḍa by Nemicandra with Hemarāja's Hindi comm. I.O. San. 2909 (2)
1213. Karmaprakṛti by N., incompl., with Add. 25,022 (1)

Dilārām's Persian comm.

1214. Tribhangisāra by Nemicandra	Burnell 430 (3)
1215. Siddhāntasāra [by Jinacandra]	Burnell 430 (1)
1216. Siddhāntasāra with Prabhācandra's Kanarese comm.	Burnell 430 (2)
1217. Trilokasāra by Nemicandra	Burnell 417
1218. Trilokasāra by Nemicandra with Mādhavacandra Traividya's comm.	Burnell 381
1219. Trilokasāra by Nemicandra with M. T.'s comm., incompl.	I.O. San. 1033
1220. Trailokyadīpikā by Indravāmadeva, with lacunas	I.O. San. 2583
1221. [Trailokyadīpikā by Indravāmadeva], incomplete	Or. 15892
1222. Parīkṣāmukha by Māṇikyanandin	Or. 2134 (D,3)
1223. Prameyakamalamārtāṇḍa by Prabhācandra	Burnell 246 & 247
1224. Ratnakaraṇḍaka by Samantabhadra	Burnell 433 (4)
1225. Ratnakaraṇḍaka by Samantabhadra with a gloss in Kannada	Burnell 433 (1)
1226. Ācārasārasaṁgraha by Vīranandin	Or. 3348 (A)
1227. Samādhitantra by Pūjyapada with a Guj. comm. by Parvata	I.O. San. 1399
1228. Subhāṣita-ratna-sandoha by Amitagati	I.O. San. 669
1229. Sadbodhacandrodaya by Padmanandin	I.O. San. 1564g
1230. Sajjanacitta-vallabha by Malliṣeṇa	Burnell 433 (5)
1231. Doharā (Ap.) by Suprabhācārya with Skt. comm.	Or. 13221 (10)
1232. Gṛhasthācāradharma	I.O. San. 3245 (k)
1233. [Unidentified] (Skt.)	I.O. San. 3545

3. Narrative literature

1234. Ādi-purāṇa by Jinasena & Uttara-purāṇa by Guṇabhadra	Burnell 354, 355, 356
1235. Ādi-purāṇa & Mahā-purāṇa (chap. 1-47)	I.O. San. 2470
1236. Ādi-purāṇa (chap. 1-25)	Mackenzie XII.3
1237. Ādi-purāṇa (chap. 1-40)	Mackenzie XII.1
1238. Ādi-purāṇa (chap. 40-47)	Mackenzie XII.4
1239. Uttara-purāṇa (chap. 48-76)	Mackenzie XII.2
1240. Harivaṁśa-purāṇa by Jinasena	I.O. San. 3414 (A)
1241. Harivaṁśa-purāṇa by Jinasena	Or. 3350
1242. Śānti-purāṇa by Asaga, sargas 1-12	I.O. San. 372 (B)
1243. Neminātha-purāṇa by brahmaNemidatta	Or. 3348 (B)
1244. Bhārata-bhāṣā (= Pāṇḍava-purāṇa) (H.) by Lāla Bulākīdāsa	MSS. Hin. C 8
1245. Yaśodharacarita by Sakalakīrti	I.O. San. 2363
1246. Hanūmac-caritra by brahma Ajita	Or. 2129 (C)
1247. Dhanyakumāracaritra-bhāṣā by Khusyālacanda	Or. 16132/13
1248. Kṣatracūḍāmaṇi by Vādībhasiṁhasūri with Tamil comm.	Burnell 235

1249. Bhujabali-caritra (Skt.) [by Doḍḍaiya], incomplete	Mackenzie XII.10

4. Hymns

1250. Svayambhū-stotra by Samantabhadra	I.O. San. 3532 (3)
1251. Akalankāṣṭaka by Akalanka	Burnell 229
1252. Yugādideva-aṣṭottara-sahasra-nāma-stotra by Jinasena	Or. 13221 (2)
1253. Aṣṭasahasranāma-stotra by Jinasena	I.O. San. 3532 (4)
1254. Jinasahasranāma-(laghustotra)	Or. 13221 (1)
1255. [Vṛṣabhagadya]	I.O. San. 3532 (5)
1256. Ekībhāva-stotra by Vādirāja	Or. 13221 (6)
1257. Ekībhāva-stotra by Vādirāja	I.O. San. 3532 (6)
1258. Viṣāpahāra-stotra by Dhananjaya	Or. 13221 (7)
1259. Viṣāpahāra-stotra by Dhananjaya	I.O. San. 3532 (7)
1260. Bhūpāla-pacīsī by Bhūpāla	Or. 13221 (8)
1261. Bhūpāla-pacīsī by Bhūpāla	I.O. San. 3532 (8)
1262. Bhaktāmara-stotra by Mānatunga	Or. 13221 (4)
1263. Kalyāṇamandira-stotra by Siddhasena divākara	Or. 13221 (5)
1264. Paramānanda-stotra with Guj. comm.	Or. 16132/5 (1)
1265. Pancaparameṣṭhi-stuti (H.) by Vindodilāl	Or. 13221 (12)
1266. Tīsa covīsī jina-nāma	Or. 13221 (9)
1267. Jina-stotra (Skt.)	Burnell 433 (2)
1268. [Collection of Jain hymns] (Skt.), frag.	I.O. San. 3532 (1)
1269. Padas (H.) by Navala Rāma	MSS. Hin. A 5

5. Vrata literature & Ritualistic works

1270. Ādityavāra-kathā by Gangadāsa	Or. 14290
1271. [Collection of four vrata-kathās (H.) by Brahma Jñānasāgara]	I.O. San. 1596 (C)
1272. Puṣpānjali-rāsa (Guj.) by Brahma Jinadāsa	I.O. San. 1596 (D)
1273. Pratiṣṭhā-tilaka by Nemicandrasūri	Mackenzie XII.13 (A)
1274. Pratiṣṭhā-tilaka by Nemicandrasūri	Mackenzie XII.12
1275. Sakala-kriyā	Mackenzie XII.13 (B)
1276. Śāntihoma	Mackenzie XII.6
1277. Nityābhiṣekavidhi	Mackenzie VIII.72 (A)
1278. Pūjā-vidhi	Mackenzie VIII.72 (B)
1279. Pūjā-vidhi	Mackenzie VIII.72 (C)
1280. [Daśakuṇḍa-lakṣaṇa] (Skt.)	Mackenzie XII.14 (A)
1281. Vāstupūjā-vidhi	Mackenzie XII.14 (C)

6. Works by Banārasīdāsa

1282. Samayasāra-nāṭaka	I.O. San. 2112 (A)
1283. Samayasāra-nāṭaka with a lacuna	I.O. San. 1596 (A)
1284. Samayasāra-nāṭaka, incomplete	Add. 26,358 (E)
1285. Samayasāra-nāṭaka, with a lacuna	MSS. Hin. B 3 (1)
1286. Banārasī-vilāsa by Banārasīdāsa, an anthology	Add. 22,393

1287. [Jinasahasranāma and ten other poems] MSS. Hin. B 3 (2-11)

7. Varia

1288. [Malliṣeṇa's epitaph] Bühler 308
1289. Rāgamālā by Harṣakīrti Or. 13221 (11)
1290. Inscribed Yantra OA 1880-4057 (BM)

III. Belles-lettres and Śāstric disciplines

1. Anthologies and floating verses

1.1. Anthologies

1291. Vajjālagga by Jayavallabha I.O. San. 1363 (A)
1292. Praśnottara-ratna-mālikā by Vimala Or. 3347 (C,4)
1293. Sūktimuktāvalī (Sindūraprakāra) by Somaprabhācārya Or. 2148 (B)
1294. Sūktimuktāvalī (S.) by Somaprabhācārya, incompl. I.O. San. 3614 (A)
1295. Sūktimuktāvalī (S.) by Somaprabhācārya with Mānasāgara's comm. Or. 13791
1296. Prabodhacintāmaṇi by Dharmasundara I.O. San. 2468 (C)
1297. Dhanarāja-prabodha-mālā by Jayasiṁhasūri Or. 2138 (C)
1298. Sūktāvalī Or. 2138 (B)
1299. Sūktāvalī Or. 2138 (A,1)
1300. Śatakatraya by Bhartṛhari with Dhanasāra's comm. Or. 5236
1301. Śatakatraya by Bhartṛhari with a Guj. comm. Or. 13773
1302. Śloka-subhāṣita (Pkt. & Skt.) Or. 16133/3 (C)
1303. [Prakrit verses and moral sentences] MSS. Guj. 2 (2)

1.2. Floating or unidentified verses

1304. [kṣipto hastāvalagnaḥ] & [tārā viṣṇū raṇatvid] Add. 26,358 (B,2; C,2)
1305. [sāraṁ sāraṁgalocanā] Add. 26,461 (7)
1306. [tasmāj jāgṛta jāgṛta] Or. 15633/102 (2)
1307. [pāpī ne pratibodhatāṁ] Or. 15633/30 (Suppl.)
1308. [sajana phala jo phūla jo] Or. 15633/132 (Suppl.)
1309. [rāmakali] I.O. San. 3614 (N)

2. Commentaries of non-Jain *kāvyas*

1310. Kālidāsa's Raghuvaṁśa with Dharmameru's comm., incomplete Add. 14353
1311. Meghadūta with an *Avacūri* Or. 2145 (C)
1312. Ṛtusaṁhāra by Kālidāsa with glosses I.O.San. 2525 (A)
1313. Cāritravardhana's comm. on Naiṣadhīyacarita, frag. Add. 26,446 (A)
1314. Gītagovinda by Jayadeva (Jain scribe) Or. 2145 (D)
1315. Nalacampū of Trivikrama with Guṇavinayagaṇi's comm. Or. 3351
1316. Khaṇḍapraśasti-kāvya by Hanūmanta with Guṇavinayagaṇi's comm. I.O. San. 3408

3. Grammar

1317. Jainendra-vyākaraṇa — Bühler 134
1318. Śabdānuśāsana of Śākaṭāyana, chapters 1-4 — Burnell 454
1319. Kātantra with Bhāvasena's Laghuvṛtti — Burnell 461
1320. Kātantra-vistara by Vardhamāna on Śarvavarman's *Kātantra* (*Kṛdanta*) — Or. 13775
1321. [A comm. on the Kṛdanta section of the Kātantra], frag. — Add. 26,452 (O)
1322. Kātantra-vibhramasūtra with Cāritrasiṁha's *Avacūri*, incompl. — I.O. San. 2341 (C)
1323. Śabdānuśāsana by Hemacandra, *sūtras* only — Add. 26,443 (C)
1324. Śabdānuśāsana by Hemacandra with *Bṛhadvṛtti*, incomplete — Or. 13500
1325. Śabdānuśāsana by Hemacandra with *Laghu-vṛtti* (I.1-III.2) — Or. 5248
1326. Śabdānuśāsana by Hemacandra with *Laghu-vṛtti* (I.1-III.2 + V.1-4) — Or. 5247
1327. Śabdānuśāsana by Hemacandra with *Laghu-vṛtti*, incomplete — Add. 26,434 (B)
1328. Śabdānuśāsana by Hemacandra with *Laghu-vṛtti* (I.1.14-IV.4.112) — Or. 13481
1329. Śabdānuśāsana by Hemacandra with *Laghu-vṛtti* (III.3-IV.4) — Or. 2142 (C)
1330. Śabdānuśāsana by Hemacandra with *Laghu-vṛtti* (III.3-IV.4) — Add. 26,434 (C)
1331. Śabdānuśāsana by Hemcandra with *Laghuvṛtti* (VIII), incomplete — Bühler 140
1332. Lingānuśāsana by Hemacandra with auto-comm., frag. — Add. 26,434 (D)
1333. Lingānuśāsana by Hemacandra with a comm. — Or. 5240
1334. Nyāyamanjūṣā-nyāsa by Hemahaṁsa — Or. 5227
1335. Nyāyamanjūṣā-nyāsa by Hemahaṁsa — Or. 5228
1336. Sārasvatī-prakriyā by Anubhūtisvarūpācārya, beg. missing — Or. 13496
1337. Sārasvata-vyākaraṇa by Anubhūtisvarūpācārya, incomplete — Or. 15633/186
1338. Sārasvata-prakriyā by Anubhūtisvarūpācārya, frag. comm. and [Sandhi-prakriyā], a brief fragment of Guj. explanations — Add. 26,452 (K)
1339. Vākya-prakāśa by Udayadharma with Jinavijaya's comm. — Or. 2143 (B)
1340. Vākya-prakāśa by Udayadharma with a comm. — Or. 2143 (C)
1341. Kriyāratnasamuccaya by Guṇaratnasūri — Or. 5204
1342. Dhāturatnākara by Sādhusundaragaṇi with auto-comm., incomplete — Or. 5222
1343. Kriyākalāpa by Vijayānanda, incomplete (chap. 2-4) — I.O. San. 2527 (B)
1344. Kavirahasya by Halāyudha with Ravidharman's comm. — Bühler 118

1345. [Nāma-rūpāvali], beginning only — Add. 26,452 (L)

4. Lexicography

1346. Abhidhānacintāmaṇi by Hemacandra — Or. 2141
1347. Abhidhānacintāmaṇi by Hemacandra — Or. 5196
1348. Abhidhānacintāmaṇi by Hemacandra, incomplete — Or. 2142 (A)
1349. Abhidhānacintāmaṇi by Hemacandra with auto-comm. — Or. 5197
1350. Abhidhānacintāmaṇi by Hemacandra with Śrīvallabhagaṇi's *Nāmasāroddhāra* — Or. 4530
1351. Abhidhānacintāmaṇi by Hemacandra with Śr.'s *Nāmasāroddhāra* — Or. 13806
1352. Abhidhānacintāmaṇi by Hemacandra with glosses, incomplete — Add. 26,436 (A)
1353. Anekārthasaṁgraha by Hemacandra — Add. 26,424 (E)
1354. Anekārthasaṁgraha by Hemacandra with comm. — Sloane 4090 (E)
1355. Deśīnāmamālā by Hemacandra with auto-comm. — I.O. San. 3280
1356. Pancavargasaṁgrahanāmamālā by Śubhaśīlagaṇi — Or. 2142 (B)
1357. Uṇādināmamālā by Śubhaśīlagaṇi — Or. 5200
1358. Śabdaprabheda by Maheśvara with Jñānavimalagaṇi's comm., incompl. — Or. 5246
1359. Nāmamālā by Harṣakīrti — Burnell 474 (1)
1360. Anekārthanāmamālā by Harṣakīrti — Burnell 474 (2)
1361. Śabdānekārtha by Harṣakīrti — Burnell 474 (3)
1362. Nāmamālā or Nighaṇṭusamaya by Dhananjaya — Or. 5224 (2)
1363. Anekārthadhvanimanjarī (3 chap.) — Or. 5224 (1)
1364. Anekārthakośa — Or. 16132/8
1365. Anekārthadhvanimanjarī (4 chap.) — Add. 26,434 (E)
1366. Ratnakośa, incomplete — I.O. San. 864 (C)
1367. Ratnakośa — Aufrecht 87

5. Metrics

1368. Prākṛtachandaḥkośa by Ratnaśekhara — Or. 8061
1369. [Chando'nuśāsana] by Hemacandra with auto-comm. (chap. 3-8) — Or. 2140 (E)
1370. Chandoratnāvalī by Amaracandrasūri — Or. 2140 (D)
1371. Chandaḥ-prastāra-vidhi with a Guj. comm. — Add. 26,464 (B)
1372. Vṛttaratnākara by Kedārabhaṭṭa with Somacandragaṇi's *Chandovṛtti* — Or. 13774
1373. Vṛttaratnākara by K. with Kṣemahaṁsagaṇi's *Samāsānvayaṭippana* — Or. 2140 (C)
1374. Śrutabodha in the version by Kāntivijayagaṇi — Or. 2140 (F)

6. Poetics

1375. Vāgbhaṭālaṁkāra Or. 5241
1376. Vāgbhaṭālaṁkāra Or. 13542
1377. Vāgbhaṭālaṁkāra with Jinavardhanasūri's comm., incomplete Or. 13497
1378. Vāgbhaṭālaṁkāra with Jinavardhanasūri's comm., incomplete Or. 2146 (C)
1379. Vāgbhaṭālaṁkāra with Siṁhadevagaṇi's comm., incomplete Or. 11747
1380. Vāgbhaṭālaṁkāra with an *Avacūri* Or. 2146 (B)
1381. Kāvyānuśāsanavṛtti or Alaṁkāratilaka by Vāgbhaṭa with auto-comm. I.O. San. 2543 (A)
1382. Kāvyakalpalatā-vṛtti by Amaracandra Bühler 119
1383. Alaṁkāracūḍāmaṇi by Hemacandra Bühler 111
1384. Alaṁkāracūḍāmaṇi by Hemacandra, beg. missing Bühler 112
1385. Alaṁkāracūḍāmaṇi by Hemacandra Bühler 113

7. Riddles

1386. Vidagdhamukhamaṇḍana by Dharmadāsa, frag. Add. 26,452 (B,1)
1387. Praśnottara by Jinavallabha with an *Avacūri* Or. 5231
1388. [Samasyā-padyāni] (Skt.) Add. 26,452 (B,2)

8. Mathematics

1389. Līlāvatī by Bhāskarācārya Or. 13457 (A)
1390. Līlāvatī by Lālacandagaṇi Or. 13639
1391. Līlāvatī by Lālacandagaṇi Add. 26,373
1392. Gaṇitasārasaṁgraha by Mahāvīrācārya, 1-3 Mackenzie VIII.50
1393. Gaṇitasārasaṁgraha by Mahāvīrācārya, 1-2 Mackenzie V.19
1394. Gaṇitasārasaṁgraha by M., 1-4, with Kannada comm. Mackenzie XII.9a

9. Astronomy, Astrology

1395. Ārambha-siddhi by Udayaprabhadevasūri Or. 5199
1396. Ārambha-siddhi by U. with Hemahaṁsagaṇi's comm. Or. 2139
1397. Ārambha-siddhi by Udayaprabhadevasūri with an *Avacūrṇi* Or. 2140 (A)
1398. Nāracandra-yantroddhāra-ṭippaṇa, incomplete I.O. San. 3384 (A)
1399. Jyotiḥsāra by Naracandra with a Guj. comm. I.O. San. 3315
1400. Grahabhāvaprakāśa or Bhuvanadīpaka by Padmaprabhasūri I.O. San. 742 (A)
1401. Grahabhāvaprakāśa by Padmaprabhasūri, with a lacuna Or. 13635
[1401[a]. Grahabhāvaprakāśa by P. with Siṁhatilakasūri's comm. I.O. Suppl. 3]
1402. Grahabhāvaprakāśa by P. with Guj. comm. I.O. San. 2049 (D)
1403. Dhruvabhramayantra by Padmānabha with Or. 5223

auto-comm.

1404. Yantrarāja by Mahendrasūri — I.O. San. 1528 (A)

1405. Yantrarāja by Mahendrasūri with Malayendu's comm. — I.O. San. 2343 (B)

1406. Yantrarāja by Mahendrasūri with Malayendu's comm. — I.O. San. 1845

1407. Yantrarāja by M. with Malayendu's comm., incomplete — I.O. San. 2343 (A)

1408. Jyotiṣa-sāroddhāra by Harṣakīrtisūri — I.O. San. 2049 (A)

1409. Jyotiṣa-sāroddhāra by Harṣakīrtisūri (chap. 1) — Or. 5210

1410. Jātakadīpikāpaddhati by Harṣavijayagaṇi with a Guj. comm. — Or. 13487

1411. Jātakakarmapaddhati by Śrīpati with Sumatiharṣagaṇi's comm. — Or. 5208

1412. Ratnamālā by Śrīpati (Jain scribe) — Or. 5209

1413. Karaṇakutūhala by Bhāskarācārya with Sumatiharṣagaṇi's *Ganakakumudakaumudī* — Or. 5201

1414. Tājikasāra by Haribhaṭṭa — Or. 3354 (C)

1415. Bhūgola-śāstra (Guj.) — Or. 13540

1416. Sāmudrika-śāstra — Add. 26,461 (D)

1417. Bāra-rāsa nuṁ phala — I.O. San. 3400 (ea)

1418. [Janma-kuṇḍalī] — Or. 13639 (Suppl.)

1419. Bhāvādhyāya (Ratnadīpaka) — I.O. San. 1530 (I)

10. Medicine

1420. Yogacintāmaṇi by Harṣakīrtisūri — Or. 8150

1421. Vaidyamanotsava (H.) by Nayanasukha, incomplete — Add. 26,454 (E)

1422. Yoga-ratnākara-caupaī (Guj.) by Nayanaśekhara-muni — I.O. San. 2511

1423. Vaidyavallabha, frag. — Add. 26,452 (D)

11. Music

1424. [Verses, unidentified source] — Or. 8061 (Suppl.)

IV. A Vijñaptipatra in the Oriental collections

1425. Invitation scroll from Sirohi — Or. 16192

Description of composite manuscripts or codices

A composite manuscript or codex is defined as an identical material (paper or palm-leaf) serving for more than one text written by the same scribe (see Introduction II.). The original idea of the scribe is to present a consistent collection or selection of texts making a unity (section A, below). Complex instances of cases where different scribes have put their hands in the same codex are exceptional in the collection and are reviewed in section B. They can be called collective manuscripts. Such situations are distinct from cases where a given text is followed by supplements meant to fill the last page or for other reasons and written from a different hand than the main work, for which see section C.

In most catalogues published so far, the material description of composite manuscripts appears with the entry which happens to be the first. This method, however, is not very convenient especially when the catalogue is of important size. This is the reason why we have only used the phrase 'Contains N texts' in the corresponding entries, referring the reader to the present section for the full description of a given manuscript.

A. Composite manuscripts

N.B.: The basic organizing criterion in this part, which collects information both about manuscripts having the Indian format and manuscripts bound in book form or codices, has been the number of texts (from 2 to 25). Within each group, we follow the alphabetical order and the numerical sequence of the shelfmark.

In most of the catalogues of Jain manuscripts it is not easy to analyze the functioning of composite items or to draw some observations from the descriptions which are given. A noteworthy exception is the Strasbourg catalogue where Appendix 1 'Correspondence table of numbers' (pp. 377-380) can be used for this purpose and for purpose of comparison.

The overwhelming majority of situations exhibited by the composite manuscripts of our corpus are those where the number of texts amounts to two, i.e. the minimal pattern for a composite manuscript. This is also the general pattern in the Strasbourg collection. Whatever the number of texts, consistency and complementarity are the two principles governing groupings of texts. The following types of patterns can be distinguished:

- Text and commentary or texts and commentaries.
- Texts belonging to the same category: e.g., five *angas* (no example in our collections, but see Strasbourg under Ser. No. 1 and Indian collections), two Prakīrṇakas, two or more *prakaraṇas*, two or more *vrata-kathās*, etc. A certain amount of freedom is possible. But there are also recurring fixed sets, illustrated, for instance, by the vast number of manuscripts containing five or six *Karmagranthas* (several examples in our corpus; see also Strasbourg under Ser. No. 116), and those having seven or nine hymns, always the same, which are known as *Sapta-* and *Nava-smaraṇas*.
- Texts by the same author, equivalent to our 'collected works' or 'collected papers' by so and so.

The majority of manuscripts or codices containing more than five texts, and often more than ten, are the equivalent of *pūjā* or *svādhyāya* manuals, or private prayer manuals. They are meant to include everything which is useful in the context of daily ritual and religious life for any pious layman, from textbooks on the doctrine (such as the *Tattvārthasūtra*) to narrative texts, hymns and *vidhis* (see examples below; Strasbourg under Nos. 280, 101, 245, 306, 163, 278, from 5 to 11 texts). They are marked by multilingualism, since they often exhibit side by side Sanskrit or Prakrit texts *and* Gujarati compositions. Thus the person for whom they are meant is exposed to all these languages at the same time, and uses them, at least for memorization. On the other hand, the way the texts are transmitted together cannot be without consequence on the linguistic level of those who write: how could it be possible not to introduce Gujarati elements in the Sanskrit and the Prakrit, and *vice versa*? Such a situation is also evidenced in *Āvaśyaka* manuscripts (*Pratikramaṇa-sūtra*, etc.) where Prakrit formulas alternate with hymns in vernacular languages.

'Harley 415' which contains a total of 25 texts in Gujarati (narratives and hymns, anonymous or by different authors) is an extreme case in our collection. But it is by no way unique (see the *Vividhakavi-*

racita-sajjhāya-ślokâdi-saṁgraha, ed. Muni Kalyāṇakīrtivijaya in *Anusandhān* [Ahmedabad] 24, 2003, pp. 41-78, with 15 texts).

Boundary cases (one text/several texts) are illustrated by the *Āvaśyaka* manuscripts. The combination of formulas and hymns they produce is virtually unique in each item, although the formulas and the hymns themselves can exist independently. We have considered these manuscripts as forming one unit described under one entry. Thus they are not detailed in this section. For another boundary case see **Cat. No. 24** (*Bhagavatī-sajjhāya*) or the *Banārasī-vilāsa*, a collection of works by the same author which are also liable to exist independently from one another.

Two texts

— **Add. 25022**. Contains 2 texts. Book form. Paper. MEF: 1-224. Devanāgarī script and Prakrit for the *mūla*. Persian script and language for the commentary. The book is to be read from the end (like a Persian book)! Only B sides are written. Some pages have Nāgarī, followed by Persian, some only Persian, some Persian and Nāgarī alternately. 24 x 15 cm.; 18 x 9 cm. 11-12 lines. Red used for daṇḍas. Good condition. Dated: V.S. 1852.

1	1B-63B	Karmaprakṛti (**Cat. No. 1213**)
2	65B-224	Pancāstikāyasāra (**Cat. No. 1201**).

Fol. 64 is blank on both sides. Two Digambara treatises with a Persian commentary written for the French General Claude Martin.

— **Add. 26,450, MS. C**. Contains 2 texts. Bound with Add. 26,450 A, B and D. Paper. OFN: 2-17; MEF: 56-71. 25,5 x 10,5 cm; 22 x 10 cm. 18 lines. Double-ruled red margins. No central space. Marginal title 'Gajasaṁgha' throughout. Cursive script. Good condition. Dated: V.S. 1657.

1	2A-17A	Gajasiṁha-kumāra-caupaī (**Cat. No. 790**)
2	17A-17B	Śrīmallarṣi-stavana (**Cat. No. 1047**).

One story, one hymn.

— **Add. 26,452, MS. B.** Contains 2 texts. Yellow paper. OFN: 9///12-15-(16); MEF: 27-32. 25 x 10 cm.; 18,6 x 7 cm. 11 lines. Triple-ruled red margins. Usual blank space in the centre filled with akṣaras. Red used for numbers, riddles types. Good condition but script at places rubbed off, text illegible. Folios damaged, mostly repaired. No date.

1	9A-16A	Vidagdhamukhamaṇḍana (**Cat. No. 1386**)
2	16A6-B4	[Samasyā-padyāni] (**Cat. No. 1388**).

Two texts on riddles.

— **Add. 26,452, MS. M.** Contains 2 texts. Brownish paper. OFN: nil; MEF: 54. 25 x 9,5 cm.; 22 x 8,5 cm. 15 lines (A), 13 lines (B). Orange pigment used. Ink rubbed off. No date.

1	A1-B7	Sālibhadrajī nī sajjhāya (**Cat. No. 751**)
2	B8-13	Kāya-jīva-gīta (**Cat. No. 498**).

Two short Gujarati poems.

— **Add. 26,452, MS. P.** Contains 2 texts. Brownish strip of paper. No margin drawn. OFN: nil. MEF: 59. 10,6 x 26,7 cm.; 10 x 23,4 cm. 32 lines (A), 14 lines (B). Akṣaras on the border missing because the manuscript has been pasted on new paper. Good condition. No date.

1	A1-25	Nemīśvara-bhāsa (**Cat. No. 981**)
2	A25-B14	Sthūlibhadra-bhāsa (**Cat. No. 822**).

Both works are by the same author, Ṛddhivijaya.

— **Add. 26,455, MS. AI.** Contains 2 texts. The thirty-fifth manuscript in a bundle. Paper. OFN: 1-3; MEF: 110-112; 20,5 x 11 cm.; 16,5 x 9 cm. 13 lines. Triple-ruled red margins on 1; margins not drawn on fols 2-3. Ink rubbed off. Cursive script.

1 1A-3A Keśi-Pradeśi-vicāra (**Cat. No. 73**)
2 3A6-3B [Guru-stavana] (**Cat. No. 1044**).

— **Add. 26,459**. Contains 2 identifiable texts. Book form. American paper. MEF: 1-180 (OFN not written or obscured by the binding). 31,5 x 20,5 cm.; 29 x 19,5 cm. 16-17 lines (text), 23-25 (comm.). Fol. 2 written on the recto only. Fol. 1 is the title page of the volume and is blank. Interlinear commentary. Clear script. Good condition. No date.

1 2A and 3A-35A Jambū-carita by Padmasundarasūri with Guj. comm. (**Cat. No. 716**)
2 35B-180A Kalpā-sūtra with ṭabo (**Cat. No. 121**).

— **Bühler 282**. Contains 2 texts. Paper. OFN: 1-49 (folio numbers are not always visible because the folios have been mounted on new paper). 21 x 8,5 cm.; 17 x 6 cm. 10-24 lines. Double-ruled black margins. Square blank space in the centre. Red used over numbers, titles. Good condition. No date.

1 1B-34B Daśavaikālika with Avacūri (**Cat. No. 203**)
2 34B-49A Pākṣika-sūtra (**Cat. No. 236**).

— **I.O. San. 1372**, MS. B. Contains 2 texts. Brownish rough paper. OFN: 124-292; MEF: 124-292. 25 x 11 cm.; 20,5 x 9,5 cm. 16-17 lines. Tripāṭha. Double-ruled black margins. Lozenge-shaped blank space filled with akṣaras. Red used for titles, verse numbers and colophon. Blank space in the centre, partially filled with letters from the adjacent lines. Marginal glosses or additions at places rather numerous. Clear script. Good condition. Dated: V.S. 1659.

In its present form, the ms. contains only the last two Karmagranthas with the auto-commentary. But the pagination, the title written at the end from another hand 'Karmagrantha saṭīka' and the final colophon at the end of the *Saptatikā* (q.v.) show that it was meant to contain all the six Karmagranthas, and that Nos. 1 to 4 have been lost.

1 124A-213B Śataka (**Cat. No. 448**)
2 214A-292B Saptatikā (**Cat. No. 463**).

— **I.O. San. 1564g, h**. Contains 2 texts. The two library numbers correspond to one and the same ms. Grey paper. OFN: 1-11; MEF: 1-11. 26 x 11 cm.; 24,5 x 9 cm. 11-12 lines. Double-ruled black margins. Red used over verse numbers. Rectangular central space. Good condition. Dated: V.S. 1475.

1 1A-3A Sadbodhacandrodaya by Padmanandin (**Cat. No. 1229**)
2 3B-11B Yogasāra (**Cat. No. 505**).

Two Digambara works on general teaching.

— **I.O. San. 2527, MS. E**. Contains 2 texts. Paper. OFN: 1. 25 x 10 cm.; 14 lines. Pancapāṭha. Double-ruled margins. Bad condition (partly torn). No date.

1 A1-11 Praśnagarbha-pancaparameṣṭhi-stotra with comm. (**Cat. No. 920**)
2 A12-B Vardhamāna-stotra with comm. (**Cat. No. 998**).

Two hymns of the *citrakāvya* type by the same author, Jayacandrasūri; the same hymns in a Pune ms. (see Notes *ad locum*).

— **I.O. San. 2909.** Contains 2 texts. Bound in book form. The two texts have an individual pagination starting with 1. They seem to be written by the same hand. 15 x 20 cm.; 11,5 x 16 cm. 19 lines. Red used for daṇḍas. Page number in the corner of the verso (like in a European book). In the second part, Arabic numbers in the margin indicating the verse number of the *mūla*. On the verso of the last page, something written in Persian along with a red stamp indicating 'CLAUD MARTIN' (*sic*). Dated: V.S. 1716 at the end of the second text. Collection of J. Leyden.

1 1-167B Pancāstikāya with Hemarāja's Hindi comm. (**Cat. No. 1200**)
2 1-89 Karmakāṇḍa with Hemarāja's Hindi comm. (**Cat. No. 1212**).

— **I.O. San. 3177**. Contains 2 texts. Paper. OFN: 1-154. 29 x 9 cm.; 23 x 5 cm. 6 lines. Twofold ms. with three margins of 2 cm., two on the sides, and one as a separation between the two parts of the ms. Good condition. 'It is written with silver on 113 leaves, most of which are painted alternatively black and red. ...

There are many pictures in the text, and arabesques on the margin. (MSS. of this kind are not unfrequent with the Jainas' (Jacobi's edition. Leipzig, 1879, introd. p. 28). The leaves are indeed lavishly decorated. Their background are either black or pink. Fol. 2 is written in golden letters with a somewhat cream background. Borders are also sometimes richly decorated. The same is true with the middle margin which separates the leaf into two parts. Reading sometimes difficult since letters may be more or less erased. Dated: V.S. 1485.

1	1B-113A	Kalpasūtra (**Cat. No. 96**)
2	114B-149A	Kālakācārya-kathānaka (**Cat. No. 708**).

Two works which traditionally go together.

— **I.O. San. 3394**. Contains 2 texts. Bound with I.O. San. 3383, 3390, 3393 and 3396 Light brownish paper. OFN: 1-7. 26,5 x 11 cm.; 25 x 9 cm. 7 lines. Double-ruled red margins. Bad condition. Mounted on new paper. Folio numbers mostly not visible. Hence misbound. Partly mixed with I.O. San. 3396 (= *Bhaktāmarastotra*) under the same binding. No date.

1	1A-5B5	Dāna-śīla-tapo-bhāvanā (**Cat. No. 625**)
2	5B6-7B9	Ekonatriṁśati-bhāvanā (**Cat. No. 612**).

Two works of the category *bhāvanā*.

— **I.O. San. 3395**. Contains 2 texts. Paper. OFN: 6-9; MEF: 1-4. 28 x 12,5 cm.; 23 x 10 cm. There are broad spaces inbetween the lines to permit the insertion of a gloss, which is not written. Good condition. No date.

1	6A1-3	Navatattva, frag. (**Cat. No. 565**)
2	6A3-end	Cauvīsadaṇḍaka (**Cat. No. 342**).

Two *prakaraṇas* among those which are part of basic teaching.

— **MSS. Guj. 2**. Contains 2 texts. See **Cat. No. 818** for description.

1	1B-20A	Vīrangada-caupaī (**Cat. No. 818**)
2	20A5-21B8	Prakrit verses (**Cat. No. 1303**).

— **MSS. HIN. B 3**. Contains 2 texts. Works by Banārasīdāsa. See **Cat. No. 1285** for description.

1	1A-113B	Samayasāra-nāṭaka (**Cat. No. 1285**)
2	114B-end	Various poems (**Cat. No. 1287**).

— **MSS. Guj. 14.** Contains 2 texts. Paper. OFN: 1-3. 26,6 x 11,5 cm.; 21,6 x 12 cm. 12 lines. Good condition. No date.

1	1-2A4	Neminātha Reṣatā-chanda (**Cat. No. 985**)
2	2A5-3	Dhyāna-chattīsa (**Cat. No. 615**).

Two works by the same author, Ṛṣi Gurudāsa.

— **Or. 1385, MS. A.** Contains 2 texts. Palm-leaf ms. See **Cat. No. 158** for description.

1	1A-9A	Jītakalpasūtra (**Cat. No. 158**)
2	9A-B	Sāvaya-pacchitta (**Cat. No. 161**).

Both texts are connected through their contents and are complementary. No. 1 belongs to the Chedasūtras and deals with atonements for the monks; No. 2 deals with atonements for lay people.

— **Or. 2112, MS. A.** Contains 2 texts. Paper. OFN: 1-16; MEF: 1-16. 27,2 x 11,5 cm.; 24 x 8,5 cm. 15 lines. Triple-ruled red margins. Lozenge-shaped blank space. Red used for daṇḍas and numbers. Marginal title 'Nava'. Clear script. Good condition. No date.

1	1A-1B7	Navatattva-prakaraṇa, *mūla* (**Cat. No. 563**)
2	1B7-16B	Navatattva-bālāvabodha (**Cat. No. 572**).

A text followed by its commentary.

— **Or. 2120, MS. C.** Contains 2 texts, described together. See the relevant entry (**Cat. No. 652**) for description.

1	MEF: 107-127	Śrāddha-vidhi-viniścaya by Harṣabhūṣaṇa
2	MEF: 127B9-13	[Aṣṭāhnikā-mahiman].

— **Or. 2123, MS. C.** Contains 2 texts. Thin paper. OFN: 1-75 (328-402); MEF: 195-269. 26,4 x 11 cm.; 22,5 x 9 cm. 21 lines. Double-ruled black margins filled with red. One red disk (A), three red disks (B). Orange pigment on numbers. Fine script. Good condition. Dated: 1471 V.S.

1	1A-75B	Triṣaṣṭiśalākāpuruṣa-caritra, VIII.1-12 (**Cat. No. 690**)
2	75B	Virāṭa-parva (**Cat. No. 841**).

One long narrative work in Sanskrit, one shorter text in Gujarati, both connected with Ariṣṭanemi and the Pāṇḍavas.

— **Or. 2138, MS. A.** Contains 2 texts. Paper. OFN: 1-9; MEF: 1-9. 25 x 11,5 cm.; 21 x 7 cm. 18-20 lines. Marginal space but margins are not drawn. No central blank space. No red used. Good condition. No date.

1	1B-9A3	Sūktāvalī (**Cat. No. 1299**)
2	9A3-9A13	Śāntinātha-stavana (**Cat. No. 961**).

One longer work, a hymn as a shorter supplement.

— **Or. 5131**. Contains 2 texts. Bound with Or. 5134. Thin paper, light cream colour. OFN: 1-10. 25,5 x 10,8 cm.; 21 x 8 cm. ca. 16 lines. One red disk on A sides, three on B sides. Four-ruled margins filled with red. Red used for daṇḍas. Marginal title 'Anta° vṛ°' then 'Aṇutta° vṛ'. Good condition. No date.

1	1B-8A	Antakṛd-daśāḥ (**Cat. No. 44**)
2	8A-10A	Anuttaropapātika-daśāḥ (**Cat. No. 51**).

Two *angas*, Nos. 7 and 8.

— **Or. 5147**. Contains 2 texts. Bound with Or. 5146 and 5148. Paper. OFN: 1-14; MEF: 1-14; 26 x 10,5 cm.; 11 lines. Good condition. Cruciform central design with a red disk. Red disks in the margins of some of the folios.

1	1B-8B	Bhaktaparijñā-prakīrṇaka (**Cat. No. 220**)
2	9A-14A	Saṁstāraka-prakīrṇaka (**Cat. No. 221**).

Two Prakīrṇakas having a common topic: fasting to death.

— **Or. 5151**. Contains 2 texts. Paper. OFN: 1-176; MEF: 1-176. 26,5 x 13 cm.; 20 x 9 cm. 15 lines. Double-ruled red margins. No margins drawn on fol. 94-110. Marginal title 'Kalpadrumaka°' (up to 168B) then 'Kālikācārya°', with folio number. Titles are marked with red. No punctuation. Sporadic marginal corrections. Clear script. Good condition. Dated: V.S. 1903.

1	1B-166B3	Kalpasūtra with commentary (**Cat. No. 115**)
2	166B3-176A	Kālakācārya-kathā (**Cat. No. 713**).

— **Or. 5182**. Contains 2 texts. Paper. Pancapātha. OFN: 1-4; MEF: 1-4. 26,5 x 11 cm.; 25,5 x 10 cm. Varying number of lines: 12 for the mūla; 4-5 in the upper part, 4-7 in the lower part, 27 in the left and right margins. Lozenge-shaped blank space. Orange pigment on numbers, and also on some words in the commentary. Clear and neat script. Good condition. Dated in the commentary: V.S. 1646.

1	1A-2B	Karmastava with avacūri (**Cat. No. 495**)
2	2B-4B	Bandhasvāmitva with the comm. by Sādhukīrti (**Cat. No. 415**).

Two Karmagranthas.

— **Or. 5224**. See **Cat. Nos. 1362** and **1363** for description.

Two lexicographical works.

— **Or. 13548**. Contains 2 texts. Brownish paper. OFN: 1-20; MEF: 1-20. 26 x 11 cm.; 22 x 8 cm. 13 lines. Double-ruled red margins. Red disks: 1 (A sides), 3 (B sides). Different scripts. Occasional corrections in the margins. Good condition. No date.

1 1A-12B Ratnaśekharanṛpa-Ratnavatī-kathā by Dayāvardhana (**Cat. No. 1098**)
2 12B-20B Dhanyakathā by Dayāvardhana (**Cat. No. 753**).
Two works by the same author.

— **Or. 15633/4**. Contains 2 texts. Paper. OFN: 1-3; MEF: 29-31. 26 x 11,5 cm; 20,3 x 8,5 cm. 11 lines.

1 1B-2B Pāṁca-Pāṇḍava-sajjhāya by Kaviyaṇa (**Cat. No. 842**)
2 2B-3A Rājimatī-sajjhāya by Somavimalasūri (**Cat. No. 833**).
Two Gujarati narrative poems.

— **Or. 15633/10**. Contains 2 texts. Paper. OFN: 1-2; MEF: 4-5. 27,5 cm. x 11,6 cm.; 23,2 x 9,5 cm. 10 lines. Double-ruled red margins. Red for numbers and daṇḍas. No central blank space. Bold script. Good condition. No date.

1 1A-2A8 Daśaśrāvaka-sajjhāya (**Cat. No. 40**)
2 2A9-2B Ajitanātha-stavana (**Cat. No. 1013**).

— **Or. 15633/12**. Contains 2 texts. Paper. OFN: 1-4; MEF: 13a-13d. 28 x 11,8 cm; 23 x 9,5 cm. 10 lines. Double-ruled red margins. Red used for daṇḍas and numbers. Good condition. Dated: V.S. 19x3.

1 1A-3B Navakāra no rāsa (**Cat. No. 264**)
2 3B-4A Dhanā-Kākandi-sajjhāya (**Cat. No. 53**).

— **Or. 15633/40**. Contains 2 texts. Paper. OFN: 1-13; MEF: 55-67. 28,5 x 12 cm; 23 x 9,5 cm. 9 lines. Double-ruled red margins filled with yellow. Red for daṇḍas, refrains, etc. First and last folios with ornamental motives. Bold script. Good condition. Dated: V.S. 1889.

1 1A-13A Navatattva-bhāṣā-ḍhāla-bandha (**Cat. No. 578**)
2 13A-13B Śankheśvara-Pārśvanātha-stavana (**Cat. No. 1082**).

— **Or. 15633/43**. Contains 2 texts. Paper. OFN: 1; MEF: 2. 24,7 x 11,3 cm.; 19,3 x 8,5 cm. 11 lines. Good condition. No date.

1 1A-1B4 Dṛṣṭi-rāgopari svādhyāya (**Cat. No. 598**)
2 1B4ff. Cauda-guṇa-thāṇā nī sajjhāya (**Cat. No. 482**).

— **Or. 15633/52**. Contains 2 texts. Paper. OFN: 1; MEF: 11. 27,5 x 11,5 cm; 23 x 7,5 cm. 10 / 7 lines. Triple-ruled red margins. Red for daṇḍas. No date.

1 1A1-10 [amalakalpa udyāna māṁ devācī nārī] by Rāmavijaya (**Cat. No. 1012**)
2 1B1-7 Ṛṣabha-jina-vinatī by Udayaratna (**Cat. No. 1132**).

— **Or. 15633/54**. Contains 2 parts, described together, of a larger work by Udayaratna. See **Cat. No. 630** for description.

1 Samakita nī sajhāya
2 Māna upara sajhāya.

— **Or. 15633/58**. Contains 2 texts. Paper. OFN: 1; MEF: 17. 26 x 12,2 cm.; 21 x 9,3 cm. 4-12 lines. Clear script. Good condition. No date.

1 1A1-7 Santoṣa nī sajjhāya by Kaviyaṇa (**Cat. No. 608**)
2 1A7-1B4 Śāntijina-stuti by Rūpavijaya (**Cat. No. 965**).

— **Or. 15633/67**. Contains 2 texts, described together and both forming a part of a *Caityavandanastuti*. See **Cat. No. 929** for description.

1 Tīrthaṁkara-janma-tithi
2 Jina-lānchana.

— **Or. 15633/68**. Contains 2 texts. Paper. OFN: 1; MEF: 27. 26 x 11,7 cm; 21,7 x 8,5 cm. 8-10 lines. Clear script. Good condition. No date.

1 1A Aṣṭamī-svādhyāya by Devavijaya (**Cat. No. 1128**)
2 1B Pancamī-tapa-mahimā-sajjhāya by Devavijaya (**Cat. No. 1114**).
Two works by the same author, having a common topic: *vratas*.

— **Or. 15633/79**. Contains 2 texts. Paper. OFN: 1; MEF: 38. 25,8 x 12,8 cm; 20,5 x 10 cm. 4-11 lines. Clear script. Good condition. No date.

1 1A1-7 Śānti-stavana by Rūpacanda (**Cat. No. 969**)
2 1A8-1B4 Neminātha-stavana by Hīravijaya (**Cat. No. 978**).

— **Or. 15633/81**. Contains 2 texts. Paper. OFN: nil; MEF: 40. 27 x 13 cm; 21,5 x 8,4 cm. 10 lines. No margins drawn. Good condition. No date.

1 Siddhagiri nī horī (H.) by Rūpacanda (**Cat. No. 1067**)
2 Siddhagiri no vasanta (H.) by Dharmacandra (**Cat. No. 1068**).
Two short compositions having a common topic: Shatrunjaya.

— **Or. 15633/87**. Contains 2 texts. Thin paper. OFN: nil; MEF: 46. 25 x 12 cm.; 22,4 x 9 cm. 10 lines (A), 4 lines (B). Good condition. No date.

1 A1-6 [prabhāte pankhiḍāṁ bole] by Lakṣmī/Rāmavijaya (**Cat. No. 958**)
2 A6-B4 Siddhācala-stavana by Jñānavimalasūri, Guj. (**Cat. No. 1058**).

— **Or. 15633/88**. Contains 2 texts. Paper. OFN: 1. 25,5 x 12 cm.; 20 x 9,2 cm. 9 lines. Double-ruled red margins. Red for numbers, titles, etc. Clear large script. Good condition. No date.

1 1A1-7 Cāmara-pūjā by Kuśalakṣema (**Cat. No. 1154**)
2 1A8-1B10 Viṁśati-tīrthapada-pūjā by Vijayasaubhāgya (**Cat. No. 1149**).

— **Or. 15633/89**. Contains 2 texts. Paper. OFN: 1; MEF: 47. 26 x 11,6 cm.: 21,5 x 9 cm. 11 lines (A), 3 lines (B). Double-ruled red margins forming a frame around the page. Red used for numbers and colophon. Good condition. No date.

1 1A-1-9 Sujātajina-vasanta by Nyāyasāgara (**Cat. No. 1035**)
2 1A10-B3 Mahāvīra-phāga by Vimalavijaya (**Cat. No. 1003**).
Both short compositions are by different authors, but both are outpouring of joy connected with the games of spring in a Jain context.

— **Or. 15633/105**. Contains 2 texts. Paper. OFN: 1; MEF: 63. 26,8 x 11,4 cm; 22 x 8,5 cm. 9-10 lines. Double-ruled red margins. Red for numbers, daṇḍas, refrains. Large clear script. Good condition. No date.

1 1A1-1A7 Simandharajina-stuti (**Cat. No. 1030**)
2 1A8-1B10 [Ātmopadeśa-]sajjhāya (**Cat. No. 604**).

— **Or. 15633/113**. Contains 2 texts. Paper. OFN: 1; MEF: 71. 26,5 x 10,5 cm.; 22,5 x 8 cm. 12 lines (A), 10 lines (B). Clear script. Good condition. No date.

1 1A-8 Aṣṭa-karama cūraṇa karī by Devavijaya (**Cat. No. 472**)
2 1A8-B10 Navapada-mahimā by Vimalavijaya (**Cat. No. 1142**).

— **Or. 15633/128**. Contains 2 texts. Paper. OFN: 1-9; MEF: 35-43. 27 x 12,7 cm; 22 x 9 cm. 11 lines. Clear script. Good condition. No date.

1 1B-9A Dīpālikā-kalpa by Guṇaharṣa (**Cat. No. 1110**)
2 9B Vīra-stavana (**Cat. No. 999**).

— **Or. 15633/144**. Contains 2 texts. Paper. OFN: 1-4; MEF: 26-29. 27,8 x 13,2 cm; 20,5 x 10,5 cm. 12 lines. Double-ruled red margins. No blank space in the centre. Red used for daṇḍas and numbers. Folio numbers are decorated, and written twice, also in the upper left margin. Clear script. Good condition. No date.

1 1A-3A Sīmandhara-stuti by Sakalacandra (**Cat. No. 1028**)
2 3A-4A Alpabahutva-stavana (**Cat. No. 495**).

— **Or. 15633/183**. Contains 2 texts. Paper. OFN: 1-48; MEF: 17-64. 27 x 11,3 cm; 21,3 x 10 cm. Lines: 2 (m), 5-7 (ṭ). Mūla in larger script, comm. cleanly written, divisions into compartments clearly marked in red. Good condition. No date.

1 1B-47A Sambodha-saptatikā (**Cat. No. 592**)
2 47B-48A [jīva-dayā jiṇa-dhammo], 3 Pkt. verses with a Guj. ṭabo (**Cat. No. 562**).

— **Or. 15633/192**. Contains 2 texts. Paper. OFN: 1; MEF: 73. 26,6 x 11,5 cm.; 22,3 x 8,7 cm. 9 lines (A), 5 lines (B). Good condition. No date.

1 1A [Śānti jiṇinda avadhārīe] by Ratnavijaya (**Cat. No. 970**)
2 1B [merā nehā lagyā Nābhinandana] (**Cat. No. 957**).

— **Or. 16132/5**. Contains 2 texts. Paper. OFN: 1-8. 26,5 x 12,5 cm.; 22 x 9,5 cm. 15 lines on fol. 1; 4 lines and interlinear on the other fols. Marginal title 'Caracāpatra' and fol. number.

1 1B1-5A1 Paramānanda-stotra with Guj. comm. (**Cat. No. 1264**)
2 5A2-8B Prastāvika-gāthā (**Cat. No. 636**).

— **Or. 16133/4**. Contains 2 texts. Paper. One unnumbered folio (most probably to be identified as fol. 11 of Or. 16133/2). MEF: 7. 28 x 11 cm.; 25 x 9 cm.; 16 lines. Fragile. No date.

1

A1-3 [Pārśva-stavana], fragment (**Cat. No. 992**)
2 A4-B Gajasukumāla-carita by Nannasūri (**Cat. No. 46**).

— **Or. 16133/5 (G)**. Contains 2 texts. Strip of paper. 10 x 43 cm. 52 lines. Written on both sides. Cursive script. No date.

1	A1-B20	[Kaliyuga-sajjhāya] (**Cat. No. 607**)
2	B21-	[Unidentified] (**Cat. No. 1045**).

— **Or. 16133/9 (L)**. Contains 2 texts. Paper. OFN: 1. 23 x 11 cm.; 21 x 10 cm. 10 lines. No margin drawn. Red used for daṇḍas. Large script. Good condition. No date.

1	1A1-10	Siddhagiri-jātrā-phala-stavana by Jñānavimala (**Cat. No. 1060**)
2	1A11-1B6	[Unidentified] by Śubhavīra (**Cat. No. 1116**).

Some unwritten space is left on B.

Three texts

— **Burnell 430**. Contains 3 texts. Book form (bound by L. Joshua, Mangalore). European blue paper. Kannada script. Folio numbers in roman script at the top of the page in the centre. 15 x 19,5 cm.; 12 x 14,5 cm. 13 lines. Black and violet ink. Modern copy. Good condition. No date.

1	1-7	Siddhāntasāra, 80 vss. (**Cat. No. 1215**)
2	8-46	Siddhāntasāra-vṛtti (**Cat. No. 1216**)
3	47-80	Tribhangisāra by Nemicandra (**Cat. No. 1214**).

Three Digambara works (from the tradition prevailing in Karnatak).

— **Burnell 474**. Contains 3 texts. Devanāgarī. Paper. OFN: 1-85. 25 x 12,7 cm. 7 lines. Good condition. No date (written about 1840 CE, I.O. Cat.).

1	1-48	Nāmamālā by Harṣakīrti (**Cat. No. 1359**)
2	48B-62A	Anekārthanāmamālā by Harṣakīrti (**Cat. No. 1360**)
3	62B-85	Śabdānekārtha by Harṣakīrti (**Cat. No. 1361**).

Three lexicons by the same author.

— **I.O. San. 1561a,c**. Bound with I.O. San. 1564. Manuscript C. Contains 3 texts. Brownish paper. OFN 1-11. 28 x 11,5 cm.; 27 x 11 cm. Pancapāṭha up to 9A; 11 lines (text, in the central part), 18-20 (comm., upper and lower parts and margins). Triple-ruled black margins. The comm. starts in the right margin. Blank space in the centre filled with red circle surrounded by red dots. Same pattern in both margins. Red used for daṇḍas, verse numbers and titles. Pṛṣṭhamātrā-script. Generally good condition, but fol. 1 is slightly damaged. No date, but looks old.

1	1A-5B6	Indriyaparājayaśataka (**Cat. No. 585**)
2	5B6-9B2	Ādināthadeśanoddhāra (**Cat. No. 559**)
3	9B2-11B	Paryantārādhanā (incomplete) (**Cat. No. 223**).

About 10 verses are missing in Text 3. Thus the ms. had probably 12 fols. in its complete form.

— **I.O. San. 1564 C**. Contains 3 texts. Paper. OFN: 1-16; 25,5 x 10,8 cm.; 21 x 8,5 cm. 17 lines. Double-ruled red margins. Red used over headings, numbers, etc. Good condition. Dated: V.S. 1764.

1	1-16	Anjanasundarī-caupaī by Punyasāgara (**Cat. No. 825**)
2	16B1-9	Nandiṣeṇamuni-sajjhāya by Jinaharṣa (**Cat. No. 798**)
3	16B9-17	Setrunjaya-maṇḍana Śrīyugādideva-stavana by Nayavimala (**Cat. No. 1079**).

— **Or. 2126, MS. D.** Contains 3 texts. Yellowish paper. OFN: 1-24. 24 x 10,5 cm.; 21 x 7 cm. Four-ruled black margins. Lozenge blank space. No red used. Angular script. Average condition. Some folios have been mended. Some are damaged by water.

1	1B1-15B3	Ratnaśekhara-Ratnavatī-kathā (**Cat. No. 1099**)
2	15B4-23B10	Dhanyakathā (**Cat. No. 754**)
3	23B11-24A	Nandiṣeṇa-kathā (from another hand) (**Cat. No. 799**).

At the end of l. 10 on 23B a new story is introduced, but not narrated: *dānaṁ dattvā yaḥ paścāttāpaṁ karoti tad-arthe bhrātṛ-traya-kathā.*

— **Or. 15633/8**. Contains 3 texts. Paper. OFN: 1-3; MEF: ii-iv. 26,5 x 13,2 cm.; 22 x 10,7 cm. 15 lines. Double-ruled red margins. Orange pigment used on verse numbers, refrains, etc. Visarga used as punctuation-mark. Folio numbers with ornamental motives.

1	1A-1B	Krodha, māna, māyā, lobha nī sajjhāya (**Cat. No. 629**)
2	1B-2A	Sīmandharasvāmi-stavana (**Cat. No. 1032**)
3	2A-3A	Kuguru-pacīsī (**Cat. No. 638**).

— **Or. 15633/23**. Contains 3 texts. Paper. OFN: 1-6; MEF: 10-15. 26,5 x 12 cm.; 20,7 x 9 lines. Good condition. Dated: V.S. 1872.

1	1B-2A	Siddha-cakra-stavana (**Cat. No. 1138**)
2	2A-3B	Tīrthaṁkara-anantaguṇāḥ (**Cat. No. 931**)
3	3B	Ātmā nī ātmatā (**Cat. No. 512**).

— **Or. 15633/26**. Contains 3 texts. Paper. OFN: 1-8; MEF: 42-49. 26,5 x 11,5 cm.; 21,2 x 9 cm. 10 lines. Double-ruled red margins, and extra red lines separating the written part from the blank marginal space. No blank space in the centre. Red used for numbers, daṇḍas and colophons. Large clear script. Good condition. No date.

1	1A-3A	Jñānapancamī-stavana (**Cat. No. 1113**)
2	3A-8A	Panca-kāraṇa-bola-Mahāvīra-stavana (**Cat. No. 1007**)
3	8A-8B	Keśī-Gautama-adhyayana-sajjhāya (**Cat. No. 190**).

— **Or. 15633/50**. Contains 3 texts. Paper. OFN: 1; MEF: 9. 26 x 11,7 cm.; 20,6 x 8,3 cm. 13 lines (A), 6 lines (B). Good condition. No date.

1	1A1-12	Aṣṭamī-caityavandana by Kṣamāvijaya (**Cat. No. 1127**)
2	1A	Tīrthaṁkara-dehamāna-varṇa-stavana by Jñānavimala (**Cat. No. 930**)
3	1A	Aṣṭa-mahāprātihārya-nāmāni (**Cat. No. 1180**).

— **Or. 15633/70**. Contains 3 texts. Yellowish paper. OFN: 1; MEF: 29. 26,4 x 11,8 cm.; 20,8 x 10 cm. 13 lines. Triple-ruled red margins. Red used for daṇḍas, numbers, titles. Clear script. Good condition. Dated: V.S. 1890.

1	1A	Puṇḍarīkagiri-stotra (**Cat. No. 1057**)
2	1A-B	Ṛṣabhajina-stuti (**Cat. No. 951**)
3	1B	Siddhagiri-stavana (**Cat. No. 1059**)

— **Or. 15633/97**. Contains 3 texts. Brownish paper. OFN: 1; MEF: 55. 26 x 11,6 cm.; 21,6 x 8,5 cm. 13/14 lines. Triple-ruled red margins. Central lozenge filled with akṣaras. Red used for titles, numbers, daṇḍas. Good condition. No date.

1	1A	Guru-bhāsa-phūlaḍāṁ (**Cat. No. 1043**)
2	1A	Vīrajina-stavana (**Cat. No. 1000**)
3	1A	Siddhacakra-pūjā-stavana by Padmavijaya (**Cat. No. 1141**)

— **Or. 15633/154**. Contains 3 texts, described together. Bhāṣya-traya. See **Cat. No. 256** for description.

1	1B-4B	Caityavandana-bhāṣya
2	4B-8B	Guruvandana-bhāṣya
3	8B-12A	Pratyākhyāna-bhāṣya

— **Or. 15633/155**. Contains 3 texts, described together. Bhāṣya-traya. See **Cat. No. 255** for description.

1	1B-4B	Caityavandana-bhāṣya
2	4B-6B	Guruvandana-bhāṣya
3	6B-9A	Pratyākhyāna-bhāṣya

— **Or. 15633/177**. Contains 3 texts. Paper. OFN: 2-42; MEF: 2-42. 27,4 x 12 cm.; 21,3 x ca. 10 cm. 4 lines (text), ca. 13 (comm.). Triple-ruled red margins. Marginal title 'Karmagrantha ṭa' with folio number. Folio numbers with decorative floral motives. Compartments for the comm. are delineated. Red used for numbers, colophons, titles.

1	2A-7A	Bandhasvāmitva with Guj. comm. (incomplete) (**Cat. No. 421**)
2	7A-22B	Ṣaḍaśītikā with the Guj. comm. of Dhanavijaya (**Cat. No. 435**)
3	22B-42B	Śataka with a Guj. comm. (**Cat. No. 453**).

Three Karmagranthas, all by Devendrasūri, all with Gujarati commentary by Dhanavijaya.

— **Or. 15633/182**. Contains 3 texts, described together. Bhāṣya-traya. See **Cat. No. 258** for description.

1	1A-7B	Caityavandana-bhāṣya
2	7B-12A	Guruvandana-bhāṣya
3	12A-16B	Pratyākhyāna-bhāṣya.

Four texts

— **Add. 26,519**. Contains 4 independent elements. Book form, bound and stuck. OFN on B sides in the left corner. Includes blank pages (99, 101, 102, 108-112A, 114-115) and pages with personal notes rather than full-fledged texts. OFN not written from 100 onwards.

	OFN/MEF	
1	1-65A/2-66A	Śukasaptati (**Cat. No. 851**)
	65B-97B/66B-98B	Śukasaptati (contin., another hand)
2	MEF 100A	Jina-stavana (**Cat. No. 928**)
3	103-107	Illustrations (see below)
4	112B-113A	Udāvarta-vāyu-cikitsā (not described)
	117B	Table of contents of the first part of the Śukasaptati (*paṁ° Kesarasāgareṇa likhitaṁ*).
	118A	Scribal Remark (very cursive script).

3: Illustrations: paintings of Tīrthaṁkaras (14 x 23 cm.) in various colours: orange, green, blue, black, olive, crimson, dark grey: Ādinātha (103A), Śāntinātha (104A) in light cream, Neminātha (105A) in blue, ☞Pārśvanātha (106A) in green, Mahāvīrasvāmī (107A) in grey. Each Tīrthaṁkara is sitting and attended by people worshipping him (monks, nuns, laymen, laywomen). People preparing food are represented in the lower parts of fol. 105, 106, 107. The landscape is represented by trees and flowers.

— **I.O. San. 1596, MS. C.** Contains 4 texts. Described under the same entry, **Cat. No. 1271**. Four *vrata-kathās* written by the same author, brahma Jñānasāgara, a Digambara.

— **Or. 2134, MS. D.** Contains 4 texts. Paper. OFN: 1-54; MEF: 38-91. 26,5 x 11 cm.; 20 x 7,5 cm. 13 lines. Rectangular space in the centre on fol. 1B, then lozenges. No numbers, no red used. Marginal title

'Pramāṇamīmāṁsā patra 54' on fol. 54. Clear script. Good condition; the edges of the folios are bound with pieces of paper. Dated at the end of Text 2: V.S. 1486. However the script used throughout is the same. Clear pṛṣṭhamātrā script. On the last page 'Mar. 1880' is written with a pencil, and '2160' in nāgarī-script.

1	1B-2A8	38-39	Pramāṇamīmāṁsā (sūtra) (**Cat. No. 675**)
2	2A8-43B13	39-80	Pramāṇamīmāṁsā-vṛtti (**Cat. No. 676**)
3	44A1-47A2	81-84	Parīkṣānāmaprakaraṇa (= Parīkṣāmukha) (**Cat. No. 1222**)
4	47A2-54B	84-91	Sarvajñasiddhiprakaraṇa (**Cat. No. 674**).

Note the same grouping of texts (without the P.m.-vṛtti) in the Jaisalmer palm-leaf ms. No. 367 p. 158 (Puṇyavijaya's Cat.).

— **Or. 15633/13**. Contains 4 texts. Paper. OFN: 1-7; MEF: 14-20. 26 x 12,7 cm.; 20,5 x 10 cm. 12 lines. Good condition. No date.

1	1A-5B	Aṣṭa-karmaprakṛti-bola-vicāra-stavana by Nagāgaṇi (**Cat. No. 474**)
2	5B-6A	Dīvālī nuṁ stavana (**Cat. No. 1109**)
3	6A-7A	Karmaprakṛti-prathama-sajjhāya (**Cat. No. 475**)
4	7A-7B	Karmaprakṛti-tṛtīya-sajjhāya (**Cat. No. 475**).

Five texts

— **Burnell 433**. Contains 5 texts. Book form (bound by L. Joshua, Mangalore). European blue paper. Kannada script. Folio numbers in roman script at the top of the page in the centre. 20,8 x 28 cm.; 15 x 22,5 cm. 20 lines. Verses numbered in roman script. Black and violet ink. Modern copy (about 1865 CE). Good condition.

1	2A-37B	Ratnakaraṇḍaka-śrāvakācāra with comm. (**Cat. No. 1225**)
2	37B4-19	Jina-stotra (**Cat. No. 1267**)
3	38B-42B	Dvādaśānuprekṣā by Kundakunda (**Cat. No. 1203**)
4	42B-53A	Ratnakaraṇḍaka (**Cat. No. 1224**)
5	53A-55B	Sajjanacittavallabha (**Cat. No. 1230**)

Four Digambara works. On 56B is the 'Scribal Remark'.

— **MSS. Guj. 6**. Contains 5 texts. Thin paper. The smallest ms. of the collection. OFN: 1-24 (fol. 16 missing); MEF: 1-24. 16,4 x 9 cm.; 14 x 6 cm. 10 lines. Double-ruled black margins filled with red. No central blank space. Marginal title 'Ārādhanā' all along. Red used for daṇḍas, numbers, titles; folio numbers in small script. Angular script. Good condition. No date.

1	1A1-5A9	Ārādhanā-vidhi (**Cat. No. 288**)
2	5A10-10A3	Samyaktva (**Cat. No. 595**)
3	10A4-12B2	Samudghāta-vicāra (**Cat. No. 366**)
4	12B2-24A10	Sthirīkaraṇa° (**Cat. No. 497**)
5	24A10-B10	Śrāvakavidhi-rāsa (**Cat. No. 603**).

— **Or. 2106, MS. B**. Contains 5 texts. Collection of 5 Karmagranthas. Paper. Pancapāṭha. OFN: 1-25; MEF: 18-42. 26 x 11 cm.; 25,5 x 10 cm. (Very small margins). 8-10 lines. Double-ruled red margins filled with yellow. Lozenge-shaped blank spaces filled with disks or floral motives. Some folios are damaged. Fol. 9 is misbound. Clear pṛṣṭhamātrā script. Dated: V.S. 1583.

1	1A-4B7	Karmavipāka + comm. (**Cat. No. 389**)
2	4B7-7B4	Karmastava + comm. (**Cat. No. 403**)
3	7B4-9B1	Bandhasvāmitva + comm. (**Cat. No. 417**)
4	9B1-15A4	Ṣaḍaśītikā (**Cat. No. 433**)

5	15A4-25B	Śataka (**Cat. No. 451**).

— **Or. 5168**. Contains 5 texts. Collection of 5 Karmagranthas. Yellowish paper. OFN: 1-193. 26,5 x 10,5 cm. 22 x 8,5 cm. Folio numbers also in the left-hand margin. Lozenge-shaped blank space. Orange pigment on final colophons of each of the texts. The text of the vss. is directly followed by the comm. The five works immediately follow each other. Marginal titles 'Karma vivṛ', 'Karmasta vṛ', 'Laghubandha vṛ', 'Ṣaḍaśīti vṛ', 'Śataka vṛ'. Clear script. Good condition. Dated: V.S. 1659.

1	1B-34B7	Karmavipāka with auto-comm. (**Cat. No. 386**)
2	35A1-51B7	Karmastava with auto-comm. (**Cat. No. 401**)
3	51B8-59B7	Bandhasvāmitva with anon. comm. (**Cat. No. 416**)
4	60A1-112B16	Ṣaḍaśītikā with auto-comm. (**Cat. No. 431**)
5	113A1-193A	Śataka (**Cat. No. 447**).

— **Or. 5188**. Contains 5 texts. Collection of 5 Karmagranthas. Yellowish paper. OFN: 1-38; MEF: 1-38. 25,5 x 11,5 cm.; 25,5 x 10 cm. 16-17 lines. Lozenge-shaped blank space. Triple-ruled red margins. Orange pigment over numbers. Small clear pṛṣṭhamātrā script. Some marginal glosses in Sanskrit and Gujarati. Some charts and diagrams. OFN not always visible. Good condition, but the upper corner of fol. 19 is repaired. Dated: V.S. 1500.

1	1A-6B	Karmavipāka with an avacūri (**Cat. No. 390**)
2	7A-13A	Karmastava with an avacūri (**Cat. No. 404**)
3	13A-16A	Bandhasvāmitva with an avacūri (**Cat. No. 418**)
4	16A-22A	Ṣaḍaśītikā with an avacūri (**Cat. No. 434**)
5	22A-38A	Śataka with an avacūri (**Cat. No. 450**).

— **Or. 15633/176**. Contains 5 texts. Collection of 5 Karmagranthas. Paper. OFN: 1-86; MEF: 1-86. 26 x 11,5 cm.; 21 x 7 cm. 3 lines (text), ca. 10 lines (comm.). Double-ruled red margins. Interlinear commentary with compartments drawn. Incomplete manuscript.

1	1B-13B	Karmavipāka with Guj. comm. (**Cat. No. 392**)
2	13B-23A	Karmastava with Guj. comm. (**Cat. No. 407**)
3	23A-31A	Bandhasvāmitva with Guj. comm. (**Cat. No. 420**)
4	31A-58A	Ṣaḍaśītikā with Guj. comm. (**Cat. No. 436**)
5	58B-86B	Śataka with Guj. comm. (incomplete) (**Cat. No. 452**).

Six texts

— **I.O. San. 1350**. Contains 6 texts. Collection of 6 Karmagranthas. Paper. OFN: 1- 31; MEF: 1-31. 28 x 12 cm.; 18 x 8,5 cm. 9-10 lines. No central blank space. Triple-ruled red margins. Red used for titles, headings and verse numbers. Some tables on fol. 20A, 21A but the boxes are not filled. Colophons and titles in Sanskrit. Occasional Sanskrit glosses or chāyā above the line. Clear script. Nicely spaced. Good condition. Dated: V.S. 1827. Stamp 'E.I. Comp's Library'. Colebrooke collection.

'I.O. San. 1350 a, b' on the back, described separately in the I.O. Cat., respectively II,2 No. 7511 1350a., fol. 26, The four treatises on karman by Devendrasūri and II,2 No. 7559 1350b, The Saptatikā. In fact, there is only one ms. with continuous folio numbering containing a set of the 6 Karmagranthas.

1	1B1-5A9	Karmavipāka (**Cat. No. 385**)
2	5A10-7B6	Karmastava (**Cat. No. 400**)
3	7B6-9B6	Bandhasvāmitva (**Cat. No. 414**)
4	9B6-16A2	Ṣaḍaśīti (**Cat. No. 430**)

5	16A2-26A5	Śataka (**Cat. No. 446**)
6	26A5-31B	Saptatikā (**Cat. No. 458**).

— **Or. 2106, MS. A**. Contains 6 texts. Collection of 6 Karmagranthas. Paper. OFN: 1-17; MEF: 1-17. 25 x 10,8 cm. 13 lines. Triple-ruled red margins on fol. 1. Double-ruled black margins afterwards. The paper of fol. 1 is different from the rest, but the text is continuous. Marginal title 'Karmma sū'. Marginal glosses or additions. Good condition. No date.

1	1B-3B12	Karmavipāka (**Cat. No. 379**)
2	3B12-5A9	Karmastava (**Cat. No. 395**)
3	5A10-6B1	Bandhasvāmitva (**Cat. No. 409**)
4	6B1-10A4	Ṣaḍaśītikā (**Cat. No. 424**)
5	10A5-13B13	Śataka (**Cat. No. 441**)
6	13B13-17A	Saptatikā (**Cat. No. 456**).

— **Or. 2106, MS. D**. Contains 6 texts. Collection of 6 Karmagranthas with the avacūri by Guṇaratna. Yellowish paper. OFN: 1-59; MEF: 51-109. 25,8 x 11 cm.; 23 x 9 cm. 19 lines. Triple-ruled red margins. Lozenge-shaped blank space in the centre. Clear, neat and rather small pṛṣṭhamātrā script. Good condition. No date.

1	1A-6B3	Karmavipāka + comm. (**Cat. No. 388**)
2	6B3-10B13	Karmastava + comm. (**Cat. No. 402**)
3	10B13-13B6	Bandhasvāmitva (**Cat. No. 419**)
4	13B6-24A7	Ṣaḍaśītikā (**Cat. No. 432**)
5	24A-41B7	Śataka (**Cat. No. 449**)
6	41B8-59B	Saptatikā (**Cat. No. 464**).

— **Or. 13552**. Contains 6 texts. Collection of 6 Karmagranthas. Bound with Or. 13551 and 13553. Yellowish paper. OFN: 1-6. 25,5 x 11 cm; 22 x 9,5 cm. 22 lines. Rather small script. Square-shaped design in the middle area. A few marginal annotations. Folio numbers are written both in the upper left corner and the lower right corner of B folios. Some folios are discoloured by water. Tolerable condition, but some folios have been repaired by stripes of paper pasted so that parts of the text are not visible. In some cases the text has been rewritten on these stripes.

1	1A-1B	Karmavipāka (**Cat. No. 383**)
2	1B-2A	Karmastava (**Cat. No. 399**)
3	2B	Bandhasvāmitva (**Cat. No. 413**)
4	2B-4A	Ṣaḍaśītikā (**Cat. No. 428**)
5	4A-5B	Śataka (**Cat. No. 445**)
6	5B-6B	Saptatikā (**Cat. No. 461**).

— **Or. 13623**. Book form, unbound. The whole is placed in a cover made of brown cotton, not in a very good condition, placed over a cardboard. But it is here possible to talk of two manuscripts since B is just placed within A. For the description of A see **Cat. No. 823**. B contains 6 elements written by 6 different hands. 108 pages. Triple-ruled red margins. Careful script except MEF 85 which is cursive. Some parts may be missing in the lower sides because folios have been torn and repaired. Blank folios between 96 and 108.

1	MEF 61-85	24 Jina-stava by Yaśovijaya (**Cat. No. 925**)
2	86A	Ghaṇṭakarṇa-mantra (**Cat. No. 1159**)
3	86B-87A	Kuguru- (**Cat. No. 1046**)

4	90B-91A	Kuṇḍalī (no entry in the present catalogue)
5	93A-93B	The past Jinas (**Cat. No. 1175**)
6	95A-95B	The future Jinas (**Cat. No. 1175**).

On 87B, 88A-90A, assortment of lists of items, written in a very cursive script and hardly legible. On 90B-91A, a horoscope concerning a person named Bhagulāla and its description. On 91B-92A list of items concerning the 24 Jinas in three columns, dated V.S. 1884. On 97A-97B, 98A, paṭṭāvalī of Devardhikṣamākṣamaṇa ācārya. On 99B, 100A, 100B, an illegible account. On 101A-108B, tables, accounts, charts written but not legible.

— **Or. 15633/150**. Contains 6 texts. Collection of 6 Karmagranthas. Paper. OFN: 1-33; MEF: 44-76. 26,6 x 12 cm.; 20,6 x 9,5 cm. 10 lines. Triple-ruled red margins. Red for numbers, daṇḍas. Folio numbers with ornamental motives. No central blank space. Dated: V.S. 1942.

1	1B-5B	Karmavipāka (**Cat. No. 380**)
2	5B-8A	Karmastava (**Cat. No. 396**)
3	8A-10B	Bandhasvāmitva (**Cat. No. 410**)
4	10B-17A	Ṣaḍaśītikā (**Cat. No. 425**)
5	17A-25A	Śataka (**Cat. No. 442**)
6	25A-33A	Saptatikā (**Cat. No. 459**).

— **Or. 15633/151**. Contains 6 texts. Collection of 6 Karmagranthas. Paper. OFN: 1-30; MEF: 1-30. 26,5 x 12 cm.; 20,8 x 9,5 cm. 11 lines. Fol. 1 damaged a little.

1	1B-5A	Karmavipāka (**Cat. No. 381**)
2	5A-7B	Karmastava (**Cat. No. 397**)
3	7B-9A	Bandhasvāmitva (**Cat. No. 411**)
4	9B-15B	Ṣaḍaśītikā (**Cat. No. 426**)
5	15B-23A	Śataka (**Cat. No 443**)
6	23A-30B	Saptatikā (**Cat. No. 460**).

— **Or. 15633/156**. Contains 6 texts. Collection of 6 Karmagranthas. Paper. OFN: 1-26; MEF: 1-26. 26 x 12 cm.; 20,2 x 9,5 cm. 10 lines.

1	1B-6B	Karmavipāka (**Cat. No. 382**)
2	6B-9A	Karmastava (**Cat. No. 398**)
3	9A-11B	Bandhasvāmitva (**Cat. No. 412**)
4	11B-18B	Ṣaḍaśītikā (**Cat. No. 427**)
5	18B-26B	Śataka (**Cat. No. 444**)
6	26B	Saptatikā (vss. 1-2 only) (**Cat. No. 462**).

Eight texts

— **I.O. San. 3532**. Contains 8 texts. Kannada script. Palm-leaf. OFN: 1-143. 23,5 x 4,5 cm. 5 lines. The leaves are numbered on the verso. The wooden boards are ornamented with a coloured floral design. Very fragile. Ink often very pale. Pieces of ms. missing. About 1625-26 CE (I.O. Cat.).

1	1A-95A	[Collection of Jain hymns] (**Cat. No. 1268**)
2	95A-106	Tattvārtha-sūtra (**Cat. No. 1205**)
3	106-119	Svayambhū-stotra (**Cat. No. 1250**)
4	119-127	Aṣṭasahasranāma-stotra (**Cat. No. 1253**)
5	128-132B	Vṛṣabha-gadya (**Cat. No. 1255**)

6	132B-135B	Ekībhāva-stotra (**Cat. No. 1257**)
7	135B-139B	Viṣāpahara-stotra (**Cat. No. 1259**)
8	140-143	Bhūpāla-pancaviṁśati (**Cat. No. 1261**).

— **Or. 2122, MS. D**. Contains 8 texts, described together. See **Cat. No. 253** for description.

1	1B-4A	Samyaktva-vidhi
2	4A-6A	Saṁgha-kṣāmaṇaka
3	6A	Saraṇa-gamaṇa & cattāri mangala
4	6A	iha bhaviyaṁ anna bhaviyaṁ (5 vss.)
5	6AB	Sukṛtānumodanā (3 vss.)
6	6B	Anaśanoccāra-vidhi
7	6B-7A	Ancalagaccha-vidhipakṣa-ārādhanā
8	7A-8A	Kṣāmaṇā-kulaka.

Ten texts and more

(Alphabetical order of the shelfmark)

— **Add. 22,393**. A collection of Banārasīdasa's works described under the same entry. See **Cat. No. 1286**.

- **Add. 26,461**. Contains 17 texts (but see below). Written and bound like a European book. 13 x 23,5 cm.; 9,5 x 20,5 cm.; 22-24 lines. Double-ruled red margins. Verse numbers marked with red ink. Clear script. Good condition. One illustration (on MEF 93A = OFN 230A). Dated: V.S. 1733 (at the end of the last text).

Different and parallel original folio numbers are used and hint at different hands. OFN: 137-140. [141 & 142 not used] 143-197 [154-197 also as 12-55]. 198 [also as 56]. 199-229 [also as 1-31]-230-231-242 [also as 1-12]-243-248. [2]58-263. Four main texts were surely copied for Sā Hīracandra, perhaps by different scribes, only one of them has given his name. Therefore we use the modern European folio numbering: *1-*117.

Only five texts have been dealt with in Blumhardt (BM) 56.I-II-III-IV-V (pp. 34-36).

TEXT	MEF	Brief Title
1	*1A-B	Ādinātha-abhiṣeka (Ap.) by Ratnākara, vss. 2-11 (**Cat. No. 941**)
2	*1B-2A	Mahāvīra-kalaśa (**Cat. No. 1001**)
3	*2B-5B20	Ādiśvara-stavana (Guj.) by Lāvaṇyasamaya (**Cat. No. 950**)
	*6A blank	
4	*6B-61A I	Navatattva-vicāra-caupaī (**Cat. No. 576**)
	*61B blank	
5	*62A-93A II	Sāmudrika-śāstra with Guj. comm. (**Cat. No. 1416**)
	*93B blank	
6	*94A-106A12 III	Giranāra-tīrthoddhāra-mahimā (Guj) by Nayasundara (**Cat. No. 1071**)
7	*106A13-16	[sāraṁ sāraṁgalocanā], floating Skt. verse (**Cat. No. 1305**)
8	*106B-109A13 IV	Śaṁkheśvara-Pārśvanātha-stavana (Guj.) by Haṁsabhavana (**Cat. No. 1083**)
9	*109B1-111A4 V	[hamāṁ caḍī] by Vardhamāna paṇḍita (**Cat. No. 956**)
	*111B	blank
10	*112A-113B18	Jīrāulā-Pārśvanātha-stavana (Guj.) by Lāvaṇyasamaya (**Cat. No. 1089**)
11	*113B19-114B14	[Kusumānjali] by Bhāna (**Cat. No. 1151**)
12	*114B14-115B4	Ādinātha-abhiṣeka (Ap.) by muni Ratnākara (**Cat.No. 940**)
13	*115B5-13	Ṛṣabhanātha-vivāha (Guj.) (**Cat. No. 946**)

14	*115B13-117B1	Mahāvīra-kalaśa (**Cat. No. 1002**)
15	*117A10-117B1	Lūṇa-pāṇi-vidhi (Pkt.) (**Cat. No. 1152**)
16	*117B1-9	Ārātrika (Ap.)
17	*117B9-17	Snātra-vidhi (Pkt.)

Texts 15 to 17 have been described in the same entry (**Cat. No. 1152**) since they form a group of mnemonic verses which normally follow each other in the actual performance of *pūjā*.

— **Harley 415**. Contains 25 texts. Bound in the European way. Paper. OFN: 3-41; MEF: 1-39. 21 x 13,5 cm.; 18 x 11,5 cm. 15 lines. Central lozenge with one red disk on each side. Triple-ruled red margins. Red used for daṇḍas and colophons. Clear dark script, throughout the same. Good condition. Dated: V.S. 1673, Śāka 1540 (see **Cat. No. 750** for the Scribal Remark). 'HARL. 415 Or. 41 A f.'. Stamp: 'Museum Britannicum'. Probably the oldest Jain manuscript to have entered a non Indian library, see Introduction.

Collection of Guj. Jain hymns, songs of various sorts.

1	3A	Tīrthamālā-stavana, frag. (**Cat. No. 1076**)
2	3AB	Pārśvanātha-vinatī (**Cat. No. 994**)
3	3B-4B	Śāntinātha-stavana (**Cat. No. 963**)
4	4B-5B	Ādinātha-Śatrunjaya-maṇḍana-stavana (**Cat. No. 1080**)
5	5B-6B	Śāntinātha-vinatī (**Cat. No. 964**)
6	6B-7B	Cauvīsa-tīrthaṁkara-vinatī (**Cat. No. 927**)
7	7B-8A	Jīrāula-Pārśvanātha-vinatī
8	8A	Sīmandharasvāmi-stavana (**Cat. No. 1033**)
9	8A-9A	Śāntinātha-vinatī (**Cat. No. 967**)
10	9A-10B	Vaṭapadra-maṇḍana-śrīCintāmaṇi-Pārśvanātha-vinatī (**Cat. No. 1087**)
11	10B-11A	Śatruṁjaya-maṇḍana-śrī-Ādinātha-vinatī (**Cat. No. 1081**)
12	11A-12A	Aṣṭāpada-stavana (**Cat. No. 1072**)
13	12A-14B	Aṣṭāpada-ṛddhi-varṇana-stavana (**Cat. No. 1073**)
14	14B-24A	Ṛṣabhadeva-dhavalabandha-vivāhalu (**Cat. No. 943**)
15	24A-26B	Gautamasvāmi-rāsa (**Cat. No. 705**)
16	26B-27A	Sikhāmaṇi nī caupaī (**Cat. No. 601**)
17	27A	Ādinātha-gīta (**Cat. No. 947**)
18	27A-28B	Ārdrakumāra-vivāhalu (**Cat. No. 785**)
19	28B	Kamalā-gīta (**Cat. No. 1038**)
20	29A-31A	Āṣāḍhabhūti-gīta (**Cat. No. 786**)
21	31A-31B	Meghakumāra-gīta (**Cat. No. 811**)
22	31B-32A	Śivakumāra-gīta (**Cat. No. 819**)
23	32A-33A	Thāvaccāputra-gīta (**Cat. No. 797**)
24	33A-34A	Gajasukumāra-sajjhāya (**Cat. No. 791**)
25	34A-41A	Śālibhadra-caupaī (**Cat. No. 750**).

— **Or. 2137, MS. B.** Contains 14 texts. Paper. OFN: 1-40; MEF: 16-54. 26,5 x 11,5 cm.; 22 x 8 cm. 15 lines. Central middle areas are of different shapes, filled with red geometrical designs (circles, rectangles, squares, lozenges). A noticeable one on fol. 8A. Double black-ruled margin filled with red. Red disks in both margins of folios B. Careful handwriting. Good condition. No date.

1	1A-9A13	Saṁgrahaṇīratna (**Cat. No. 322**)
2	9A13-13B1	Karmavipāka (**Cat. No. 378**)
3	13B1-14B14	Karmastava (**Cat. No. 393**)
4	14B14-15B8	Karmastavabhāṣya (**Cat. No. 394**)
5	15B8-18A10	Āgamikavastuvicāra-prakaraṇa (**Cat. No. 422**)

6	18A10-19B5	Ṣaḍaśīti-laghubhāṣya (**Cat. No. 423**)
7	19B5-20B15	Bandhasvāmitva (**Cat. No. 408**)
8	20B15-23B4	Śataka (**Cat. No. 437**)
9	23B4-24A11	Śatakabhāṣya (**Cat. No. 438**)
10	24A11-29B4	Sārdhaśataka-prakaraṇa (**Cat. No. 439**)
11	29B5-30A8	Sārdhaśataka-bhāṣya (**Cat. No. 440**)
12	30A8-32B2	Saptatikā (**Cat. No. 457**)
13	32B2-34B13	Sattarīsāra (**Cat. No. 466**)
14	34B13-40A3	Sattarībhāṣya (some folios are misbound, but the text is continuous) (**Cat. No. 455**).

A remarkable collection. Except for the first text, which is a cosmological work, all works are Karmagranthas (old or new). Another ms. with a very similar arrangement is represented by the L.D. Institute of Indology (Ahmedabad) ms. shelfmark No. 1394 *Karmagrantha tathā Karmagrantha bhāṣyāṇi*, 26 fols., dated V.S. 1530 (which was consulted in March 2005). Since the individual entries are scattered over the L.D. Catalogues, the description of this ms. in its sequential state is given below:

1	1A-4A12	Karmavipāka-prakaraṇa (L.D. Ser. No. 3177)
2	4A12-5B2	Karmastava (L.D. Ser. No. 3179)
3	5B2-6A8	Karmastava-bhāṣya (L.D. Ser. No. 3181)
4	6A-8A14	Āgamikavastuvicāra-prakaraṇa (L.D. Ser. No. 3194)
5	8A15-9A10	Ṣaḍaśīti-bhāṣya (L.D. Ser. No. 3195)
6	9A10-13B7	Sārdhaśatakanāma-prakaraṇa (L.D. Ser. No. 7586)
7	13B8-14A10	Sārdhaśataka-bhāṣya (L.D. Ser. No. 7587)
8	14A10-15B1	Bandhasvāmitva-prakaraṇa (L.D. Ser. No. 3186)
9	15B1-17B12	Śataka-prakaraṇa (L.D. Ser. No. 3202)
10	up to 18A15	Śataka-bhāṣya (L.D. Ser. No. 3203)
11	up to 20A15	Saptatikā (L.D. Ser. No. 3212)
12	20B1-22B1	Sattarīsāra (L.D. Ser. No. 3243)
13	22B1-26B	Sattari-bhāṣya (L.D. Ser. No. 3213).

— **Or. 3347, MS. C** like an anthology contains 17 texts. Yellowish paper. OFN: 1-79; MEF: 351-432. 25,5 x 10,5 cm.; 20,7 x 8 cm. 9 lines. Large clear script. No date.

1	1A-6A3	Karma-vipāka (**Cat. No. 384**)
2	6A4-14A9	Vivekamanjarī by Āsaḍa (**Cat. No. 593**)
3	14A9-20B3	Sambodha-saptatikā by Jayaśekhara (**Cat. No. 589**)
4	20B3-22B3	Praśnottara-ratna-mālikā by Vimala (**Cat. No. 1292**)
5	22B4-29A3	Indriyaparājaya-śataka (**Cat. No. 584**)
6	29A4-42B6	Ādinātha-deśanoddhāra (**Cat. No. 558**)
7	42B6-43B4	Vairāgya-sandhi (**Cat. No. 582**)
8	43B5-45B1	Upadeśa-sandhi by Hemasāra (**Cat. No. 532**)
9	45B1-47A1	Hemavimalasūri-stuti (**Cat. No. 1048**)
10	47A2-47B8	Upaśamarasa-kulaka (**Cat. No. 627**)
11	47B8-52A9	Catuḥśaraṇa-prakīrṇaka (**Cat. No. 214**)
12	52A9-57B3	Paryantārādhanā (**Cat. No. 222**)
13	57B3-62A3	Kesī-Gotama-sandhi (**Cat. No. 191**)
14	62A3-64A3	Upadeśaratnakośa (**Cat. No. 531**)
15	64A3-67B2	Śīla-sandhi by a pupil of Jayaśekhara (**Cat. No. 619**)
16	67B2-75B8	Śīlopadeśamālā by Jinavallabha (**Cat. No. 533**)
17	75B9-79A9	Saṁvigna-Sāmācārī-kulaka (**Cat. No. 298**)

Collection of didactic texts of various lengths, mostly short, in Prakrit and Apabhraṁśa.

— **Or. 5192, MS. A.** Contains 15 texts. Paper. OFN: 1-79; MEF: 1-79. 25,5 x 8,4 cm.; 20,4 x 5,8 cm. 12 lines. Tripāṭha. Double-ruled black margins. Orange pigment used but not throughout. Punctuation marked by wider spaces. Cursive round script. Good condition. Date: A and B are two different mss., with a different pagination. Both are separated by a yellowish paper of European origin. But both look quite alike and use a similar script. The same date, V.S. 1916 (see **Cat. No. 251**), is given at the end of A (Texts 1, 9, 13, 14) and B.

1	1B-16B	Bhaktāmara-stotra (**Cat. No. 880**)
2	17A-21A	Laghuśānti-stava (**Cat. No. 867**)
3	22A-32B	Ajita-Śānti-stava (**Cat. No. 864**)
4	32B-37B	Ullāsika-stava (**Cat. No. 875**)
5	38A-41A	Bhayahara-stavana (**Cat. No. 894**)
6	41B-44B	Taṁ-jayau-stotra (**Cat. No. 895**)
7	45A-49A	Maya-rahiyaṁ-stotra (**Cat. No. 896**)
8	49A-51A	Siggham-avaharau-stotra (**Cat. No. 897**)
9	51A-51B	Upasargahara-stotra (**Cat. No. 899**)
10	52A-54A	Navagraha-stotra (**Cat. No. 921**)
11	55A-62A	Sarvajina-stotra (**Cat. No. 905**)
12	62B	Jina-stuti (**Cat. No. 901**)
13	63A-66A (66B blank)	Tijaya-pahutta-stotra (**Cat. No. 902**)
14	67A-73B	Jaya-tihuyaṇa-stotra (**Cat. No. 904**)

(In the upper left corner 'Jayati° ṭī' and a separate pagination OFN 1-7).

15	74A-79A	Bṛhacchānti-stavana (**Cat. No. 870**).

(In the upper left corner 'Bṛhacchāṁtīṭi°' and a separate pagination OFN 1-6).

— **Or. 13221.** Small book (8 x 12 cm.) in a European format, the pages of which are thus written vertically. Page numbering in the right-hand corner on sides B. On the binding: 'B.L. Jain Texts Skt./Hindi'. The paper is either white-yellow or brown. White or silver ink used at times.

Starts with three pages which are not originally numbered (MEF: 1-3) and contain a kind of table of rāgas to be used for the singing of some of the texts which come later. Then contains 12 texts. Total number of pages: OFN: 1-364; MEF: 1-361.

1	1A-6B	Jinasahasranāma (**Cat. No. 1254**)
2	6B-29A	Yugādideva-aṣṭottara-sahasranāma-stotra (**Cat. No. 1252**)
3	29A-56B	Tattvārthasūtra (**Cat. No. 1204**)
4	56B-67A	Bhaktāmarastotra (**Cat. No. 1262**)
5	67A-77A	Kalyāṇamandirastotra (**Cat. No. 1263**)
6	77A-83B	Ekībhāvastotra (**Cat. No. 1256**)
7	84A-91A	Viṣāpahārastotra (**Cat. No. 1258**)
8	91A-98A	Bhūpāla-pācīsī (**Cat. No. 1260**)
9	98A-119A	Tīsa covīsī jina nāma (**Cat. No. 1266**)
10	119A-162A	Doharā by Suprabhācārya with ṭīkā (**Cat. No. 1231**)
11	162B-353B	Rāgamālā by Harṣakīrti (**Cat. No. 1289**)
12	353B-364A	Pancaparameṣṭhi-stuti by Vinodilāl (**Cat. No. 1265**).

Hence this ms. is a collection of religious texts which are of current use. In view of the specifically Digambara character of some of them (Nos. 10-11), it can be said that it was more probably meant for Jains belonging to Digambara circles.

— **Or. 13642.** Book form. Bound. Contains 11 texts. Much longer than wider. Triple-ruled dark pink margins on the four sides. External side of this colour too.

1	1-21B	1-21	Gītagovinda (not described)
2	22A-25A6	22-25	Goḍī-Pārśvanātha-stavana (**Cat. No. 1086**)
3	25A6-25B13	25	Kunthu-stavana (**Cat. No. 1020**)
4	25B13-25B22	25	Tantrākhyāla (**Cat. No. 1161**)
5	26A1-34B25	26-34	Avantisukumāla (**Cat. No. 784**)
6	35A1-35B9	35	Kunthu-stavana (**Cat. No. 1020**)
7	35B9-36A1	35	Pārśvajina-stavana (**Cat. No. 989**)
8	36A1-37B	36-37	[Bharata-Bāhubali-sajjhāya] (**Cat. No. 804**)
9	38A1-20	38	Pārśvajina-stavana (**Cat. No. 989**)
10	(38)A20-(38)B6	38	Navakāra-s. (**Cat. No. 267**)
11	1A1-2Aend	39-40	Rājācanda no rāsa (**Cat. No. 794**)

No. 11 is numbered separately. The rest of the book is empty.

— **Or. 14064, MS. B.** Contains 25 texts: a collection of Gujarati *stavans* and *sajjhāyas*. Bound like a small notebook. 10,2 x 11,5 cm.; 10 x 10 cm. 13 lines. Red used for figures and titles. Various handwritings are used, cursive script. Good condition. 22 pages, but there are problems: MEF 1 = OFN 3; OFN 9 is missing, so that there is a gap; MEF 15 is probably bound wrongly; MEF 21 and 22 are probably to be inverted. In two cases, the texts do not continue on the next page, but on its verso. But this misbinding is perhaps original, for the ms. is a *guṭakā* with small margins. OFN written in the lower right corner of B sides and/or in the upper left corner of B sides, but not written after OFN 13. Sometimes no colophon in between the different texts. Hence limits are difficult to see.

No.	OFN/MEF	Title
1	2A/2A	Ṛṣabhadeva-laghu-stavana (no entry in our Catalogue)
2	2A-3B/2A-1B	Jambūsvāmi-sajjhāya (**Cat. No. 719**)
3	3B-4A/1B-3A	Araṇikamuni-sajjhāya (**Cat. No. 783**)
4	4B/3B	Simandhara-stavana (Jinarāja) (**Cat. No. 1034**)
5	5A-6A/4A-5A	Sālibhadra-sajjhāya (**Cat. No. 752**)
6	6B-8B/5B-7B	Āvyaprabodha-sajjhāya (**Cat. No. 600**)
7	8B-10A/7B-8A	*Unidentified* (see below; no entry in the present cat.).
8	10A-10B/8A-8B	Ṛṣabha-stuti (Mayācanda) (**Cat. No. 938**)
9	10B-11A/8B-9A	Abhinandanajina-stavan (Mayācanda) (**Cat. No. 1016**)
10	11A-13B/9A-11B	Mahāvīra-sajjhāya (**Cat. No. 1006**)
11	MEF 12A-14A	Neminātha-bāramāsa (Tilakaśekhara) (**Cat. No. 977**)
12	14A-14B+15B	Nemaji-sajjhāya (?) (Hīramuni) (**Cat. No. 974**)
13	15A1-8	Ṛsabha-sajjhāya (**Cat. No. 939**)
14	15A9-16	*Unidentified* (see below; no entry in the present cat.).
15	15B11-17	*Unidentifed* (see below; no entry in the present cat.).
16	16A1-9	Mantra (see below; no entry in the present cat.).
17	16A10-16B11	Sāntinātha-stavana (**Cat. No. 966**)
18	16B12-17B7	Manakamuni-sajjhāya (**Cat. No. 809**)
19	17B8-19B5	Nemi-jina-stavana (**Cat. No. 979**)
20	19B6-17	Nemijinavara-stavana (**Cat. No. 980**)
21	20A1-14	Rājimati-sajjhāya by Nārāyaṇa (**Cat. No. 834**)
22	21A1-14	Sambhavajina-stavana (**Cat. No. 1014**)
23	21A15-21B19	Nemi-Rājimati-sajjhāya (**Cat. No. 975**)
24	20A15-20B17 + 22A1-3	Pārśvajina-stavana (**Cat. No. 993**)

25 22A4-22B16 Mana-bhamara-sajjhāya (**Cat. No. 499**)

- Text 7 (OFN 8B4-10A6; 9 is missing): Unidentified

(8B4) *vakaṭa pantha dura āgaliṁ* || *vīsamo che re ghāṭa* || *āpaṇutī ho ko nahī* || *je deṣā lere vāṭa 1*, etc. *praṇī prayāṇo āvīu ra* || *nagaṇe vāra kuvāra* || *bhahya bharaṇa jogaṇī* || *śani sāha mokāla 4 māra///* (10A1) *jīva duhi lomā nava avatāra* || *ha* ||*2 dharma na cukīyai re* ||*2*||, etc. *ruḍī dayā kṣamā taṇo parasāda* ||*2 avicila sukha pāmase re* ||*6*||.

- Text 14 (15A9-16): Unidentified

pravacana vacana sumaṇā re, je sa bhalāvesāra re
catu . nā deta jugata karī bujhave lāla, sevo śrī 1 aṇagarā. pura nara 1
sādhu-sangaṭha kījīeṁ re lāla, etc. *jāya re |2| ca sādhu-saṁgata nata kījīya///*

- Text 15 (15B11-17): Unidentified. Very cursive and untidy script.

kālāeṁ kamala kama, etc. ... *vāṇī* 1 ///

- Text 16 (16A1-9) Mantra: *śrīSāradāya nama* | *praṇamī deva Ambāi* | *pancāyaṇa gāma* | *vīrasarva sūrāsurai ... oṁ hrīṁ śrīsarvâriṣṭa-praṇāśāya ... sarva-labdhi ... śrīGotamāya namo namo 1 iti* |

— **Or. 15633/5.** Contains 11 texts. Paper. OFN: 1-10; MEF: 31a-31j. 22,8 x 12 cm.; 17 x 9 cm. 15 lines. Triple-ruled red margins. Folio numbers with ornamentation. No punctuation used. Orange pigment over numbers. Good condition. No date.

1	1B-3B	Pārśvanātha-covīsa-daṇḍaka (**Cat. No. 988**)
2	3B-4A	Ātma nī sajjhāya (**Cat. No. 510**)
3	4A-4B	Ātma nī sajjhāya (**Cat. No. 511**)
4	4B-5A	Caitrī nī thoya (**Cat. No. 1131**)
5	5A-5B	Śrāvaṇa-śukla-pancamī nī thoya (**Cat. No. 1133**)
6	5B-7A	Niścaya-vyavahāra nī sajjhāya (**Cat. No. 686**)
7	7A-8A	Jina-stavana (**Cat. No. 955**)
8	8A-8B	Pratyākhyāna-sajjhāya (**Cat. No. 284**)
9	8B-9B	Ātmā ne hita-śikṣā sajjhāya (**Cat. No. 509**)
10	9B-10A	Ṛṣabhanātha thoya (**Cat. No. 954**)
11	10A-10B	Olī nī thoa (**Cat. No. 1143**)

All the texts written in this manuscript are rather short. The presence of an individual who really aimed at preparing a consistent collection of Gujarati hymns and simple doctrinal texts for daily use can be felt from various signs: the initial phrase *atha paṁca* at the beginning of Text 5, the fact that there are two hymns by the same author, Ṛṣabhadāsa (Nos. 5 and 10), or that Cakreśvarī is addressed in more than one of them (e.g. Nos. 4 and 11). Moreover, the name Vajakuara, for whose reading the ms. has been written, appears thrice: in Texts 1, 7 and 11.

— **Or. 15633/185**. Contains 10 texts. Paper. OFN: 1-77; MEF: 1-77. 27,8 x 12 cm; 22 x ca. 9 cm. 3 lines (mūla), ca. 9 (comm.). Double-ruled red margins. Red used for daṇḍas and colophons. Good condition. Dated: V.S. 1911.

1	1B	Navakāra-mantra (**Cat. No. 262**)
2	1B-3A	Upasargahara-stotra (**Cat. No. 900**)
3	3A-6A	Śānti-stavana (**Cat. No. 874**)
4	6A-9A	Tijayapahutta-stotra (**Cat. No. 903**)
5	9A-15B	Bhayahara-stotra (**Cat. No. 893**)
6	15B-31B	Ajita-Śānti-stava (**Cat. No. 865**)
7	31B-47B	Bhaktāmara-stotra (**Cat. No. 885**)

8	47B-52B	Laghu-Śānti-stava (**Cat. No. 868**)
9	52B-61A	Bṛhacchānti-stotra (**Cat. No. 871**)
10	61A-77A	Kalyāṇamandira-stotra (**Cat. No. 889**)

— **Or. 16133/2.** Contains 18 texts. Paper. OFN: 12-19. 29 x 11,5 cm.; 23 x 10 cm. 16 lines. No date.

1	12A1-6	Gajasukumāla-caritra (**Cat. No. 46**)
2	12A6-13A7	[Unidentified] (**Cat. No. 514**)
3	13A7-B13	Bāra-bhāvanā-sajjhāya (**Cat. No. 611**)
4	14A1-B4	Nava vāḍī-sajjhāya by Hīrānanda (**Cat. No. 621**)
5	14B4-15A10	Ādijina-stavana by Sahajasundara (**Cat. No. 953**)
6	15A10-15B7	Tamāṣū-sijjhāi (**Cat. No. 647**)
7	15B8-16A13	[Unidentified] (**Cat. No. 624**)
8	16A13-B9	Sīla-gīta (**Cat. No. 623**)
9	16B10-17A3	Sīla-gīta by Ajitadevasūri (**Cat. No. 622**)
10	17A3-B2	Nema-Rājimatī-sajjhāya (**Cat. No. 976**)
11	17B2-8	[Unidentified] by Brahma (**Cat. No. 300**)
12	17B8-18A1	[Unidentified] (**Cat. No. 606**)
13	18A1-11	[Unidentified] (**Cat. No. 291**)
14	18A11-B3	[Unidentified] (**Cat. No. 937**)
15	18A4-B6	Vairāgya-gīta by Māladeva (**Cat. No. 583**)
16	18B8-19A8	Bhramara-gīta by Māladeva (**Cat. No. 499** [a])
17	19A8-11	Stavana (**Cat. No. 959**)
18	19A11-B	Mahāvīra-stavana, incomplete (**Cat. No. 1009**).

B. Collective manuscripts or codices

— **I.O. San. 3400**. Book form (*guṭakā*), 334 pages. An intricate case. All pages have the same size but the margins, the script and the decoration are not identical throughout. Hence in the following description we use the term 'Hand so and so'. One hand may have written more than one text. The original folio numbers are not always written. The book is shared between full texts neatly written and fragments written in very cursive script and not occupying the whole pages, looking more like personal notes than real texts meant for others' reading. The fact that the original folio numbering is continuous (e.g. below 1-173) does not necessarily mean that all the texts coming under this numbering have been written by the same hand. — The sigla (a, aa, etc.) are those given in Blumhardt.

HAND A. Double-ruled red margins. Red disks in the centre and the margins. Red used for daṇḍas. Pigment over numbers. Clear script. MEF: 1-190. Dated: V.S. 1603.

	OFN/MEF	
a	2-10/1-9	Pratikramaṇa-sūtra (Contains 3 texts: 1. Āvaśyaka; 2. Nāgadrahasvāmī-vinatī; 3. Śītalanātha-deva-vinatī, **Cat. No. 244, 1092, 1018**)
aa	10-19/10-19	Śrīsāra-sīkhāmaṇa-rāsa (**Cat. No. 602**)
b	1-97/20-116	Viveka-vilāsa (**Cat. No. 682**)
c	1-74/117-190	Pancākhyāna with Guj. comm. (**Cat. No. 849**)

HAND B. Triple- or double-ruled black margins. Lozenge-shaped blank space in the centre. MEF: 191-290.

ca	75-96/191-213	Gajasiṁha-kumāra-rāja-caritra (incompl.) (**Cat. No. 789**)
cb	97-117/214-234	Mangalakalaśa-rāsa (**Cat. No. 805**)
cc	118-131/235-248B	Rātrībhojana-caupaī (**Cat. No. 814**)
cd	131-142/248-259	Vidyāvilāsa-rāsa (**Cat. No. 817**)

ce 142-163/259-280 Mṛgāṅkalekhā-satī-caupaī (**Cat. No. 830**)
cf 163-173/280-290 Jambūsvāmī-caupaī (**Cat. No. 718**)

HAND C. Cursive script. MEF: 291A-293A.

cg *śrīsarvajñāya namaḥ*...Disconnected notes (see Blumhardt No. 135 p. 125). Two dates (V.S. 1628 and V.S. 1645) are mentioned along with the name of Hīravijayasūri and a few other monks. (No entry in the present catalogue).

HAND D. Cursive script (different than Hand C). MEF: 293B-294A.

d Yogaśāstra, frag. (**Cat. No. 551**)

HAND E. Cursive script. MEF: 294B-295A. See Blumhardt No. 133 (294B-305A).

da Aticāras of the layman's vows (**Cat. No. 280**)

HAND F. MEF: 296A-298A.

HAND G. MEF: 298A-300A + 302A-B. Cursive script.

Stories of Ānanda and two other laymen adapted from the *Uvāsagadasāo* (see **Cat. No. 280**).

HAND H. MEF: 300B-301B.

HAND I. MEF: 303A (303B-304A are blank).

HAND J. MEF: 304B. Astrological notes. *||§O|| śrīHīravījaasūrī-gurubhyo namaḥ | Sarasatī matī nīramala dīu jaga-jīvana me re ... ||1|| ... bāra rāsa nā nāma ... gṛha no vicāra.* (No entry in the present catalogue).

HAND K. MEF: 305A. Two tables of nakṣatras (no entry in the present catalogue).

HAND L. Double-ruled black margins. Orange pigment used over numbers. MEF: 305B-311A.

db 305B-306B Vadodarā Pārśva-Jina-stuti (**Cat. No. 1088**)
e 306A-307A2 Astrological poem in 17 vss. (no entry in the present catalogue).
ea 307A3-13 Bāra-rāsa nuṁ phala (Guj.) (**Cat. No. 1417**)
eb 307A-308A Bimba-pratiṣṭhā-vidhi (**Cat. No. 1156**)
ec 308A9- Buddhirāsa (**Cat. No. 599**)
ed Ṛsabhadeva-namaskāra (**Cat. No. 952**)

HAND M. MEF: 311B-321B

f 311B-321B Ṛsimandala-stotra (**Cat. No. 913**)

HAND N. MEF: 322A.

g Sanskrit medical stanza (not included in the present catalogue).

HAND O. MEF: 322B-323A. Astrological notes. *|§O| sūrya bhānu gaṇaye cāndraṁ saptamī mārge mā haret ... mṛgā-svāti-puṣya-nakṣatre punar vasu ca hastānurādhā ... svāti sārṇa viśākhā ca nilanga mana varjayet ||1||*

HAND P. Cursive script. No daṇḍas.

ga Jīvadayā (frag.) (**Cat. No. 492**)

HAND Q. MEF: 324A-B.

gb Gautamasvāmī (Blumhardt No. 52 and **Cat. No. 492**).

HAND R. MEF: 325A-B.

gc Vimśatisthānaka (**Cat. No. 1148**)

HAND A'. OFN: 1-2; MEF: 326A-327A.

gd Jinastuti (incomplete) (**Cat. No. 923**)

HAND S. MEF: 327B-328A.

ge Akbar's coin (no entry in the present catalogue).

HAND T. MEF: 328B.

gf Fragments (see Blumhardt No. 75).

HAND U. MEF: 329A (see Blumhardt No. 75).

HAND V. MEF: 329B-330A.

h Catuḥṣaṣthī-yoginī (**Cat. No. 1162**)

i Mantra (**Cat. No. 1160**)

HAND W. MEF: 330B-334B. Cursive script.

Ayurvedic recipes and lists of ingredients (see Blumhardt No. 136 p. 126; no entry in the present catalogue).

— **Or. 15633/102**. Contains 3 texts, all by different hands. Paper. OFN: 1; MEF: 60. 25-25,6 x 11,6-11,8 cm; 22,2 x 9 cm. 9 lines (A), 2 + 7 lines (B).

1 1A1-9 [āja mhārā prabhujī re] by Jñānavimala (**Cat. No. 926**)

2 1A Floating verse (**Cat. No. 1306**)

3 1A [huṁ to mohyo re jina] by Nityalābha (**Cat. No. 1015**).

— **Or. 15633/139**. Contains 2 texts, by different hands. Paper. OFN: 1-3.4; MEF: 32-35; 25 x 12 cm; 20,5 x 9,5 cm. 12 lines. No marginal lines drawn. Good condition. No date.

1 1A-4A Sādhu-aticāra (**Cat. No. 277**)

2 4A8-4B2 Aṣṭamī-sajjhāya (**Cat. No. 1129**).

C. Main texts with supplements

Sometimes the supplement(s) are written in a very careless manner and are extremely difficult to read and identify. Such a case (not included in the present list) is provided by I.O. San. 3383 (**Cat. No. 816**): the main text is the *Vidyāvilāsa-kathā*. After the Scribal Remark come three additions from three different hands: 1) about Sarasvatī, 2) a story about a foolish man (*ajānamūḍha-kathā*), 3) the 12 vows to be taken by the Jain layman.

— **I.O. San. 2341 (D)**. See **Cat. No. 325** and **Cat. No. 1119** [a] for description.

Main text	1A-11A	Saṁgrahaṇiratna
Supplement	11B	Maunaikādaśī-stuti.

— **I.O. San. 3287 (B)**. See **Cat. No. 239** for description.

Main text	1B-4A	Śramaṇasūtra
Supplement	4A	Hymn (unidentifiable).

— **I.O. San. 3362**. See **Cat. No. 729** for description.

Main text	1B-40A	Mahīpāla-caritra by Vīradevagaṇi (**Cat. No. 729**)
Supplement 1	40B1-9	Śāntinātha-stavana by Āc. Manahara (**Cat. No. 962**)
Supplement 2	40B10-16	Neminātha-stavana (**Cat. No. 984**).

— **I.O. San. 3391**. See **Cat. No. 215** and **Cat. No. 987** for description.

Main text	1B-8A	Catuḥśaraṇa-prakīrṇaka
Supplement	8A-8B	Hymn to Pārśvanātha.

— **Or. 2106, MS. C**. See **Cat. No. 391** and **Cat. No. 971** [a] for description.

Main text	1A-8B	Karmavipāka
Supplement	8B	[Śānti sadā sukhadāyī], by another hand in order to finish the page.

— **Or. 2120, MS. E**. See **Cat. No. 654** and **Cat. No. 81** for description.

Main text	1B-9A	Śrāvakavidhi-prakaraṇa *or* Dharma-tattva-vicāra-huṇḍī
Supplement	9A	Prajñāpanā, vs. 131, Malayagiri's vṛtti, frag. (post-colophon supplement)

— **Or. 2122, MS. E**. See **Cat. No. 224** and **Cat. No. 687** for description.

Main text	1B-7A	Paryantārādhanā with Guj. comm.
Supplement	7B	[Darśana-bheda].

— **Or. 5171**. See **Cat. No. 922** and **Cat. No. 972** for description.

Main text	1B-15A	Caturviṁśati-Jina-stava by Jinaprabhasūri with Kanakakuśala's comm.
Supplement	15A-15B	[Hymn to Neminātha].

— **Or. 13639**. See **Cat. No. 1390** and **Cat. No. 1418** for description.

Main text	1B-17A	Līlāvatī by Lālacandagaṇi
Supplement	17B-18	[Janma-kuṇḍalī].

— **Or. 13697, MS. B**. See **Cat. No. 872** and **Cat. No. 891** for description.

Main text	1A-1B4	Sāntikara-stotra
Supplement	1B6-	Bhayahara-stotra, beg.

— **Or. 15633/30**. See **Cat. No. 478** for description.

Main text	1B-13A	Jambū-pṛcchā *or* Karma-phala
Supplement	13A	[pāpi ne pratibodhataṁ] post-colophon verse.

— **Or. 15633/132**. See **Cat. No 971** for description.

Main text	1A-2A	Śāntinātha-snātra by Jñānavimala
Supplement	2A	[sajana phalajo...] post-colophon verses.

Appendices

1. Selected Scribal Remarks

Two ordinary instances

A) Ms. of the *Ekaviṁśasthāna-prakaraṇa* by Siddhasena with Guj. commentary. Shelfmark: I.O. San. 3401 - **Cat. No. 643.**

sakala-bhaṭṭāraka-purandara-sundara-Tapāgacchâdhirāja-bhaṭṭāraka-śrīVijayasenasūri-śiṣya-mukhya-mahôpādhyāya-śrīKīrttivijayagaṇi-śiṣya paṁ° Jinavijayagaṇinā likhataṁ I saṁvat 1722 varṣe Aśvina-māse kṛṣṇa-pakṣe ṣaṣṭyāṁ budhe I śrīĀgarā-nagare

(*Second hand, between the lines*:) e Ikavīsaṭhāṇa-prakaraṇa-sampūrṇa thayauṁ I sakala- śrāvikā-mukhya-śrāvikā śrīKamalājī-paṭhanârtham I Āgarā-nagara-madhye II

Translation
Copied by Pandit Jinavijayagaṇi, pupil of the great preceptor Kīrtivijayagaṇi, foremost among the disciples of Vijayasenasūri, pontiff leader of the Tapāgaccha, the best and foremost among all pontiffs. In the year (V.S.) 1722, in the month of Āśvina, on the sixth day of the dark fortnight, on Wednesday, in the city of Agra. (*Second hand*) The treatise Ikavīṣaṭhāṇa is now complete. For the reading of Kamalā, a laywoman who is the foremost among all laywomen. In the city of Agra.

B) Ms. of the *Antakṛddaśāḥ*. Shelfmark: I.O. San. 3358 - **Cat. No. 42.**

saṁvat 1674 varṣe Āsauṁja śudi pancamī bāru Bṛhaspatavāru śubha-dine likhattaṁ Malūkacada ṛṣi Śrīmāla ātmā-arthe śubhaṁ bhavāt kalyāṇam astu I likhaka bāṁcijayoṁ Ambakāpura-madhye caturmāsā kīdhā tadi likhī prati II

Translation
In the year V.S. 1674, in (the month of) Āśvina, in the bright fortnight, on the fifth day, on Thursday, on an auspicious day, copied by Malūkaca(n)da ṛṣi from the Śrīmālī (caste) for himself. May there be auspiciousness. May there be good fortune to the scribe and to the reader. This manuscript was copied in Ambakāpura when (he) was spending the rainy season.

Comments
The reference to the place of stay during the rainy season strongly suggests that Mālukacandaṛṣi was a monk. The title *ṛṣi* indicates that he could have been a Sthānakvāsin (or a member of the Lonkāgaccha), but he could not be identified more precisely.

*A Kalpasūtra manuscript in silver letters, Nālhā, a lay follower of Jinabhadrasūri of the Kharataragaccha : verse-*praśasti *(V.S. 1484 = 1427 CE)*

Ms. of the *Kalpasūtra* followed by the *Kālakācārya-kathā*. Shelfmark: I.O. San. 3177 (originally belonging to H. Jacobi) - **Cat. Nos. 96 and 708.**

See I.O. Cat. II No. 7481 p. 1261 for some quotations and indications about the contents. The full text is worth presenting, despite several obscure points in reading and understanding for the following reasons. There are problems in the verse numbering. The ink has become so pale at places that several akṣaras are hardly legible. Nalini Balbir, who is planning a larger study of the *praśastis* and scribal remarks of *Kalpasūtra* manuscripts in the wider context of patronage, interaction between monks and laymen, and modes of prestige among important Jain families, will revert to this manuscript at a later stage in the hope of filling the lacunae and of correcting erroneous interpretations.

Note: for the Scribal Remark proper, with the name of the scribe and the date of copying (V.S. 1485) see **Cat. No. 708.**

150B: II§OII arhaṁ I
Ūkeśa-vaṁśe vimale viśāle gotre bhavaty Aṁgaṭikêti nāmni

śraddhālu dhuryo Dhanapāla-nāmā putras tadīyo Mahaṇādisiṁhaḥ ||1
prathamo Devasiṁhâkhyo Moṣâbhikhyo dvitīyakaḥ
Vikramo Devasiṁhaś ca catvāra iti tat-sutāḥ ||2
abhūvān Devasimhasya trayaḥ putrā guṇôjvalāḥ
Salaṣâkhyaś ca Sāmantas tṛtī(151A)yaḥ Sājaṇâbhidhaḥ ||3
bhāryā Mahigaladevī Moṣā-śrāddhasya guṇa-gaṇaika-nidheḥ
Ṭhākurasī-Suhaḍâbhikhyau Samarā iti tat-sutāḥ ||4
bhāryā Ṭhākurasiṁhasya Sāru-nāmnī guṇaikabhūḥ
putras tayoḥ Sāyarâkhyaṁ śrīdeva-guru-bhakti-bhāk ||5
Jina-bhaktiṁ guru-bhaktiṁ śruta-bhaktiṁ yo mano-'vanau dhatte
bahu-mūlya-ratna-jāta-prapūritaṁ saṁnidhānam iva ||6||
Suhaḍâkhyasya tasyâbhūt preyasy Aṁbiṇī[1] nāmikā
yā sādhu-Rāmadevasya nandanī vinayaikabhūḥ ||7
ekas tad-udbhūtir udāra-cetā Mahīpati m++tamo-mahīśāṁ
svayaṁ dvitī(151B)yaḥ param advitīyo Nālhâbhidhānaḥ kamaṇīya-kīrttiḥ ||8
karma-karma-manu-mite varṣe sādhu-mahīpatiḥ
yātrā yenânvitākārṣij Jirāpallyā mahodayā[2]
yaḥ satra-śālāṁ viṣame 'pi kāle kuṭhāra-dhārām iva tejayitvā
durbhikṣa-vṛkṣān alunād dayāluḥ śraddhālu-cūḍāmaṇitāṁ dadhānaḥ ||9
caityāni caturaśītiṁ gurūṇi guru-vatsalaḥ
ātmīya-vasu-jātena kārāyām āsa yaḥ kṛtī ||1
tatraiva yaḥ prājja-Jina-pratiṣṭā-mahotsavaṁ vismaya-kāri-rūpaṁ
acīkarad dravya-vaya-vyayena karttavyam etat sudṛśām yad āhuḥ ||10
dharmmma-sthānair bhuvaḥ kīrttyā vyomnaś candra-rucêva ca
pātālasya pratāpeṇa śṛngāro yena kalpitaḥ ||11
+i++ṁviśe (152A) tvaraṁ (?) (cai)tyāni[3] gurūṇi guru-vatsalaḥ
ātmīya-vasu-jātena kārayām āsa yaḥ kṛtī ||12
netra-ṛṣi-manu-saṁkhyāte vatsare yo nyaveśayat
Jirāpallyāṁ caitya-garbbhe Pārśvanāthaṁ Jineśvaraṁ |12[4]
akṣa-ṛṣi-manu-me varṣe <te>[5] mahīpatir nyadhāpayat
śrīJinabhadrasūrīṇāṁ ≍ ≍ ≍[6] padavī-mahaṁ ||13
athângaṇā-yogya-guṇair ameyā Mahīpate Rohiṇī nāmadheyā
saujanya-sārasyânu Nālhā-sādhoḥ priyāś catasraś caturā +vanti[7]||14
Nāmaladevī Līlādevī kila Kautigâdidevī ca
Anupamadevī turyā +uṁmāvatī+ (?) imāḥ sutāḥ ||15
Kautigade-kukṣibhavo Jinadatto nāma nandano vijayī
madhye ga(152B)rbbhâṁgīkṛta-saṁgha-padavīka iva jātaḥ ||16

---

[1] The reading and understanding *Preysasyaṁdhiṇi* of the I.O. Cat. are very unlikely. Ambiṇī as the name of the wife is supported by external evidence: see Comments below.

[2] Unnumbered verse written above the text, very close to the top of the folio, so that some mātrās indicating the vowel signs are hardly visible. The indication 'x 1' means that the verse has to be inserted in line 1 of 151B.

[3] The syllable 'cai' is added in the margin.

[4] This verse in the upper margin in golden letters with a x indicating that it should be inserted in the text in line 1.

[5] A sign indicating that this should be erased is written on the top.

[6] What remains visible in the ms. suggests something including the syllables *ya* and *na*.

[7] *bhavanti* could have been expected, but the first syllable, which is very faint, does not look like *bha*.

yataḥ

yaḥ ++āra-sphuṭa-bhāgya-bhānur a+u+u++nyāmbu-pāyī
punaḥ suptaḥ pālana ki+u+u+u-madhura-śrīman-mukhâmbhoruhaḥ
śrīŚatruṁjaya-Raivatâcala-mahātīrtheṣu saṁghânvito
yātrā-kīrttanam ādhadād akalayat saṁghâdipatyaṁ tathā ||17
Anupamade-jātaḥ punar aneka-satkarma-karaṇa-jāta-yaśāḥ
Saubhāgya-Rāmacandro nararatnaṁ Ratnapālaś ca ||18
nija-pitaram anuharantyau priya-vādinyau sa-lakṣaṇe su-bhage
Nāmaladevī-prabhave paddīpo+ punaḥ putryau ||19
kiṁcâdbhutaṁ kuśala(153A)-karmma valakṣa-rāṇa-vyāpāra-karmma kaṭhinaṁ ca
vitanvato 'sya Nālhasya puṇya-puruṣasya punaḥ
sakhayo 'bhūvann amī sakala-kārya-dhurā-dhurīṇāḥ ||20
eko dharmmo Dharmmamūrttir mmahātmā, Tolākaś câdvaita-buddhir dvitīyaḥ
Kānhâbhikhyaḥ śrīsahāyas tṛtīyaḥ pṛthvīṭhā+adasya sarvākuṭumbaṁ ||21
ityādi-sāra-parivāra-samanvitaḥ sā-lakṣmī-vilāsa-kamalaṁ vimala-svabhāvaḥ
śrīsaṁgha-gaccha-gata-kāryāṁ vidhānas tad-dhāraś ciraṁ vijayate kila Nālharājaḥ ||22

itaś ca ||

Cāndre kule śrīJinacandrasūriḥ, siddhānta-vettâbhayadeva(153B)-sūriḥ[1]
sad-vallabhaṁ[2] śrīJinavallabho 'pi, yuga-pradhāno Jinadatta-sūriḥ ||23
bhāgyôdbha(v)aḥ[3] śrīJinacandra-sūriḥ, sūrîśvaraḥ śrīJinapaty-abhikhyaḥ[4]
Jineśvaraḥ sūrir udāra-cetā,[5] Jinaprabodho 'pi tamo'panetā[6]||24
gurûttamaḥ[7] śrīJinacandra-nāmā sūrir Jinādiḥkuśalo jitâtmā[8] padmāpadaṁ[9] śrīJinapadma-sūrir, labdhi-nidhānaṁ Jinalabdhi-sūriḥ ||25
vairangikaḥ[10] śrīJinacandra-sūrir Jinodayaḥ sūrir abhūd bhūriḥ[11]
śamī kṣamī śrī[12]Jinarāja-sūrir yo daśanaś (?) cāru-caritra-ratnaṁ ||26[13]
sarvasya saṁghasya viśāla-kīrttir bhadraṁkaraḥ śrīJinabhadra-sūriḥ

---

[1] From here onwards we note the variants found in the two Jaisalmer *praśastis* in Muni Punyaviajaya's article and in A. Nahta's article (for which see below Comments). Jaisalmer Nos. 8 and 426: *saṁvigna-bhāva*; Nahta: *saṁvijña°*.

[2] For *sad-vallabhaḥ* (= Jaisalmer No. 8, Nahta, Punyavijaya; Jaisalmer No. 426: *vairangikaḥ*).

[3] Jaisalmer Nos. 8 and 426: *bhāgyâdhikaḥ*; Nahta and Punyavijaya: *bhāgyâdbhūtaḥ*.

[4] Jaisalmer Nos. 8 and 426, Nahta: *kriyā-kaṭhoro Jinapattisūriḥ*.

[5] Nahta: *udāra-vṛttaḥ*.

[6] London = Jaisalmer No. 426; Jaisalmer No. 8 and Punyavijaya: *duritâpanetā*; Nahta: *duritānnibṛttaḥ* (?).

[7] Jaisalmer Nos. 8 and 426, Nahta: *prabhāvakaḥ*; Punyavijaya: *saṁvegikaḥ*.

[8] Jaisalmer Nos. 8 and 426, Punyavijaya: *Jinādiḥ kuśalâvasānaḥ*; Nahta: *Jinādiḥ kuśalânta-śabdaḥ*, i.e., who has Jina at the beginning and Kuśala at the end (of his name).

[9] Nahta: *padmānidhiḥ*; Punyavijaya: *padmāśritaḥ*.

[10] Jaisalmer No. 8 and Nahta: *saṁvegikaḥ*; No. 426: *saiddhāntikaḥ*; Punyavijaya: *mahôpakārī*.

[11] = Jaisalmer No. 426 and Nahta; Jaisalmer No. 8: *Jinodayaḥ sūri babhūva sūriḥ*; Punyavijaya: *Jinodayaḥ sūrir udagra-bhāgyaḥ*; (*bhūriḥ* of the London ms. makes better sense than the repetition of *sūri*; it was probably intended also in the Jaisalmer ms. The difference may be due to the reading: *bha* and *sa* can be very close to each other in certain handwritings).

[12] J Punyavijaya: *praśānta-mūrtir J.*

[13] Jaisalmer Nos. 8, 426, Nahta and Punyavijaya have a different formulation for Jinarājasūri and Jinabhadrasūri.

(154A) saṁsāra-sāre Jina-śāsane 'smin nitānta-saumyaḥ sugurur vibhāti ||27|
tadīya-vaktrād upalabhya samyak śuddhôpadeśaṁ sa hi Nālha-sādhuḥ
granthān anekān api lekhayitvā Kalpâgamaṁ lekhayati sma harṣāt ||28
tataḥ śrīmajJinabhadra-sūrīṇāṁ rīṇa-rephasāṁ
śrāddhaḥ saṁkalpayām āsa kalpavit Kalpa-pustakaṁ ||29
vedâṣṭamanu-saṁkhyāte varṣe Vikramato gate | 1484 |
rūpyeṇa Kalpasiddhānta-pustakaṁ yo vyalekhayat |29[1]
sthūla-muktāphala-prāya-rūpya-varṇāvalī-yutaṁ
vyāpāryamāṇaṁ caturaiḥ pustakaṁ nandatād iti |30|
iti śrīKalpâgama-praśasti samāptā ||

Translation

1. In the Ukeśa line, pure, immense, in the family-clan named Aṁgaṭika there is (a man) named Dhanapāla, a foremost believer. His son Mahaṇasiṁha.[2]

2. First Devasiṁha, second Moṣa, Vikrama and Devasiṁha (were) his four sons.

3. Devasiṁha had three sons bright with virtues: Salaṣa, Sāmanta, and the third Sājaṇa.

4. Mahigaladevī was the wife of the layman Moṣa, a real treasure of numerous virtues. Ṭhākurasī, Suhaḍa (and) Samara were their sons.

5. Ṭhākurasiṁha's wife, named Sāru, was good qualities only. Their son Sāyara was fully devoted to gods (= Jinas) and religious teachers.

6. The one who carries devotion to the Jinas, devotion to the teachers and devotion to the scriptures in the depth of his mind is like a good storehouse, filled with jewels of great value.

7. The one named Suhaḍa had a dear wife named Ambinī, modesty only, who was the daughter of the merchant Rāmadeva.

8. One, born of them, noble-minded, Mahīpati ... second, but without a second, Nālhā by name, of desirable reputation.

9. (By building) a house for the poor, even in a difficult time, as if sharpening the edge of an axe, he cut off the trees of famine, full of compassion, becoming the best among laymen.

1. Full of affection for the religious teachers he caused eighty-four majestic temples to be built, with his own money, pious as he was.

10. There he organized important ceremonies for the installation of Jina (images), of a wondrous type, spending money. This is what should be done for (/by?) the handsome ones, as it is said.

11. Through places of dharma (= temples) he embellished the earth with his fame, the sky through a brightness as great as moonlight, and the lower regions through his ardour.

12. ... Full of affection for the religious teachers he caused to be built ... majestic temples, with his own money, pious as he was.

12. In the year counted in eyes-seers-Manus (1472) he installed the Jina Pāśvanātha in Jirāpallī in the inner sanctum.

13. In the year measured in dice (*akṣa*)-seers-Manus (1475) this king (of laymen) organized the celebration for Jinabhadrasūri's (attainment of the) rank (of *ācārya*).

[1] '31' originally written, then corrected into '29'.

[2] Text: *Mahaṇādisiṁha.* In Jain texts, the word *ādi* is commonly used as a separator without any specific meaning, especially in proper names. Several instances will be met with in our Scribal Remarks.

14. And Mahīpati had (a wife) named Rohiṇī, immeasurable in the virtues appropriate to ladies. On the side of the merchant Nālhā, the essence of goodness, were four beloved clever wives:

15. Nāmaladevī, Līlādevī and Kautigadevī, Anupamadevī the fourth ... Their children were:

16. From Kautigade's womb was born a son named Jinadatta, the victorious, as if he had already accepted the title of leader of the community while in his mother's womb.[1]

Indeed

17. ... Accompanied by the community to the important Jain sacred places of Śatrunjaya and Girnar, he guaranteed the fame of the pilgrimage and earned the title of leader of the community as well.

18. From Anupamade, on the other hand, was born Ratnapāla, a jewel of a man, and also Saubhāgya and Rāmacandra (?).[2] His reputation came from accomplishing various good deeds.

19. Taking after their father, of pleasant speech, with auspicious marks, fortunate, two daughters were born from Nāmaladevī.

20. Moreover, for the accomplishment of amazing good acts and the difficult task of business, the meritorious Nālhā also had the following companions who held the yoke of all the works.

21. One, a pious man, of great soul, Dharmamūrti, the second, Tolāka, whose intelligence was peerless, Kānha, the friend of Fortune, the third.

22. Thus accompanied by money and entourage, pure-natured, lotus for the joy of Fortune, managing the affairs of the religious group and the community, Nālhā, the king, supporting them, is long victorious.

On the other hand

23. In the Candra line, Jinacandrasūri; Abhayadevasūri, the knower of the Scriptures. Dear to the good was Jinavallabha; Jinadattasūri, foremost of the era.

24. Son of good fortune was Jinacandrasūri; the lord among the pontiffs called Jinapati. The pontiff Jineśvara was noble-minded. As for Jinaprabodha, he was a dispeller of darkness.

25. Jinacandra, the best among religious teachers; the pontiff Jinakuśala, self-subdued; abode of good fortune, Jinapadmasūri; storehouse of magical powers, Jinalabdhisūri.

26. Free from attachments was Jinacandrasūri; the pontiff Jinodaya was great. Patient, indulgent was Jinarājasūri ... jewel of pleasant conduct.

27. Of great fame to all the community, causing prosperity Jinabhadrasūri, the good teacher, extremely gentle, shines in the Jain doctrine, which is the essence of the world.

28. It is after he learnt the pure teaching from the mouth of this man that this merchant Nālhā, who had already commissioned the writing of several works, commissioned the writing of this sacred book, the *Kalpasūtra*, with joy.

29. Then the layman, who knows the rule, destined this manuscript of the *Kalpa(sūtra)* to Jinabhadrasūri who has eliminated the wicked.

29. In the year counted in Vedas-8-Manus (1484) from Vikrama, with his money he got the manuscript of the *Kalpasūtra* copied.

30. May this manuscript with silver letters resembling big pearls rejoice, being handled by intelligent people.

---

[1] Meaning: he was destined to be as generous in spending money for religious works as his grandfather, and, as a consequence, to hold a prominent position within the community.

[2] Uncertain whether these words are also proper names.

Comments

The author of the *praśasti* is not mentioned anywhere in the manuscript and is not known. The structure is clear and threefold:

A. the lay patron's family and activities (1-22),

B. the monk's insertion within the succession of pontiffs of his religious group (23-27),

C. the specific circumstance where both interacted, i.e., the present manuscript (28-30).

This is a formalized structure, which is by no means unique to our document. It can be found in several contexts, especially at the end of *Kalpasūtra* manuscripts containing illustrations and/or written in gold or silver letters (*suvarṇākṣarī, raupyākṣarī*), which were precious objects involving considerable expense. The sponsors of such manuscripts were particularly keen to give information about the identity and place of the partners, from the instigator to the donor, which led to such impressive results. The texts of two *praśastis* of this type provide conveniently accessible instances of relevance. They are reproduced in Muni Punyavijayaji's *Catalogue of Sanskrit and Prakrit Manuscripts. Jesalmer Collection* (Ahmedabad, 1972, L.D. Series 36): No. 426 pp. 178-180 (Kalpasūtra with the comm. Sandehaviṣauṣadhi, 102 fols., dated V.S. 1497, Paṁca no bhaṇḍāra) and No. 8 pp. 359-360 (palm leaf KS in golden letters, dated V.S. 1524, Tapāgacchīya Jñānabhaṇḍāra). A third, found at the end of a golden *Kalpasūtra* copied in V.S. 1517 in Patan, has also been published by Muni Punyavijaya in an independent article: 'Suvarṇākṣarī Kalpasūtra nī prati nā antamā nī vistṛta praśasti' in *Jñānāṁjali. Pūjya Muni Śrī Puṇyavijayajī Abhivādana Grantha*. Bombay, 1969, Gujarati Section No. 23, pp. 207-211. A fourth one, closing a golden *Kalpasūtra* dated V.S. 1487, is published in A. Nahta's article entitled 'Mahopādhyāya Jayasāgara' (Maṇidhārī śrīJinacandrasūri aṣṭama śatābdī smṛti grantha, ed. A. Nahta, Bh. Nahta, Delhi, 1971, pp. 84-88).

Section B amounts to a versified *paṭṭāvalī* of the Kharataragaccha, from Jinacandrasūri to Jinabhadrasūri, i.e., from No. 41 to No. 56.[1] Note that the designation 'Kharataragaccha' does not appear explicitly. The purpose of the text is to characterize briefly each of the leaders in turn. The choice of epithets seems to be largely determined by the desire to create attractive puns on the leader's name. They could not be rendered in the translation. They are found in almost identical terms in the two Jaisalmer *praśastis* pointing to a stereotyped and formalized style current among scribes or authors of such *praśastis* (see above for individual variants). Brief biodata of the pontiffs mentioned in the three documents are as follows[2]:

Jinacandrasūri, author of the *Saṁvegarangaśālā* in V.S. 1125 - Abhayadevasūri, died V.S. 1135, the commentator of the Canon - Jinavallabhasūri, *sūri* V.S. 1167; died six months later - Jinadattasūri, born V.S. 1132, *dīkṣā* V.S. 1141, *sūri-pada* V.S. 1169, died V.S. 1211 - Jinacandrasūri, born V.S. 1197, *dīkṣā* V.S. 1203, *ācārya* V.S. 1211, died V.S. 1223 - Jinapatisūri, born V.S. 1210, *pada-sthāpanā* V.S. 1223, died V.S. 1277 -Jineśvarasūri, born V.S. 1245, *dīkṣā* V.S. 1255, died V.S. 1331 - Jinaprabodhasūri, born V.S. 1285, dīkṣā V.S. 1296, died V.S. 1341 - Jinacandrasūri, born V.S. 1326, *dīkṣā* V.S. 1332, *pada-mahotsava* 1341, died V.S. 1376 - Jinakuśalasūri, born V.S. 1337, *dīkṣā* V.S. 1347, *sūri* V.S. 1377, died V.S. 1389 - Jinapadmasūri, born V.S. 1381, *nandī-mahotsava* V.S. 1389, died V.S. 1400 - Jinalabdhisūri: pontiff in V.S. 1400, died V.S. 1406 -Jinacandrasūri, *nandī-mahotsava* 1406, died V.S. 1415 Jinodayasūri, born V.S. 1375 - died V.S. 1432 - Jinarājasūri, *sūri-pada* V.S. 1432, died V.S 1461 - Jinabhadrasūri: see below.

Four dates are given in the document, all expressed in the form of chronograms.

1) V.S. 1488: accompanying a pilgrimage to Jirāpallī (vs. not numbered).

2) V.S. 1472: installation of the image of Pārśvanātha in Jirāpallī (vs. 12).

3) V.S. 1475: celebration of Jinabhadrasūri's attainment of the rank of *sūri* (vs. 13).

[1] The serial numbers do not appear in the mss. under consideration. They may vary according to the *paṭṭāvalis*. Jinacandrasūri can also be No. 44 or No. 45, and Jinabhadrasūri can also be No. 59 or 60.

[2] All information based on J. Klatt, *Specimen of a literary-bibliographical Jaina-Onomasticon*.

4) V.S. 1484: sponsorship of the *Kalpasūtra* manuscript (vs. 29).

The date occurring first in the text is not the first in the chronological order (unless the chronogram is misinterpreted by us but *karma* normally means 8 in the Jain context). This may be due to the fact that the verse has been added afterwards. It is not written in the text but above. Jirāpallī is located at about 48 kms. from the station of Abu Road. It is closely connected with Pārśvanātha. Its history (and legend) go back far in the past. It is highly probable that documents such as inscriptions, *caityaparipāṭīs*, *praśastis*, etc., dealing with this sacred place would provide evidence corroborating or supplementing the facts mentioned in the London *praśasti*. Unfortunely, none of those which could be consulted so far has given the expected result.

The event referred to by the third date, however, is supported by parallel sources. Although three syllables are unclear in the corresponding verse of the manuscript, *padavī-mahaṁ* and the name of Jinabhadrasūri are sufficient to suggest that Nālhā was instrumental in an event connected with the attainment of a given religious status by the monk. Indeed, both the year and Nālhā's name have been preserved in connection with Jinabhadrasūri's biography in the *paṭṭāvalīs* of the Kharataragaccha: see J. Klatt, *Specimen of a literary-bibliographical Jaina-Onomasticon*, p. 28. According to the manuscripts consulted by Klatt, Jinabhadrasūri was born in V.S. 1449, took *dīkṣā* in V.S. 1461, became *sūri* in V.S. 1475: '*māgha sudi 15 budhe* (another MS. 1468 cavada-saya-aḍa-saṭṭhai māha sudi 15), *Bhāṇasauli-grāme sā° Nālhā-kārita-nandyāṁ śrī-Sāgaracandrācāryaiḥ sthāpitaḥ*', and died in V.S. 1514. Other sources for the information of our interest are: *Yugapradhāna Dādā Jinadattasūri aṣṭama śatābdī samāroha kī puṇyasmṛti meṁ prakāśita Kharataragaccha kā Itihāsa* (in Hindi, introduction by A. Nahta), Ajmer, 1959, p. 188; *Kṣamākalyāṇôpādhyāyādi-sankalita Kharataragaccha-paṭṭāvalī-sangraha*, 1st ed. by Muni Jinavijaya; reed. by Mahopādhyāya Vinayasāgara, Jaipur: Prakrit Bharati Academy, 2000, p. 6 vs. 82 (versified *gurvāvali*):

> *bāṇa-ṛṣi-vedêndu-mite ca varṣe Māghasya rākā-divase 'janiṣṭa*
> *paṭṭotsavo Bhāṇasapallikāyāṁ naṁnaumi taṁ Jinabhadrasūrim.*

Further, p. 12 (prose *paṭṭāvali*), and another *paṭṭāvali* (quoted in Muni Jinavijaya, *Vijñaptitriveṇi*, Bhavnagar, 1916, p. 48): *saṁ. 1475 (varṣe) Māgha sudi pūrṇimāsyāṁ Bhaṇasālika-Nālhā-sāha-kārita-sapāda-lakṣa-rūpaka-vyaya-rūpa-nandimahotsavena sūri-pade sthāpitavān*, where the amount of money spent in the event (one lakh and a quarter) is specified.

The event is also narrated in a *Jinabhadrasūri-paṭṭābhiṣeka-rāsa* (not seen). The contents of this work is given in Hindi by A. Nahta (pp. 188-189):[1]

> In Bhāṇasaulīpura lived the merchant (*sāhukāra*) Nāliga, whose father was Suhaḍā and whose mother was Ambiṇī [see vs. 7 of the London ms.]. Līlādevī's husband, Nālhigaśāha [see vss. 14-15 of the London ms.] sent a ceremonial letter everywhere. The community started coming from outside. In V.S. 1475 at an auspicious moment Sāgaracandrasūri granted the status of *sūri* to Kīrtisāgara [the name given to the future Jinabhadrasūri at the time of *dīkṣā*]. Nālhigaśāha organized the celebration of this coronation (*paṭṭābhiṣeka*) with great pomp. Various musical instruments were played and beggars were satisfied with whatever presents they wanted.

Jinabhadrasūri was undoubtedly a prominent and extremely influential figure. His activity as an instigator of the consecration of images or foundation of temples (in Jaisalmer and elsewhere) need not detain us here. On the other hand, his concern for having manuscripts copied and preserved is well rooted in the tradition. In one of the *paṭṭāvalis* mentioned above he is credited with the establishment of libraries in different places: *sthāne sthāne pustaka-bhāṇḍāgāra-sthāpakāḥ śrīJinabhadrasūrayaḥ*.[2] In his case, this is much more than a literary expression. According to Muni Jinavijaya (p. 57), no other *ācārya* could perhaps compete with him in this field. He has not been forgotten in the *praśastis* written by several Jain authors. He taught laypeople how to restore or handle manuscripts, and got hundreds or even thousands of manuscripts copied between V.S. 1475 and V.S. 1515, a period during which his name as instigator very often appears. Jaisalmer, Javalpur, Daulatabad, Ahipura, Patana, Mandavgarh, Ashapalli, Karnavati (= Old

[1] No reference is given by A. Nahta, but this is likely to be the same as the *Jinabhadrasūri paṭṭābhiṣeka rāsa* composed by Samayaprabha mentioned in JGK 1 p. 45.

[2] Quoted in Muni Jinavijaya, *Vijñaptitriveṇi* p. 48.

Ahmedabad) and Cambay are some of the many places where he urged the laity to set up libraries. Among the faithful laymen encouraged by him is Dharaṇāka, who, alone, installed a library in Cambay, and is also responsible in Jaisalmer for the so-called 'Great Library' (officially named 'Jinabhadrasūri Jaina Granthabhaṇḍāra').[1]

The London manuscript is one of the two illustrated *Kalpasūtra* manuscripts which were made to be copied at the instigation of Jinabhadrasūri during the same year, V.S. 1484, or, more precisely, at a few months' interval. The brother of the London manuscript (not seen so far) is reported to be in the collection of Seth Anandji Kalyanji ni Pedhi, Palitana. Its description is given in Sarabhai Manilal Nawab & Rajendra Sarabhai Nawab, *Jaina Paintings* (vol. II), Ahmedabad, 1985, pp. 26-27 (located after a brief description of the London manuscript, probably not seen by the authors). Illustrations of the Palitana manuscript are also reproduced in the book. They include a painting of Jinabhadrasūri found at the end of the manuscript (fig. 179, black and white plate No. 33). The text of the Scribal Remark proper is quoted and translated (p. 27 and n. 57). Only the last two verses of the *praśasti* are quoted and translated:

sac-citrâcitra-kṛta-puṁsāṁ sauvarṇâkṣara-dhāriṇī
eṣâhlādayati cetaḥ satāṁ vācayatāṁ satām || *32*
śrīJinabhadrasūrīṇāṁ guruṇāṁ upadīkṛtā
vācyamānā ciraṁ jīyād ācandrârkam iyaṁ budhaiḥ ||*33*
iti śrīKalpa-pustikā praśasti || ☒ ||

saṁvata 14 Āṣāḍhâdi 84 pravarttamāne Kārttika vadi 9 guro śrīmadAṇahilapuranagara-vāstavya śrīcaturvidha-śrīsangha-prasādāta tri. Vaikunṭha || *śrīKalpa-pustikā likhitā* || *x* || ||☒|| *śrīsanghāya kṣemaṁ bhūyāt.*

	London ms.	Palitana ms.
Texts	KS + Kālakācārya-kathā	KS + Kālakācārya-kathā
Size	154	162 folios
Paintings	34	25
Letters	Silver	Gold
Scribe	Trivedi Vaikuṇṭha	Trivedi Vaikuṇṭha
Place	Patan	Patan
Date	*V.S. 1485 Caitra sudi 5 ravi*	*V.S. 1484 Kārttika vadi 9 guru*
Praśasti	31 vss. + 2-3 unnumbered vss.	33 verses

It would be worth going deeper into the comparison, and identifying if possible the family who commissioned the Palitana manuscript, given the similarity of the ornamentation of the two manuscripts.

A piously active family (V.S. 1571 = 1494 CE)

Ms. of the *Vandāru-vṛtti*. Shelfmark: Or. 2104 - **Cat. No. 245.**

(See below Comments for the parallel texts mentioned in the notes).

(50B2): saṁvat 1571 varṣe Pauṣa vadi 1 some | śrīĀgamagacche śrīJayānandasūri | tat-paṭṭe śrī-Devaratnasūri tat-śiṣya śrīŚīlarājasūri | śrīŚīlavarddhanasūri tat-paṭṭe śrī-Śīlaratnasūri tat-paṭṭ(e) nabho-gaṇa-maṇḍana-dinakara-samāna saṁyama-yoga-sādhana-sâvadhāna-virājamāna-gacchanāyaka-bhaṭṭāraka-śrīVivekaratnasūrīṇām ugra-deśena ācārya-śrīSaṁyamaratnasūri upādhyāya śrīVidyāratna-sāṁnidhyena ca śrīGaṁdhāra-mandira-vāstavya śrīPragvāṭa-vaṁśa-śṛgāra vyavahāri-vara śrīācāryapada-upādhyāyapada-bimbapratiṣṭā-śrītīrthayātrā-saṁghapatipada-samyaktva-śīlavratôccaraṇa-mahotsava | aneka-prāsāda-

[1] Quotations and analysis in Muni Jinavijaya, *Vijñaptitriveṇi* pp. 56-62; Muni Jambuvijaya, introduction to the Jaisalmer catalogue p. 6 for the Jaisalmer library.

pauṣadhaśālôddharaṇâdy-aneka-mahāpuṇya-karaṇīya-kārakābhyāṁ[1] | śrīvya°[2]Pethaḍa-saṁtāne vya° Ṭhāīā-kula-dīpakābhyāṁ vya° Sahasavīra vya° Poīā- Udayakaraṇa-bāī Kakū {Vālhī ajī Rahī}-Poṣī-pramukha-samasta-kuṭamba-yutābhyāṁ[3]saṁghapati-vya° Parabata-vya° Kānhābhyāṁ ||

śrī-jñāna-bhaktaye 1[4]

vya° Ḍuṁgara śreyo-'rthaṁ ca śrīṢaḍāvaśyaka-vṛttir lekhitā | vācyamānā ciraṁ nandatāt | śrīr astu lekhaka-vācakayoḥ || śrī: || ☒ || ga.|| śrīḥ || kī || cha || śrīḥ || vi || ☒|| ma || śrīḥ || la || śrī.

Translation

In the year V.S. 1571 in (the month of) Pauṣa in the dark fortnight on the 1st, on Monday. In the Āgamagaccha the pontiff Jayānandasūri, his successor Devaratnasūri and his disciple Śīlarājasūri. Śīlavardhanasūri, his successor Śīlaratnasūri. Following the compelling teaching of the pontiff Vivekaratnasūri, the leader of the group, remarkable for his purity and meditation, the efficient practice of yoga and self-restraint, resembling the sun embellishing the sky, who belonged to the line of Śīlaratnasūri, in the presence of the teacher Vidyāratna and of the teacher Saṁyamaratnasūri, the commentary on the six Āvaśyakas was caused to be copied for the good of the merchant Ḍungara, out of devotion for good knowledge, by the merchants Parabata, leader of his community, and Kānha, residents of Gandhāra, excellent merchants, ornaments of the Pragvāṭa line, who belonged to the family line of the merchant Pethaḍa and illuminate the family of Ṭhāī. Both (Parabata and Kānha) accomplished various tasks of great merit, such as celebrations on the occasion of (a monk's attaining) the status of teacher or preceptor, installation of images, pilgrimages to sacred places, celebrations for the status of leader of the community, for solemnly uttering (adhesion to) right faith or to the vow of chastity, or restoration of several temples and halls for fasting. They were joined by the complete family, starting with the merchants Sahasavīra and Poīā, Udayakaraṇa, the lady Kakū ... Radī and Poṣī, etc.

Being read may (this manuscript) be a source of joy. Prosperity to the scribe and to the reader. Prosperity.

Comments

The London manuscript is not the only one where both the religious teachers of the Āgamagaccha and the lay family are mentioned together, in the same year, at exactly the same date, or in years close to V.S. 1571. They recur together in several other manuscripts. So far six of them have been traced.

- Ms. of the *Caityavandanasūtra-vivaraṇa* from Patan, dated V.S. 1659 (certainly a mistake for 1569, or, rather, 1571; 5th day of the dark fortnight of the month of Caitra, Monday): No. 633 p. 161 in Shah, *Praśasti-saṁgraha*.
- Ms. of the *Praśnavyākaraṇāṅgasūtra-vivṛti*: Pune: BhORI 17.1 No. 168 pp. 152-155, dated V.S. 1571.
- Ms. of the *Sandehaviṣauṣadhi* from Patan, dated V.S. 1571, first day of the dark fortnight of the month of Pauṣa, on Monday: No. 272 pp. 79-80 in Shah, *Praśasti-saṁgraha*.
- Ms. of the *Oghaniryukti*, dated V.S. 1571, from Ahmedabad: No. 270 pp. 76-79 in Shah, *Praśasti-saṁgraha*.
- Ms. of Somaprabhasūri's *Yatijītakalpa* with Sādhuratnasūri's commentary, dated V.S. 1571: Ahmedabad: L.D. Inst., vol. 4, coll. of Āc. Shri Kṣāntisūri, No. 103, *Praśasti* pp. 46-49.

[1] Shah No. 272: *jinabimbapratiṣṭhā-tīrthayātrā-śrīKalpaśrutalekhana-vācana-śrīsamyaktve śīlavratâdaraṇa-nandimahotsava-ācāryapada-upādhyāyapada-pradāpanâdi-sadutsa(va)-vidhānâdi-vihita-bahu-satkartavya*; Pune No. 247 (and Shah No. 633): *śrīācāryapada-bimbapratiṣṭhā-tīrthayātrâdi-mahāpuṇya-karaṇīya-kārakābhyāṁ.*

[2] Abbreviation *vya°* for *vyavahārin, vyavahārika.*

[3] The reading of the passage noted { } is uncertain. No such list in Pune No. 247 or Shah No. 633; Shah No. 272: *vya° Sahasavīra-vya° Poiyā-vya° Udayakaraṇa-śrā° Kakū-śrā° Raḍhī-śrā° Poṣī-pramukha-kuṭumba-yutābhyāṁ.*

[4] The figure '1' (absent in the parallel text of Pune: BhORI No. 247) could mean that these words are the beginning of a verse.

- Ms. of the *Jambūdvīpaprajñapticūrṇi*: Pune: BhORI 17.1 No. 247 p. 235, dated V.S. 1576, first day of the dark fortnight of the month of Pauṣa, on Monday.

In the two Ahmedabad manuscripts and in Pune No. 168, the information is given in the form of an extremely detailed verse-*praśasti* (33 vss.) of the Pragvāṭa line going further back than Parvata and Kanhā, the main donors. In the two Patan manuscripts (Shah Nos. 272 and 633) and in Pune No. 247 the information is supplied in the form of a prose scribal remark, the wording of which is very close to that of the London manuscript.

The laypeople involved are merchants from the coastal city of Gandhāra in Gujarat. The type of business they were doing is not specified. But, given the place where they lived, it could well have been maritime commerce. The merchant Ṭhāī (married to Varamaṇakāī, not mentioned in the London manuscript, see *praśastis* vs. 21) was the father of three sons: Parvata, Ḍungara and Narabada. The role played by the third is not specified. Parvata and Ḍungara organized the consecration of a Jina image and organized the celebration of the attainment of the status of *vācaka* (of one of the religious teachers of the Āgamagaccha) in V.S. 1559 (*praśastis*, vs. 25). In V.S. 1560 they organized pilgrimages to Jīrāpallī, Abu, etc. (*praśasti* vs. 26). In the city of Gandhāra they managed to get copies of the *Kalpasūtra* widely distributed and read (vss. 27-28). At the instigation of Vivekaratnasūri, they decided to observe the vow of chastity (vs. 29). Then Parvata and Kānha (the son of Ḍungara and his wife Mangādevī, vs. 24) called people from all over to organize the ceremony connected with the status of *sūri* (vs. 31). This explains why their names are met with in more than one document. Following the teaching of Vivekaratnasūri, Parvata and Kānha had decided to get copied all the scriptures. The year V.S. 1571 was the time when they started this undertaking:

Āgamagaccha-bibhratāṁ sūri-Jayānanda-sadguroḥ kramataḥ
śrīmadVivekaratnaprabha-sūrīṇāṁ sad-upadeśāt
śaśi-muni-tithi (1571)-mita-varṣe samagra-siddhānta-lekhana-parābhyām
vyavahāri-Parvata-Kānhābhyāṁ sukṛta-rasikābhyāṁ ... (vss. 32-33).

The comparison of the verse-*praśasti* with the prose scribal remarks shows that the compounds where the family's religious activities are listed are not a literary embellishment, but as many allusions to historic events.

The verse-*praśasti* shows a curious shift. The activities undertaken in V.S. 1559 and V.S. 1560 involve Parvata and Ḍungara. Later on, Parvata and Kānha are involved. The two brothers have been replaced by the uncle and the nephew. This element, combined with the mention 'for the sake of Ḍungara' in the prose scribal remarks could suggest that Ḍungara was no longer alive, and had been replaced by his son, Kānha, worthy of his father in religiosity. Further, Parvata's and Kānha's project could have been a commemoration project, with transfer of merit.[1]

Other members of the family mentioned in the verse-*praśasti* are Sahasravīra and Poiā (vs. 23), in connection with Parvata, but in a rather vague manner. None of them seems to be his son. This could perhaps explain Parvata's association with his nephew, Kānha. The other names appearing in the London manuscript also appear in the Patan manuscript (Shah No. 272). They designate members of the family (°*pramukha-kuṭumba*) who collaborated in the undertaking, but none of the available documents gives their specific position within the family.

All the evidence shows a close connection between the family and the Āgamagaccha. The main specificity of this religious group is that their followers do not worship the *kṣetrapāla* deity while performing *pratikramaṇa*. It was started in V.S. 1250 by Śīlaguṇasūri and Devabhadrasūri, and is not among those which are best represented in epigraphy or manuscripts.

[1] Tentative hypothesis, all the more so as the date of the Patan ms. (Shah No. 633) is problematic (see above).

A brotherly undertaking: uniting efforts for the best way of spending money (V.S. 1691 = 1634 C.E.)

Ms. of the *Bhagavatī-sūtra* with Abhayadeva's commentary. Shelfmark: Or. 5124 - **Cat. No. 23.**

Versified donor-praśasti following the *granthāgra* number.

(342B5): ||śrīmad-Ūkeśi-vaṁśâgrasāra-mauktika-sannibhaṁ
gotraṁ Parīkṣakaṁ vittaṁ viśvasmin bhāti viśvake |1|
tasminn ajaniṣātāṁ ca pitṛvya-bhrātṛ-naṁdanau
Rājapālaḥ Sivādrājaś côbhāv āhita-lakṣaṇau |2|
sukṛjo (*sic*) Rājapālasya śāradāś sūnavas trayaḥ
suśriyo Rayaṇadevī-kāmya-kukṣi-samudbhavāḥ |3|
Amarâhvas tv ādimaṁs teṣu deva-gurvvor upāsakaḥ
Varddhamānâbhidheyo 'nyo Lālâbhidhas tṛtīyakaḥ |4
prauḍha-saṁpattayaḥ paṁca Sivarājasya sūnavaḥ
Sindūradevī-satkukṣi-śukti-muktā-phalāny atha |5
teṣv ādimo 'sti Sārdūlo 'nyas Suratāṇa-saṁjñakaḥ
tārtīyas Sajjanas turyo Vasatâbhidha ity asau |6
Paṁcānanâbhidho yo hi paṁcamo 'mī adhiśriyaḥ
dhani-mukhyās sadā dakṣās sadgurûpāsane 'niśaṁ |7
sugatāḥ bhrātaras sarve dāna-śauṁḍā dvipā iva
śubhôdarkkās tu caṁdrârkkās + + + +hayālavaḥ |8
ebhis subhrātṛbhis sarvvair ātmanaś śreyasaḥ kṛte
śrīmad-Bhagavatīsūtra-ṭīkā-pratir vihāritā |9
Kharataragaṇa-rājānāṁ śrīmajJinacaṁdrasūri-saṁjñānāṁ
āmnātināṁ ca satsūrīṇāṁ maṁtre mahārtha-yute |10
Harṣakuśala-nāmabhyaś śiṣya-mukhyebhya āditaḥ
svāyatibhyaś śubhodarkebhyo ?nūcānebhya? ādarāt |11 tribhiḥ kulakaṁ
ṣoḍaśa-śataika-navatau 1691 māsi Nabhasye caturthikā-ghasre
puṇyâhe sudinâhe valakṣa-pakṣīya-uccêndau |12
śrīmad-Ghogha-pure draṁge {śreyaś śātrava} jetari {uncertain}
rājyaṁ kurvati bhūpīṭhe Gajasiṁhe 'tirājani |13
tair eva pāvitā lakṣmīs tair janiḥ saphalī-kṛtā
yaiḥ svīyaṁ draviṇaṁ bhūyaḥ pradattaṁ pustakâdiṣu |14
tejasvinī pravarttete yāvac caṁdrârkka-maṁḍale
naṁdyād eṣā pratis tāvad vācyamānā manīṣibhiḥ |15
dadānās saṁti bhūyāṁso dravyam aihika-karmaṇi
puṇya-kṣetre prayacchaṁti te nūnaṁ paṁca-ṣā narāḥ |16
svôpārjitaṁ dhanaṁ yais tu sapta-kṣetryām avāpi na
bhūyād ajananīs teṣāṁ mātṛ-kleśa-vidhāyināṁ |17
Bhagavaty-ādi-sūtrasya pratīr vihārya sādha(*continues in the right hand margin*:)ve śṛṇvaṁti sauva-karṇṇābhyāṁ dhanyās te dhanina (*uncertain*) naraḥ ||18||
iti praśastiḥ ||

2nd Hand (*right-hand margin top*): 1137 varṣe

3rd Hand (*right-hand margin bottom*): 18616 (graṁthāgra in Guj. figures)

4th Eur. Hand (*upper margin*): saṁvat 1691.

Translation

1. Resembling a pearl taking the lead of the glorious Ūkeśi line, the celebrated family clan Parīkṣaka (= mod. Pārakh, Pārekh) shines in the whole universe.

2. In this line were born the two cousins[1] Rājapāla and Śivarāja, both known for their good qualities.

3. The virtous Rājapāla had three modest sons, fortunate, born from the womb of the lovable Rayaṇadevī.

4. Amara, the first of them, was devoted to the gods (= the Jinas) and the religious teachers, another one was named Vardhamāna, and the third Lāla.

5. Considerably rich were Śivarāja's five sons, pearls in the shell which was Sindūradevī's womb. As follows:

6. Among them the first is Śārdūla, another one is named Suratāṇa, the third is Sajjana, and the fourth has the name of Vasata.

7. As for the fifth he is Pancānana. They were exceedingly rich, always foremost among the wealthy, continuously expert in their service to good religious teachers.

8. Well-bestowed all the brothers were intoxicated by generosity, like elephants intoxicated by rut.[2] Having the brightness of the sun, (as many?) moons and suns ...

9-11. For their own sake, following the advice full of deep meaning of the leader of the Kharataragaccha, named Jinacandrasūri, a good monk of the tradition (?), all these good brothers, with full consideration, presented this copy of the *Bhagavatī-sūtra* with commentary to his main disciple, named Harṣakuśala, a monk of perfect steadiness having the brightness of the sun [...].

12. In (V.S.) 1691, in the month of Bhādrapada, on the fourth day, an auspicious day, a good day, as the moon was high during the bright fortnight,

13. in the city of Ghoghapura, while the king Gajasiṁha was ruling on the throne, victorious (over his enemies?),

14. these brothers purified their wealth, they made their life fruitful, they who gave their money several times for manuscripts.

15. May this manuscript, being read by intelligent people, rejoice as long as the orbs of the sun and the moon will continue to shine.

16. Numerous are those who give their money for secular activities. Indeed, not more than five or six men offer it for a meritorious field.

17. Those who have not sown the money they earned in the seven fields, may they cease to exist, these tormentors of their mothers!

18. Having presented the manuscript of the *Bhagavatī-sūtra* to a monk, fortunate are the rich men who listen (to it) with their own ears.

End of the *praśasti*.

Comments

Interesting because of the precise information it includes, but also because of the final verses praising the use of money for manuscripts and their lively tone. Reference to the 'seven fields' (vs. 17) is far from being unique in such *praśastis*. The fields are: 1) Jaina images, 2) Jaina temples, 3) Jaina scriptures, 4)

---

[1] Lit. 'the son of the brother and of the father's brother'. In India, this means they are brothers. Indeed, the word *bhrātṛ*, and no other, is used throughout the text.

[2] Word-play (*śleṣa*) on *dāna*.

monks, 5) nuns, 6) laymen, 7) laywomen (R. Williams, *Jaina Yoga* p. 165). But spending for the scriptures is often emphasized in manuscripts.

Ghoghapura, located in Saurashtra, at a distance of fourteen miles from Bhavnagar, is a Jain sacred place characterized by the presence of a so-called 'Navakhaṇḍa Pārśvanātha'. References to this place in inscriptions or *praśastis* are available since the beginning of the 12th century (cf. Muni Viśālavijayajī, *ŚrīGhoghātīrtha*. Bhavnagar, 1958, Yaśovijaya Jaina Granthamālā, 32 pages).

For another reference to king Gajasiṁha, see Ahmedabad: L.D. Inst. No. 7098 (*Praśasti* p. 441), at the end of a commentary composed in V.S. 1692 in Padmāvatīpattana:

> *rājā hy utkaṭa-vairi-nāga-damane rāṣṭrôḍu-vaṁśôdbhavaḥ*
> *śrīmān śrīGajasiṁha-bhūpati-varo 'sti śrīMeror maṇḍale.*

The specific mention of the king's heroism, as in the London manuscript, is worth noting. It may be stereotyped, it may also reflect a historical reality.

So far the members of the family mentioned here could not be traced elsewhere. Emphasis is laid on the male elements, those who earn the money and decide how to spend it. No financial indication is given, but the fact that five persons of considerable wealth had to join in the venture is enough to suggest that commissioning the copy of a manuscript of 342 pages was expensive.

The Jinacandrasūri of the manuscript was the 61st (or 64th, 65th) pontiff of the Kharataragaccha, who is known for his influence on Akbar. He was born in V.S. 1595 and died in V.S. 1670. Thus, he was no longer alive when the manuscript was copied. His role could only have been that of an instigator or an advisor (vs. 10, not fully clear). The recipient of the manuscript was his disciple Harṣakuśala. For another reference to him, also in connection with his teacher Jinacandrasūri, see the final verses of the *Meghakumāra-copāī*, composed in V.S. 1686 by Sumatihaṁsa, a disciple of Harṣakuśala (JGK 3 p. 275).

Focus on a lady

Ms. of the *Anekāntajayapatākā*. Shelfmark: Or. 2111 - **Cat. No. 670.**

> ||oṁ namaḥ||
> Prāgvāṭânvaya-saṁghapa-Bholāvārū-samudbhavā dayitā
> śreṣṭhī-Narapāla-Rūpādevī-tanayasya Bhīmasya ||1||
> Lūṇâhvaya-saṁghapater bhaginī Jāūḥ kula-dvaya-viśuddhā
> sadguṇa-gaṇa-prasiddhā nityaṁ śrī-dharma-karma-parā ||2
> sūtraṁ vrttiṁ tippanakaṁ cAnekāntajayapatākāyāḥ
> śrīSomasundara-guror girâśva-gaja-ratna-1487-vatsare 'lekhīt ||3
> (bh)ātaḥ pradīpavad yāvad rodasī bhavanôdare
> candrârkau, vācyamāno 'yaṁ tāvan nandatu pustakaḥ ||4||
> śrīḥ|| śrīḥ|| śrīḥ|| bhadraṁ bhavatu śrīśramaṇasaṁghāya|| maṁgalaṁ mahāśrī. (*See below 'Father and sons as collectors of manuscripts' for the remark by the second hand*).

Translation

1. Daughter of Bholāvārū, a leader of the community of the Prāgvāṭa line, wife of Bhīma, the son of the merchant Narapāla and (his wife) Rūpadevī,

2. Jāū, the sister of the leader of the community named Lūṇa, a lady whose two sides of the family are perfect, well-known for her innumerable good virtues and always intent on religious acts,

3. following the order of the religious teacher Somasundara, copied the aphorisms, the commentary and the gloss on the *Anekāntajayapatākā* in the year horse-elephant-jewels (1487).

4. Being read, may this manuscript rejoice as long as the sun and the moon shine, similar to lights, in the heart of the world, on heaven and earth.

Prosperity. Prosperity. Prosperity. May there be auspiciousness on the mendicants' community. Auspiciousness, great prosperity.

Comments

Noteworthy for the focus on a lady apparently belonging to a prominent family. Ordinary for the fact that she is throughout defined by dependence on the male members of the family: father, husband, brother.

Although the religious affiliation of Somasundarasūri is not specified in the manuscript, given the date it is extremely likely that he is the same as the 50th pontiff of the Tapāgaccha, also the author of several works, especially commentaries (see Index 2: Authors). He was born in V.S. 1430, became pontiff in V.S. 1457, and died in V.S. 1499 (cf. J. Klatt, 'Extracts from the historical records of the Jainas', *Ind. Antiquary* 11, 1882, p. 256).

A lady's initiative (V.S. 1696 = 1639 CE)

Illustrated ms. of the *Kalpasūtra* and the *Kālakācārya-kathā*. Shelfmark: Or. 13959 - **Cat. No. 104**.

Scribal Remark*(From a second hand)*: ||§0|| saṁvata 1696 varṣe Jyeṣṭa vadi 11 dine | guruvāre | śrīRājanagare śrīPūrṇṇimā-pakṣe | bhaṭṭāraka-śrī6Vimalacandrasūri | tat-paṭṭi bhaṭṭāraka-śrī6-śrīśrīLakṣmīcandrasūri tat-paṭṭe ācārya-śrīSaubhāgyacandrasūri-vijaya-rājye | vācanācārya-vā°-śrīDevasundaram-upadesena | śrīŚrīmālajñātīya-vṛddhi-śāṣāyāṁ phaḍīyāsīhā śrīBhīmā bhāryā Līlāde putra sā° śrīJesanga bhā° Vāhalabāi tathā bāī Bacī putra Kalyāṇa bhā° Vīramade puṇyārthaṁ bāī Bacīkena pitākasya pāriṣa sā° Dhanajī bhā° Dhanāde putrī Bacīkena puṇārthaṁ dattaṁ || vaḍāūyā (?) pāriṣa Ratana bhā° Ratanāde-pramuṣa-parivāra-puṇyârthaṁ | Pancamī-udyāpanena | bāī Cāmpā Meghabāī teja vābaḍīkasya puṇyârthaṁ idaṁ pustakaṁ bāī Bacīkena kṛtaṁ | vācyamāna ciraṁ nindyāt śrīPārśvanātha-prasādāt ||⊠||

Translation

In the year V.S. 1696, on Thursday, the 11th day of the dark fortnight of (the month of) Jyeṣṭha, in Rājanagara (= Ahmedabad). In the Pūrṇimāpakṣa, during the victorious reign of Saubhāgyacandrasūri, successor of the pontiff Lakṣmīcandrasūri, himself successor of the pontiff Vimalacandrasūri, himself successor of the pontiff Vimalacandrasūri, following the instruction of the specialist teacher Devasundara. In the elder branch of the Śrīmāla caste, ... Bhīmā, his wife Līlāde, (their) son the merchant Jesanga, his wife the lady Vāhala and the lady Bacī, his son Kalyāṇa (and his) wife Vīramade. For the sake (of all these people). It was given by the lady Bacīka - the lady Bacīka's father side: the merchant Dhanajī and his wife Dhanāde - Bacīka, (their) daughter, for the good - for the good of the family, starting with Ratana and his wife Ratanāde, (representing) the side of ... For the good of the lady Cāmpā, the lady Meghā, and ..., along with the performance of the complementary ritual of (Knowledge)-the Fifth, this manuscript was made by the lady Bacīka. Being read, may it rejoice for long, with the favour of Pārśvanātha.

Comments

The Scribal Remark is from a different hand than the rest of the manuscript and could be later than the manuscript as a whole. The redaction is rather clumsy, with repetitions and sinuous sentences taking the same elements again.

The names mentioned are not easily traced in other sources. A whole family belonging to the 'elder' branch of the Śrīmālīs is involved in the process. The main person concerned is a lady named Bacī who acted in the name of her relatives and whose genealogy is given here. What she did exactly is not fully clear: what is meant by *kṛta*?

The manuscript was commissioned on a specific occasion, namely the conclusion of the (Jñāna)pancamīvrata, when having manuscripts copied is considered specially meritorious and is frequently done, since this vow and the connected festival are meant to celebrate scriptural knowledge and books.

A layman's affair (V.S. 1604 = 1547 CE)

Ms. of the *Bhagavatī-sūtra*. Shelfmark: Or. 5123 (A) - **Cat. No. 19**.

saṁvat 1604 varṣe Aśva sudi sukla-pakṣe sanivāsare tṛtīyā-dine pātisāha-Sāha Salema-rājya-pravarttamāne Caudharī-śrīVaradeva, tat-putra śrīCaüdharī-Sahajapāla, tat-putra doi: ci°[1] Bhavānīdāsa, ci° Deidāsa, ci° śrīśrīVāirāvo (*recte:* Varadevo?) sva-punyârthaṁ liṣāpitaṁ śrīBhagavatīsūtraṁ, liṣāpitaṁ śubhaṁ bhavatu, māgalyaṁ (*sic*) dadātu‖ liṣitaṁ Udayakalasa ‖ māṁgalyaṁ dadātu‖ ☒

Scribal Maxim: jādṛsaṁ pustakaṁ dṛṣṭvā tādṛsaṁ liṣitaṁ mayā
jadi suddham asuddhaṁ vā mama doṣo na dīyate‖ ‖ ☒

Translation

In the year (V.S.) 1604, in Āśvina, on Saturday, the third day of the bright fortnight, while the Emperor Salim Shah was ruling (r. 1545-1553 CE; common title of Islam Shah or Jalal Khan, the son of Sher Shah; see Index 3), Varadeva Caudhari, his son Sahajapāla Caudhari, who himself had two sons: Bhavānīdāsa and Deidāsa. Vāirāvo caused the *Bhagavatīsūtra* to be copied for his own good. Having been caused to be copied may it be auspicious, may it bring prosperity. Copied by Udayakalasa. May it bring prosperity.

As I saw in the manuscript, so exactly has it been written by me. Whether it is correct or incorrect, please do not blame me.

Monks as scribe and painter (V.S. 1783, Śāka 1648 = 1726 CE)

Ms. of the *Śālibhadra-caupaī* by Matisāra. Shelfmark: Or. 13524 - **Cat. No. 747**.

samâgni-nāgâdri-candra-pramitâbde, Śāṁke vasv-abdhi-rasaike pravarttamāne । mahā-māngalya-prada-Bāhulaka-māse dhana-trayodaśyāṁ karmavāṭyāṁ ‖ cāndri-vāsare ‖ śrīmajJesala-peśala-durgge sakala-śobhā-vijita-svargge śrīmatVṛhatKharatara-vegaḍa-gacche ‖ bhaṭṭāraka-śrīJinesvara-sūri-santāne । bhaṭṭāraka-śrī105śrīJinasundara-sūri-paṭṭâlaṁkāra-yuga-pradhāna-bhaṭṭāraka-śrīmajJinodaya-sūri-vijaya-rājye prājya-saṁmrājye ‖ śrī ‖ śubhaṁ bhavatu lekhaka-pāṭhakayoḥ ‖ śrīr astu ‖ śrī ‖ śrī ‖ śam astu ‖ paṇḍita Devakuśalena likhitā pratir iyam । paṁ° Kanakakīrtti-muninā ca citritāṁ । vivekâtireka-nipuṇa-Muṁkaurapālasa-parivāra-pāṭhanāya darśanāya jñāna-vṛddhy-arthaṁ likhāpitā: ‖

Translation

In the year measured in fire-elephant-mountain-moon (= 1783), in the current Śāka year Vasu gods-ocean-taste-one (= 1648), in the month of Kārttika, bestower of great aupiciousness, in the 13th lunar mansion, on the civil day[2] Monday, in the beautiful fort of Jesala (= Jaisalmer), the splendour of which excels that of heaven, in the 'Great Kharataragaccha', during the significant reign, in the victorious reign of Jinodayasūri, pontiff of the era and ornament of the seat of Jinasundarasūri, himself pontiff from the line of the pontiff Jineśvarasūri. Good fortune. May it be auspicious for the scribe and for the reader. May good fortune be. May there be happiness. This manuscript was written by Pandit Devakuśala, and it was illustrated by Pandit Kanakakīrti, a monk. It was caused to be written for the sake of increasing knowledge to be seen (and) read by the Muṁkaurapālasa family, remarkable for their extreme judgment.

---

[1] Abbreviation for *ciraṁjīvin*, used when referring to living people (especially one's own children) as a way to protect them from all dangers.

[2] The work *karmavāṭī* is not a toponym, as thought by some (see Index 5). It always appears before or after a numeral in the expression of the date. References in the London collections are **Cat. Nos. 15, 246, 722, 747, 1065**. The word is far from being limited to our corpus. In many cases, a clear place name (in the form X-*madhye*) follows. Hence it is certain that the word has some connection with the precise date in the week, the *tithi* and not with a place name. Indeed, *k.* is recorded as a synonym of *tithi* in Hemacandra's *Abhidhānacintāmaṇi*: *tithiḥ punaḥ karmavāṭī* (2.61), the first edition of which was published by O. Böhtlingk and Ch. Rieu (1847). This explains that it is also recorded in the Petersburg dictionary (with reference to Hemacandra's lexicon and only to this) and then in Monier-Williams and Apte. [The word will be further discussed in a specific article by Nalini Balbir].

Comments

Very carefully written in red. Interesting for the literary flavour given by the two chronograms, the *kāvya*-like evocation of the beauty of Jaisalmer, and the fact that the person who illustrated the manuscript is clearly a monk. The identity of the family and the reasons for the epithet are unclear. They would need to be supported by external evidence.

Monastic collaboration

Ms. of the *Jñātādharmakathānga* with Abhayadeva's commentary. Shelfmark: Or. 5126 - **Cat. No. 27**.

(*in red*): ||§O|| saṁ° 1600 varṣe dvitīya-Bhādrapada-kṛṣṇa-pakṣe 9 dine śrīKharatara-gacche svacche vācanâcārya-śrīKṣemakīrtti-śāṣāyāṁ śrīJinamāṇikyasūri-vijayarājye śrīPūrṇṇacaṁdra-mahopādhyāyānāṁ śiṣya-muṣya-śrīśrīśrī-ācāryaśrīPuṇyaratnasūrīṇāṁ śiṣya-vā°Ratnakīrttigaṇi-vā°Kṣamābhadragaṇi-paṁ°Puṇyasuṁdaragaṇi-paṁ°Lakṣmīmeru-muninā lipīkṛtā sva-puṇyârthaṁ vācanârthaṁ. śrīr astu leṣaka-pāṭhakayoḥ|| subhaṁ bhavatu|| ||

Scribal Maxims: adṛṣṭa-doṣān mati-vibhramād vā, yad artha-hīnaṁ likhitaṁ mayâtra
tat sādhu-mukhyair api sodhanīyaṁ, kopo na kāryaḥ khalu lekhakāya ||1||
yādṛśaṁ pustake dṛṣṭaṁ tādṛśaṁ likhitaṁ mayā |
yadi suddham asuddhaṁ vā mama doṣo na dīyate ||1||
|| śrīrāyārāya-śrīMāladeva-vijayarājye| śrīNāgapura-madhye śrīJñātādharmakathâṁga-bṛhadvṛtti likhitā|| vācyamānaṁ ciraṁ naṁdyāt || ||śrī||
sarva-maṁgala-māṁgalyaṁ sarva-kalyāṇa-kārakaṁ
pradhānaṁ sarvva-dharmāṇāṁ jai<ya>naṁ jayatu sāsanaṁ||1||
paṁ°Rūpakalasa-paṭhanârthaṁ|| ☒||

Translation

In the year V.S. 1600, in the dark fortnight of the second Bhādrapada, on the ninth day, in the perfect Kharataragaccha, in the branch of the specialist teacher Kṣemakīrti, during the victorious reign of Jinamāṇikyasūri, copied for their own merit, for reading, by the monk Pandit Lakṣmīmeru, the gaṇi Pandit Puṇyasundara, the gaṇi specialist Kṣamābhadragaṇi and the gaṇi specialist Ratnakīrtigani, (himself) disciple of the teacher Puṇyaratnasūri, (himself) main disciple of the great teacher Pūrṇacandra. May there be auspiciousness to the scribe and to the reader. May there be auspiciousness.

Whatever meaningless (thing) I have written in this manuscript, whether it was through oversight or through mental confusion, this should be corrected by the foremost among the best. Indeed, one shoud not be angry with the scribe.

I have written exactly what I have seen in the manuscript. Whether it is correct or incorrect, please do not blame me.

During the victorious reign of Māladeva, king among kings. The large commentary on the *Jñātādharmakathānga* was written in Nāgapura. Being read, may it rejoice. Prosperity.

Auspicious among all things auspicious, creating all that is good, foremost among all religions, may the Jain teaching be victorious!

For the reading of Pandit Rūpakalasa.

Comments

Jinamāṇikyasūri (born V.S. 1549, died V.S. 1612) was the 60th (or 63rd, 64th) pontiff of the Kharataragaccha.

Among Sthānakavāsīs (V.S. 1821 = 1764 CE)

Ms. of the *Bhaktāmarastotra* with Guj. commentary. Shelfmark: Add. 26,453 (B) -**Cat. No. 883.**

li° pūjya-pravara-paṁḍita-maṁḍalâcāryya-sthavira-śrī-mahāṁta-śāsaṇôdyotakāraka-stha°-śrī-108śrī-Bhīmasenajījī-tat-paṭṭe vidyamāṁna-pūjya-pravara-paṁḍita-sthavira-pada-dhāraka-jagaj-jīva-tāraka-pū°-sthavirajī-śrī-ṛ-śrī5śrī-Sujāṁṇajījī-tad-aṁtevāsī-ṛ-Dayārāṁmasya lekhi vācanârtha śiṣya-ṛ-Rāyacaṁdasya hetoḥ. saṁ. 1821 nā mitī Āso vadi pratipad-dine śrīBagasara-pura, Kāṭhiyāvāḍa-deśa-madhyeǁ

Translation

Copied - in the lineage of the respected elder Bhīmasenajī, the expounder of the great teaching among the Pandits, the teachers of groups of monks and the elders, Dayārāma, the attendant of the venerable elder the monk Sujānajī who helps the souls of the world to cross over, who holds the position of an elder, a respected and excellent Pandit of our time, copied (this text) for the reading of the monk Rāyacanda, (Sujānajī's) disciple. In the year V.S. 1821, in (the month of) Āśvina, on the first day of the dark fortnight, in the town of Bagasara, in the region of Kathiawar.

Comments

We assume that these monks belonged to a Sthānakavāsī (or Lonkāgaccha?) lineage, but we have not been able to find supporting information from other sources at our disposal.

Among Lonkāgaccha monks (V.S. 1650 = 1593 CE)

Ms. of the *Prajñāpanāsūtra*. Shelfmark: I.O. San. 3351 — **Cat. No. 77.**

atha pancāsat-saṁvatsare māse Caitra badi dvutīyāyāṁ bhauma-vāsvare liṣitam idaṁ śāstraṁ Prajñāpanâkhyaṁ śrīmadUttarādhīsâcārya Saravara-munīndrâkhya tasya śikhya Arjunâbhiddhaḥ tat-chikhya ciram ānandatu suddhī Durggadāsâkhya-gaṇīsa tac-chikhya Megharāja-munir abhūta pūrvve buddhimān tac-chikhya Raṇamallâkhya-muninâleṣi śrīmalLābhapure sthite ǁ sati śrīmān Akkavara-narindra-rājye Mudgalânvaye vidimāna varttate.

Translation

And this treatise called *Prajñāpanā* was written in V.S. (16)50 on the second day of the dark fortnight of the month of Caitra, a Tuesday. The monk named Saravara, teacher leader of the Northern (branch). His disciple named Arjuna. May his disciple rejoice for a long time, the wise (or pure?) monk Durgadāsa. There was his disciple, the intelligent monk Megharāja. His disciple the monk named Raṇamalla copied (this manuscript). It happened when His Royal Highness Akbar, the king of kings in the Mughal dynasty, was in Lahore.

Comments

The reading *atha* is clear. The date is not expressed in full, but is certain. The same Durgadāsa, disciple of Arjuna, himself disciple of Saravara, is known from other sources. He belongs to the Northern branch of the Lonkāgaccha known as 'Lāhorī Uttarādha Lonkāgaccha' (JGK 9 pp. 135-136, with further references). He composed a *Khandakakumāra sūri copai* in V.S. 1635 in Lahore (JGK 2 pp. 163-164). Nothing can be said about the other names.

A Śvetāmbara author, a Digambara monk as the copyist (V.S. 1849 = 1792 CE)

Ms. of Hemacandra's *Abhidhānacintāmaṇi*. Shelfmark: Or. 2141 - **Cat. No. 1346.**

83A:

saṁvadi randhra-sindhv-aṣṭêndu 1849-mite Mārghaśīrṣake
māsi śukle vare pakṣe pratipad-divase gurau 1
Uṇiyārâbhidhe grāme deśe Nāgara-cālake
rāveśa Bhīmasiṁhasya rājye śrīMūlasanghake 2

Sarasvatī śubhe gacche Bālātkārâhvaye gaṇe
Naṁdyāmnāye tathā Kundakunda-sūri-mahānvaye 3
ambāvatī su-paṭṭôttha-bhaṭṭāraka-śiromaṇiḥ
Kṣemendrakīrttideva āsīt kṣema-karo bhuvi 4
tat-paṭṭâcala sūryyābha Surendrakīrtti-jiṣṇunā
śiṣya-vargge supāṭhârthaṁ kautukī likhita tv iyam 5
ā-candra-sūryam eṣā sā Nāmamāle vyaprastikā
vācyamānā jalāt taulāj jaḍād bhūyāḥ sthirā vudhaḥ 6
samāptā cêyaṁ Nāmamālā śubhaṁ.

2nd Hand: idaṁ pustakaṁ *(ca. 20 syllables written and fully covered with ink)* paṭhanârthaṁ saṁ. 1904 kā madhye likhāpitam.

Translation

1. In the year measured hole-ocean-eight-moon (1849), in the month of Mārgaśīrṣa, in the bright fortnight, the best, on the first day, on Thursday,

2. In the village named Uṇiyāra, in the region of Nāgaracāla, during the reign of Bhīmasiṁha, in the Mūlasangha,

3. in the good religious group of Sarasvatī, in the group known as Bālātkāra, in the tradition 'Nandi', and in the great lineage of Kundakunda,

4. there was the best of pontiffs coming from a good spiritual lineage ..., the respected Kṣemendrakīrti, bringer of prosperity on earth.

5. A true sun on the mountain of his spiritual line, the victorious Surendrakīrti copied this interesting manuscript for good reading among his pupils.

6. Being read, may this manuscript, the 'Garland of nouns' last (*sthirā*) as long as the sun and the moon [the rest is strongly reminiscent of the scribal maxim inviting to protect a manuscript against 'water', 'oil', and against 'fools', although the words are not in their standard shape].

This 'Garland of words' is now complete. Auspiciousness.

(Second hand) This manuscript had been caused to be copied in V.S. 1904 for the reading of ...

Comments

Grammars and lexicons transcend sectarian boundaries, and Hemacandra's works are valuable for all, especially for teaching junior monks (mentioned in vs. 5). The scribe, a monk, copied this work for this purpose.

Kṣemendrakīrti and Surendrakīrti are also mentioned together in the scribal remark of a manuscript of Hariṣena's *Bṛhatkathākośa* dated V.S. 1868 (Johrapurkar, *Bhaṭṭāraka Sampradāya* No. 276). Both these pontiffs belong to the Delhi-Jaipur branch of the Balātkāragaṇa. Kṣemendrakīrti became pontiff in V.S. 1815. He was succeeded by Surendrakīrti in V.S. 1822 and remained in this position until V.S. 1852 (Johrapurkar p. 111). The latter is known to have written a Sanskrit commentary on the *Jambūdvīpaprajñapti* in 1776 CE. Bhīmasiṁha (vs. 2) ruled in Udaipur from 1767 to 1828 CE (Johrapurkar No. 395; K.C. Sogani, *Jainism in Rajasthan* p. 147).

A Digambara layman's reading

Composite manuscript (*guṭakā*) containing the *Tattvārthasūtra* and a collection of hymns or basic works forming a private book of prayer. Shelfmark: Or. 13221 - **Cat. No. 1265** (reference of the last text).

atha subha saṁvatsare saṁvat 1811 varṣe māsôttama-Māgha-māse śukla-pakṣe vasanta-ṛto pancamī dina śukravāre pustaka sampūrṇaḥ ǁ ǁ śubhaṁ bhavatu ǁ suśrāvaka-punya-prabhāvaka devaguru-bhakti-kāraka-sanghanāyaka sangha-mukhya-dharma-vṛddhī-upadesa-karaṇa sādhami Ugrasena Pātharīvāla Pānīpatha-madhye dharmavṛddha-karana-arthe pustaka likhāpitaṁ paṭhanârthaṁ ǁ śrīr astu ǁ kalyāṇaṁ°

Translation

So in the auspicious year V.S. 1811, in the month of Māgha, the best of the months, in the bright fortnight, during the season of spring, on the fifth day, on Friday, this manuscript was completed. May it be auspicious. This manuscript was caused to be copied in Panipat in order to be read, with the intention of expanding the (Jain) faith, by Ugrasena Pātharīvāla, a propagator of good deeds among good laymen, a leader of the community acting for the sake of devotion to the gods (= the Jinas) and the religious teachers, a fellow Jain (concerned by) teaching to increase the Jain faith in the community. May there be auspiciousness. May there be prosperity.

The manuscript as an object of financial transaction

Ms. of the *Pancasaṁgraha* by Candrarṣi with the auto-commentary. Shelfmark: Or. 2107 (B) - **Cat. No. 468.**

2nd Hand: bhaḷśrī-Punyasāgarasūriṇā gṛhīto 'yaṁ graṁtha ru. 2 mullyena.

Translation

This book has been acquired by the leader Puṇyasāgarasūri at the price of two rupees.

From copying to the library

Ms. of the *Daśavaikālika-sūtra* with Haribhadra's commentary. Shelfmark: Or. 2101 - **Cat. No. 199.**

savat 1699 varṣe Jyeṭha vadi 6 ravau laṣataṁ Māḍavī nī pola madhye celā Jeṭhāǁ ǁ☒ǁ ǁ☒ǁ

2nd Hand: gaṇiSuṁdarasāgara-nīṣṭā-pratiḥ iyaṁ śrīpūjya-pārśve.

3rd Hand: ǁ sakala-bhaṭṭāraka-śirovataṁsāyamāna-bhaṭṭāraka-śrī5śrī-Rājasāgara-sūrîśvara-śiṣya-gaṇi-Suṁdarasāgareṇa svakīyā pratir bhaṁḍāre nyastā saṁvat 1721 varṣe Mārggaśīrṣa sita caturthyāṁ śanau puṣya-nakṣatre śreyase 'stu ǀ

Translation

In the year (V.S.) 1699, in (the month of) Jyeṣtha, on the 6th (day) of the dark fortnight, on Sunday, copied by the junior Jeṭhā in the Māḍavī area.

(*Second Hand*): This manuscript belonging to Sundarasāgaragaṇi (was handed over?) to his respected (superior).

(*Third Hand*): Sundarasāgaragaṇi, pupil of the pontiff Rājasāgarasūri, the best leader among all leaders, deposited the copy belonging to him in the library in the year V.S. 1721 in (the month of) Mārgaśīrṣa, on the fourth (day) of the bright (fortnight), on Saturday, during the lunar mansion Puṣya. May it be for the better.

Interconnected manuscripts

1. Ms. of the *Nirayāvaliyāo*. Shelfmark: Or. 13599 - **Cat. No. 95.**

saṁvat 1865 nā varṣeṁ Āsu-māseṁ śukla-pakṣe trayodasyāyāṁ tithau bhṛgu-vāsare śrīKacha-dese śrīBhuja-nagara-madhyeṁ likhataṁ Travāḍī Khīmajī Chaganajī āṁṇī ǁ

2. Ms. of the *Niśīthasūtra*. Shelfmark: Or. 13600 - **Cat. No. 157.**

saṁvat 1865 nā varṣe Āsu māse śukla-pakṣe dvitīyāyāṁ tithau sukra-vāsare śrīKacha-dese śrīBhujanagara madhye likhataṁ Travāḍī Khīmajī Chaganajī āṁṇī ||

3. Ms. of the *Kisana-bāvanī*. Shelfmark: Add. 26,376 - Non-Jain work, not included in our Catalogue.

saṁvat 1865 nā varṣe Caitra śuda 2 bhṛgau || likhitaṁ Travāḍī-Chagana suta-Ṣīmajī-paṭhanârthaṁ || ⊠ || leṣaka-pāṭhakayoḥ śubhaṁ bhūyāt.

4. Ms. of the *Anuttaropapātika-daśāḥ* with Guj. commentary. Shelfmark: Or. 13598 - **Cat. No. 52.**

saṁvata 1861 nā varṣe Baisākha-māse śukla pakṣe dvitīyāyāṁ tithau bhoma-vāsare śrīKacha-dese śrīBhuja-nagara-madhye likhataṁ Travāḍī Haradevajī Chaganajī āṁṇī.

Comments

Three manuscripts written in Bhuj, in Cutch. This probably applies also to No. 2, where the place of copying is not specified.

Three manuscripts written during the same year, at a few months' interval, and two of them written during the same month, at a few days' interval.

Interrelated persons all belonging to the same clan (Travāḍī): according to one manuscript, Khīmajī is the son, and Chaganajī the father. The relation is not fully clear in the other documents. Only No. 3 is clear about who is the scribe (Chagana) and who is the reader (Khīmā). Nos. 2 and 4 have an identical wording (but the function of *āṁṇī* is not transparent: 'at the instruction of'?). In No. 4 a new person intervenes: Haradevajī.

Father and sons as collectors of manuscripts: Sahasakiraṇa, Varddhamāna, Śāntidāsa.[1]

The names of these three persons appear at the end of several manuscripts which are now scattered in different collections. Originally, the manuscripts were meant to build a family library. Sahasakiraṇa, the father, was the initiator. What he did was either for his elder son, Vardhamāna, or for Vardhamāna and his younger brother, Śāntidāsa. Either he had the manuscripts copied directly for him, or he bought them afterwards, when they had already been commissioned and copied long ago. The seven London manuscripts provide evidence for both situations: No. 232 was copied in V.S. 1680 and No. 664 (a special case, see below) in V.S. 1674; the five other manuscripts had been written much before Sahasakiraṇa and his sons were born (see the dates below). Thus, the Scribal Remark containing their names appears in red, written by a second hand, playing the role of an *ex libris*.

The texts available from various sources show that Sahasakiraṇa wanted to build a scholarly library, containing specialized or difficult works in Prakrit and Sanskrit (and not common reading material). Indeed, the family was not an ordinary one. It was a representative of the intelligentsia of the time, and took part in religious controversies. Thus, in the vivid polemic and complex debate opposing the followers of Dharmasāgara, the so-called 'Sāgara' side, leading to the banishment of some texts, and the main trend of the Tapāgaccha, Śāntidāsa took side with the Sāgaras, and looked for official state support for spreading their ideas (see the *praśasti* of **Cat. No. 664**; cf. *Aitihāsika Rāsa-saṁgraha [Vijayatilakasūri-rāsa]*, vol. 4. Bhavanagar, V.S. 1977, pp. 83ff.). A prominent figure of the beginning of the 17th century, Sahasakiraṇa's family, whose role in business and religious affairs was inseparable, is the ancestor of another prominent businessman and *mécène* of the 20th century, Kasturbhai Lalbhai.

Ms. of the of the *Viśeṣāvaśyaka-bhāṣya* with Hemacandra Maladhārin's commentary. Shelfmark: Or. 2103 - **Cat. No. 232.**

saṁvat 1680 varṣe Bhādrapada-māse śukla-pakṣe 2 ri(!)vau likhitaṁ | śrī-Tapāgacchâdhirāja-bhaṭṭāraka-śrī6śrī-Vijayasenasūri tat-paṭṭâlaṁkāra-bhaṭṭāraka-śrī6śrī-Vijayadevasūri-rājye paṁḍita-prakāṁḍa-maṁḍalī-śiromaṇi-paṁḍi[ta]-śrī5śrī-Śrīsaubhāgyagaṇi-śiṣya-paṁḍita-śrī5śrī-Satyasaubhāgya-gaṇi-vācanârthaṁ

[1] Brief summary of what is more detailed in Nalini Balbir, 'Sur les traces de deux bibliothèques familiales jaina au Gujerat', *Anamorphoses, Mélanges en l'honneur de Jacques Dumarçay,* Paris: EFEO / Les Indes Savantes, 2006.

idaṁ pustakaṁ Osavāla-jñātīya-Sā°-Sahasrakiraṇa-suta-Sā°-Śāṁtidāsa-puṇyârthe likṣyāpitaṁll vācaka ciraṁ jīyātll Veganapura-vāstavya Udīcya-jñātī-Rāūla-Govyaṁda likhitaṁ:ll ☒:ll śrī śrī:l

Translation

Copied in the year V.S. 1680, in the month of Bhādrapada, in the bright fortnight, on the second (day), on Sunday. This manuscript has been caused to be copied for the merit of Śāntidāsa, son of Sahasrakiraṇa of the Osval caste, to be read by the Pandit Satyasaubhāgyagaṇi, disciple of the Pandit Saubhāgyagaṇi, the crest jewel in the circle of the excellent Pandits, during the reign of Vijayadevasūri, a pontiff who is the ornament of the seat of Vijayasenasūri, the pontiff leader of the Tapāgaccha. Being read, may it have a long life. Copied by Rāula Govinda, of the Udīcya caste, resident of Veganapura.

Comments

The reference to Vijayadevasūri is meaningful in connection with the religious atmosphere prevailing in the Tapāgaccha of the time, and with the position taken by Sahasakiraṇa's family. Vijayadevasūri was not recognized as a worthy successor by Vijayasenasūri (the 59th pontiff), who preferred to favour Vijayatilakasūri (who thus became the 60th pontiff).

Ms. of the *Anekāntajayapatākā*. Shelfmark: Or. 2111 - **Cat. No. 670**.

See above 'Focus on a lady' (ms. dated V.S. 1487).

2nd Hand (in red): Sāhā śrīVacchā bhāryā bāī-Gurude suta-Sahasakiraṇena bhaṁḍāre gṛhītvā su°-Varddhamāna-Śāṁtidāsa-paripālanârthaṁll

Translation

Sahasakiraṇa, son of Vacchā and his wife Gurude, acquired (this manuscript) for his collection, for his sons Vardhamāna and Śāntidāsa to preserve.

Ms. of the *Śrīpāla-kathā*. Shelfmark: Or. 2126 (A) - **Cat. No. 731**.

Lāvaṇyaratna-gaṇinā likhitā ll śrīḥ l saṁvat 1544 varṣe mārgaśīrṣa vadi 11 dine budhavāre pūjya-Bhadrahaṁsa-gaṇi-kṛte Dadhyālaya-nagare lilikhāna ll ciraṁ nandatāt. sāha śrīVacchā- suta sāha Sahisakaraṇa svapuṇya[*hole in the paper; prob.* ârthe*]* bhaṇḍāri kāritā ll suta-Varddhamāna pustaka-pratipālanârthaṁ ll śubhaṁ bhavatu ll

Translation

Copied by Lāvaṇyaratnagaṇi. Prosperity. In the year V.S. 1544 in (the month of) Mārgaśīrṣa, in the dark fortnight, on the 11th day, on Wednesday, copied in the town of Dadhyālaya for the venerable Bhadrahaṁsagaṇi. May it rejoice for long. Sahasakiraṇa, the son of Vacchā, had the manuscript put into his collection for his own merit, for his son Vardhamāna to preserve.

Ms. of the *Praśamarati-prakaraṇa*. Shelfmark: Or. 2098 (B) - **Cat. No. 516**.

2nd Hand (in red): Sāha-śrīVacchā-bhāryā-bāī-Gorade-tat-pūtra-Sāha-Sahasakiraṇe(na) sakala-śāstra-bhāṁḍāra kārāpitaṁ l idaṁ pustakaṁ lisyāpita pūtra-yugma-Varddhamāṁna-laghu-bhrātra-Śāṁtidāsa-paripālanârthall idaṁ pustakaṁ Aṁbāvīdāsa likhitaṁll rastu:ll graṁ° 350.

Translation

Sahasakiraṇa, son of Vacchā and his wife Gorade, commissioned a collection/library containing all books. This manuscript was caused to be copied for his two sons, Vardhamāna and his younger brother Śāntidāsa, to preserve. This manuscript was copied by Ambāvīdāsa. Prosperity. Grantha number 350.

Ms. of the *Praśamarati-prakaraṇa* with a commentary. Shelfmark: Or. 2098 (A) - **Cat. No. 517**.

2nd Hand (in red): Sāha-śrīVacchā-suta-Sā° Sahasrakiraṇena puṇyârthaṁ pustakam idaṁ likhāpitaṁ suta-Varddhamāna-Śāṁtidāsa-paripālanârthaṁll

Ms. of the *Caityavandana-bhāṣya* by Śāntyācārya. Shelfmark: Or. 2109 (B) - **Cat. No. 268**.

śrī saṁvat 1631 varṣe posa vada 3 guru leṣaka-pāṭhakayo śubhaṁ bhavatu kalyā<ṁ>ṇam astull ll☒ll ☒ll śrī 1l☒

2nd Hand in red: Sāha śrī-Vacchā-suta-Sāha-Sāha Sahiṁsakaraṇa-puṇyârthi pustaka ḍaṁ bhaṁḍāri laṣāpitaṁ suta-Varddhamāna-pratipālanârthaṁ.

2. *Alphabetical index of Scribal Maxims*

See Introduction II for general observations on the scribal maxims. References given to other manuscripts having the same maxim have been given only to indicate the degree of frequency or popularity. They are by no means exhaustive. 'Ahmedabad' refers to the Praśasti section of the catalogues of manuscripts in the L.D. Institute of Indology, published as Appendices to vols 1-3 (unless otherwise indicated), and to vol. 4.

akhara-paya-hīnaṁ, 181.

akkhara-mattā-hīṇaṁ, 21; 125.

akṣara-mātra-pada-svara-hīnaṁ, 1240. Kapadia 1938 p. 26 and compare Tripathi, Strasbourg No. 10 or No. 106.

Anjaṇī-garbha-sambhūtaṁ, 571 (Homage to Hanumān from a scribe who is a Kāyastha).

adṛṣṭa-doṣān mati-vibhramād vā, 27. See Kapadia, 'The Jaina Manuscripts' (1938) p. 27; Strasbourg No. 114.

anābhogāt kiṁcit kim api, 97. See Ahmedabad No. 654 (almost identical) and compare Strasbourg Nos. 220 and 39; Pune BhORI 17.2a p. 121 and 201.

udakânala-caurebhyo, 689. See Kapadia, 'The Jaina manuscripts' (1938) p. 27, Ahmedabad No. 4828.

eka jināvara īda, 696.

kāṇau ankhihi jāṇiyai, 1343.

kihāṁ kancaṇa kihāṁ maliyā-girī, 775. Compare for the general idea Kapadia BhORI 19.2.1 p. 429.

gātraṁ sankucitaṁ gatir vigalitā, 882.

ciraṁ nandatu bhū-pīṭhe, 535.

jāisaṁ pustakaṁ, 126 (cf. *yādṛśaṁ pustakaṁ dṛṣṭvā*), 126.

jaba laga Meru aḍagaiṁ, 843. See Kapadia, 'The Jaina manuscripts' p. 29 and Strasbourg No. 212.

jaba lagga Meru thīra rahi, 1108. Identical as Pune: BhORI 19.2.1 p. 32. Compare with Ahmedabad No. 361 and Pune: BhORI 19.2.1 p. 428.

jarā jāva na pīḍei, 186 (orthographical transformation of *Daśavaikālika* 8.35!).

jalā rakhe tailā rakhe, 186.

jalād rakṣet (numerous orthographical variants or deformations), 20, 87, 126, 131, 353, 854, 1247. See Kapadia, 'The Jaina manuscripts' (1938) p. 27.

jahāṁ lage Mera aḍiga rahai, 115. Variant of *jaba laga Meru aḍagaiṁ* (above). Pune: BhORI 17.3a p. 264.

jihāṁ dru sāyara, 87 (*duharo*). Same as Ahmedabad No. 2644 and vol. 4 p. 91 No. 807.

jñānavān jñāna-dānena, 1243. See Ahmedabad Nos. 2953, 3527 and Strasbourg, introduction p. 48: typical of Digambara manuscripts of Western India, as rightly observed there.

telaṁ rakṣe, 119. See next.

tailād rakṣaṁ, 132, 171, 535, 735 (t. rakṣe), 775 (t. raṣyem), 843, 1211. See Kapadia, 'The Jaina manuscripts' p. 27.

pada-akṣara-mattāi ahiyaṁ, 11, .

pothī pyārī, 735.

bhagna-pṛṣṭhi kaṭi-grīvā, 14, 71, 87, 171, 175, 353, 735, 774. See Kapadia, 'The Jaina manuscripts' (1938) p. 28.

mangalaṁ bhagavān Vīraṁ, 843.

mangalaṁ lekhakānāṁ ca, 39, 1247.

yādṛśaṁ pustakaṁ dṛṣṭvā / yādṛśaṁ pustake dṛṣṭaṁ (numerous orthographical variants or deformations), 19, 21, 27, 36, 52, 71, 77, 78, 87, 94, 102, 109, 110, 112, 115, 116, 172, 175, 196, 213, 308, 309, 326, 352, 353, 535, 541, 578, 602, 616, 678, 679, 708, 713, 743, 843, 854, 888, 1052, 1108, 1211, 1228, 1243, 1245, 1247.

yāvan Meruḥ pavitro jinavara-janana°, 689 [*sragdharā*, four pādas, although the manuscript counts two verses]. Kapadia BhORI 19.2.1 p. 360 (at the end of a manuscript of the same work as the present one, although not a part of the work).

yāval Lavaṇoda°, 160.

ye likhayanti narā dhanyā, 353.

lipeḥ kutrâpi daurllakṣyāt ... nyūnito 'py uparārye yaḥ (yugmam), 662.

vanka-grīvā kaṭī bhagnā, 77, 78, 102, 119.

saṁkociya-kara-caraṇaṁ, 1211. See Kapadia, 'The Jaina manuscripts' (1938) p. 28 and Strasbourg No. 68.

sarva-mangala-māngalyaṁ, 27. See Pune: BhORI 17.4 p. 116 and note: a verse found in various hymns.

sarve riṣṭa-praṇāśāya ... śrīGautama-svāmineṁ nama, 843.

sūrya-candramasau yāvad, 888. Same stanza in Ahmedabad Nos. 2941, 2943, 3271, 4797. Only first pāda identical in Ahmedabad Nos. 920, 2559.

3. List of dated manuscripts

(Unless otherwise indicated, the date is the date of copying)

3.1. Vikrama era

Date (V.S.)	Catalogue number
1258	159 (palm-leaf)
1349	678 (also below 3.2)
1381	1384
1408	1384 (second hand)
1471	690
1474	680
1475	505
1477	552
1478	225
1483	323, 689
1484-85	708 (see Selected Scribal Remarks)
1486	506, 676
1487	670
1500	450
1502	97
1506	226
1507	1377
1514	1296
1515	1381
1520	330
1521	98
1523	227, 671
1524	1324
1526	307, 1320
1533	671
1539	518
1542	328
1543	527
1544	731
1545	99
1547	170
1549	1375
1554	522
1556	555
1560	82
1563	163
1571	98, 245
1576	1104
1577	714
1578	1246
1579	100
1583	451
1586	684
1590	101

Date (V.S.)	Catalogue number
1593	229
1594	179, 308
1598	166
1599	70
1600	27, 465
1601	586
1603	602, 682 (also below 3.2)
1604	19, 209
1607	85
1608	61, 269
1610	789
1611	172, 242, 486
1614	102, 331
1616	10, 587
1617	25
1618	801
1619	321
1620	216, 524
1621	36, 313
1622	13, 702
1623	1211
1626	91, 196 (also below 3.2)
1627	720
1629	195, 743
1631	268
1635	1246
1636	325
1638	1396
1640/1647	665 (autograph?)
1643	186, 1343
1646	415
1647	181, 296, 853
1648	704
1650	77
1651	14
1652	348
1653	541
1654	1312
1655	84, 530
1657	495, 535, 790
1659	74, 447, 463, 1150
1660	171, 1387
1661	898
1662	48, 1330
1664	297

Date (V.S.)	Catalogue number
1668	317, 653, 654, 840
1669	92
1671	33, 773
1672	103, 770, 888
1673	94, 729, 750 (also below 3.2), 869
1674	42 (chronogram and number), 109
1675	177, 571
1680	232
1681	11, 110
1682	591
1683	626
1685	37, 78, 253, 660
1686	7, 304
1687	1240
1688	1290
1691	23 (donation)
1693	728
1694	1376
1695	642
1696	104
1697	816, 1389 (also below 3.2)
1699	199, 327, 768
1700	326, 367
1702	83, 89
1703	29
1705	748, 997, 1415
1706	744, 803
1708	1419
1711	1401
1713	119, 1054
1715	597
1716	1212
1717	1245
1718	320, 844
1721	199 (donation), 334
1722	643
1723	781, 1316
1724	815
1728	75
1731	309
1732	471, 828 1083
1733	950, 1152
1734	250, 1285
1735	217
1736	1350

Date (V.S.)	Catalogue number
1740	887
1741	1413
1742	1380
1743	699
1744	1412
1746	1339
1747	188, 850, 1342
175x	59 (one digit missing, 1750? or 1705?)
1750	748, 1418
1751	832, 1399
1755	491, 1347
1756	846
1761	132
1762	294, 1301
1763	72
1764	825, 1339
1765	154, 749, 1283
1766	60
1768	1291
1771	30
1773	1336
1774	574, 924
1775	67, 69 (donation to the same person)
1781	742
1783	747 (chronogram; also below 3.2)
1785	525
1786	1106
1787	120, 823
1790	925, 1208
1793	573 (also below 3.2)
1794	71 (also below 3.2), 352, 1374
1796	545
1798	1247
17xx	20 (unclear, chronogram)
1801	507, 858
1802	4, 39, 1390
1803	131
1804	15 (chronogram and number), 18 (see Notes)
1807	887 (second hand), 1300
1810	349, 1220
1811	246, 1265
1814	854

Date (V.S.)	Catalogue number
1816	182
1818	1391
1819	876
1821	126, 883, 1108
1822	112
1823	185
1825/1828	116 (see Notes)
1826	316
1827	458
1828	774, 1144
1829	1241, 1372
1832	1293
1833	1243
1836	736 (also below 3.2), 1036
1838	1065
1839	368 (also below 3.2)
1842	239
1843	721
1844	1228
1848	1120
1849	1270, 1346
1850	87
1851	792, 922 (also below 3.2), 1122
1854	275
1856	481
1857	513
1858	735
1859	696 (also below 3.2)
1860	1085
1861	52, 679
1862	338
1863	1421
1864	568, 775
1865	95, 157
1866	1269
1867-68	636
1868	1069
1869	336
1870	1410
1871	1111
1872	454, 464 (acquisition and donation), 512
1875	1053
1877	807, 843
1878	478, 971, 1226
1880	240

Date (V.S.)	Catalogue number
1886	1139
1888	838, 1112
1889	578
1890	1004, 1041, 1059
1891	480
1893	219
1897	712
1901	429
19(0)3	264 (uncertain, 1903? or 1930?)
1903	713, 1101 (uncertain; see Notes)
1904	255, 1346
1905	360
1907	567
1908	259
1910	638, 1315
1911	734, 889
1913	293, 906, 995
1915	835
1916	641, 880, 902, 904; 251, 899 (also below 3.2)
191x	1202
1926	787
1927	210
1928	1202
1930	318, 644
1931	485
1932	759
1936	248, 736 (see also below 3.2),
1937	91, 180
1938	1355
1941	344
1942	256, 459, 566
1943	777
1944	503
1948	371[a]
1954	218
1956	282, 283, 350
1957	345, 357
1958	1049
1960	207
1965	1005, 1147
1970-71	645

3.2. Vikrama era and Śāka era

V.S. 1349 Śāka 1214	678
V.S. 1603 Śāka 1468	682
V.S. 1626 Śāka 1491	196
V.S. 1673 Śāka 1540	750 (slightly problematic correspondence between the two eras)
V.S. 1697 Śāka 1563	1389
V.S. 1783 Śāka 1648	747 (chronogram)
V.S. 1793 Śāka 1659	573
V.S. 1794 Śāka 1659	71
V.S. 1836 Śāka 1701	736
V.S. 1839 Śāka 1705	368
V.S. 1851 Śāka 1716	922
V.S. 1859 Śāka 1724	696
V.S. 1878 Śāka 1743	1226
V.S. 1916 Śāka 1781	251, 899

3.3. Dates in South Indian manuscripts

The few dated South Indian manuscripts from the London collections use the sixty-year cycle of Bṛhaspati (Jupiter), which is common in the region. Either they use the nominal Jupiter year only, in which case it cannot be converted into any other era, or the Jupiter year accompanied by a date in the Śaka era. Cf. H. Jacobi, 'The Computation of Hidu Dates in Inscriptions, &c.', *Epigraphia Indica = Kleine Schriften* II, p. 969ff. (Wiesbaden, 1970) for the individual names, modes of calculation and tables, D. Sircar, *Indian Epigraphy*, Delhi: Motilal Banarsidass, 1965, pp. 267-269, and R. Salomon, *Indian Epigraphy*, Oxford University Press, 1998, pp. 197-198.

sarvadhāri-nāma saṁvatsaraṁ	1236 ('doubtless = A.D. 1768-69', I.O. Cat. No. 7625); 'sarvadhāri' is the name of year 22 of the Jupiter cycle if starting from Prabhava, 55 if starting from Vijaya).
prabhava-saṁvatsarad	1237; 'prabhava' is year 1 or year 34 of the Jupiter cycle.
śaka 1601 saṁvat siddhārtha-s.	1273; the calculation is correct if 'siddhārtha' is year 26 of the Jupiter cycle, i.e., if the cycle starts with Vijaya, as according to the *Bṛhatsaṁhitā* (and not with Prabhava). According to the I.O. Cat. the ms. is not as old as indicated by Śaka 1601 = 1679 CE
1608 kṣayābde	1275; same observation as in the preceding case. 'Kṣaya' is here year 33.
abde kṣaye	1281; probably the same year as in the preceding case, but here there is no Śaka date.

4. Chronograms

We list pure chronograms, where all numbers are represented by words designating things, as well as mixed chronograms, where *bhūtasaṁkhyā* alternate with numerals in words (*dvi*, *tri*, etc.). See Introduction II, 'Date' for more details.

Among the numerous sources where chronograms and their significations are listed (e.g., D.C. Sircar, *Indian Epigraphy*, pp. 228-233), the following ones are worth mentioning in the context of Jain manuscripts: H.R. Kapadia, Pune: BhORI 17.5, Appendix VI (a) and 19.1.2 Appendix VI (a); H.R. Kapadia, 'Outlines of Palaeography' (1938), pp. 109ff.; ŚrīMahāvīrācārya-viracita, *Gaṇitasārasaṁgraha*, ed. L.C. Jain, Sholapur, 1963 (Jīvarāja Jaina Granthamālā 12), Appendix 1, pp. 1-10; Jambuvijaya Muni (ed.), *A Catalogue of Manuscripts in Jaisalmer Jain Bhandars*, Delhi, 2000, Appendix 9, pp. 574-579.

4.1. List in chronological order

Dates of copying

1487	aśva-gaja-ratna, 670
1618	tri-ṣaḍ-kalā-candra, 1419 (if read 3x6 = 18, kalā = 16, 'candra' left out; uncertain)
1647	candra-rasa-samudra-kula, 1414 (from left to right; but see notes: 1461 ŚS?)
1660/1665	sara-rtu-rasa-vidhu, 1395 (problematic, see notes)
1688	siddhaguṇâṣṭa-kāya-rajanīrāja, 1405
17xx	saṁjama-gandha-vaṇṇakkattiya-ravi, 20 (unclear)
1723	tri-nayana-muni-candra, 1316
1736	rasânilasakhâcala-vasatîśa, 1350
1747	sapti-payodhi-śaila-vasudhā, 1342
1747	muni-yuga-bhojana, 850
1804	abdhi-khaṁ-vyāla-candraiḥ 1804, 15
1829	nidhi-yugma-diggajêndu, 1241
1849	randhra-sindhv-aṣṭêndu, 1346

Dates of composition

1036 ŚS	rasa-guṇa-pūrṇa-mihī, 1413
1129	nava-kara-hara, 172
1214 ŚS.	manu-ravi, 678
1227	muni-nayana-taraṇi, 160
1242	kāra-sāgara-ravi, 544
1248	vasu-jalahi-diṇesa, 593
1293	guṇa-navâditya, 616
1312/1412	ravi-viśva, 700 (see notes)
1324	vāridhi-pakṣa-yakṣa, 725
1329	nanda-kara-kṛpīṭayoni-bhū, 1372
1334	jinâtiśaya-yakṣa, 746
1364	strīkalā-viśvedeva, 109
1440	khâbdhi-yugêndu, 231
1441	ekâbdhi-bhuvanâbde, 80
1457	aśvêśu-manu, 124
1459	nandêśu-manu, 464
1463	agni-rasa-guṇasthāna, 753
1466	ṣaḍ-rasa-Pūrva, 1341
1483	agni-dvīpa-viśva 1483, 1104 (see notes), 1105, 1106, 1108 (read as 1383)
1492	dvy-anka-manu, 762
1497	viśva-nanda-ṛṣi, 764 (note the order)
1502	yugma-vyomêndu pancabhiḥ, 1144 (note the order)

1506	rasa-dyo-tithī, 275
1507	muni-gagana-śarêndu, 1339-1340
1512	hasta-candra-śara-candra, 1296
1527	muni-karêśu-dhara, 1297
1543	tri-catus-tithi, 527
1553	vahni-śarâśugôḍupa, 914
1579	nidhi-muni-śarêndu, 346-348
1583	guṇa-śāsanajananī-tithi, 9
1602	dvi-kha-rasa-niśākara, 469
16(0)5	prāṇa-kāyêndu-śaradi, 486 (problematic, see notes)
1615	bāṇa-rayaṇîsa-rasa-bhū, 658-659
1625	bāṇâśvi-ṣaḍ-indu, 1322
1629	nava-hattha-kāya-rāy'aṁkia, 656-657 (explanation about the meaning of the words and the way to read the chronogram in 657)
1630 ŚS	guṇaṁga-mahī, 1410 (no chronogram to express '0'; see comm. for the numerical equivalent)
1641	vidhu-vāridhi-rasa-śaśadhara, 1316
1647	svara-sarasvat-tarkka-śakra, 1315
1647	muny-abdhi-saccandrakalā, 665
1647	muni-vārddhi-rasêndu, 579
1652	nayana-bāṇa-rasa-candraiḥ, 887, 922
1663	vahni-kāya-rasêndu, 128
1654	Caturānanavadanêndriya-rasa-vasudhā, 1358
1654	veda-bāṇa-rtu-candra, 701
1659	nanda-bāṇa-rasêndu, 15
1665	vāṇa-tarka-rasa-glau, 1361
1667	sapta-ṣaṣṭi-ṣaṭ-candra, 1350-1351 (only the last word is a chronogram)
166x	ūṣāpati-rasa-leśyā-mahi, 1055 (see notes and below s.v. *ūṣāpati*)
1673	rāma-munîśa-ṣoḍaśa, 1411
1674	abdhi-adri-ṣaṭ-candra (but '1684' in figures!), 664
1674	vedâdri-rasa-śitâṁśu, 110
1678	mangalyâdri-kalā, 1413
1680	vyoma-siddhi-rasa-kṣoṇī, 1342
1680	kha-vasu-kalānidhikalā, 334-335 (the last compound has to be understood as 'the digits of the abode of digits, i.e. of the moon' and has to be interpreted as redundant in the context of a play on words. If *kalānidhi* and *kalā* are understood separately, the chronogram would have to be read as 1 16 80).
1685	bāṇâṣṭa-darśanêndu, 111
1692	nitta-nanda-rasa-candramā, 992 (nitta = netra = 2)
1693	Īsaranayana-nidhana-surasa-sasi, 844
1694	yuga-nidhi-kāya-śaśānka, 1339
1696	rasa-nidhi-rasa-śaśi, 114
1700	saṁyama-śatami, 435
1703	bhojana-nabha-guṇa, 610
1706	bheda-saṁjama bhoma ... varasa chatrīsa nuṁ varaga-mūla, 973 (17 0 + 6 which is the square root of 36)
1716	rasêndu-naga-bhū, 850
1723	sattara saṁvata vahni locana, 1007 (read as 1723, but note the order, which is a mixture of *vāma-gati* and left to right sequence; or to be read as 1732?)

1763 guṇa-rasa-muni-vidhu, 1105
1765 śara-rasa-muni-candra, 1410
1773 guṇa-muni-munîndu, 565
1781 candra-gajâdri-dakṣaja, 525
1782 nayana-vasu-turaga-himakara, 1052-1053
1801 candra-ghanâśrayâṣṭaka-mahī, 721
1812 āditya-siddha-śasaṁka, 578
1849 nidhi-abdhi-vasu-sasī, 1085
1915 nanda-sasī paṇa-indūṁ 1915, 1094 (note the sequence, from left to right, in two pairs)

4.2. Numerical significations of individual words

agni, 3 (753-754, 1104-1106, 1108)
acala, 7 (1350)
anka, 9 (762)
anga, 6 (1410)
adri, 7 (110, 525, 664 [understood as 8, '1684' in figures], 1413)
anilasakha, 3 (1350)
abdhi, 4 (15, 80, 231, 664, 665, 1085)
aśva, 7 (124, 670)
Aśvin, 2 (1322)
āditya, 12 (578, 616)
āśuga, 5 (914)
indu, 1 (15, 111, 128, 231, 346-348, 486, 575, 579, 850, 1094, 1144, 1241, 1322, 1339-1340, 1346)
indriya, 5 (1358)
iṣu, 5 (124, 464, 1297)
Īsara-nayana, 3 (844)
uḍupa, 1 (914)
ūṣāpati, ? (1055). 'Uṣāpati' (if the word intended here is this) is a designation of Aniruddha, i.e. Pradyumna's son, according to the *Amarakoṣa*. However, the possible numerical value remains unclear.
ṛtu, 6 (701, 1395)
ṛṣi, 7 (764)
kara, 2 (172, 1297, 1372)
kalā, 16 (334-335, 1413, 1419)
kalānidhi, 1 (334-335)
kāya, 6 (128, 486, 656-657, 1339, 1405)
kāra, 2 (544)
kula, 7 (1414)
kṛpīṭayoni (a rather literary designation of the fire), 3 (1372)
kṣoṇī, 1 (1342)
kha, 0 (15, 231, 334-335, 469)
gagana, 0 (1339-1340)
gaja, 8 (525, 670)
gandha, ? (20)
guṇa, 3 (9, 575, 610, 616, 1105, 1410, 1413)
gunasthāna, 14 (753-754). Jain technical term.
glau ('moon' or 'earth'), 1 (1361)

ghanâśraya, 0 (721)
Caturānana-vadana, 4 (1358)
candra, 1 (15, 525, 664, 701, 721, 887, 922, 701, 1296, 1316, 1350-1351, 1410, 1414, 1419)
candrakalā, 16 (665)
candramā, 1 (992)
jalahi, 4 (593)
jinâtiśaya, 34 (746). Jain technical term referring to the extraordinary powers of a Jina.
taraṇi, taraṇī, 12 (160)
tarka, 6 (1315, 1361)
tithi, 15 (9, 275, 527)
turaga, 7 (1052-1053)
dakṣaja, 1 (525)
darśana, 6 (111)
diggaja, 8 (1241)
diṇesa, 1 (593)
dyo, 0 (275)
dvipa, dvīpa, 8 (1104; 1105, comm. aṣṭa; 1106, comm. dvipa hāthī 8; 1108)
dharā, 1 (1297)
naga, 7 (850)
nanda, 9 (15, 464, 764, 992, 1094, 1372)
nabha, 0 (610)
nayana, 2 (160, 887, 922, 1052-1053, 1316)
nidhana, 9 (844)
nidhi, 9 (114, 346-348, 1085, 1241, 1339)
niśākara, 1 (469)
pakṣa, 2 (725)
payodhi, 4 (1342)
pūrṇa, 0 (1413)
Pūrva, 14 (1341). Jain technical term: a body of 14 'ancient' Scriptures which are lost].
prāṇa, 5 (486)
bāṇa, 5 (15, 111, 658-659, 701, 887, 922, 1322, 1361)
bhuvana, 14 (80)
bhū, 1 (658-659, 850, 1372)
bhojana, 17 (610, 850)
bhoma (Guj.), 0 (973)
mangalya, 8 (1413)
manu, 14 (124, 464, 678, 762)
mahī, 1 (721, 1055, 1410, 1413)
muni, 7 (575, 850, 160, 346-348, 665, 579, 1105, 1297, 1316, 1339-1340, 1410); munîśa (1411)
yakṣa, 13 (725, 746)
yuga, 4 (231, 850, 1339)
yugma, 2 (1144, 1241)
rajanīrāja, 1 (1405)
ratna, 14 (670)
randhra, 9 (1346)
rayaṇîsa (Pkt.), 1 (658-659)
ravi, 12 (544, 678, 700)

rasa, 6 (15, 110, 114, 275, 469, 579, 658-659, 753-754, 844, 850, 887, 922, 992, 1055, 1105, 1316, 1341, 1342, 1350, 1358, 1361, 1395, 1410, 1413, 1414)
rāma, 3 (1411)
rāya (Pkt. = Skt. rājan), 1 (656-657)
leśyā, 6 (1055). Jain technical term: the six colours of the soul depending on the amount and type of karman.
locana, 2 (1007)
vaṇṇa, 5 (20)
vasatîśa ('the lord of the night', i.e. the moon), 1 (1350)
vasu, 8 (334-335, 593, 1052-1053, 1085)
vasudhā, 1 (1342, 1358)
vahni, 3 (128, 914, 1007)
vāridhi, 4 (725, 1316)
vārddhi, 4 (579)
vidhu, 1 (1105, 1316, 1395)
viśva, 13 or 14 (700), 764, 1104-1106 (= 14; 1106, viśva jagata 14, comm.), 1108 (= 13)
viśvedeva, 13 (109)
veda, 4 (110, 701)
vyāla, 8 (15)
vyoma, 0 (1144, 1342)
śakra, 1 (1315)
śara, 5 (346-348, 914, 1296, 1339-1340, 1410)
śaśadhara, 1 (1316)
śaśānka, 1 (578, 1339)
śaśi, 1 (114)
śāsana-jananī, 8 (9). Jain technical term: the '8 mothers of the Teaching', i.e. the five *samitis* and the three *guptis*. See for instance, *Uttarādhyayana*, chap. 24.
śitâṁśu, 1 (110)
śaila, 7 (1342)
samudra, 4 (1414)
saṁyama, 17 (435, 20); bheda-saṁjama, 17 (973). Technical meaning in the Jain context: see, for instance, **Cat. No. 1184**.
sara, 5 (1395)
sarasvat, 4 (1315)
sasi, 1 (844, 1085, 1094)
sāgara, 4 (544)
siddha, siddha-guṇa, 8 (578, 1405)
siddhi, 8 (1342)
sindhu, 4 (1346)
strīkalā, 64 (109)
svara, 7 (1315)
hara (= the eleven Rudras), 11 (172)
hasta (Pkt. hattha), 2 (656-657, 1296)
himakara, 1 (1052-1053)

4.3. Words used to express particular numbers

0 kha, gagana, ghanâśraya, dyo, nabha, pūrṇa, bhoma, vyoma
1 indu, uḍupa, kalānidhi, glau, candra, candramā, diṇesa (Pkt.), niśākara, rajanīrāja, rayaṇîsa (Pkt.), ravi, rāya (Pkt.), vasatîśa, vidhu, śaśadhara, śaśānka, śaśi, śitâṁśu, sasi, himakara,

	dakṣaja; kṣoṇī, glau, dhara, bhū, bhūmi, mahī, vasudhā; kula; śakra
2	yugma; Aśvina; kara, kāra, hasta; nayana, nitta (= netra), locana; pakṣa
3	agni, anilasakha, kṛpīṭayoni, vahni; Īsara-nayana; guṇa; rāma
4	abdhi, jalahi (Pkt.), payodhi, vāridhi, vārddhi, samudra, sarasvat, sāgara, sindhu; yuga; Caturānana-vadana; veda
5	indriya, prāṇa; iṣu, bāṇa, śara, sara, āśuga; vaṇṇa (Pkt.)
6	ṛtu; rasa; kāya; tarka, darśana; leśyā
7	acala, adri, kula, naga, śaila; ṛṣi, muni; aśva, turaga; dvipa; svara
8	gaja, diggaja, dvīpa, vyāla; mangalya; vasu; śāsana-jananī; siddha, siddhaguṇa, siddhi
9	anka; nanda; nidhana, nidhi; randhra
11	hara
12	āditya, ravi, taraṇi
13	yakṣa; viśva, viśvedeva
14	guṇasthāna; Pūrva; Manu; ratna; viśva, bhuvana
15	tithi
16	kalā, candrakalā, kalānidhi-kalā
17	saṁyama, bhojana
34	jinâtiśaya
64	strī-kalā

5. List of illustrated manuscripts

(The numbers within brackets refer to the entries of our Catalogue. See List of illustrations for those which are reproduced in the plates of this volume or as digital images on the CD)

5.1. With one or several miniatures

Kalpasūtra manuscripts

I.O. San. 1622 (Cat. No. 116; one ill.)
I.O. San. 3177 (Cat. No. 96)
Or. 5149 (No. 98)
Or. 11921 (No. 99)
Or. 12744 (No. 100)
Or. 13341 (No. 138), isolated leaves
Or. 13342 (No. 139), isolated leaves
Or. 13455 (No. 106)
Or. 13700 (No. 97)
Or. 13701 (No. 122)
Or. 13950 (No. 140)
Or. 13959 (No. 104)
Or. 14262 (No. 141), isolated leaves
Illustrated folios at the Victoria and Albert Museum (Nos. 142-147)
Illustrated folios at the British Museum (Nos. 148-153)

Uttarādhyayana manuscripts

Or. 5257 (No. 164; one ill.)
Or. 13362 (No. 178)
Or. 13476 (No. 179, two ills.)
Victoria and Albert Museum IS 2-1972 (No. 165)

Cosmological texts

Add. 26374 (No. 316), Kṣetrasamāsa
Add. Or. 1812 (No. 371[a]), Aḍhāī-dvīpa
Add. Or. 1814 (No. 372), Aḍhāī-dvīpa
Burnell 417 (No. 1217), Trilokasāra (Dig.)
I.O. San. 2583 (No. 1220), Trailokyadīpikā (Dig.)
I.O. San. 3409 (No. 308), Laghu-kṣetra-samāsa
Or. 2116 C (No. 337), Saṁgrahaṇīratna
Or. 2117 A (No. 310), Laghu-Kṣetrasamāsa (diagrams)
Or. 2117 B (No. 320), Laghu-Kṣetrasamāsa (diagrams)
Or. 2117 C (No. 314), Laghu-Kṣetrasamāsa (diagrams)
Or. 13294 (No. 369), Jambūdvīpa
Or. 13454 (No. 327), Saṁgrahaṇīratna
Or. 13456 (No. 336), Saṁgrahaṇīratna
Or. 13459 (No. 367), Saṁgrahaṇī-yantra (tables and diagrams only)
Or. 13937 (No. 370), Aḍhāīdvīpa
Or. 13974 (No. 368), Lokapuruṣa
Or. 15892 (No. 1221), Trailokyadīpikā (Dig.)
Victoria and Albert Museum IS 35-1971 (No. 339), Saṁgrahaṇīratna

Narratives

I.O. San. 3177 (No. 708), Kālakācārya-kathā
Or. 2123 B (No. 689), Triṣaṣṭiśalākāpuruṣa-caritra
Or. 2125 (No. 1051), Śatrunjaya-māhātmya
Or. 2126 A (No. 731), Sirivāla-kahā
Or. 5189 (No. 1050), Śatrunjaya-māhātmya
Or. 13745 (No. 709), Kālakācārya-kathā
Or. 13524 (No. 747), Śālibhadra-caupaī
Or. 13622 (No. 737), Śrīpāla-rāsa
Or. 13950 (No. 710), Kālakācārya-kathā
Or. 14064 A (No. 808), Madanakumāra-caupaī
Or. 14290 (No. 1270), Ādityavara-kathā
Or. 14687 1 (No. 860), Ḍholā-Marū
Or. 14687 2 (No. 859), Madhavanala kī copaī
Or. 15289 (No. 792), Candana-rāja-caupaī
British Museum BM 1959-4-11-04 (No. 711)

Other texts (mostly one or two illustrations)

Add. 26,461, 5 (No. 1416), Sāmudrika-śāstra
Add. 26,519 (see the section 'Description of composite manuscripts'), Images of the Jinas
Or. 7619 (No. 76), Prajñāpanā
Or. 13457 (No. 1389), Līlāvatī (image of Sarasvatī)
Or. 13477 (No. 250), Ṣaḍāvaśyaka-bālāvabodha
Or. 13478 (No. 876), Bhaktāmara-stotra (small vignettes)
Or. 13623 (No. 925), Caturviṁśatijina-stava
Or. 13696 (No. 645), Saptati-śata-sthānaka
Or. 13697 C (No. 836), Neminātha-stavana
Or. 13741 (No. 884), Bhaktāmara-stotra (yantra)
Or. 13806 (No. 1351), Abhidhānacintāmaṇi (image of Sarasvatī)
BM 1926-3-16-01 (No. 1188), illustrated folio

Vijñaptipatra

Or. 16192 (No. 1425)

5.2. With ornamental designs (*citrapṛṣṭhikā*)

Citrapṛṣṭhikā is the technical term for full pages illustrated with ornamental motifs, especially flowers, trees, birds. They serve as opening or closure of manuscripts.

I.O. San. 1363 D (No. 36) Upāsakadaśāḥ
I.O. San. 1522 (No. 163), Uttarādhyayana
I.O. San. 1530 K (No. 815), Rātribhojana-rāsa
I.O. San. 1564 E (No. 274), Sāmāyika-pratikramaṇa-vidhi
I.O. San. 1992 (No. 548), Yogaśāstra
I.O. San. 2646 A (No. 130), Kalpāntarvācya
I.O. San. 2646 B (No. 131), Kalpasūtra
I.O. San. 3315 (No. 1399), Nāracandra-ṭippaṇa
Or. 2116 B (No. 321), Saṁgrahaṇīratna

Or. 2116 C (No. 337), Saṁgrahaṇīratna
Or. 2122 I (No. 722), Bhuvanabhānukevali-caritra
Or. 2125 (No. 1051), Śatrunjaya-māhātmya
Or. 2132 F (No. 346), Vicāraṣaṭtriṁśikā
Or. 2137 A (No. 666), Siddhāntālāpaka
Or. 5123 A (No. 19), Bhagavatī-sūtra
Or. 5257 (No. 164), Uttarādhyayana-sūtra
Or. 7619 (No. 76), Prajñāpanā
Or. 11921 (No. 99), Kalpasūtra
Or. 13179 (No. 586), Ṣaṣṭiśataka
Or. 13454 (No. 327), Saṁgrahaṇīratna
Or. 13457 A (No. 1389), Līlāvatī
Or. 13477 (No. 250), Ṣaḍāvaśyaka-bālāvabodha
Or. 13479 (No. 520), Upadeśamālā
Or. 13498 (No. 581), Vairāgyaśataka
Or. 13598 (No. 52), Anuttaropapātika-daśāḥ
Or. 13599 (No. 95), Nirayāvalikāsūtra
Or. 13950 (No. 140), Kalpasūtra folio
Or. 13600 (No. 157), Niśīthasūtra
Or. 15633/2 (No. 207, Daśavaikālika-sajjhāya
Or. 13605 (No. 28), Jñātādharmakathā
Or. 13609 (No. 87), Jambūdvīpaprajñapti
Or. 13622 (No. 737), Śrīpālarāsa
Add. 26,462 (No. 71), Rājapraśnīya
IS 35-1971 V&A (No. 339), Saṁgrahaṇīratna

See also Sections I.8.2 and II.7 of the Catalogue for objects.

5.3 Images on CD

Cat. No	CD Image numbers	Cat. No	CD Image numbers
76	101, 107	708	112, 115
96	11, 16, 18, 21, 30	709	109, 110, 111, 113, 114, 116
97	6, 10, 26, 32	737	93, 117, 118
99	29, 14, 19, 20, 28, 23, 31, 34, 33, 3	747	119, 120, 121, 122, 123, 124
100	15, 17, 35, 36	792	140, 141, 142, 143
104	13, 24, 27, 22	859	138, 139
122	92, 4, 5, 7, 8, 9, 37, 85, 12, 25	860	132, 133, 134, 135, 136, 137
165	146, 147, 148, 149, 150	872	96
178	38-68, 74, 69, 84, 70	928	99
179	100, 106	1050	95
327	80, 79, 81, 108, 71, 82, 83	1051	104
337	91, 76, 77, 78, 73, 72, 75, 103, 2	1053	94
549	102	1194	145
586	1	1220	86, 87, 88, 89, 90
645	98	1270	125, 126, 127, 128, 105, 129, 130, 131
689	97	1290	144

Indexes

(Indian alphabetical order)

1. Titles of works described

Chando'nuśāsana 1369

Chandoratnāvalī 1370

Jagaḍūcarita 767[a], 767[b]

[Janma-kuṇḍalī] 1418

[Janma-mahimā] 88

Jambūcarita 715, 716

Jambūdvīpa-prajñapti 86; Jīvavijayagaṇi's comm. 87

Jambūdvīpa-saṁgrahaṇī 305

Jambū-pṛcchā 478

Jambusāmī-sajjhāya 719

Jambūsvāmī-caupaī (Depāla) 717-718

Jaya-tihuyaṇa-stotra 904

Jayantī-śrāvikā nī guṁhalī 829

Jayānanda-caritra 796

Jātakakarmapaddhati 1411

Jātakadīpikāpaddhati 1410

Jina: lists or tabular presentations 1171, 1172, 1173, 1174, 1175

Jina-caritra *see* Kalpasūtra, Kalpāntarvācya *and* [Sketches of the lives of five Jinas]

Jina-nāma-yantra 1176

Jina-parivāra-stavana (Jñānavimala) 934

Jinapratimā-caityavandana-phala (Vinayavijaya) 271

Jinavāṇi-stavana 1017

Jinaśataka (Jambūguru) 916, 917, 918

Jinasahasranāma-(laghustotra) 1254

Jina-stavana 928 (Rāmavijaya), 955 (Guṇasāgara)

Jina-stuti 901 (Skt.), 923 (Guj.)

Jina-stotra 1267

Jina-snātra-vidhi 1150

Jītakalpa-sūtra 158; cūrṇi 159; bṛhaccūrṇivyākhyā 160

Jīrāulā-Pārśvanātha-vīnatī 1090

Jīrāulā-Pārśvanātha-stavana 1089

[Jīva-dayā] 492

[Jīva-dayā jiṇa-dhammo] 562

[Jīva-dravya-]sajjhāya (Maṇicanda) 504

Jīvavicāra (Śāntisūri), Skt. comm. 486, 487; Guj. comm. 488, 489, 490

Jīva-vicāra-sāra 491

Jīvābhigama-sūtra with Malayagiri's comm. 74

Jainendra-vyākaraṇa 1317

Jñātā-upanaya-kathāḥ 32

Jñātādharmakathāṅga 25-26; Abhayadeva's comm. 27-28; Kanakasundara's comm. 29; anon. Guj. comm. 30, 31

Jñānakalā-caupaī (Sumatiranga) 597

Jñānapancamī-kathā 1111

Jñānapancamī-sajjhāya 1115

Jñānapancamī-stavana 1113

Jyotiṣasāroddhāra 1408, 1409

Jyotiḥsāra (Naracandra) 1399

Ḍhālasāgara 843

Ḍhola-Māru-copaī 860

Taṁ-jayau-stotra 895

Tattvataranginī 658-659 (with auto-comm.)

Tattvaprabodha-prakaraṇa 650

Tattvārtha-sūtra 515 (with Bhāṣya), 1204 (Dig.), 1205 (Dig.), 1206 (Bhāskaranandin's comm.)

Tantrākhyāla 1161

Tapaś-caraṇāni 1137

Tapāgaccha-paṭṭāvalī 1169

Tamāṣū-sijjhāi 647

Tarkataranginī 683

[tasmāj jāgṛta jāgṛta] 1306

Tājikasāra 1414

[tārā viṣṇū raṇatvid] 1304

Tijaya-pahutta-stotra 902 (Skt. comm.), 903 (Guj. comm.)

Tīna-covīsī-vandana *see* 1025

Vicāraṣaṭtriṁśikā *see* Cauvīsadaṇḍaka

Vijñaptipatra 1425

Vidagdhamukhamaṇḍana 1386

Vidyāvilāsa-kathā 816

Vidyāvilāsa-rāsa 817

Vipākasūtra with Guj. comm. 59, 60

Vimalanāthacarita 694

Vimalācalatīrtha-mālā 1069

Viṁśati-tīrthapada-pūjā 1149

[Viṁśati-sthānaka] 1148

Viṁśatisthānaka-pūjā-vidhi 1146

Viṁśatisthānaka-vicāra 1145

Viṁśatisthānaka-vicārāmṛta-saṁgraha 1144

Viṁśatisthānaka-vidhi 1147

Virāṭa-parva 841

Vividha-śāstra-vicāra-subhāṣita-gāthā 561; 669

Vivekamanjarī 593

Vivekavilāsa 680, 681, 682 (with Guj. comm.)

Viśeṣāvaśyakabhāṣya 232

Viṣāpahāra-stotra 1258-1259

Vītarāga-stotra 861

Vīrajina-stavana 1000

Vīra-stavana 999

[Vīra hamaṇe āve che māre maṁdirīe] 999

Vīrāngada-caupaī 818

Vṛttaratnākara 1372, 1373

[Vṛṣabhagadya] 1255

Vetāla-pacīsī 854

Vetāla-pacīsī-rāsa (Devaśīla) 853

Vaidyamanotsava 1421

Vaidyavallabha 1423

Vairāgya-gīta (Māladeva) 583

Vairāgyaśataka 579, 580, 581; *see* Śataka-traya

Vairāgya-sandhi 582

Vairāgyasāra 1231

Vrata-kathā (Dig.) 1271

Śaṁkheśvara-Pārśvanātha-chanda 1084

Śaṁkheśvara-Pārśvanātha-stavana 1083

Śaṁkheśvara-Pārśvanātha-stotra 1082

Śataka 437

Śataka (Devendrasūri) 441-446; auto-comm. 447-448; Guṇaratna's comm. 449-450; Skt. comm. 451; Guj. comm. 452, 453

Śataka-karmagrantha-sūcīyantra (Sumativardhana) 454

Śataka-traya 1300, 1301

Śataka-bhāṣya 438

Śatrunjaya-Ādinātha-namaskāra 1077, 1078

[Śatrunjaya-uddhāra-rāsa] 1056

Śatrunjaya-giri-stavana 1061

Śatrunjaya-maṇḍana-śrīĀdinātha-vinatī 1081

Śatrunjaya-māhātmya 1050-1051

Śatrunjaya-māhātmyollekha 1052-1053

Śatrunjaya-sāroddhāra 1054

Śabdaprabheda 1358

Śabdānuśāsana (Śākaṭāyana) 1318

Śabdānuśāsana (Hemacandra) 1323; 1324 (Bṛhadvṛtti), 1325-1331 (Laghuvṛtti)

Śabdānekārtha 1361

Śāntikara-stotra 872

[Śānti jiṇinda avadhārīe] 970

Śāntijina-chanda 968

Śāntijina-stuti 965

Śāntināthacarita 695 (Ajitaprabhasūri), 696 (Bhāvacandra), 697

Śāntinātha-vīnatī 964 (Sādhuhaṁsa), 967

Śāntinātha-stavana 873-874 (Munisundarasūri), 963 (Lakṣmaṇa), 966 (Jinacanda), 969 (Rūpacanda), 971[a] (Vijayasaubhāgya)

Śāntinātha-snātra 971

2. Authors of works described

Abbreviations: Ag. = Ancalagaccha; Dig. = Digambara; Khg. = Kharataragaccha; Lg. = Lonkāgaccha; Pp. = Pūrṇimapakṣa; Tg. = Tapāgaccha - The school affiliation of a given author is mentioned in order to avoid confusions in case of homonyms only when certain from the work described or from external sources.

Akalaṅka (Dig.) 1251

Ajita brahma (Dig.) 1246

Ajita/Harṣa 582

Ajitadevasūri 622

Ajitaprabhasūri 695

Anubhūtisvarūpācārya 1336-1338

Abhayadeva-sūri 14, 23, 27-28, 37-38, 44, 51, 56, 63-64, 292-293, 455, 493, 902, 904

Amara (Lg.) 274

Amarakīrti (Tg.) 591

Amaracandrasūri (Vāyaḍag.) 1370, 1382

Amitagati (Dig.) 1228

Amṛtacandra (Dig.) 1197-1198, 1199

Amṛtavijaya (Tg.) 835, 836, 1069

Arisiṁha 765

Aśoka muni 625

Asaga (Dig.) 1242

Ānandaghana 1019

Ānandavijaya 297

Ānandasevaka (?) 1047

Āsakaraṇa (Lg.) 274

Āsaḍa 593

Indravāmadeva (Dig.) 1220-1221

Ugrasenasūri 491

Uttamavijaya 999-1000 (?), 1017 (?), 1039

Udayacandra 510

Udayadharma (Tg.) 1339-1340

Udayaprabhasūri 1395-1397

Udayaratna 511, 620, 629, 630, 1062, 1084, 1132, 1143

Udayaruci (Tg.) *see* 246

Udayavijaya (Tg.) 189, 190

Udayavīra (Tg., laghupauṣadhaśālikā śākhā) 701

Uddyotavijaya 284

Umāsvāti vācaka 515, 516-518 ; Umāsvāmi (Dig.) 1204-1206

Ṛddhivijaya 822, 981

Ṛṣabhadāsa (Tg.) 954, 1133

Kanakakīrti vācaka (Khg.) 844

Kanakakuśala (Tg.) 887, 905, 922, 1111

Kanakasundara (Tg.) 29

Kanakasoma 483, 806

Kapūravijaya 13.4

Kalyāṇavimala 1025

Kaviyaṇa (Tg.) 608, 842

Kāntivijaya 299, 646, 1117 (Tg.)

Kāntivijayagaṇi 1374

Kālidāsa 1310, 1312

Kīrtisāgara *see* 663

Kundakunda (Dig.) 1197-1203

Kumudacandra 1263

Kulamaṇḍana 80

Kuśalakṣema 1154

Kuśalalābha upādhyāya (Khg.) 858-859, 860

Kuśalalābha 265

Kedārabhaṭṭa 1372-1373

Keśavajī (?) 73

Kesarakavi 792

Kṣamāvijaya (Khīmavijaya) 951, 1063, 1127, 1145

Kṣemasundaragaṇi 997

Kṣemahaṁsagaṇi 1373

Khusyālacanda 1247

Gangadāsa (Dig.) 1270

Gajasāra 342-355

Gargarṣi 378

Jñānavimala (Tg.) 40, 266, 926, 930, 932-933, 934, 971, 1023-1024, 1031, 1058-1059, 1060, 1109, 1113, 1118-1119, 1139; (pupil of) 1061

Jñānavimalagaṇi (Khg.) 1358

Jñānasāgara (Tg.) 231, 694

Jñānasāgara brahma (Dig.) 1271

Tattvahaṁsagaṇi 721

Tārācanda 248

Tilakaśekhara 977

Tilakācārya (Candrag.) 230

Tejapāla 638

Trivikrama 1315

Dayāvardhana 753, 1098-1099

Dayāvimala 1095-1096

Dayāsiṁhagaṇi 317

Dilārām 1201, 1213

Dīpa muni (Lg.) 801

Dīpavijaya 1093

Durgadāsa 935 (?)

Depāgara (Lg.) *see* 274

Depāla 717-718, 785, 797

Devacandra(gaṇi) 545, 577

Devacandrasūri 708

Devaprabhasūri 840

Devabhadra 328

Devavijaya 472, 1114, 1128

Devaśīla (Tg.) 853

Devasūri 294

Devendra/Nemicandra 170-175

Devendra-sūri 254-258, 259, 379-392, 395-407, 409-421, 424-436, 441-453, 540, 617-618, 639-640

Devendrācārya 692

Doḍḍaiya 1249

Dolatasāgara 1049

Dhananjaya 1258-1259

Dhananjaya 1362

Dhanavijaya (Tg.), 110, 435

Dhanasāra 1300

Dhaneśvarasūri (Rājag.) 1050-1051

Dharmakumāra (Nāgendrag.) 746

Dharmaghoṣasūri 911-915

Dharmaghoṣasūri (pupil of Devendrasūri) 162, 360, 484-485

Dharmacandra 1067

Dharmadāsa-gaṇi 519-528

Dharmadāsa 1386

Dharmaprabhasūri 707

Dharmameru 336, 1310

Dharmavardhana 948; *see also* Dharmasiṁha

Dharmaśekharagaṇi 470

Dharmasamudragaṇi (Khg.) 814-815

Dharmasāgara 656-657, 658-659, 660-661, 663, 1165[a], 1166

Dharmasiṁha 988; *see also* Dharmavardhana

Dharmasiṁhamuni 4

Dharmasundara (Ūkeśag.) 1296

Dhavalacandra *see* Gajasāra

Nagāgaṇi 474

Nannasūri (Koraṇṭag.) 46-47, 527

Nandiṣeṇa 863-865

Nayanaśekharamuni 1422

Nayanasukha 1421

Nayavijaya 1074-1075

Nayavimala 1079, 1100 (= Jñānavimala)

Nayasundara (Tg.) 1054, 1071

Naracandra 1398, 1399

Navala Rāma (Dig.) 1269

Nārāyaṇa muni 834

Nityalābha 989, 1015

Māṇikyacandra 888

Māṇikyanandin (Dig.) 1222

Māṇikyasūri 726-727

Mādhavacandra Traividya (Dig.) 1218-1219

Mānatunga 876-886, 892, 894, 1262

Mānadeva 866-868, 902-903; *see also* 869-871

Mānavijaya 24, 631

Mānasāgara (Tg.) 1295

Māla 983, 1022

Māladeva 499[a], 583, 788, 802, 818

Municandra 873

Municandrasūri 238, 270

Munidevasūri 698

Munisundarasūri 872

Megharāja ṛṣi (Pārśvacandrag.) 15, 827; *see also* 71

Meghavijaya (Tg.) 850

Memanda 499

Merutunga 755-756

Merutungasūri (Ag.) 848

Meruvijaya 273

Merusundara (Khg.) 535

Mohanavijaya 793-794, 810

Yaśaḥsoma (pupil of) *see* Jayasoma

Yaśodhīra 849

Yaśovijaya vācaka/upādhyāya (Tg.) 282-283, 293, 482, 500, 596, 598, 734-738, 740-741, 925, 990; *see* 73

Rangavijaya 838, 995, 1085

Ratnamandiragaṇi 530

Ratnavijaya 957, 970

Ratnaśekhara (Bṛhad Tg., Nāgapurīya) 308-320, 481, 556, 588-590, 591-592, 637, 731-733, 1368

Ratnasundara (Pp.) 851-852

Ratnākara vācaka 486

Ratnākara 905, 906, 940

Ravidharman 1344

Rājakīrtigaṇi 560, 744

Rājacandra 65

Rājavallabha 768

Rājaśekharasūri (Harṣapurīyag.) 759- 761, 772

Rājasamudra *see* Jinarāja

Rājahaṁsa 1018

Rājendrasāgara (?) 854

Rāmadāsa ṛṣi (Lg.) 828

Rāmavijaya (pupil of Vimalavijaya) 804

Rāmavijaya vācaka (Tg., pupil of Sumativijaya) 525, 928, 1011-1012, 1014

Rūpacanda 969, 982, 1067

Rūpavijaya 192, 782, 813, 965

Lakṣmaṇa *see* Lakhamaṇa

Lakṣmīvalllabhagaṇi (Khg.) 115-116

Lakṣmīvijaya 958

Lakhamaṇa 963, 1080

Labdhivijaya 787, 809, 1130, 1131, 1135, 1136

Lālacandagaṇi 1390-1391

Lāla Būlākīdāsa 1244

Lālavijayagaṇi 605, 1005

Lāvaṇyacandra (Ag.) 1086

Lāvaṇyasamaya (Tg.) 950, 1089

Vacchavācho 830

Vardhamāna paṇḍita 956

Vardhamānasūri (Candrag.) 693

Vardhamāna 1320; 1004 (?)

Vallabha-muni 839

Vasatā muni 628

Vāgbhaṭa 1375-1380, 1381

Vādirāja (Dig.) 1256-1257.

Vādībhasiṁhasūri 1248

3. *Names of persons in Scribal Remarks*

Terms: disciple (a monk or a nun who is mentioned in relation with his or her religious teacher; king (also for emperors); monk & nun (with titles such as *guru*, *guruṇī*, *muni*, *sādhu*, *sādhvī* and their orthographical variants, e.g., *garaṇaji sāheba*, Or. 15633/2); patron (the person who want a ms. to be copied); layman; laywoman (with title *bāi* often prefixed); scribe; teacher (a monk or a nun who is mentioned in relation with his or her disciple(s)); user (the person for whom a ms. is copied). — Abbreviations: Ag. = Ancalagaccha; Āgg. = Āgamagaccha; Dig. = Digambara; Khg. = Kharataragaccha; Pp. = Pūrṇimapakṣa; Tg. = Tapāgaccha. — Some names are of uncertain reading.

Akabara (Mughal emperor, r. 1556-1605 A.D.), 181, 1211 (V.S. 1623)

Akkavvara (Mughal emperor), 77

Akhayacandrasūri (Pārśvacandrasūrig.), 507

Ajabābdhi/Ajabajjhi (paṇḍita), 850

Aṇandarāma (scribe, V.S. 1828), 774

Anupamadevī (wife of Nālhā), I.O. San. 3177 (Appendix 1)

Anopasarījī (nun, user), 259

Anopasāgaragaṇi (scribe & user, V.S. 1870; alias Anopābdhi), 1410

Abhayacanda (teacher, Khg.), 209

Abhayasundara (scribe, V.S. 1755), 1347

Abhayasundaramuni (disciple of Bhaktivimalamuni, scribe, V.S. 1761), 132

Amara (patron), 23

Amarananda (paṁ., scribe), 334

Amaramuni (disciple of Siṁgharāja), 119

Amararatnasūri (leader of Āgg., V.S. 1524), 1324

Amaravijayajī (monk, patron & user), 360

Amarasāgara-sūri (pontiff of Ag.), 75

Amarasī gola-Vachā (?, father), 171

Amarasundara (paṁ., scribe), 25

Amarasena (ṛṣi, instigator), 729

Amīcaṁda (owner), 172

Amṛtavijaya (paṁ., scribe), 1111

Amṛtavijaya (teacher), 735

Amṛtasirī (nun, user), 1069

Ambāvīdāsa (scribe), 516

Ambiṇī (wife of Suhaḍa, mother of Nālhā), I.O. San. 3177 (Appendix 1)

Ayāci Jesaṁkara Mulajī (scribe), 272

Arjuna (disciple), 77

Allāvadīn (sultan, V.S. 1500), 703

Aśvarāja (ṭhakkura, V.S. 1408), 1384

Āṇanda (monk, scribe, V.S. 1731), 309

Ānandarāma (layman, patron?), 1078

Āṇandalakṣmī (?, user), 285, 829

Āṇandavijayagaṇi (V.S. 1724), 815

Āryākosanāṁ (?, user), 581

Āsakarṇa (scribe), 334

Āsogāta (?, recipient of ms.), 85

Indrasāgaragaṇi (monk), 1390

Ugrasena Pātharīvāla (Dig., layman, patron, V.S. 1811), 1265

Ugrasena (disciple of Sundaradāsa), 728

Uṇasarā (laywoman?), 202

Uttamacanda (teacher), 828

Uttamavijaya (scribe, V.S. 1790), 925

Uttamavijayajī (teacher of Devendravijaya), 736

Udayakaraṇa (vya°), 245

Udayakalasa (scribe), 19

Udayacandra (scribe), 507

Udayarāja (monk, Ag.), 1403

Udayasāgara (disciple of Indirasāgara, scribe, V.S. 1802), 1390

Udayasaubhāgyagaṇi (user), 201

Udayasaubhāgyagaṇi (recipient of ms., V.S. 1686, disciple of Śankarasaubhāgya), 304

Udayaharṣagaṇi (V.S. 1764), 798

Udiyavimalasūri (pontiff), 217

Udiyahaṁsa (monk), 1419

Udharaṇa, 1329

Ūjala (sā°, user, resident of Patan), 82

Ṛkṣavacchā (user), 1246 (Dig.)

Ṛddhivijaya (second scribe, with Vīravijaya), 1053

Ṛddhivijayagaṇi (disciple of Lālavijayagaṇi), 1105

Ṛddhīvījayajī (scribe; prob. monk), 53

Ṛṣabhadāsa (ṛṣi, scribe, VS. 1859), 696

Ṛṣabhasainī (Dig., user), 1202

Kautigadevī (wife of Nālhā), I.O. San. 3177 (Appendix)

Kakkasūri (Ūesag.), 1296; 1377 (V.S. 1507)

Kaṁku (laywoman, user), 460

Kakū (laywoman), 245

Kanakakīrtimuni (artist), 747

Kanakadharmagaṇi (scribe), 260

Kapūraśaśadharamuni (V.S. 1687), 1240 (Dig.)

Kamalakīrttiśiva (V.S. 1647), 853

Kamalabhuvanagaṇi (user), 746

Kamalavijayagaṇi (disciple of Dayāvijayagaṇi), 1054

Kamalaharṣa, 1342

Kamalājī (laywoman of Agra, reader), 643

Kamī (āryā, nun, user), 286

Karamacanda (*cela*, user), 75

Karamasī (ṛṣi), 572

Karamasī (ṛṣi, user), 635

Karmasīha (ṛṣi, teacher), 36; 102 (V.S. 1614)

Kalā Śivadāna (scribe), 965

Kalyāṇa (layman), 104

Kalyāṁṇa(ka)(vi)malajī (?), 1025

Kalyāṇanidhāna (teacher), 1408.

Kalyāṇavijayagaṇi (teacher), 1054

Kalyāṇasāgarasūri (pontiff Ag., V.S. 1697), 1389

Kalyāṇasāgarasūri (V.S. 1821), 1108

Kalyāṇaharṣagaṇi (disciple of Dayāśekharagaṇi, V.S. 1761), 132

Kāṁṭāhādākayāra (?, merchant), 518

Kāntivijaya (teacher of Lakṣmīvijaya), 735

Kānhā (patron; see Appendix 1), 245

Kānhā (colleague of Nālhā), I.O. San. 3177 (Appendix 1)

Kāsibhoja (?), 182

Kīrtiratnasūri (leader of a branch, V.S. 1825), 116

Kīrtivijayagaṇi (Tg., disciple of Vijayasenasūri, V.S. 1722), 643

Kīrtisāgara (pupil of Labdhisāgaragaṇi, scribe), 257

Kīsturavijaye gaṇi, 107

Kuṁvarajī Sūṁdarajī (ṛṣi, scribe), 477

Kumbhakarṇa (ṛṣi, teacher), 176

Kurāaśrī (?, disciple of Vīrūjī, scribe & user), 626

Kulahaṁsamuni (disciple of Labdhisamudragaṇi, scribe), 671

Kuśalavijaya (monk, reader), 815

Kṛṣṇa (ṛṣi, user), 1294

Kṛṣṇadāsa (scribe, disciple of Cokṣacandrajitka, V.S. 1829), 1241 (Dig.)

Keśava (śaivācārya, scribe), 1384

Keśava (ṛṣi, scribe & user), 37, 78

Keśavajī (ṛṣi, teacher), 71

Kesarī (āryā, nun, user), 626

Kesarīsiṁha (layman, Kasliwal, builder of a temple), 1241 (Dig.)

Keso/// (scribe? disciple of Lakṣmīdāsa, V.S. 1672), 103

Kesodāsa (contemporary of Shahjahan, scribe), 831

Koṭhārī Rāṁmacaṁda (scribe), 638

Korapāla (?), 70

Krasanā (ṛṣi, scribe), 289

Kṣamābhadragaṇi (teacher, Khg.), 27

Kṣamāratna (disciple of Devaratna, scribe, V.S. 1590), 101

Kṣamālābhagaṇi (Khg., scribe), 1350

Kṣemakīrti (leader of a śākhā), 27

Kṣemarāja (Khg.), 586

Kṣemendrakīrtideva (Dig., V.S. 1849), 1346

Khemasāgara (teacher), 186

Gaṁgavijaya (V.S. 1790), 925

Gaṁgavinaya (Bṛ. Khg., V.S. 1916, scribe & user), 251, 880

Gangā (laywoman), 965

Gaṁgābāī (laywoman, owner), 177

Gajakuśalagaṇi (V.S. 1700, scribe), 326

Gajasāra (muni, scribe), 1409

Gajasiṁha (king, V.S. 1691), 23

Gargācārya (reader), 513

Galābavije (monk, scribe), 605

Gahilā (scribe), 82

Giradhara (scribe) or Sevaka Giradhara, 926, 1149

Guṇavarddhana (Koranṭag., scribe), 527

Guṇaśrī (nun, disciple of Vaniśrī, user), 250

Guṇasundaragaṇi (Khg., V.S. 1773), 1336

Guṇasundarasūri (bha°, brahmaṇīyāg., V.S. 1576), 1104

Gumānīrāma (mahātmā, scribe), 1226

Gurudāsa (scribe), 615

Gurude (laywoman, mother of Sahasakiraṇa), 670, 516 [Gorade]

Gulāva (layman, scribe & user), 568

Gulāvacanda (son of Dayārāmajī, V.S. 1833), 1243 (Dig.)

Gokaladāsa (svāmi, V.S. 1718), 320

Goḍīdāsa (patron?), 39

Gopālaṛṣi (contemporary of Shahjahan, user), 831

Gopālarāya (Dig.), 1202

Gorajī Ṛddhīvijayajī (scribe), 219

Govarddhana (ṛṣi, scribe), 971 + 1308

Gharusiṁha (muni, teacher), 33

Ghāsī (second son of Candrabhāṇa), 1245 (Dig.)

Caudharī-śrīVāradeva (father, benefit of), 19

Caudharī-Sahajapāla (son), 19

Cakracūḍāmaṇi (paṁ.), 746

Caturabhoja ṛṣi (disciple of Amarasena ṛṣi, scribe), 729

Candaṇasīrijī (nun, teacher, user), 311, 312, 906, 1010, 1093

Candrakīrti (Rudrapallīyag.), 524

Candrabhāṇa (patron, V.S. 1717), 1245 (Dig.)

Candravijejī (monk, scribe), 578

Cāṁpā (scribe), 196

Cāmpā (lady), 104

Cāratrakalaśajī (monk, Ūpakeśag., teacher), 92

Cāritrasundara (scribe, disciple of Jaiśīlajī, V.S. 1825), 116

Cārulabdha (vācaka), 1342

Ciraṁchajamala (?, scribe), 924

Cetanadāsa (muni, scribe, V.S. 1629), 743

Coṣā (ṛṣi, scribe), 181

Chaganajī (patron? see Appendix 1), 52, 95, 157

Chaju (sā°, user), 82

Jagajivaṇa Pāṁnācaṁda (scribe), 1093

Jagadbhūṣaṇadeva (Dig. teacher), 1290

Jayakīrti (scribe), 129

Jayanidhāna (muni, scribe, disciple of Rājacandragaṇi, V.S. 1646), 415

Jayamūrttigaṇi (monk), 203

Jayavijayagaṇi (disciple of Kalyāṇavijayagaṇi), 1054

Jayasāgaragaṇi (teacher), 1295

Jayasāgara (Khg., recipient of a ms.), 228

Jayasāgara (ga°, scribe, V.S. 1661), 898

Jayahaṁsakṣullaka (paṁ.), 586

Jayānandasūri (Āgg., V.S. 1571), 245

Jasavijaya (Tg., disciple of Nayavijaya, recipient of ms.), 1395

Jasavije (V.S. 1801, scribe), 858

Jasovīvī (wife of Dayācandajī, V.S. 1828), 774

Jahāngīra (Mughal emperor, r. 1605-1627 A.D.), 11 (V.S. 1681); see also Salema

Jāū (laywoman, patron; see Appendix 1), 670

Jāsalade (laywoman, wife of Jiṇā), 228

Jiṇadharma (reader), 597

Jiṇā (sā°, layman), 228

Jinakuśalasūri (monk, benediction of), 33

Jinakuśalasūri (pontiff of Khg.), I.O. San. 3177 (Appendix 1)

Jinaguṇaprabha (disciple of Jineśvarasūri, Khg., corrector), 1387

[1]Jinacandrasūri (pontiff of Khg.), I.O. San. 3177 (Appendix 1)

Jinacandrasūri (pontiff of Khg., died V.S. 1223), I.O. San. 3177 (Appendix 1)

Jinacandrasūri (pontiff of Khg., died V.S. 1376), I.O. San. 3177 (Appendix 1)

Jinacandrasūri (pontiff of Khg., died V.S. 1415), I.O. San. 3177 (Appendix 1)

Jinacandrasūri (pontiff of Khg.), 23 (V.S. 1691), 84 (Akbar's contemporary), 132 (V.S. 1761), 246 (V.S. 1811), 334 (V.S. 1721), 1350 (V.S. 1736), 1387 (V.S. 1660), 1342, 109 (V.S. 1674)

Jinacandasūri (V.S. 1408), 1384

Jinadatta (son of Nālhā and Kautigadevī), I.O. San. 3177 (Appendix 1)

Jinadattarṣika (owner of a ms.), 827; Jinadattarṣi (owner), 1283

Jinadattasūri (Khg.), I.O. San. 3177 (Appendix 1)

Jinadharmasūri (V.S. 1742), 1380

Jinapatisūri (Khg.), I.O. San. 3177 (Appendix 1)

Jinapadmasūri (pontiff of Khg.), I.O. San. 3177 (Appendix 1)

Jinaprabodhasūri (pontiff of Khg.), I.O. San. 3177 (Appendix 1)

Jinaprabhasūri (Khg., V.S. 1604), 209

Jinabhaktisūri (Khg., V.S. 1801), 1425

Jinabhadrasūri (pontiff of Khg. in V.S. 1484-85), I.O. San. 3177 (Appendix 1)

Jinabhadrasūri (pontiff, contemporary of Emperor Salim), 269

Jinamāṇikyasūri (pontiff of Khg.), 27 (V.S. 1600), 586 (V.S. 1601)

Jinaratnasūri (Khg., V.S. 1736), 1350

Jinarājasūri, 1342

Jinarājasūri (pontiff of Khg.), I.O. San. 3177 (Appendix 1)

Jinalabdhisūri (pontiff of Khg.), I.O. San. 3177 (Appendix 1)

Jinavallabhasūri (Khg.), I.O. San. 3177 (Appendix 1)

Jinavijaya / Jinavije (paṁ., Tg., scribe), 1004, 1041

Jinavijayagaṇi (Tg., scribe, V.S. 1722), 643

Jinasiṁhasūri (pontiff, V.S. 1671), 1314

Jinahaṁsa (ga°, Ūesag., scribe), 1296

Jineśvarasūri (pontiff of Khg.), I.O. San. 3177 (Appendix 1)

Jinesvarasūri (Khg.), 747

Jinodayasūri (Khg.), 747

Jinodayasūri (pontiff of Khg.), I.O. San. 3177 (Appendix 1)

Jivanta (ṛṣi), 587

Jītasāgaragaṇi (teacher, disciple of Jayasāgaragaṇi), 1295

[1] All Jinacandrasūris mentioned in I.O. San. 3177 are different pontiffs of the Kharataragaccha having this name.

Dānacandragaṇi (disciple of Māṇikyacandragaṇi, V.S. 1705, scribe), 1415

Dānadharmagaṇi (scribe, V.S. 1774), 924

Dāsagovindadāsa (scribe), 1126

Divākara (ṛṣi, disciple of Lālacandramuni, V.S. 1672, user), 103

Dīpavijayaga (user of a ms. bought for him), 464

Dugarasakte (paṁ., scribe?), 318

Duṁgarasījī (?), 69

Durggadāsa (āc.), 20, 77, 78, 773

Durgadāsamuni (V.S. 1699), 768

Dūda/Dūdā (monk, disciple, scribe & user), 92

Deīdāsa (son, patron), 19

Devakuśala (paṁ., scribe), 747

Devacanda Meghajī (ṛṣi, user, V.S. 1839), 368

Devajī (scribe?), 1395

Devaratna (V.S. 1590), 101

Devaratnasūri (Āgg.), 245

Devavijaya (teacher), 495

Devavijayagaṇi (scribe), 504

Devavimalagaṇi (monk, scribe), 1059, 1139

Devasiṁha (first and fourth sons of Mahaṇasiṁha), I.O. San. 3177 (Appendix 1)

Devasundara (vā°, Pp., instigator), 104

Devasaubhāgyamuni (V.S. 1787), 120

Devasaubhāgyagaṇi (owner of ms.), 701

Devasūrata (ṛṣi, user), 72

Devīdāsa (ṛṣi, V.S. 1718), 320

Devendravijaya (monk, scribe), 736

Dolatarakha (?, disciple), 57

Dolatavjagaṇi (V.S. 1862, scribe & user), 338

Doli (laywoman), 471

Dhanakuyara (layman, user), 1036

Dhanacandragaṇi (disciple of Ratnacandragaṇi, scribe), 1150

Dhanajī (layman), 104

Dhanapāla (Ūkeśavaṁśa), I.O. San. 3177 (Appendix 1)

Dhanarāja (pupil of Jayahaṁsakṣullaka, co-scribe, V.S. 1601), 586

Dhanarāja (paṁ., scribe, V.S. 1832), 1293

Dhanavijayagaṇi (user), 681

Dhanāde (wife of Dhanajī), 104

Dharamavimalajī (monk, scribe), 1135

Dharma (colleague of Nālhā), I.O. San. 3177 (Appendix 1)

Dharmakallola (monk, Khg., V.S. 1594, patron & user), 308

Dharmakīrtigaṇi (disciple of Dharmanidhāna, Khg., corrector of ms.), 109

Dharmakīrttideva (Dig. teacher), 1290

Dharmadāsa (ṛṣi, patron, V.S. 1653), 541

Dharmanidhāna-upādhyāya (disciple of Jinacandrasūri, Khg.), 109

Dharmasundara (Ūesag.), 1296

Dhurābhāi Khoḍābhāi (layman, patron?), 1037

Nathā (sā°), 304

Nannasūri (Koraṇṭag.), 527

Nayakunjara (monk, disciple of Bhāvaprabhasūri, user), 616

Nayanabhadra (muni, scribe & user), 812

Nayanabhadra (disciple of Somanandana), 116

Nayavijayagaṇi (paṁ., Tg., teacher of Yaśovijaya), 1395

Nayavijayagaṇi (Khg., disciple of Guṇasundaragaṇi, scribe, V.S. 1773), 1336

Narapati (?, Nāgapurīya-Tapāg., scribe), 1358

Narapāla (merchant), 670

Navala (lady, reader), 1066

Nāṁnacandajī (māhātmā, scribe), 256, 344, 459, 501, 566

Nākara (ṛṣi, user), 216

Nāthībāī (laywoman, patron & user), 459

Beṁnakorabā (laywoman, user), 255 [Behena Mel Nāmkora], 1306

Boḍā Punamacaṁda (scribe), 210

Bhairaiṁ Māthurānya (scribe?), 1329

Bhaktiranga (paṁ., one of the scribes), 486

Bhaktilābha (?), 1120

Bhaktivimalamuni (V.S. 1761), 132

Bhaktiviśāla (paṁ., scribe), 254

Bhaktiviśālagaṇi (disciple of Udayaharṣagaṇi, V.S. 1764), 798

Bhaktīvījayagaṇi (scribe), 240

Bhagatuḥ (?), 70

Bhadra (ṛṣi, V.S. 1668, scribe), 1240

Bhadrahaṁsagaṇi (user, V.S. 1544), 731

Bhavāṁnajī (ṛṣi), 722

Bhavānīdāsa (son, patron), 19

Madi (laywoman, user), 36

Bhāūjī (scribe), 642

Bhāṁnulabdhigaṇi (user), 1375

Bhāgyavaṁtī (āryā, nun teacher, user), 185

Bhāvaranga (teacher), 175

Bhāvaśāra Keśavajī Mangalajī, 353

Bhāvaśekharagaṇi (Ag., scribe), 1389

Bhāvasarījī (nun, user), 838

Bhāvasekharagaṇi (Ag., user), 75

Bhāvodaya (V.S. 1761, user), 132

Bhīma (son of Narapāla & Rūpadevī), 670

Bhīma (do°, Osval layman from Surat, V.S. 1668), 81

Bhīma (Śrīmālī layman from Ahmedabad, V.S. 1696), 104

Bhīmajī (V.S. 1839, scribe ? and user), 368

Bhīmasiṁha (king?, V.S. 1849), 1346

Bhīmasenajī (ṛṣi, leader of a lineage, V.S. 1821), 883

Bhuvanaśekhara (monk, Ag., user), 1389

Bhojaka Ujama Narabherāṁma (scribe), 282, 283, 350

Bhojaka Giradhara Saṁkara (scribe), 1042

Bhojaka Giradhara Hemacanda (scribe), 829

Bhojaka Saṁkara (scribe), 995

Bholāvārū (layman, *sanghapa*), 670

Maganīrāma (layman, Agrawal), 1269

Maṇakāi (laywoman, wife of Rūpacanda, user), 527

Maṇivijaya (monk, scribe), 513

Matimeru-mahopādhyāya (Ag., V.S. 1545), 99

Matisoma (disciple of Tilakīrtimuni, scribe 726

Manajī Vinayacanda (ṛṣi, user), 1391

Mayalasāgara (monk, scribe, V.S. 1747), 850

Mayācandragaṇi (monk, teacher), 354

Malūkacanda (monk), 20, 42, 94

Mahaṇasiṁha (son of Dhanapāla), I.O. San. 3177 (Appendix 1)

Mahigaladevī (wife of Moṣā), I.O. San. 3177 (Appendix 1)

Mahimāvijaya (reader), 461

Mahīpati (first son of Suhaḍa and Ambiṇī), I.O. San. 3177 (Appendix 1)

Mahīmāsāgara (teacher, V.S. 1657), 535

Māiā (śre° ??), 127

Māṁṇikasāgara (scribe), 316

Māṇikyacandragaṇi (V.S. 1705), 1415

Māthura Mevariyāṭhā (Kāyastha, scribe), 571

Mādhavajī (?), 18

Mādhavajī (scribe), 971[a]

Mānavijaya (disciple of Devavijaya, scribe, V.S. 1657), 495

Mānavijaya, 1342

Māṁnavijeyagaṇi (paṁ., monk, teacher), 293, 734

Mānasāgara (muni, scribe, disciple of Jītasāgaragaṇi), 1295

Māladeva (king), 27

Mitrānandagaṇi (Khg., teacher), 586

Miśra Jīvārāma (scribe), 1269

Mīyācandra (Mayācandra, scribe, V.S. 1877), 843

Mukaṁderāya, 846

Municaturasāgara (instigator), 774

Muniratnasūri (Āgg.), 572

Munivallabha (scribe), 15

Munivijaya (teacher of Darśavijaya, V.S. 1654), 1312

Mūla**vijaya (disciple of Śivavijaya), 229

Meghajī (ṛṣi, disciple of Ṣemajī), 71

Meghana (ṛṣi, scribe), 290

Meghabāī (laywoman), 104

Megharāja (monk, disciple of Sakhara), 77

Meghā (pāṁḍyā, scribe), 172

Mehā (ṛṣi, disciple, scribe), 11

Mehā (instigator?), 607

Mehāṛṣi (user), 343

Moṭībāī (laywoman, user), 1021

Moticanda (mahātmā, patron), 485

Motilāla (scribe), 644

Motivijaya (disciple of Kīsturavijaye gaṇi, owner of ms. + scribe?), 107

Motivijayajī (paṁ., scribe), 1112

Motivijayajejī (paṁnyāsa, scribe), 478 + 1307

Motivīje (monk, patron), 318

Motiśāgara (paṁ., scribe), 641

Moṣā (second son of Mahaṇasiṁha), I.O. San. 3177 (Appendix 1)

Mohaṇa (scribe), 597

Mohanavijejī (ga°, patron), 1121

Mohānalala (scribe), 182

Maukitkasaubhāgya (scribe & owner of ms.), 470

Yaśorangamuni (scribe), 803

Rangade (laywoman), 572

Rangapramoda (paṁ., monk, scribe), 1283

Rajjakuṁyara (āryā, nun teacher), 185

Raṇamalla (monk, scribe), 77

Ratana (layman), 104

Ratnakalaśa (paṁ., scribe & user, V.S. 1807), 1300

Ratnakīrtigaṇai (teacher, Khg.), 27

Ratnacanda (scribe, prob. monk), 714

Ratnacandra (paṁ., disciple, user), 354

Ratnacandragaṇi (teacher, lineage of Śānticandragaṇi), 1150

Ratnapāla (son of Anupamadevī and Nālhā), I.O. San. 3177 (Appendix 1)

Ratnapāla (muni, scribe, Vijayagaccha, Agra, V.S. 1762), 821

Ratnavijayagaṇi (paṁ., disciple of Vijayānandasūri, Tg.), 327

Ratnasiṁghasūri (teacher), 1050

Ratnasiṁha (son of Jīvarāja, co-scribe), 109

Ratnasigha (disciple of Muniratnasūri, Āgg.), 572

Ratnasindha (or °gha?; son of Jīvā, V.S. 1674, user), 109

Ratnahaṁsa (muni, disciple, user), 217

Ratanāde (wife of Ratana), 104

Ratnasaubhāgya (disciple of Devasaubhāgya, V.S. 1787, scribe), 120

Rayaṇadevī (wife of Rājapāla), 23

Ravajī (do°, Surat, V.S. 1668), 81

Ravidāsa (father of Rāmacandra), 13

Rahiyā (disciple of Ṣemajī), 71

Rahiyā (son of Nathā, scribe, 304

Rahī (?, layman), 245

Rāula-Gadā (scribe), 226

Rāula-Govyaṁda (scribe), 232

Rāghavaka (monk, scribe), 888

Rājacandragaṇi (teacher, V.S. 1646), 415
Rājadhara (ṛṣi, scribe), 30
Rājapāla (saṁ°, donor of ms.), 171
Rājapāla (layman), 23
Rājalade (laywoman, user), 229
Rājasāgarasūri (teacher), 199
Rājasāgaragaṇi (Khg., V.S. 1773), 1336
Rājasundaragaṇi (Khg., V.S. 1721), 334
Rājahaṁsagaṇi (V.S. 1843), 721
Rājahaṁsa (pupil of Harṣatilaka, V.S. 1608), 269
Rājahaṁsa (brother in religion of Udiyahaṁsa), 1419
Rājendrasāgara (muni, scribe, V.S. 1814), 854
Rādhākṛṣṇa (scribe), 239
Rāṁmajī (ṛṣi, disciple of Syāṁmajī, scribe), 1391
Rāmakṛṣṇa (paṁ., Dig.), 1202; 1242 (Dig., homage to)
Rāmacandra (scribe, son of Ravidāsa), 13
Rāmadeva (father of Ambiṇī), I.O. San. 3177 (Appendix 1)
Rāmasangha (scribe), 906
Rāmāuja (homage to), 1242 (Dig.)
Rāyakuvara (ṛṣi, disciple, scribe), 36
Rāyakuvara (nun, user), 774
Rāyacanda (ṛṣi, V.S. 1821, user), 883
Rāyamallajī (sāha, patron), 548
Rāyamala (donor of ms.), 171
Rāvata-Gorā (scribe), 216
Rāvata-Gorā (V.S. 1622, scribe), 702
Rīṇḍāguru° (ga°), 1347
Rudrasivacanda (scribe), 735
Rūpa (ṛṣi, teacher), 807
Rūpakalasa (paṁ., user), 27
Rūpacanda (sā°, layman, V.S. 1543), 527
Rūpacanda (°sundara?; V.S. 1743, scribe), 699
Rūpadevī (wife of Narapāla), 670
Rūpavijaya (muni, scribe, V.S. 1724), 815
Rūpavijaya (V.S. 1848), 1120
Rūpavijayagaṇi (disciple of Gangavijayagaṇi, V.S. 1790), 925
Rūpavijye (scribe), 1121
Rūpasakta (paṁ. or Lakṣmīrūpasakta, V.S. 1851, scribe), 1122
Rūṣamāṁ (user), 808
Rohiṇī (wife of Mahīpati), I.O. San. 3177 (Appendix 1)
Lakṣmai (? laywoman, recipient of ms.), 722
Lakṣmīkīratigaṇi (V.S. 1744), 1412
Lakṣmīcandrasūri (Pp.), 104
Lakṣmīdāsa (disciple), 78
Lakṣmīdāsa (ṛṣi, teacher, V.S. 1672), 103
Lakṣmīmeru (monk, Khg., scribe), 27
Lakṣmīvallabhagaṇi (V.S. 1744), 1412
Lakṣmīvijaya (scribe, disciple of Kamalavijayagaṇi), 1054
Lakṣmīvijaya (reader, disciple of Kāntivijaya), 735
Lakṣmīvimala (user), 1353
Lakṣmīsāgara (muni, brahmaṇīyāg., scribe, V.S. 1576), 1104
Lakṣmīsāgaragaṇi (Ag., teacher), 2
Lakṣmīsāgarasūri (pontiff, Tg., V.S. 1547), 170
Lakṣmīsāgarasūri (gacchanāyaka), 260
Lakṣmīsundariganinī (nun), 330
Lakhūka (muni, disciple of Nihālacandramuni, scribe & user, V.S. 1687), 1240 (Dig.)
Lachamaṇa (paṁ., scribe, V.S. 1903), 713
Labdhicandra (scribe), 1408.
Labdhisāgaragaṇi (teacher), 257
Lalubhāī Rūpacanda (layman, patron and user), 1029

Vinayasomagaṇi (recipient of ms.), 171
Vinayahaṁsa (gaṇi, teacher), 217
Vindrāvanadāsajī (paṁ.), 1243 (Dig.)
Vimalacandrasūri (Pp., V.S. 1696), 104
Vimalaprabhasūri (teacher, V.S. 1657), 535
Vimalasāgaragaṇi (scribe, V.S. 1796), 545
Vimalasī (celā, disciple of Mahimāsāgara, V.S. 1657, scribe), 535
Vivekaratnasūri (V.S. 1571, pontiff, Āgg., instigator), 245
Vivekavijaya (monk, disciple of Ṛddhivijayagaṇi, scribe), 1105
Vivekaśeṣaragaṇi (Ag., teacher), 75
Vivekaśekharagaṇi (Ag., V.S. 1697), 1389
Vivekaśrīji (nun, teacher), 207, 357 (user?), 1049 (user)
Vivekasāgaragaṇi (Ag., disciple, patron & user), 2
Vivekasāgaragaṇi (Ag., scribe, V.S. 1685), 253
Viśeṣasāga (!, gaṇi), 316
Viśvanātha (scribe), 1285
Viśvamangū (scribe, disciple of Ugrasena, V.S. 1693), 728
Vīramade (wife of Kalyāṇa), 104
Vīravijayagaṇi (scribe), 1053
Vīru (?), 57
Vīrūjī (kavi, poet), 626
Vīvekavijayagaṇi (monk, scribe), 1101, 1123
Vṛddhavijaya (monk, disciple of Satyavijaya, user), 327
Vṛddhivijaya (disciple of Subhavijaya, deposited ms. in library), 557
Vṛddhisaubhāgya (monk, user), 304
Vṛddhihaṁsagaṇi, 721
Vegā (ṛṣi, scribe, V.S. 1672), 770
Vela (laywoman), 588
Vyāsa-Dungara (scribe), 230
Vyāsa-Ratnāka (scribe), 518
Śaktikalasa (paṁ., scribe), 594
Śankarasaubhāgyagaṇi (V.S. 1686), 297, 304
Śavatilaka (muni, recipient of ms., V.S. 1657), 535
Śāntikuśalagaṇi (paṁ., scribe), 1106
Śānticandragaṇi (teacher), 1150
Śāntidāsa (layman, son of Sahasakiraṇa and brother of Vardhamāna), 232 (V.S. 1680), 516, 517, 670, 731; see also 664
Śāntivijaya (monk, Tg.), 1405
Śirojñāna (paṁ., user), 720
Śivagaṇe (disciple, user), 176
Śivajī (do°, elder brother, V.S. 1668, Surat), 81
Śivajīrāma (Dig., owner of ms.), 1226
Śivadattarṣika (owner of ms.), 448, 748
Śivanidhānagaṇi (Khg., corrector), 84
Śivarāja (layman), 23
Śivavarddhanagaṇi (disciple of Lakṣmīvallabhagaṇi, V.S. 1744), 1412
Śivavijayagaṇi (disciple of Śāntivijaya, Tg., scribe), 1405
Śivavijayagaṇi (disciple of Padmavijayagaṇi), 229
Śivasī (ṛṣi), 587
Śīlabhūṣaṇadeva (Dig. teacher), 1290
Śīlaratnasūri (Āgg.), 245
Śīlarājasūri (Āgg.), 245
Śīlavardhanasūri (Āgg.), 245
Śyāmaliyā (member of the Śrīmālī caste, scribe), 888
Śrīpuṁjā (paṁ., user), 720
Ṣimajī (ṛṣi, scribe, V.S. 1657), 790
Ṣimāsomajī (reader, disciple of Dayāsomajī), 735
Ṣillū (V.S. 1671), 773
Ṣīvasī (paṁ., recipient of ms.), 69
Ṣemacanda (scribe), 787

Ṣemajī (ṛṣi, teacher), 71

Saka (ṛṣi, owner of ms.), 587

Sakalakīrti (paṁ°, scribe, disciple of Sukhanidhāna), 1314 (V.S. 1671), 1373

Sakalamāla (paṁ. ?, V.S. 1700), 326

Saktiranga (muni, one of the scribes), 486

Sakhirakha (?), 60

Sakhīsyajī (mendicant), 57

Sangrāma (= Sanga Singha, rāṇā of Mewar, 1508-1527, *see* Blumhardt No. 84), 714 (V.S. 1577)

Sajjana (patron), 23

Satarāiṁ (layman, user), 290

Satyavijayagaṇi (brother in religion of Ratnavijayagaṇi, Tg., patron), 327

Satyasāgara (disciple of Nayanabhadra), 116

Satyasaubhāgyagaṇi (Tg., V.S. 1680, user), 232

Sadā (ṛṣi, disciple of Pherū, scribe, V.S. 1706), 744

Sadānandamuni (disciple of Supharacandramuni, V.S. 1713, scribe), 119

Sadānanda (ṛṣi, user, V.S. 1699), 768

Sadāranga (āc., ṛṣi, user), 195

Samayanandi (muni), 348

Samayanidhāna (paṁ., scribe, V.S. 1700), 367

Samara (son of Moṣā), I.O. San. 3177 (Appendix 1)

Samalagaṇi (scribe, V.S. 1638), 1396

Samayahaṁsa (pupil of Rājahaṁsa, V.S. 1608, scribe), 269

Samācanda (user), 239

Saṁyamaratnasūri, 245

Saravara (Lg.), 77

Saravijaijī (?, V.S. 1743), 699

Sarāhī (laywoman, user), 25

Salaṣa (son of Devasiṁha), I.O. San. 3177 (Appendix 1)

Salema (sāha, sāhi; Mughal emperor), 1. = Islam Shah (r. 1545-1553 A.D.; title taken by Jalāl Khān, second son of Sher Shāh): 19 (V.S. 1604), 269 (V.S. 1608) - 2. = Jahangir (r. 1605-1627): 840 (V.S. 1668), 773 (V.S. 1671)

Sahajakalaśagaṇi (Khg., patron), 209

Sahaja(or: na?)sāgara (user), 702

Sahasakiraṇa (layman, father of Śāntidāsa), 232, 268, 516, 517, 670, 731; see also 664

Sahasavīra (vya°), 245

Sāṁvalā (cailā, V.S. 1708, scribe), 1419

Sājaṇa (third son of Devasiṁha), I.O. San. 3177 (Appendix 1)

Sāmanta (second son of Devasiṁha), I.O. San. 3177 (Appendix 1)

Sāmīdāsu (ṛṣi, teacher, patron), 181

Sāyara (son of Ṭhākurasiṁha), I.O. San. 3177 (Appendix 1)

Sāru (wife of Ṭhākurasiṁha), I.O. San. 3177 (Appendix 1)

Sārdūla (patron), 23

Sālīvāḍāmāḥ (?, son, user), 163

Sāhajahān (Mughal emperor, r. 1628-1658, elder son of Jahangir, original name Khurram), 78 (Jahāṅgīra-suta', V.S. 1685), 831 (no date)

Siṁhakīrttideva (Dig. teacher), 1290

Singharāja (Uttarādhag.), 119

Singharājyarṣi (disciple of Karmasīharṣi, scribe, V.S. 1614), 102

Siddhācārya (leader, Ūesag.), 1296

Sindūradevī (wife of Sivarāja), 23

Sindharāju (or: gha°; son of Haradāsu, scribe), 1211

Sivadattarṣi (owner of ms.), 211

Sivadattṛṣika (owner of ms.), 579, 812

Sītārāma (paṁ., recipient of ms.), 1243 (Dig.)

Sīpā (paṁ.), 746

Sīhameru (paṁ., Ag., owner of ms.?), 99

Sukhanidhānagaṇi (teacher of Sakalakīrti), 1314, 1373
Sugālacandajī (sā°, layman, patron), 316
Sugālacandragaṇi (monk, teacher), 354
Suguṇacandra (acquired a ms.), 908
Sugyāṁnajī (ṛṣirāja, lineage of Bhīmasenajī, V.S. 1821, author?), 883
Sujāṁṇajī, see Sugyāṁnajī
Sudānanda (scribe & user), 677
Sudhā (disciple of Rūpā, scribe), 807
Sundaradāsa (āc. V.S. 1693), 728
Sundaramuni, 119
Sundarasāgara (gaṇi, disciple of Rājasāgara, owner of ms., deposited in coll.), 199
Sundarasaubhāgya (ga°, scribe, V.S. 1733), 950
Supharacandramuni, 119
Subhavijaya (teacher), 557
Sumatimerugaṇi (Khg., V.S. 1721), 334
Sumativimalagaṇi (Khg.), 1414
Sumatisādhusūri (pontiff, Tg., V.S. 1547), 170
Sumatisundaramuni (disciple of Sumativimalagaṇi, Khg.), 1414
Sumatihemamuni (disciple of Sumatisundaramuni, Khg., scribe), 1414
Surajasarī (nun, reader), 479
Suratacanda (paṁ., scribe & user, V.S. 1856, Bikaner), 481
Suratāṇa (patron), 23
Surendrakīrti (Dig., V.S. 1849), 1346
Suhaḍa (son of Moṣā), I.O. San. 3177 (Appendix 1)
Sūṁnā (laywoman, patron? user), 248
Sūrajasari (nun, user), 219 (patron & user?), 578, 1112
Sūrajika (do°, Surat, V.S. 1668, patron & user), 81
Sūratarṣa (scribe, disciple of Prāhlāda, V.S. 1765), 154
Sūratā (paṁ., V.S. 1851, scribe), 922
Sūrati (ṛṣi, scribe & user), 119
Sūrasarī (nun), 293
Sūrttirāma (son of Gulāvacanda, scribe), 1243 (Dig.)
Sūryakuṁyara (laywoman), 504
Sūryavijaya (paṁ., scribe), 609
Sūryaśrī (nun, user), 1004, 1041
Sobhāgacandajī (user), 925 (V.S. 1790), 823 (V.S. 1787)
Sobhāgyasariji (nun, disciple, user), 207, 357
Soṁmajī (disciple of Bhavāṁnajī), 722
Somajī (ṛṣi, teacher), 177
Somanandanajī (religious teacher, lineage of Kīrtiratnasūri), 116
Somasundara (teacher, V.S. 1487, Tg.; see Appendix 1), 670
Somasundarasūri (teacher, V.S. 1523), 671
Saukhyavardhana (disciple of Jinadharmasūri, V.S. 1742, scribe), 1380
Saubhāgyagaṇi (Tg., contemporary of Vijayadevasūri, V.S. 1680), 232
Saubhāgyacandragaṇi (one of the scribes), 486
Saubhāgyacandrasūri (Pp., pontiff V.S. 1696), 104
Saubhāgyavije (monk, scribe?), 391
Sthiraharṣa (paṁ.°, user), 1316
Sthivara (ṛṣi), 642
Syāṁmajī (ṛṣi), 1391
Haṁsagiri (saṁnyāsī, scribe), 548
Haṁsaratna (paṁ., scribe, V.S. 1794), 1374
Hameravijaya (teacher), 736
Harakuvaryabāī (laywoman, patron), 906, 1010
Harajī (ṛṣi, scribe), 635
Haradāsu (Dig., layman), 1211
Harikalaśamiśrāḥ (u°, teacher, Khg.), 209

4. *Names of social and religious groups in Scribal Remarks*

Agravāla (Dig.), 1202, 1211; Agravāra, 1269

Aṁgaṭika (?, name of a gotra), I.O. San. 3177 (Appendix 1)

Ancalagaccha, 2; 7, 75, 99 (V.S. 1545), 253, 1403; see also Vidhipakṣa

Āgamagaccha, 245, 572, 1324 (Āgamapakṣa)

Ābhyantaranāgara (jñātīya), 82

Utarādhagaccha, 11 (V.S. 1681), 20, 119; Auttarādhikag., 773 (V.S. 1671), 1240 (Dig.)

Uttarādhīsācārya, 77

Udīcya (jñāti), 232

Usa (vaṁsa-jñātīya), 1411

Ūkeśa (vaṁśa), I.O. San. 3177 (Appendix 1), 23

Ūesagaccha, 1296

Ūpakesagaccha, 92

Odīcya (jñāti, connected with Patan), 230

Osavāla (jñāti), 81 [vṛddhaśākhā], 232

Audīcya (jñāti, connected with Patan), 226

Kāyastha, 571

Kāsalīvāla (gotra), 1241 (Dig.)

Kundakundasūri-anvaya (Dig.), 1246, 1290, 1346

Koraṇṭagaccha, 527

Kharataragaccha, 23 (V.S. 1691), 27 (Kṣemakīrti-śākhā), 84, 109, 209, 228, 308 (V.S. 1594), 586, 1336 (V.S. 1773), 1350, 1414, 1425 (V.S. 1801) —— Bṛhat-Kharataragaccha, 69, 334 (V.S. 1721), 251 (V.S. 1916), 747

Candra-sākhā, 75

Cauhāṇa (vaṁśa), 216, 702

Ḍīsāvāla (jñāti), 518

Tapāgacha, 170, 232 (V.S. 1680), 326 (V.S. 1700), 327 (V.S. 1699), 643 (V.S. 1722), 678, 888 (Tapagaṇa), 1004, 1395 (Tapagaṇa), 1405 —— Nāgapurīya-T., 1358

Travāḍī, 52, 95, 157, 610

Daśāḍīya (?), 530

Nandyāmnāya (Dig.), 1346

Parīkṣaka (gotra), 23

Pārasa-gotrīya, 69

Pārśvacandragaccha, 507

Pūrṇimāpakṣa, 104 (V.S. 1696), 714 (Pūnyama-gacha, V.S. 1577), 720 (V.S. 1627)

Prāgvāta (jñāti), 82, 245, 670

Balātkāra (Dig.), 1211, 1246, 1290, 1346

Brahmaṇīyāgaccha, 1104 (V.S. 1576)

Bhāṇasālī (gotra), 109

Bhāvaśāra, 353

Mudgalānvaya, 11; 77, 773

Muṁgala, 181

Mūlasangha (Dig.), 1211, 1246, 1290

Moḍha (jñāti), 163

Rudrapallīyagaccha, 524

Vāya (or: tha?)cāra (gotra), 304

Vijayagaccha, 294

Vidhipakṣagaccha, 1389 (V.S. 1697)

Vṛdgaccha, 1413

Śrīmāla, 42, 94, 768, 888

Śrīmālī (jñāti), 104 (elder branch), 610, 679

Saṁghavī, 171, 202

Sadārangagaccha, 10

Sarasvatīgaccha (Dig.), 1211, 1246, 1290, 1346

Sindhala (gotra, Dig.), 1211

Sonī (gotra, Dig.), 1290

5. Toponyms in Scribal Remarks

The purpose of this appendix is primarily to provide basic information on the location of the places where the manuscripts were copied (see also the map placed at the beginning of this volume). In cases where no identification could be made, an attempt has been made to give references to other manuscripts (or inscriptions) where the same place is mentioned so as to ascertain the reading and show that the reference is not unique. This explains why more references or details are given in the case of less known places than in the case of famous ones. Help has been drawn from A.P. Shah's book Jain Tīrtha Sarva Saṁgraha *published by the Anandji Kalyanji Trust (I, II,1, II,2. Ahmedabad, 1953) and from individual surveys and history of Jain institutions conducted by the same trust (see under Pāṭaṇa, Rājanagara and Ṣambhāyata). Names obviously referring to the same place have been given under the same entry (Pattana, Pāṭaṇa, both corresponding to mod. Patan, etc.).*

Ajīmaganja 116 (V.S. 1825), 275 (V.S. 1854) — Mod. Azhimganj in the district of Murshidabad in Eastern Bengal, on the bank of the Ganges (*Jain Sarva Tīrtha Saṁgraha* II pp. 491-492). This is one of the five main Jain sacred places of Bengal. Its rather recent history goes back to the 18th century when it was developed thanks to the installation of Marwari Jain communities in the region.

Ajhāharī 690. Other references: Ajāhari, *Praśasti Saṁgraha* II p. 83 No. 291; Ranakpur inscription of V.S. 1496.

Aṇahallapurapattana 82 — Aṇahilapāṭaka 14 - Aṇahillapattana (vāstavya) 708 — Mod. Patan in North Gujarat, one of the most famous places of Jain history and glory. See also under Pattana.

Amadāvāda 357, 1037 — Ahmadāvāda 13 (A.-Rājanagara), 39 — Ahammadāvāda 1350 — Ahimadāvāda 1324 — Ahmmadāvād 505 — Mod. Ahmedabad. See also under Rājanagara.

Ambakāpura 42. Other references: e.g. JGK 3 p. 390.

Alavara 308 — Alavaragaḍhadurgga 543, 789 — Ālavaragaḍha-mahā-durga 594 — Mod. Alwar in Mewar, Eastern Rajasthan.

Alāulapura 216. Other references: e.g. *Praśasti Sangraha* II p. 118 No. 449; is it the same as Alāvalapura named after Alavālakhān (cf. *Praśasti Sangraha* II p. 66 No. 250, dated V.S. 1566)?

Āgarā 294, 643, 803 — Mod. Agra in Uttar Pradesh.

Ālāratā-grāma (?) 1384.

Indraprastha 1202, 1269 — The ancient name of the heart of mod. Delhi.

Ūjeṇa 736 - Same as Ujjayinī, mod. Ujjain.

Kacha-desa 52, 95, 157 (all three mss. written by the same scribe) — Mod. Cutch in Gujarat.

Kaḍī(gāṁma) 185 — North East of Viramgam and West of Kalol, in North Gujarat.

Kapitthala (-sthita) 840

Karaṇagrāma 349. Other references: e.g. Ahmedabad No. 4764.

Karanāli 181 (mentioned in JGK 3 p. 388) - Mod. Karnal in the surrounding of Delhi?

[karmmavāṭī: among toponyms in Ahmedabad, Appendix p. 625; Pingree: Wellcome Library 2004, p. 447. This is not correct. See Appendix 1 note on Or. 13524, **Cat. No. 747**].

Kalakattā 679 - Mod. Calcutta in West Bengal.

Kumbhalameru 637 — Mod. Kumbhalmer or Kumbhalgadh in Mewar, to the North-East of Ranakpur (*Praśasti Saṁgraha* II p. 20 No. 83, dated V.S. 1515, during the reign of Rāṇaśrīkumbharāṇa; p. 55 No. 221, dated V.S. 1555, during the reign of king Rāyamalla).

Kuśapura 773.

Khambhāyata 1078 (°bindare); see Ṣambhāyata — Mod. Cambay in Gujarat.

Khayarāvāda 209. Other references: e.g. Ahmedabad No. 1693 — Mod. Khairabad, Rajasthan, to the North West of Jhalawar?

Kharaḍi (nagara) 154.

Kharaṇṭidevasthāni (?) 102.

Kharevānagara 792.

Khāravīgrāma 1295.

Gangāpurapala (?) 843.

Gajanagara 1389.

Gandhāramandira 245 (°vāstavya) — One of the five main *tīrthas* around Broach, Gujarat, on the coast, it was also an important port, especially in Akbar's time (see n. 28 pp. 25-26 of M.D. Desai's introduction to Siddhicandra's *Bhānucandracarita*. Ahmedabad, Calcutta, 1941, Singhi Jain Series 15).

Gāgaraḍhū 1293 (temple of Ādinātha).

Gujarāya (nagara) 20 (Pārśva).

Ghoghapura 23 — Mod. Ghoghā about 14 miles South-East from Bhavnagar in Gujarat. A Jain *tīrtha* with a long history dating back to the beginning of the 12th century, famous for the image called 'Navakhaṇḍa Pārśvanātha'.

Caṇḍāvali 186.

Cāṁgagrāma 636.

Cāṭasūnagara 1243. Other references: e.g. Schubring No. 847 (temple of Candraprabha) — Mod. Catsu, about 42 kms to the south of Jaipur; a place of great antiquity known as a centre of Jainism since the early Medieval period (cf. K.C. Jain, *Ancient Cities and Towns of Rajasthan*. Delhi, Varanasi, Patna: Motilal Banarsidass, 1972, pp. 203-209).

Cetrakoṭagaḍha 714 - Mod. Chittor in Rajasthan.

Chabaḍā (Chavaḍā) 126.

Cha (or:Ṭha)ndagokulanagara 586 (Ādijina).

Jagattāraṇī 844 — Mod. Jaitaran, to the East of Jodhpur between Bilara and Beawar. Other forms of the name are Jayatāraṇa, Jayatārṇi.

Jayapura 1300 — Mod. Jaipur in Rajasthan.

Jāṁnakī (puravare) 1391 (Phatesiṁghajī-vijaya-rājye).

Jāmbū 720 (°madhye) — Is it the same as Jambugrāma (L.D. I-III No. 5832, *Praśasti Sangraha* II p. 110 No. 410)?

Jīrṇadurga 1106 — Mod. Junagadh in Gujarat.

Jūneranagara 735 - Mod. Junagadh in Gujarat.

Jesalamera 1336; 304, 1380 (Jesalameru); Jesala(peśaladurga) 747 — Mod. Jaisalmer in Rajasthan, one of the richest places of Jain history, especially in the Medieval period.

Jodhapura 210, 251, 904 — Mod. Jodhpur in Rajasthan.

Jhūnjhuṇūpura 269 - Mod. Jhunjhunu in Rajasthan.

Ḍiṇḍupura 1373 — Same as Ḍiṇḍuānā (Ahmedabad, Praśasti No. 849 p. 73?).

Ḍīsāgrāma 217. Numerous references: Pune: BhORI Index s.v. Dīsānagara; Ahmedabad Nos. 1914, 3759; *Praśasti Saṁgraha* II p. 53 No. 207. — Mod. Disa (Deesa), North-East of Palanpur, North Gujarat. Information on this place is available since the 13th century. It has been visited by Hemacandra.

Takṣikapura 1226 — Same as Takṣakagaḍha identified with mod. Toda Rai Singh in Rajasthan, to the South East of Malpura?

Taḍāvigrāma 535.

Toḍānagara 1243 — Same as Toda Rai Singh in Rajasthan? See also Takṣikapura.

Thalasīmara (?)-grāma 1412.

Thallusthāna 486. Other references: e.g., Schubring No. 742.

Thirapudranagara 535 — Mod. Tharad, about 36 miles to the West of Disa. Other names are Thirapura, Thirāda, Tharāpadra, Thirāpadra (see *Jain Tīrtha Sarva Saṁgraha* I,1, pp. 40-42).

Dadhālīānagara 824; Dadhyālanagara 731. Other references: e.g. Ahmedabad No. 6194; P.C. Nahar, *Jain Inscriptions* No. 496 p. 117.

Darīyāsara 188.

Darbhāvatīnagara 573, 1085 (Loḍhaṇaprabhu: see notes); mod. Dabhoi about 30 kms. South-East from Baroda in Gujarat.

Dallapura 1174.

Dahīravāsa (madhye) 832.

Devakulapāṭaka (nagara) 677.

Devagirinagara 450 — Identified with mod. Dolatabad (JGK Index, vol. 7), but could also be one of the old names of mod. Devaliya, Rajasthan, 8 kms to the West of Pratapgarh. Other references: Ahmedabad, Praśasti p. 332.

Devarājapura 33. Other references: L.D. I-III Praśasti p. 361; JGK I p. 314.

Devavāḍāgrāma 323.

Dhanadapura 1396.

Navalasari jhāmpaḍā ni pola 508.

Nahavarakoṭṭa 812. Other references, with the spelling Navahara: Schubring No. 995, JGK Index vol. 7 Navahara/Nauhara — Same as Nohar in Rajasthan, Bikaner region? It is a small Jain site with remains of old temples (see R.V. Somani, *Jain Inscriptions of Rajasthan*. Jaipur: Rajasthan Prakrit Bharati Sansthan, 1982, p. 173).

Nāgapura 27 — Nāgora 1347 — Mod. Nagaur in Rajasthan. An old centre, a rather big town (see *Jain Tīrtha Sarva Saṁgraha* I,2 pp. 198-201.

Nāgorīsarā 1041 (N.s. madhye Rājanagare): see Rājanagara.

Nābhapura 1414.

Nautaṁpura 679 (°vāsī, in Saurāṣṭra) — Mod. Jamnagar in Saurashtra. Other old names are Nautanapura and Navānagara (see JGK).

Paṭīnagara 807.

Pattana: see Pāṭaṇa.

Pallikāpura 1409 — Mod. Pali, South East of Jodhpur, Rajasthan. An important Jain centre which was the seat of the so-called Pallīvālagaccha and of the Pallīvāla Oswals.

Pāṭaṇa 60, 360, 748, 829, 1003, 1384; 453 (Pancāsarājī), 478 (Pancāsarā Pārśvan.), 610 (P.-madhye Sonīvāḍā-madhye), 889 (Thambhaṇājī Pārśvan.), 1036 (Kokā nā pāḍā-madhye), 1146 (Śāntin.), 478 (Paulīyā) — Pāṁṭaṇanagara 357 — Pattana 226, 225, 230, 237, 250, 348, 518, 825, 1245, 1384 — Mod. Patan, 78 miles North West of Ahmedabad. A glorious and well-known site for the history of Jainism, Patan was the capital of several important dynasties of Gujarat before Ahmedabad was established. The temple of Pancāsarā Pārśvanātha which is located in the heart of the whole city (Pimplano Seri) is extremely important to the heart of the Jains as it is associated with the foundation of the city at the time of king Vanarāja (8th century). Hence no wonder that it is often referred to in *praśastis* or scribal remarks. Pancāsarā is the name of the locality where the image came from (see details in J. Cort, *Jains in the World*, pp. 35-36; p. 13 and p. 203 for the translation of two hymns). The 'Thaṁbhaṇajī Pārśvanātha' mentioned in 889, the only one having this name in the city (according to Candrakant Kadiya, *Pāṭaṇ nāṁ Jinālayo*. Ahmedabad: Sheth Anandji Kalyanji, 2000, p. 46; 276) is probably the one located near the Pancāsarā complex. The 'goldsmith area' (*Sonīvāḍā*, 610) has a temple dedicated to Śāntinātha and Mahāvīra (*ibid.* pp. 201-204). The *Kokā no pāḍā* (1036, also named *Kokāvāḍo*) is an old area of Patan, for which data are available since the beginning of the 16th cent. (*ibid.* pp. 48-50). The Śāntinātha mentioned in 1146, however, cannot be identified in the absence of the indication of any location. 'Paulīyā' (478) is probably an orthographical and phonetical variant of the *Poliyo Upāśraya*, also located in Patan (*ibid.* p. 358).

Pāṁdarīā (?) 1143.

Pānīpatha 1265 — Mod. Panipat, North of Delhi.

Pārāṣī (?) 642.

Pālaṇapura 1053 (Śāntinātha) — Pāhālaṇapura 240, 1094 — Mod. Palanpur, an important city of North Gujarat. Another old form of the name is Prahladanpur. The temple dedicated to Śāntinātha is the main old temple of the city (see *Jain Tīrtha Sarva Saṁgraha* I,1 p. 34).

Pālitāṇā 207, 475, 1049; mod. Palitana near Bhavnagar in Gujarat, at the foot of Shatrunjaya hill.

Pāvānagara 326 (Ṛṣabhajina) — Same as the famous Pāvāpurī in Bihar? Or is it a place in western India?

Pīṁḍīnagara 491.

Pīpaṇeṣāpurī 78 (same as Pīpaṣeṇā, JGK 3 p. 391?); Pāpaṇāṣā 541.

Pīrāṁnapattana 1079.

Paulīyā 478: see Pāṭaṇa.

Pharakanara 182.

Pharīdakoṭa 112 (mentioned in JGK 6 p. 424) — Mod. Faridkot in Penjab?

Phalavarddhika 15 — Mod. Phalodi, West of Nagaur in Rajasthan, a famous Jain place known for its local image of Pārśvanātha.

Bagasarapura 883 (śrīB. Kāṭhiyāvāḍa-deśa-madhye) — Mod. Bagsara, Gujarat, to the East of Junagadh and West of Palitana.

Baraṇāvenagara 320.

Baharāṇapura 18 — Other spellings: Barahānapur, Barhāṇpur, Burahānpur, Burānpur, Brahmānpur; in Gujarat, 'in the south of Dandes (Khāndeś). It is a large city three Kos distant from the Tāpti' according to the Āin Akbarī quoted n. 65 p. 44 in M.D. Desai's introduction to Siddhicandra's *Bhānucandracarita* (Ahmedabad, Calcutta, 1941, Singhi Jain Series 15). The city was founded around 1400 and was named after the Shekh Burhān-u-ddin of Daulatābād (*ibidem*).

Barhāna-pattana 1405; see previous entry.

Bārahāgrāma 815.

Bāvallīgrāma 1408.

Bīkanera 371[a] — Mod. Bikaner in Rajasthan. See also Vikramapura.

Bhayāṇaideśa 1211.

Bhābhara (?) (nagraiṁ) 1120.

Bhāvanagara 759 (Bh. bandara-madhye), 971 — Mod. Bhavnagar in Gujarat.

Bhāskara(śubhasthāna) 1211 (Bhayaṇāideśa Nemināthacaityālaya).

Bhujanagara 52, 95, 157 (all three mss. written by the same scribe) — Mod. Bhuj in Cutch.

Makasūdavāda 858 — Makṣūdāvāda 116 — Maksudāvādana 774 — Magasudābāda 316 (śrīŚiṣarajīprasādāt) — Mod. Murshidabad in the Eastern part of Bengal, on the bank of the Ganges. A town where Marwari Jain communities settled since about the 18th century and which they took as a basis to develop other Jain centres in the neighbourhood, such as Ajīmaganja and Mahīmapura (see these names; *Jain Tīrtha Sarva Saṁgraha* II p. 490).

Magalapura 587 — Mangalapura 888 (Saurāṣṭra-deśe), 1415 — Mod. Mangrol, on the South West coast of Saurashtra. Other references: *Praśasti Saṁgraha* II p. 323 No. 1264 (Saurāṣṭra-deśe).

Mathurāpurī 1269.

Mahīmāpura 1144 — Mod. Mahimpur, near Murshidabad in the Eastern part of Bengal and one of the five important Jain *tīrthas* of the region, along with Ajīmaganja (see *Jain Tīrtha Sarva Saṁgraha* II pp. 489-490).

Māthurānya (?), 'from Māthurā' (?) 1329

Maṁta 132 (°vāsinaḥ).

Māḍavī nī pola 199 — The name of the city where this area is located is not mentioned in the ms. However it could well be Ahmedabad, which has a *pola* having this name. A temple dedicated to Sametaśikhara with cloth-paintings (*paṭas*) of other Jain pilgrimage-centres is located in this area.

Mālavaṇagrāma 909.

Mubai 775 (koṁṭa-maddheṁ koṁraṭa nāṁ Mālā-madheṁ) — Mod. Bombay, Mumbai.

Mūlatrāṇa 367 — Maulatrāṇa 1399 — Mod. Multan (now in Pakistan), see *Jain Tīrtha Sarva Saṁgraha* II p. 366. An important centre of Jainism, especially in the 17th century. The famous author, Samayasundara, who belonged to the Kharataragaccha, composed several of his works in this place.

Meugrāma 71.

Meḍatā 1343 — Meḍatākoṭa 196 — Mod. Merta in Rajasthan, to the North West of Ajmer and South East of Nagaur. An important town and commercial centre.

Medanītaṭa 908 — Perhaps mod. Merta (see JGK vol. Index s.v. and vol. 2 p. 150).

Yārāṣī (?) 642.

Yodhapura 591; mod. Jodhpur.

Ratnapura 1316.

Ratnapurī 922 (Śāntinātha-pr.) — Possibly mod. Ratlam in Madhya Pradesh. The Śāntinātha temple dates back to about V.S. 1600 (see *Jain Tīrtha Sarva Saṁgraha* II pp. 314-315).

Rājanagara 7, 13 (Ahm.-R.), 104, 485, 512, 578 (Phātasī nī pola, see notes), 787, 934, 968 (Cantāmaṇaji pr.), 1041, 1306; 995 (R. Nāgorīsirā-m.) — Rāyanagara 1094 — Mod. Ahmedabad. The location of the Cintāmaṇi Pārśvanātha referred to in 968 cannot be identified precisely in absence of any other indication. The place referred to as Nāgorīsirā (995) and Nāgorīsarā (1041) is probably to be identified as mod. Nāgorīśālā, the name of an *upāśraya* located in the Ratanpol area of old Ahmedabad which once belonged to both the Devasūrigaccha and the Ānandasūrigaccha (see J.B. Shah and Candrakant Kadia, *Rājnagar nāṁ Jinālayo*. Ahmedabad: Sheth Anandji Kalyanji, 1997, pp. 170-171). There are other spellings: Nāgapurī/Nāgorī Sarāha/Sarāya (JGK Index, vol. 7). The second part of the name is a variant of *sarāī*, which was replaced in the modern name by *śālā* (see e.g., L.D. I-III No. 6747), an equivalent with approximately the same meaning.

Rājapura 1121 — Same as Rājanagara? Another town? Or an area in Ahmedabad or Baroda?

Rāḍabara 853; Rāḍavara 1376 — Mod. Radabar, in the Sirohi district of Rajasthan. The nearest railway-station is Javaibandh.

Rāṇakapura 1122 — Rāṇapura 73; mod. Ranakpur in Rajasthan.

Rādhaṇapara 248 (Kunthujina) — Rādhaṇapura, Rādhanapura 256 (Kunthujina), 266 (place of compos.), 282, 338, 344 (Kunthujina), 406, 618, 1042, 1425 — Mod. Radhanpur, to the West of Patan, not far from Cutch.

Rādhikāpura 638, 838 — Perhaps the same as Rādhanapura.

Rāmapurā, Rāmapura, 239, 846. Other references in JGK Index vol. 7.

Rāhelānagara 850.

Lābhapura 11, 77 — Lāhora 296 — Mod. Lahore (see *Jain Tīrtha Sarva Saṁgraha* II p. 358), a centre of bright history in Jainism, especially in Akbar's time.

Limbaḍī 368 - Mod. Limbdi in Gujarat, an important place in connection with the Jain tradition. Important libraries (one of which was much damaged during the earthquake of 2001).

Lūṇakaraṇasāra 334 — Mod. Lunasar in Gujarat, to the North East of Wankaner and the South West of Surendranagar.

Lodrakoṭa 626 — Mod. Lodurva, a famous Jain centre 10 miles to the North West of Jaisalmer.

Vaṭakanagara 119 — Same as next?

Vaṭapattana 470 — Same as Vaṭapadra = mod. Baroda?

Vaḍāvalīgrāma 869 — West of Gambhu, a place in North Gujarat 24 miles from Patan (see *Jain Tīrtha Sarva Saṁgraha* I,1 p. 68 note).

Vaṇathalī 253 — Mod. Vanthali in Saurashtra, South West of Junagadh. The old form of the name is Vāmanasthalī (see *Jain Tīrtha Sarva Saṁgraha* I,2 pp. 132-133).

Vangadeśa 116, 774; old name referring to the eastern part of Bengal.

Vāṁsāgrāma 1150 — Mod. Vasa in Rajasthan, 4 miles to Sarupaganj and Rohida Road (see *Jain Tīrtha Sarva Saṁgraha* I,2 pp. 257-258).

Vikramapura 447, 481 — Vīkapura 1342 — Vīkānayara 92, 1413 — Mod. Bikaner in Rajasthan.

Vidyutpura 1419.

Veganapura 232 (°vāstavya). Other references: e.g., *Praśasti Saṁgraha* p. 199 No. 702.

Śiṇalī(grāma) 132.

Śeṣapura 1054. Other references: Schubring Nos. 403, 1098, Ahmedabad, Praśasti p. 51, 77; *Praśasti Saṁgraha* II p. 302 No. 1173 - Mod. Shekhapur.

Ṣāṁṇapura 530 — Same as Khānapura to be identified with mod. Khanpur, in Rajasthan, to the North East of of Jhalawar?

Ṣaṁbhāta 568 (S.-nagre corāsī-gacha nī dharmasālā-madhe), 477 (°bindare) — Ṣambhāyata 75 (°bandara) — mod. Cambay in Gujarat. No relevant information found about the *dharmaśālā* of 568 in Candrakant Kadia, *Khambhāt nāṁ Jinālayo*. Ahmedabad: Sheth Anandji Kalyanji 2000).

Saṁkarāṇīgrāma 850.

Sajāulapura 1312.

Satyapura 325 — Mod. Sanchor (Sachor) in Rajasthan. An old site with a rich history.

Samāṇainagara 195.

Saraṣejanagara 495 — Mod. Sarkhej, 8 miles of Ahmedabad.

Sarasai 744 — Same as Sarasvatī Pattana or Sarasā Pāṭaṇ?

Sarasapurā (gāṁma) 318 — Same as mod. Saraspur, an area in Ahmedabad (see *Jain Tīrtha Sarva Saṁgraha* I,1 p. 9, 12)? Or an independent place?

Savāijayanagara 1315 — Mod. Jaipur in Rajasthan.

Sasapara 218.

Sācora-nagara 37: see Satyapura.

Sāṁṇaṁda 988, 1143. Other references: *Praśasti Saṁgraha* II p. 228 No. 1112 (Sāṇandagrāma), p. 244 No. 917 (°nagara), p. 237 No. 886, p. 285 No. 1096, etc. — Mod. Sanand, Gujarat, West of Virangam.

Sāryātīrathā (?) 343.

Sālauranagara 36.

Sīkarīpurī 84.

Sīṁgamapura 179.

Sīrohī 451, 671, 1403, 1425 — Mod. Sirohi in Rajasthan, an important place on the road to Mount Abu. Most temples date back to the 16th-17th centuries.

Sunāma(-maddhe) 729. Other references: JGK 3 p. 183 (Suṇāma).

Surata 87 (°bandareṁ) — Sūrati 352 (°bandire, śrīPārśva) — Mod. Surat in South Gujarat. The Pārśvanātha temple referred to in 352 could be the temple located in Gopipura, the heart of the Jain part of Surat (see *Jain Tīrtha Sarva Saṁgraha* I,2 p. 30). See also Sūryapura.

Sulatānapura 72.

Suhāī 696.

Sūryapura 653, 654 - Suryapura 835 (S. kānasānā pāḍo) — Is identified with mod. Surat or also with mod. Jhinjhuwada in Rajasthan (see JGK Index, vol. 7).

Sesapura 293 — Sesapūra 734.

Sojhatanagara 336. Other references: Ahmedabad No. 6957; Praśasti p. 22 — Mod. Sojat, Rajasthan, South East of Jodhpur, North East of Pali.

Saurāṣṭradeśa 679.

Stambhatīrtha 165, 327, 660 - Mod. Cambay.

Srāparanagara (?) 339.

Halaura 831 (= Lahaura?).

Havatapura 10.

Concordances

1. Concordance of shelfmarks with catalogue numbers

(Shelfmarks according to alphabetical order and number)

Shelfmark: Catalogue number

India Office and Oriental Collections

Add. 14,353: 1310

Add. 22,393: 1286

Add. 25,022 (1): 1213

Add. 25,022 (2): 1201

Add. 26,358 (B,2 and C,2): 1304

Add. 26,358 (E): 1284

Erskine collection

Add. 26,362: 701

Add. 26,363: 738

Add. 26,365: 340

Add. 26,366: 1107

Add. 26,367: 775

Add. 26,373: 1391

Add. 26,374: 316

Add. 26,375: 1052

Add. 26,378: 75

Add. 26,379: 114

Add. 26,424 (E): 1353

Add. 26,434 (B): 1327

Add. 26,434 (C): 1330

Add. 26,434 (D): 1332

Add. 26,434 (E): 1365

Add. 26,435 (B): 649

Add. 26,436 (A): 1352

Add. 26,443 (C): 1323

Add. 26,446 (A): 1313

Add. 26,450 (C,1): 790

Add. 26,450 (C,2): 1047

Add. 26,450 (D): 795

Add. 26,452 (A): 575

Add. 26,452 (B,1): 1386

Add. 26,452 (B,2): 1388

Add. 26,452 (C): 135

Add. 26,452 (D): 1423

Add. 26,452 (E): 684

Add. 26,452 (F): 185

Add. 26,452 (G): cf. 120

Add. 26,452 (H): 341

Add. 26,452 (I): 613

Add. 26,452 (J): cf. 114

Add. 26,452 (K): 1338

Add. 26,452 (L): 1345

Add. 26,452 (M,1): 751

Add. 26,452 (M,2): 498

Add. 26,452 (N): 1170

Add. 26,452 (O): 1321

Add. 26,452 (P,1): 981

Add. 26,452 (P,2): 822

Add. 26,453 (A): 65

Add. 26,453 (B): 883

Add. 26,454 (B): 30

Add. 26,454 (E): 1421

Add. 26,454 (G): 136

Add. 26,455 (AI,1): 73

Add. 26,455 (AI,2): 1044

Add. 26,455 (AP): 780

Add. 26,459 (1): 716

Add. 26,459 (2): 121

Add. 26,460: 525

Add. 26,461 (1): 941
Add. 26,461 (2): 1001
Add. 26,461 (3): 950
Add. 26,461 (4): 576
Add. 26,461 (5): 1416
Add. 26,461 (6): 1071
Add. 26,461 (7): 1305
Add. 26,461 (8): 1083
Add. 26,461 (9): 956
Add. 26,461 (10): 1089
Add. 26,461 (11): 1151
Add. 26,461 (12): 940
Add. 26,461 (13): 946
Add. 26,461 (14): 1002
Add. 26,461 (15-17): 1152
Add. 26,462: 71
Add. 26,463: 120
Add. 26,464 (A): 217
Add. 26,464 (B): 1371
Add. 26,464 (C,1): 488
Add. 26,464 (C,2): 573
Add. 26,464 (D): 942
Add. 26,464 (E): 286
Add. 26,464 (F): 609
Add. 26,519 (1): 851
Add. 26,519 (2): 928
Add. 26,542 (B): 855
Add. 26,542 (D): 973

Add. Or. 1812: 371[a]
Add. Or. 1813: 371[b]
Add. Or. 1814: 372

Aufrecht 86 (I-II): 702
Aufrecht 87: 1367

Bühler 64: 766
Bühler 90: 850
Bühler 91: 854
Bühler 111: 1383
Bühler 112: 1384
Bühler 113: 1385
Bühler 118: 1344
Bühler 119: 1382
Bühler 134: 1317
Bühler 140: 1331
Bühler 280: 49
Bühler 281 (A): 110
Bühler 281 (B): 1169
Bühler 282 (1): 203
Bühler 282 (2): 236
Bühler 282A: 204
Bühler 283: 156
Bühler 284: 1103
Bühler 284A: 1181
Bühler 285: 1166
Bühler 286: 762
Bühler 287: 763
Bühler 288: 1167
Bühler 289: 1168
Bühler 290: 1165[a]
Bühler 290A: 1165[b]
Bühler 291: 767[a]
Bühler 292: 769
Bühler 293: 704
Bühler 294: 760
Bühler 295: 761
Bühler 296: 755

Bühler 297: 756
Bühler 298: 757
Bühler 299: 758
Bühler 300: 764
Bühler 301: 847
Bühler 302: 765
Bühler 303: 779
Bühler 305: 1106
Bühler 306: 671
Bühler 307: 673
Bühler 308: 1288
Bühler 325: 767[b]

Burnell 229: 1251
Burnell 235: 1248
Burnell 245: 1202
Burnell 246-247: 1223
Burnell 354-356: 1234
Burnell 381: 1218
Burnell 417: 1217
Burnell 430 (1): 1215
Burnell 430 (2): 1216
Burnell 430 (3): 1214
Burnell 433 (1): 1225
Burnell 433 (2): 1267
Burnell 433 (3): 1203
Burnell 433 (4): 1224
Burnell 433 (5): 1230
Burnell 454: 1318
Burnell 461: 1319
Burnell 474 (1): 1359
Burnell 474 (2): 1360
Burnell 474 (3): 1361

Harley 415 (1): 1076
Harley 415 (2): 994
Harley 415 (3): 963
Harley 415 (4): 1080
Harley 415 (5): 964
Harley 415 (6): 927
Harley 415 (7): 1090
Harley 415 (8): 1033
Harley 415 (9): 967
Harley 415 (10): 1087
Harley 415 (11): 1081
Harley 415 (12): 1072
Harley 415 (13): 1073
Harley 415 (14): 943
Harley 415 (15): 705
Harley 415 (16): 601
Harley 415 (17): 947
Harley 415 (18): 785
Harley 415 (19): 1038
Harley 415 (20): 786
Harley 415 (21): 811
Harley 415 (22): 819
Harley 415 (23): 797
Harley 415 (24): 791
Harley 415 (25): 750

I.O. San. 80: 126
I.O. San. 354: 170
I.O. San. 372 (B): 1242
I.O. San. 669: 1228
I.O. San. 742 (A): 1400
I.O. San. 862 (A): 269
I.O. San. 862 (B): 296
I.O. San. 864 (C): 1366

I.O. San. 867: 128
I.O. San. 888: 699
I.O. San. 1015: 182
I.O. San. 1032: 465
I.O. San. 1033: 1219
I.O. San. 1094: 679
I.O. San. 1166: 846
I.O. San. 1350 (1): 385
I.O. San. 1350 (2): 400
I.O. San. 1350 (3): 414
I.O. San. 1350 (4): 430
I.O. San. 1350 (5): 446
I.O. San. 1350 (6): 458
I.O. San. 1354 (A): 698
I.O. San. 1354 (B): 724
I.O. San. 1354 (C): 821
I.O. San. 1354 (D): 294
I.O. San. 1357: 304
I.O. San. 1358: 1144
I.O. San. 1363 (A): 1291
I.O. San. 1363 (B): 68
I.O. San. 1363 (C): 1054
I.O. San. 1363 (D): 36
I.O. San. 1367 (B): 570
I.O. San. 1372 (A): 387
I.O. San. 1372 (B,1): 448
I.O. San. 1372 (B,2): 463
I.O. San. 1399: 1227
I.O. San. 1522: 163
I.O. San. 1524: 31
I.O. San. 1525 (B): 1199
I.O. San. 1526 (B): 237
I.O. San. 1527: 695
I.O. San. 1528 (A): 1404
I.O. San. 1530 (A): 945
I.O. San. 1530 (B): 707
I.O. San. 1530 (C): 1172
I.O. San. 1530 (D): 1179
I.O. San. 1530 (E): 1187
I.O. San. 1530 (F): 1173
I.O. San. 1530 (G): 669
I.O. San. 1530 (H): 924
I.O. San. 1530 (I): 1419
I.O. San. 1530 (J): 297
I.O. San. 1530 (K): 815
I.O. San. 1532: 29
I.O. San. 1553 (A): 748
I.O. San. 1553 (B): 333
I.O. San. 1553 (C): 827
I.O. San. 1553 (D): 491
I.O. San. 1558 (A): 241
I.O. San. 1558 (B): 243
I.O. San. 1558 (C): 187
I.O. San. 1561b: 831
I.O. San. 1561c (1): 585
I.O. San. 1561c (2): 559
I.O. San. 1561c (3): 223
I.O. San. 1561d: 802
I.O. San. 1564a: 579
I.O. San. 1564 (B): 812
I.O. San. 1564 (C,1): 825
I.O. San. 1564 (C,2): 798
I.O. San. 1564 (C,3): 1079
I.O. San. 1564 (D): 211
I.O. San. 1564 (E): 274
I.O. San. 1564 (F): 844
I.O. San. 1564g: 1229
I.O. San. 1564h: 505

I.O. San. 1564 (I): 845
I.O. San. 1564 (K): 858
I.O. San. 1565: 774
I.O. San. 1571 (B): 714
I.O. San. 1571 (C): 857
I.O. San. 1596 (A): 1283
I.O. San. 1596 (B): 944
I.O. San. 1596 (C): 1271
I.O. San. 1596 (D): 1272
I.O. San. 1599: 117
I.O. San. 1603 (A): 287
I.O. San. 1609 A: 828
I.O. San. 1609 B: 806
I.O. San. 1610: 543
I.O. San. 1622: 116
I.O. San. 1632: 856
I.O. San. 1638 (B): 102
I.O. San. 1845: 1406
I.O. San. 1952: 1158
I.O. San. 1954: 198
I.O. San. 1992: 548
I.O. San. 2049 (A): 1408
I.O. San. 2049 (D): 1402
I.O. San. 2112 (A): 1282
I.O. San. 2112 (B): 537
I.O. San. 2126 (A): 309
I.O. San. 2201: 1198
I.O. San. 2341 (A): 587
I.O. San. 2341b: 200
I.O. San. 2341 (B): 1322
I.O. San. 2341 (C): 325 + 1119[a]
I.O. San. 2343 (A): 1407
I.O. San. 2343 (B): 1405
I.O. San. 2354: 721
I.O. San. 2358 (B): 749
I.O. San. 2363: 1245
I.O. San. 2468 (C): 1296
I.O. San. 2470: 1235
I.O. San. 2511: 1422
I.O. San. 2525 (A): 1312
I.O. San. 2525 (D): 848
I.O. San. 2527 (A): 648
I.O. San. 2527 (B): 1343
I.O. San. 2527 (C): 270
I.O. San. 2527 (D,1-2): 677
I.O. San. 2527 (E,1): 920
I.O. San. 2527 (E,2): 998
I.O. San. 2527 (F): 167
I.O. San. 2530: *see* MSS. Guj. 19
I.O. San. 2539 (F): 133
I.O. San. 2543 (A): 1381
I.O. San. 2543 (B): 824
I.O. San. 2583: 1220
I.O. San. 2642: 21
I.O. San. 2646 (A): 130
I.O. San. 2646 (B): 131
I.O. San. 2646 (C): 1177
I.O. San. 2691: 113
I.O. San. 2727: 125
I.O. San. 2728 (A): 735
I.O. San. 2728 (B): 810
I.O. San. 2879: 108
I.O. San. 2909 (1): 1200
I.O. San. 2909 (2): 1212
I.O. San. 3006: 91
I.O. San. 3165: 180
I.O. San. 3177 (1): 96
I.O. San. 3177 (2): 708

I.O. San. 3245 (k): 1232
I.O. San. 3266: 1053
I.O. San. 3280: 1355
I.O. San. 3287 (A): 733
I.O. San. 3287 (B): 239
I.O. San. 3287 (C): 574
I.O. San. 3292 (B): 680
I.O. San. 3293: 523
I.O. San. 3301 (A): 5
I.O. San. 3301 (B): 183
I.O. San. 3301 (C): 16
I.O. San. 3315: 1399
I.O. San. 3348: 112
I.O. San. 3349: 119
I.O. San. 3350: 770
I.O. San. 3351: 77
I.O. San. 3352 (A): 20
I.O. San. 3353: 25
I.O. San. 3354: 541
I.O. San. 3355: 11
I.O. San. 3356: 10
I.O. San. 3357: 728
I.O. San. 3358: 42
I.O. San. 3359: 331
I.O. San. 3360: 209
I.O. San. 3361: 700
I.O. San. 3362: 729 + 962 + 984
I.O. San. 3363: 768
I.O. San. 3364: 882
I.O. San. 3365: 723
I.O. San. 3366: 72
I.O. San. 3367: 181
I.O. San. 3368: 252
I.O. San. 3369: 94
I.O. San. 3370: 59
I.O. San. 3371: 773
I.O. San. 3372: 744
I.O. San. 3374: 195
I.O. San. 3375: 48
I.O. San. 3376: 84
I.O. San. 3378: 720
I.O. San. 3379: 594
I.O. San. 3382: 907
I.O. San. 3383: 816
I.O. San. 3384: 1398 + 1171
I.O. San. 3385: 571
I.O. San. 3386: 549
I.O. San. 3387: 730
I.O. San. 3388: 88
I.O. San. 3389: 343
I.O. San. 3390: 732
I.O. San. 3391: 215 + 987
I.O. San. 3392: 17
I.O. San. 3393: 1209
I.O. San. 3394 (1): 625
I.O. San. 3394 (2): 612
I.O. San. 3395 (1): 565
I.O. San. 3395 (2): 342
I.O. San. 3396: 877
I.O. San. 3397: 561
I.O. San. 3399: 781
I.O. San. 3400 (A): 244
I.O. San. 3400 (A,a,2): 1092
I.O. San. 3400 (A,a,3): 1018
I.O. San. 3400 (A,aa): 602
I.O. San. 3400 (A,b): 682
I.O. San. 3400 (A,c): 849
I.O. San. 3400 (A',gd): 923

I.O. San. 3400 (B,ca): 789
I.O. San. 3400 (B,cb): 805
I.O. San. 3400 (B,cc): 814
I.O. San. 3400 (B,cd): 817
I.O. San. 3400 (B,ce): 830
I.O. San. 3400 (B,cf): 718
I.O. San. 3400 (D,d): 551
I.O. San. 3400 (E): 280
I.O. San. 3400 (ea): 1417
I.O. San. 3400 (L,db): 1088
I.O. San. 3400 (L,eb): 1156
I.O. San. 3400 (L,ec): 599
I.O. San. 3400 (L,ed): 952
I.O. San. 3400 (M,f): 913
I.O. San. 3400 (P and Q): 492
I.O. San. 3400 (R,gc): 1148
I.O. San. 3400 (V,h): 1162
I.O. San. 3400 (V,i): 1160
I.O. San. 3401: 643
I.O. San. 3402: 1102
I.O. San. 3404: 777
I.O. San. 3405: 776
I.O. San. 3406: 772
I.O. San. 3407: 82
I.O. San. 3408: 1316
I.O. San. 3409: 308
I.O. San. 3410: 692
I.O. San. 3411: 693
I.O. San. 3412: 745
I.O. San. 3413: 524
I.O. San. 3414: 1240
I.O. San. 3415 (A): 840
I.O. San. 3416: 727
I.O. San. 3532 (1): 1268
I.O. San. 3532 (2): 1205
I.O. San. 3532 (3): 1250
I.O. San. 3532 (4): 1253
I.O. San. 3532 (5): 1255
I.O. San. 3532 (6): 1257
I.O. San. 3532 (7): 1259
I.O. San. 3532 (8): 1261
I.O. San. 3545: 1233
I.O. San. 3600 (A): 103
I.O. San. 3606 (A): 78
I.O. San. 3606 (B): 263
I.O. San. 3610: 34
I.O. San. 3614 (A): 1294
I.O. San. 3614 (D): 886
I.O. San. 3614 (F): 1210
I.O. San. 3614 (G): 168
I.O. San. 3614 (H): 169
I.O. San. 3614 (I): 289
I.O. San. 3614 (J): 290
I.O. San. 3614 (K): 935
I.O. San. 3614 (L): 936
I.O. San. 3614 (M): 47
I.O. San. 3614 (N): 1309
I.O. San. 3614 (O): 24
I.O. San. 3614 (P): 1008
I.O. San. 3635: 1197
I.O. San. 3954 (A): 1137
I.O. San. 3954 (B): 202
I.O. San. 3954 (D): 175
I.O. San. 3954 (F): 332
I.O. San. 3954 (L): 800
I.O. Suppl. 3: 1401[a]

Mackenzie V.19: 1393

Mackenzie VIII.50: 1392
Mackenzie VIII.72 (A): 1277
Mackenzie VIII.72 (B): 1278
Mackenzie VIII.72 (C): 1279
Mackenzie VIII.93: 1206
Mackenzie XII.1: 1237
Mackenzie XII.2: 1239
Mackenzie XII.3: 1236
Mackenzie XII.4: 1238
Mackenzie XII.6: 1276
Mackenzie XII.9a: 1394
Mackenzie XII.10: 1249
Mackenzie XII.12: 1274
Mackenzie XII.13 (A): 1273
Mackenzie XII.13 (B): 1275
Mackenzie XII.14 (A): 1280
Mackenzie XII.14 (C): 1281

MSS. Guj. 2 (1): 818
MSS. Guj. 2 (2): 1303
MSS. Guj. 3: 803
MSS. Guj. 4: 6
MSS. Guj. 6 (1): 288
MSS. Guj. 6 (2): 595
MSS. Guj. 6 (3): 366
MSS. Guj. 6 (4): 497
MSS. Guj. 6 (5): 603
MSS. Guj. 7: 597
MSS. Guj. 8: 983
MSS. Guj. 9: 483
MSS. Guj. 10: 788
MSS. Guj. 11: 1022
MSS. Guj. 12: 742
MSS. Guj. 13: 832
MSS. Guj. 14 (1): 985
MSS. Guj. 14 (2): 615
MSS. Guj. 15: 614
MSS. Guj. 18: 355
MSS. Guj. 19: 793
MSS. Hin. A 5: 1269
MSS. Hin. B 3 (1): 1285
MSS. Hin. B 3 (2-11): 1287
MSS. Hin. C 8: 1244
MSS. Hin. C 17: 736
MSS. Raj. 1: 807
MSS. Raj. 2: 801

Or. 1385 (A,1): 158 + 1191
Or. 1385 (A,2): 161
Or. 1385 (B): 159
Or. 1386: 160

Bhagavandas Kevaldas / Ratnavijaya

Or. 2094: 176
Or. 2095: 177
Or. 2096: 173
Or. 2097: 174
Or. 2098 (A): 517
Or. 2098 (B): 516
Or. 2098 (C): 518
Or. 2099: 14
Or. 2100 (A): 37
Or. 2100 (B): 38
Or. 2100 (C): 41
Or. 2100 (D): 64
Or. 2101: 199
Or. 2102 (A): 231
Or. 2102 (B): 230

Or. 2103: 232
Or. 2104: 245
Or. 2105 (A): 661
Or. 2105 (B): 247
Or. 2105 (C): 226
Or. 2105 (D): 257
Or. 2105 (E): 216
Or. 2105 (F): 295
Or. 2105 (G): 162
Or. 2105 (H): 545
Or. 2106 (A,1): 379
Or. 2106 (A,2): 395
Or. 2106 (A,3): 409
Or. 2106 (A,4): 424
Or. 2106 (A,5): 441
Or. 2106 (A,6): 456
Or. 2106 (B,1): 389
Or. 2106 (B,2): 403
Or. 2106 (B,3): 417
Or. 2106 (B,4): 433
Or. 2106 (B,5): 451
Or. 2106 (C): 391 + 971[a]
Or. 2106 (D,1): 388
Or. 2106 (D,2): 402
Or. 2106 (D,3): 419
Or. 2106 (D,4): 432
Or. 2106 (D,5): 449
Or. 2106 (D,6): 464
Or. 2107 (A): 469
Or. 2107 (B): 468
Or. 2108: 657
Or. 2109 (A): 656
Or. 2109 (B): 268
Or. 2109 (C): 242
Or. 2109 (D): 238
Or. 2110: 544
Or. 2111: 670
Or. 2112 (A,1): 563
Or. 2112 (A,2): 572
Or. 2112 (B): 650
Or. 2112 (C): 658
Or. 2112 (D): 659
Or. 2112 (E): 487
Or. 2113 (A): 534
Or. 2113 (B): 535
Or. 2114 (A): 519
Or. 2114 (B): 527
Or. 2114 (C): 526
Or. 2115 (A): 536
Or. 2115 (B): 530
Or. 2116 (A): 329
Or. 2116 (B): 321
Or. 2116 (C): 337
Or. 2116 (D): 328
Or. 2116 (E): 305
Or. 2117 (A): 310
Or. 2117 (B): 320
Or. 2117 (C): 314
Or. 2117 (D): 313
Or. 2118 (A): 315
Or. 2118 (B): 317
Or. 2118 (C): 303
Or. 2118 (D): 306
Or. 2119 (A): 546
Or. 2119 (B): 547
Or. 2119 (C): 550
Or. 2119 (D): 552
Or. 2119 (E): 554

Or. 2119 (F): 553
Or. 2120 (A): 556
Or. 2120 (B): 651
Or. 2120 (C,1-2): 652
Or. 2120 (D): 653
Or. 2120 (E,1): 654
Or. 2120 (E,2): 81
Or. 2120 (F): 557
Or. 2120 (G): 663
Or. 2120 (H): 134
Or. 2120 (I): 540
Or. 2121 (A): 1150
Or. 2121 (B): 662
Or. 2121 (C): 660
Or. 2121 (D): 685
Or. 2121 (F): 506
Or. 2122 (A): 826
Or. 2122 (B): 80
Or. 2122 (C): 32
Or. 2122 (D): 253
Or. 2122 (E,1): 224
Or. 2122 (E,2): 687
Or. 2122 (F): 507
Or. 2122 (G): 292
Or. 2122 (H): 470
Or. 2122 (I): 722
Or. 2123 (A): 688
Or. 2123 (B): 689
Or. 2123 (C,1): 690
Or. 2123 (C,2): 841
Or. 2124: 691
Or. 2125: 1051
Or. 2126 (A): 731
Or. 2126 (B): 717
Or. 2126 (C): 1121
Or. 2126 (D,1): 1099
Or. 2126 (D,2): 754
Or. 2126 (D,3): 799
Or. 2127: 694
Or. 2128 (A): 697
Or. 2128 (B): 869
Or. 2129 (A): 743
Or. 2129 (B): 746
Or. 2129 (C): 1246
Or. 2130 (A): 725
Or. 2130 (B): 1120
Or. 2130 (C): 1122
Or. 2131 (C): 881
Or. 2131 (D): 888
Or. 2131 (E): 997
Or. 2131 (F): 910
Or. 2131 (G): 909
Or. 2131 (H): 919
Or. 2131 (I): 861
Or. 2132 (A): 863
Or. 2132 (B): 892
Or. 2132 (C): 898
Or. 2132 (D): 915
Or. 2132 (E): 911
Or. 2132 (F): 346
Or. 2132 (G): 1085
Or. 2132 (H): 495
Or. 2133 (A): 1105
Or. 2133 (B): 1108
Or. 2133 (C): 591
Or. 2133 (D): 590
Or. 2133 (E): 637
Or. 2133 (F): 580

Or. 2133 (G): 639
Or. 2133 (H): 640
Or. 2134 (A): 917
Or. 2134 (B): 916
Or. 2134 (C): 918
Or. 2134 (D,1): 675
Or. 2134 (D,2): 676
Or. 2134 (D,3): 1222
Or. 2134 (D,4): 674
Or. 2136 (A): 681
Or. 2136 (B): 664
Or. 2137 (A): 666
Or. 2137 (B,1): 322
Or. 2137 (B,2): 378
Or. 2137 (B,3): 393
Or. 2137 (B,4): 394
Or. 2137 (B,5): 422
Or. 2137 (B,6): 423
Or. 2137 (B,7): 408
Or. 2137 (B,8): 437
Or. 2137 (B,9): 438
Or. 2137 (B,10): 439
Or. 2137 (B,11): 440
Or. 2137 (B,12): 457
Or. 2137 (B,13): 466
Or. 2137 (B,14): 455
Or. 2137 (C): 1055
Or. 2138 (A,1): 1299
Or. 2138 (A,2): 961
Or. 2138 (B): 1298
Or. 2138 (C): 1297
Or. 2139: 1396
Or. 2140 (A): 1397
Or. 2140 (C): 1373
Or. 2140 (D): 1370
Or. 2140 (E): 1369
Or. 2140 (F): 1374
Or. 2141: 1346
Or. 2142 (A): 1348
Or. 2142 (B): 1356
Or. 2142 (C): 1329
Or. 2143 (B): 1339
Or. 2143 (C): 1340
Or. 2145 (C): 1311
Or. 2145 (D): 1314
Or. 2146 (B): 1380
Or. 2146 (C): 1378
Or. 2148 (B): 1293

Bendall

Or. 3347 (A): 696
Or. 3347 (B): 229
Or. 3347 (C,1): 384
Or. 3347 (C,2): 593
Or. 3347 (C,3): 589
Or. 3347 (C,4): 1292
Or. 3347 (C,5): 584
Or. 3347 (C,6): 558
Or. 3347 (C,7): 582
Or. 3347 (C,8): 532
Or. 3347 (C,9): 1048
Or. 3347 (C,10): 627
Or. 3347 (C,11): 214
Or. 3347 (C,12): 222
Or. 3347 (C,13): 191
Or. 3347 (C,14): 531
Or. 3347 (C,15): 619
Or. 3347 (C,16): 533

Or. 3347 (C,17): 298
Or. 3348 (A): 1226
Or. 3348 (B): 1243
Or. 3349 (A): 196
Or. 3349 (B): 712
Or. 3349 (C): 127
Or. 3350: 1241
Or. 3351: 1315
Or. 3354 (C): 1414

Miles
Or. 4530: 1350
Or. 4531: 205
Or. 4532: 246
Or. 4533: 500
Or. 4778: 759

Jacobi
Or. 5115: 1
Or. 5116: 2
Or. 5117: 3
Or. 5118: 7
Or. 5119: 8
Or. 5120: 9
Or. 5121: 13
Or. 5122: 15
Or. 5123 (A): 19
Or. 5123 (B): 22
Or. 5124: 23
Or. 5125: 26
Or. 5126: 27
Or. 5127: 33
Or. 5128: 35
Or. 5129: 43
Or. 5130: 50
Or. 5131 (1): 44
Or. 5131 (2): 51
Or. 5132: 54
Or. 5133: 55
Or. 5134: 56
Or. 5135: 61
Or. 5136: 62
Or. 5137: 63
Or. 5138: 66
Or. 5139: 67
Or. 5140: 69
Or. 5141: 74
Or. 5142: 79
Or. 5143 (A): 83
Or. 5143 (B): 89
Or. 5144: 86
Or. 5145: 92
Or. 5146: 93
Or. 5147 (1): 220
Or. 5147 (2): 221
Or. 5148: 155
Or. 5149: 98
Or. 5150: 132
Or. 5151 (1): 115
Or. 5151 (2): 713
Or. 5152: 109
Or. 5153: 210
Or. 5154: 212
Or. 5155: 213
Or. 5156: 166
Or. 5157: 172
Or. 5158: 171
Or. 5159: 188

Or. 5160: 228
Or. 5161: 193
Or. 5162: 194
Or. 5163: 201
Or. 5164: 529
Or. 5165: 302
Or. 5166: 912
Or. 5167: 914
Or. 5168 (1): 386
Or. 5168 (2): 401
Or. 5168 (3): 416
Or. 5168 (4): 431
Or. 5168 (5): 447
Or. 5169: 887
Or. 5170: 481
Or. 5171: 922 + 972
Or. 5172: 486
Or. 5173: 348
Or. 5174: 515
Or. 5175: 1207
Or. 5176: 616
Or. 5177: 569
Or. 5178: 307
Or. 5179: 778
Or. 5180: 703
Or. 5181: 542
Or. 5182 (1): 405
Or. 5182 (2): 415
Or. 5183: 878
Or. 5184: 879
Or. 5185: 538
Or. 5186: 555
Or. 5187: 560
Or. 5188 (1): 390
Or. 5188 (2): 404
Or. 5188 (3): 418
Or. 5188 (4): 434
Or. 5188 (5): 450
Or. 5189: 1050
Or. 5190: 908
Or. 5191: 330 + 365
Or. 5192 (A,1): 880
Or. 5192 (A,2): 867
Or. 5192 (A,3): 864
Or. 5192 (A,4): 875
Or. 5192 (A,5): 894
Or. 5192 (A,6): 895
Or. 5192 (A,7): 896
Or. 5192 (A,8): 897
Or. 5192 (A,9): 899
Or. 5192 (A,10): 921
Or. 5192 (A,11): 905
Or. 5192 (A,12): 901
Or. 5192 (A,13): 902
Or. 5192 (A,14): 904
Or. 5192 (A,15): 870
Or. 5192 (B): 251
Or. 5193: 678
Or. 5194: 254
Or. 5196: 1347
Or. 5197: 1349
Or. 5199: 1395
Or. 5200: 1357
Or. 5201: 1413
Or. 5204: 1341
Or. 5208: 1411
Or. 5209: 1412
Or. 5210: 1409

Or. 5211: 683
Or. 5222: 1342
Or. 5223: 1403
Or. 5224 (1): 1363
Or. 5224 (2): 1362
Or. 5227: 1334
Or. 5228: 1335
Or. 5231: 1387
Or. 5236: 1300
Or. 5240: 1333
Or. 5241: 1375
Or. 5246: 1358
Or. 5247: 1326
Or. 5248: 1325
Or. 5255: 275
Or. 5256: 668
Or. 5257: 164
Or. 5258: 347
[Jacobi's missing ms.: 672]
Or. 6832 (A): 118
Or. 6832 (B): 105

Miles
Or. 7619: 76
Or. 7620: 249
Or. 7621 (A): 240
Or. 7621 (B): 349
Or. 7621 (C): 260
Or. 7621 (D): 261
Or. 7621 (E): 1164
Or. 7623 (B): 137

Or. 8060: 635
Or. 8061: 1368 + 1424
Or. 8150: 1420
Or. 11745: 111
Or. 11747: 1379
Or. 11748: 771
Or. 11921: 99
Or. 12744: 100
Or. 13179: 586
Or. 13221 (1): 1254
Or. 13221 (2): 1252
Or. 13221 (3): 1204
Or. 13221 (4): 1262
Or. 13221 (5): 1263
Or. 13221 (6): 1256
Or. 13221 (7): 1258
Or. 13221 (8): 1260
Or. 13221 (9): 1266
Or. 13221 (10): 1231
Or. 13221 (11): 1289
Or. 13221 (12): 1265
Or. 13294: 369
Or. 13341: 138
Or. 13342: 139
Or. 13362: 178
Or. 13454: 327
Or. 13455: 106
Or. 13456: 336
Or. 13457A: 1389
Or. 13457B: 1193
Or. 13459: 367
Or. 13472: 1194
Or. 13475: 709
Or. 13476: 179
Or. 13477: 250
Or. 13478: 876

Or. 13479: 520
Or. 13480: 521
Or. 13481: 1328
Or. 13487: 1410
Or. 13495: 326
Or. 13496: 1336
Or. 13497: 1377
Or. 13498: 581
Or. 13500: 1324
Or. 13524: 747
Or. 13540: 1415
Or. 13541: 665
Or. 13542: 1376
Or. 13543: 866
Or. 13544: 726
Or. 13548 (1): 1098
Or. 13548 (2): 753
Or. 13549: 323
Or. 13550: 227
Or. 13551: 90
Or. 13552 (1): 383
Or. 13552 (2): 399
Or. 13552 (3): 413
Or. 13552 (4): 428
Or. 13552 (5): 445
Or. 13552 (6): 461
Or. 13553: 522
Or. 13598: 52
Or. 13599: 95
Or. 13600: 157
Or. 13601: 4
Or. 13602: 39
Or. 13603: 12
Or. 13604: 18
Or. 13605: 28
Or. 13606: 57
Or. 13607: 60
Or. 13608: 85
Or. 13609: 87
Or. 13610: 206
Or. 13611: 324
Or. 13612: 338
Or. 13613: 334
Or. 13614: 335
Or. 13615: 715
Or. 13616: 124
Or. 13617: 58
Or. 13618: 352
Or. 13619: 353
Or. 13620: 1208
Or. 13621: 1211
Or. 13622: 737
Or. 13623 (A): 823
Or. 13623 (B,1): 925
Or. 13623 (B,2): 1159
Or. 13623 (B,3): 1046
Or. 13623 (B, 5-6): 1175
Or. 13624: 843
Or. 13626: 123
Or. 13627: 626
Or. 13629: 642
Or. 13635: 1401
Or. 13639: 1390 + 1418
Or. 13642 (2): 1086
Or. 13642 (3) = (6): 1019
Or. 13642 (4): 1161
Or. 13642 (5): 784
Or. 13642 (7) = (9): 989

Or. 13642 (8): 804
Or. 13642 (10): 267
Or. 13642 (11): 794
Or. 13696: 645
Or. 13697 (B,1): 872
Or. 13697 (B,2): 891
Or. 13697 (C): 836
Or. 13700: 97
Or. 13701: 122
Or. 13740: 45
Or. 13741: 884
Or. 13745: 709
Or. 13773: 1301
Or. 13774: 1372
Or. 13775: 1320
Or. 13784: 70
Or. 13785: 101
Or. 13786: 225
Or. 13787: 129
Or. 13788: 1104
Or. 13789: 493
Or. 13790: 186
Or. 13791: 1295
Or. 13792: 853
Or. 13806: 1351
Or. 13937: 370
Or. 13950 (A): 710 + 1192
Or. 13950 (B,C,D): 140
Or. 13950 (E): 1192
Or. 13959: 104
Or. 13974: 368
Or. 14064 (A): 808
Or. 14064 (B,2): 719
Or. 14064 (B,3): 783
Or. 14064 (B,4): 1034
Or. 14064 (B,5): 752
Or. 14064 (B,6): 600
Or. 14064 (B,8): 938
Or. 14064 (B,9): 1016
Or. 14064 (B,10): 1006
Or. 14064 (B,11): 977
Or. 14064 (B,12): 974
Or. 14064 (B,13): 939
Or. 14064 (B,17): 966
Or. 14064 (B,18): 809
Or. 14064 (B,19): 979
Or. 14064 (B,20): 980
Or. 14064 (B,21): 834
Or. 14064 (B,22): 1014
Or. 14064 (B,23): 975
Or. 14064 (B,24): 993
Or. 14064 (B,25): 499
Or. 14064 (D): 1189
Or. 14262: 141
Or. 14290: 1270
Or. 14687 (1): 860
Or. 14687 (2): 859
Or. 15289: 792

Jambuvijaya

Or. 15633/1: 508
Or. 15633/2: 207
Or. 15633/3: 1112
Or. 15633/4 (1): 842
Or. 15633/4 (2): 833
Or. 15633/5 (1): 988
Or. 15633/5 (2): 510
Or. 15633/5 (3): 511

Or. 15633/5 (4): 1131
Or. 15633/5 (5): 1133
Or. 15633/5 (6): 686
Or. 15633/5 (7): 955
Or. 15633/5 (8): 284
Or. 15633/5 (9): 509
Or. 15633/5 (10): 954
Or. 15633/5 (11): 1143
Or. 15633/6: 454
Or. 15633/7: 782
Or. 15633/8 (1): 629
Or. 15633/8 (2): 1032
Or. 15633/8 (3): 638
Or. 15633/9: 1093
Or. 15633/10 (1): 40
Or. 15633/10 (2): 1013
Or. 15633/11: 1111
Or. 15633/12 (1): 264
Or. 15633/12 (2): 53
Or. 15633/13 (1): 474
Or. 15633/13 (2): 1109
Or. 15633/13 (3-4): 475
Or. 15633/14: 502
Or. 15633/15: 1125
Or. 15633/16: 1041
Or. 15633/17: 1036
Or. 15633/18: 357
Or. 15633/19: 852
Or. 15633/20: 620
Or. 15633/21: 1147
Or. 15633/22: 641
Or. 15633/23 (1): 1138
Or. 15633/23 (2): 931
Or. 15633/23 (3): 512
Or. 15633/24: 588
Or. 15633/25: 995
Or. 15633/26 (1): 1113
Or. 15633/26 (2): 1007
Or. 15633/26 (3): 190
Or. 15633/27: 1155
Or. 15633/28: 1139
Or. 15633/29: 982
Or. 15633/30: 478 + 1307
Or. 15633/31: 208
Or. 15633/32: 356
Or. 15633/33: 406
Or. 15633/34: 477
Or. 15633/35: 361
Or. 15633/36: 610
Or. 15633/37: 276
Or. 15633/38: 265
Or. 15633/39: 285
Or. 15633/40 (1): 578
Or. 15633/40 (2): 1082
Or. 15633/41: 890
Or. 15633/42: 1063
Or. 15633/43 (1): 598
Or. 15633/43 (2): 482
Or. 15633/44: 362
Or. 15633/45: 364
Or. 15633/46: 476
Or. 15633/47: 1031
Or. 15633/48: 1153
Or. 15633/49: 1100
Or. 15633/50 (1): 1127
Or. 15633/50 (2): 930
Or. 15633/50 (3): 1180
Or. 15633/51: 646

Or. 15633/52 (1): 1012
Or. 15633/52 (2): 1132
Or. 15633/53: 787
Or. 15633/54: 630
Or. 15633/55: 283
Or. 15633/56: 503
Or. 15633/57: 820
Or. 15633/58 (1): 608
Or. 15633/58 (2): 965
Or. 15633/59: 1084
Or. 15633/60: 272
Or. 15633/61: 1064
Or. 15633/62: 1065
Or. 15633/63: 1123
Or. 15633/64: 1037
Or. 15633/65: 1010
Or. 15633/66: 1145
Or. 15633/67 (1-2): 929
Or. 15633/68 (1): 1128
Or. 15633/68 (2): 1114
Or. 15633/69: 1025
Or. 15633/70 (1): 1057
Or. 15633/70 (2): 951
Or. 15633/70 (3): 1059
Or. 15633/71: 1101
Or. 15633/72: 1140
Or. 15633/73: 1029
Or. 15633/74: 1021
Or. 15633/75: 968
Or. 15633/76: 1074
Or. 15633/77: 829
Or. 15633/78: 628
Or. 15633/79 (1): 969
Or. 15633/79 (2): 978
Or. 15633/80: 1017
Or. 15633/81 (1): 1067
Or. 15633/81 (2): 1068
Or. 15633/82: 1049
Or. 15633/83: 1134
Or. 15633/84: 363
Or. 15633/85: 1039
Or. 15633/86: 1040
Or. 15633/87 (1): 958
Or. 15633/87 (2): 1058
Or. 15633/88 (1): 1154
Or. 15633/88 (2): 1149
Or. 15633/89 (1): 1035
Or. 15633/89 (2): 1003
Or. 15633/90: 949
Or. 15633/91: 1042
Or. 15633/92: 932
Or. 15633/93: 933
Or. 15633/94: 1182
Or. 15633/95: 1176
Or. 15633/96: 1078
Or. 15633/97 (1): 1043
Or. 15633/97 (2): 1000
Or. 15633/97 (3): 1141
Or. 15633/98: 948
Or. 15633/99: 838
Or. 15633/100: 1186
Or. 15633/101: 741
Or. 15633/102 (1): 926
Or. 15633/102 (2): 1306
Or. 15633/102 (3): 1015
Or. 15633/103: 1157
Or. 15633/104: 1020
Or. 15633/105 (1): 1030

Or. 15633/105 (2): 604
Or. 15633/106: 1061
Or. 15633/107: 1178
Or. 15633/108: 501
Or. 15633/109: 1185
Or. 15633/110: 1183
Or. 15633/111: 1184
Or. 15633/112: 813
Or. 15633/113 (1): 472
Or. 15633/113 (2): 1142
Or. 15633/114: 839
Or. 15633/115: 1077
Or. 15633/116: 271
Or. 15633/117: 1075
Or. 15633/118: 192
Or. 15633/119: 1097
Or. 15633/120: 359
Or. 15633/121: 1004
Or. 15633/122: 734
Or. 15633/123: 189
Or. 15633/124: 1005
Or. 15633/125: 796
Or. 15633/126: 1117
Or. 15633/127: 282
Or. 15633/128 (1): 1110
Or. 15633/128 (2): 999
Or. 15633/129: 471
Or. 15633/130: 358
Or. 15633/131: 605
Or. 15633/132: 971 + 1308
Or. 15633/133: 266
Or. 15633/134: 1094
Or. 15633/135: 577
Or. 15633/136: 496
Or. 15633/137: 596
Or. 15633/138: 1118
Or. 15633/139 (1): 277
Or. 15633/139 (2): 1129
Or. 15633/140: 567
Or. 15633/141: 566
Or. 15633/142: 568
Or. 15633/143: 564
Or. 15633/144 (1): 1028
Or. 15633/144 (2): 494
Or. 15633/145: 233
Or. 15633/146: 234
Or. 15633/147: 311
Or. 15633/148: 312
Or. 15633/149: 345
Or. 15633/150 (1): 380
Or. 15633/150 (2): 396
Or. 15633/150 (3): 410
Or. 15633/150 (4): 425
Or. 15633/150 (5): 442
Or. 15633/150 (6): 459
Or. 15633/151 (1): 381
Or. 15633/151 (2): 397
Or. 15633/151 (3): 411
Or. 15633/151 (4): 426
Or. 15633/151 (5): 443
Or. 15633/151 (6): 460
Or. 15633/152: 350
Or. 15633/153: 344
Or. 15633/154: 256
Or. 15633/155: 255
Or. 15633/156 (1): 382
Or. 15633/156 (2): 398
Or. 15633/156 (3): 412

Or. 15633/156 (4): 427
Or. 15633/156 (5): 444
Or. 15633/156 (6): 462
Or. 15633/157: 429
Or. 15633/158: 539
Or. 15633/159: 484
Or. 15633/160: 1146
Or. 15633/161: 197
Or. 15633/162: 485
Or. 15633/163: 248
Or. 15633/164: 293
Or. 15633/165: 617
Or. 15633/166: 618
Or. 15633/167: 489
Or. 15633/168: 490
Or. 15633/169: 480
Or. 15633/170: 318
Or. 15633/171: 259
Or. 15633/172: 644
Or. 15633/173: 632
Or. 15633/174: 218
Or. 15633/175: 219
Or. 15633/176 (1): 392
Or. 15633/176 (2): 407
Or. 15633/176 (3): 420
Or. 15633/176 (4): 436
Or. 15633/176 (5): 452
Or. 15633/177 (1): 421
Or. 15633/177 (2): 435
Or. 15633/177 (3): 453
Or. 15633/178: 351
Or. 15633/179: 354
Or. 15633/180: 528
Or. 15633/181: 467
Or. 15633/182: 258
Or. 15633/183 (1): 592
Or. 15633/183 (2): 562
Or. 15633/184: 360
Or. 15633/185 (1): 262
Or. 15633/185 (2): 900
Or. 15633/185 (3): 874
Or. 15633/185 (4): 903
Or. 15633/185 (5): 893
Or. 15633/185 (6): 865
Or. 15633/185 (7): 885
Or. 15633/185 (8): 868
Or. 15633/185 (9): 871
Or. 15633/185 (10): 889
Or. 15633/186: 1337
Or. 15633/187: 837
Or. 15633/188: 281
Or. 15633/189: 1011
Or. 15633/190: 1024
Or. 15633/192 (1): 970
Or. 15633/192 (2): 957
Or. 15633/193: 991
Or. 15633/195: 184
Or. 15633/196: 1119
Or. 15633/197: 906

Or. 15892: 1221
Or. 16132/1: 990
Or. 16132/2: 835
Or. 16132/3: 667
Or. 16132/4: 504
Or. 16132/5 (1): 1264
Or. 16132/5 (2): 636
Or. 16132/6: 1026

Or. 16132/7: 479
Or. 16132/8: 1364
Or. 16132/9: 862
Or. 16132/10: 235
Or. 16132/11: 319
Or. 16132/12: 655
Or. 16132/13: 1247
Or. 16133/1: 154
Or. 16133/2 (1): 46
Or. 16133/2 (2): 514
Or. 16133/2 (3): 611
Or. 16133/2 (4): 621
Or. 16133/2 (5): 953
Or. 16133/2 (6): 647
Or. 16133/2 (7): 624
Or. 16133/2 (8): 623
Or. 16133/2 (9): 622
Or. 16133/2 (10): 976
Or. 16133/2 (11): 300
Or. 16133/2 (12): 606
Or. 16133/2 (13): 291
Or. 16133/2 (14): 937
Or. 16133/2 (15): 583
Or. 16133/2 (16): 499[a]
Or. 16133/2 (17): 959
Or. 16133/2 (18): 1009
Or. 16133/3 (A): 986
Or. 16133/3 (B): 1091
Or. 16133/3 (C): 1302
Or. 16133/3 (D): 873
Or. 16133/3 (E): 273
Or. 16133/3 (F): 934
Or. 16133/4 (1): 992
Or. 16133/4 (2): 46
Or. 16133/5 (A): 299
Or. 16133/5 (B): 279
Or. 16133/5 (C): 1096
Or. 16133/5 (D): 301
Or. 16133/5 (E): 739
Or. 16133/5 (F): 740
Or. 16133/5 (G,1): 607
Or. 16133/5 (G,2): 1045
Or. 16133/6 (A): 1174
Or. 16133/6 (B): 1124
Or. 16133/6 (C): 1136
Or. 16133/6 (D): 1070
Or. 16133/7 (A): 1027
Or. 16133/7 (B): 1126
Or. 16133/8: 1069
Or. 16133/9 (A): 1023
Or. 16133/9 (B): 996
Or. 16133/9 (C): 1066
Or. 16133/9 (D): 513
Or. 16133/9 (E): 473
Or. 16133/9 (F): 1062
Or. 16133/9 (G): 1115
Or. 16133/9 (H): 1095
Or. 16133/9 (I): 960
Or. 16133/9 (J): 634
Or. 16133/9 (K): 1056
Or. 16133/9 (L,1): 1060
Or. 16133/9 (L,2): 1116
Or. 16133/9 (M): 706
Or. 16133/9 (N): 1130
Or. 16133/9 (O): 631
Or. 16133/9 (P): 633
Or. 16133/9 (Q): 1135
Or. 16133/9 (R): 278

Or. 16133/10: 1163

Or. 16192: 1425

Sloane 4090 (E): 1354

Victoria & Albert Museum

324-1972: 1195

Circ. 91-1970: 373

Circ. 321-1972: 377

Circ. 325-1972: 375

Circ. 326-1972: 376

IM 6-1931 & 7-1931: 144

IM 8-1931 -- 12.1931: 145

IM 89-1936: 1196

IM 161-1914: 142

IM 161A-1914: 143

IS 2-1972: 165

IS 2-1984: 374

IS 20-1978: 1190[a]

IS 35-1971: 339

IS 46-1959: 107

IS 50-1983: 1190

IS 83-1963: 146

IS 84-1963: 147

British Museum

BM 1926-3-16-01: 1188

BM 1947-7-12-02: 150

BM 1947-7-12-03: 151

BM 1948-10-9-0159: 149

BM 1959-4-11-04: 711

BM 1959-4-11-05: 148

BM 1966-10-10-05 (1): 152

BM 1966-10-10-05 (2): 153

BM OA 1880-4057: 1290

2. *List of manuscripts in individual collections*

Arranged according to numbers

(Note: Gaps in the numbering mean that the relevant mss. are non-Jain and, as such, are not described in the present catalogue - Only the manuscripts clearly belonging to a clearly marked individual collection are mentioned here).

India Office

Aufrecht collection

Pārśvanāthacarita	Aufrecht 86 I-II
Ratnakośa	Aufrecht 87

Bühler collection

Alaṁkāracūḍāmaṇi	Bühler 111
Alaṁkāracūḍāmaṇi, incompl.	Bühler 112
Alaṁkāracūḍāmaṇi	Bühler 113
Kavirahasya by Halāyudha with Ravidharman's comm.	Bühler 118
Kāvyakalpalatā	Bühler 119
Jainendravyākaraṇa	Bühler 134
Śabdānuśāsanavṛtti	Bühler 140
Aṇuttarovavāīsutta	Bühler 280
Kalpasūtra with Pradīpikā	Bühler 281
1. Daśavaikālikasūtra; 2. Pākṣikasūtra	Bühler 282
Daśavaikālikasūtra with Avacūri	Bühler 282A
Niśīthasūtra	Bühler 283
Dīpālīkalpa	Bühler 284
Gurvāvali	Bühler 285
Kumārapālacarita by Jinamaṇḍana	Bühler 286
Kumārapālacarita-bālāvabodha	Bühler 287
Gurvāvali	Bühler 288
Gurvāvali	Bühler 289
Gurvāvali	Bühler 290
Paṭṭāvali, list of names	Bühler 290A
Jagaḍūcarita	Bühler 291
Tribhuvanadīpakaprabandha	Bühler 292
Pariśiṣṭaparvan	Bühler 293
Prabandhakośa	Bühler 294, 295
Prabandhacintāmaṇi	Bühler 296, 297
Prabhāvākacarita	Bühler 298, 299
Vastupālacarita	Bühler 300
Sītācarita	Bühler 301
Sukṛtakīrtana	Bühler 302
Sudarśanakathānaka & Sampratikathānaka	Bühler 303
Akṣaracūḍāmaṇi	Bühler 304
Dīpālīkalpa	Bühler 305
Ṣaḍdarśanasamuccaya	Bühler 306
Ṣaḍdarśanasamuccaya-ṭīkā	Bühler 307
Poem by Ajitasena	Bühler 308

Burnell collection

Akalankāṣṭaka	Burnell 229
Kṣatracūḍāmaṇi by Vādībhasiṁha	Burnell 235
Aṣṭaprābhṛta with a comm. in Jaipurī	Burnell 245
Prameyakamalamārtāṇḍa (1-3) by Prabhācandra	Burnell 246
Prameyakamalamārtāṇḍa (4-6) by Prabhācandra	Burnell 247
Trilokasāra by Nemicandra with Mādhavacandra Traividya's comm.	Burnell 381
Trilokasāra by Nemicandra	Burnell 417
Siddhāntasāra by Prabhācandra	Burnell 430
Siddhāntasāra-vṛtti	Burnell 430
Tribhangisāra by Nemicandra	Burnell 430
Ratnakarakaṇḍa by Samantabhadra with a gloss in Kannada	Burnell 433
Jinastotra	Burnell 433
Dvādaśānuprekṣā by Kundakunda	Burnell 433
Ratnakarakaṇḍa by Samantabhadra	Burnell 433
Sajjanacittavallabha by Malliṣeṇa	Burnell 433
Śabdānuśāsana of Śākaṭāyana	Burnell 454
Kātantra with Bhāvasena's Laghuvṛtti	Burnell 461
1. Nāmamālā, 2. Anekārthanāmamālā, 3. Śabdānekārtha, by Harṣakīrti	Burnell 474

Mackenzie collection

Gaṇitasārasaṁgraha by Mahāvīrācārya	Mackenzie V.19
Gaṇitasārasaṁgraha by Mahāvīrācārya	Mackenzie VIII.50
Nityābhiṣekavidhi	Mackenzie VIII.72
Pūjāvidhi	Mackenzie VIII.72 (B)
Pūjāvidhi	Mackenzie VIII.72 (C)
Tattvārthasūtra with Bhāskaranandin's *Sukhabodhā*	Mackenzie VIII.93
Ādipurāṇa	Mackenzie XII.1
Uttarapurāṇa	Mackenzie XII.2
Ādipurāṇa	Mackenzie XII.3
Ādipurāṇa	Mackenzie XII.4
Śāntihoma	Mackenzie XII.6
Bhujabalicaritra	Mackenzie XII.10
Pratiṣṭhātilaka	Mackenzie XII.12
Pratiṣṭhātilaka	Mackenzie XII.13
Sakalakriyā	Mackenzie XII.13
Daśakuṇḍala-lakṣaṇa	Mackenzie XII.14 (A)
[Non Jain	Mackenzie XII.14 (B)]
Vāstupūjā-vidhi	Mackenzie XII. 14 (C)
Gaṇitasārasaṁgraha by Mahāvīrācārya with Kanarese comm.	Mackenzie XII.9a

[For mss. marked 'I.O. San.' see Introduction and individual entries]

Or. 15633/

Jambuvijaya collection

Ātmā ne hita śikṣā sajjhāya by Viśuddhavimala	1
Daśavaikālika-sajjhāya by Vṛddhivijaya	2
Saubhāgya-pancamī-deva-vandana-vidhi	3

Pānca-Pāṇḍava-sajjhāya by Kaviyaṇa and ten other texts	5
Śataka Karmagrantha-sūci-yantra by Sumativardhana	6
Araṇikamuni-sajjhāya by Rūpavijaya	7
Krodha, māna, māyā, lobha nī sajjhāya by Udayaratna and two other texts	8
[Ṛṣabhanātha-stavana] by Dīpavijaya	9
Daśa-śrāvaka-sajjhāya and Ajitanātha-stavana by Cāritravijaya	10
Saubhāgya-jñānapancamī-kathā by Kanakakuśala	11
Navakāra-rāsa and Dhanā-Kākandi-sajjhāya	12
Karmaprakṛti-dvitīya-sajjhāya and three other texts	13
[Leśyā-varṇana]	14
Rohiṇī-stavana	15
Gaṇadhara-saṁvāda-stavana by Sakalacandra	16
Anthology of *stavanas* by Padmavijaya	17
Daṇḍaka-nāma ogaṇatrīsa dvāra	18
Śukasaptati Kathā by Ratnasundara	19
Śīla nī nava vāḍa by Udayaratna	20
Viṁśati-sthānaka-vidhi	21
Ekaviṁśati-sthāna-prakaraṇa by Siddhasena	22
Siddhacakra-stavana and two other texts	23
Sambodha-saptatikā by Jayaśekhara	24
Pārśvanātha no vivāhalo	25
Jñānapancamī-stavana and two other texts	26
Sattara bheda pūjā by Sakalacandra	27
Siddhacakra-namaskāra by Jñānavimala	28
Neminātha-nava-rasa by Rūpacanda	29
Jambū-pṛcchā *or* Karma-phala by Vīrajī	30
Daśavaikālika-sajjhāya by Vṛddhivijaya	31
Trīsa dvāra	32
Karmastava by Devendrasūri with Guj. comm.	33
Āṭha karma nī 158 prakṛti	34
[Neraka-yātanā-sajjhāya]	35
Dvādaśa-bhāvanā-sajjhāya by a pupil of Yaśaḥsoma	36
[Samyaktva]	37
Navakāra-chanda by Kuśalalābha	38
Upadhāna-ḍhāla by Vinayavijaya	39
Navatattva-ḍhāla by Māyacanda muni and Śankheśvara-Pārśvanātha-stotra	40
Kalyāṇamandira-bhāṣā	41
Siddhācala-jina-stavana by Kṣamāvijaya	42
Dṛṣṭi-rāgopari-sajjhāya by Yaśovijaya and Cauda-guṇa-thāṇā nī sajjhāya	43
Bāra ārā nuṃ māna	44
Avagāhanā nu māna	45
Āṭha karma nī 136 prakṛti	46
Sīmandhara-svāmi-stava by Jñānavimala	47
Pūjā nī vidhi	48
Paryuṣaṇā-parva-stuti by Nayavimala	49
Aṣṭamī-caityavandana by Kṣamāvijaya and two other texts	50
Mātāputra-sambandha-sajjhāya by Kāntivijaya	51
[amalakalpa udyāna māṁ devācī nārī] by Rāmavijaya and Ṛṣabha-jina-vinatī by Udayaratna	52

Elāputra-sajjhāya by Labdhivijaya 53
Samakita ni sajjhāya & Māna upara sajjhāya by Udayaratna 54
Sthāpanā-kalpa by Yaśovijaya 55
Corāsī lākha jīva-jonī nāṁ prāṇa 56
Subāhu-kumāra-sajjhāya 57
Santoṣa nī sajjhāya by Kaviyaṇa and Śāntijina-stuti by Rūpavijaya 58
Śankheśvara-Pārśvanātha-chanda by Udayaratna 59
Arhad-ādi-kṣāmaṇā 60
Siddhācala-stavana by Siddhivijaya 61
Siddhācala-stavana by Padmavijaya 62
Rohiṇī-tapa-sajjhāya (by Vivekavijaya-gaṇi?) 63
Sarasvatī-stotra (Skt.) 64
[Mahāvīra-svāmī nī janmakuṇḍalī nuṁ stavana] by Śubhavīra 65
Viṁśatisthānakavicāra by Kṣamāvijaya 66
Tīrthaṁkara-janma-tithi & Jina-lānchana 67
Aṣṭamī-svādhyāya by Devavijaya and Pancamī-sajjhāya by Devavijaya 68
Tīna-covīisī-vandana by Kalyāṇavimala 69
Puṇḍarīkagiri-stotra (Skt.) and two other hymns 70
Paryuṣaṇa-hita-śikṣā-sajjhāya by (Jina)vallabha 71
Siddhacakra-stavana 72
Simandhara-jina-stavana 73
Munisuvrata-svāmi-stavana by Haṁsa(vijaya) 74
Śāntijina-chanda by Guṇasāgara 75
Siddhaśilā-sajjhāya by Nayasundara 76
Jayanti-śrāvikā nī guṁhalī by Śubhavīra 77
Rātribhojana-sajjhāya by Muni Vasatā 78
Śānti-stavana by Rūpacanda and Neminātha-stavana by Hīravijaya 79
Jinavāṇi-stavana (by Uttamavijaya?) 80
Siddhagiri nī horī by Rūpacanda and Siddhagiri no vasanta by Dharmacandra 81
Rājasāgara-guru-guṁhalī by Dolatasāgara 82
Akṣayanidhitapa-stavana by Uttamavijaya 83
Bāra ārā nuṁ stavana 84
Pīstālīsa-Āgama-stavana by Uttamavijaya 85
Tīrthapati-bhāsa 86
[prabhāte pankhiḍāṁ bole] and Siddhācala-stavana by Jñānavimalasūri 87
Cāmara-pūjā by Kuśalakṣema and Viṁśati-tīrthapada-pūjā by Vijayasaubhāgya 88
Sujātajina-vasanta by Nyāyasāgara and Mahāvīra-phāga by Vimalavijaya 89
Ṛṣabhajina-stavana 90
Guruvandana-guṁhalī by Giradhara 91
Covīsa-Jina-parivāra-stavana by Jñānavimala 92
Covīsa-Jina-parivāra-stavana by Jñānavimala 93
[Names of the 45 Āgamas and the 14 Pūrvas] 94
Jina-nāma-yantra (Skt.) 95
[Śatrunjaya-Ādinātha-namaskāra] 96
Guru-bhāsa-phūlaḍāṁ and two other hymns 97
Aṣṭāviṁśati-labdhi-maya-Ṛṣabhajina-stavana by Dharmavardhana 98
Rukmiṇī-sajjhāya by Rangavijaya 99
[Lists of names of days, months, asterisms, etc.] 100

Caturviṁśati-daṇḍaka by Gajasāra (Pkt.) 149
Set of six Karmagranthas 150
Set of six Karmagranthas 151
Vicāraṣaṭtriṁśikā by Gajasāra with Guj. comm. 152
Vicāraṣaṭtriṁśikā by Gajasāra (Pkt.) 153
Bhāṣya-traya by Devendrasūri (Pkt.) 154
Bhāṣya-traya by Devendrasūri (Pkt.) 155
Set of six Karmagranthas by Devendrasūri (No. 6 only beg.) 156
Ṣaḍaśītikā (Pkt.) 157
Dharmaratna-prakaraṇa by Śāntisūri (Pkt.) 158
Kāla-saptatikā by Dharmaghoṣasūri (Pkt.) 159
Viṁśatisthānaka-pūjā-vidhi 160
Daśavaikālikasūtra, beg. only 161
Kāla-saptatikā by Dharmaghoṣasūri with Guj. comm. 162
Ṣaḍāvaśyaka-ṭabo by Tārācanda 163
Pancanirgranthī by Abhayadevasūri with Guj. comm. 164
Śīlakulaka by Devendrasūri with Guj. comm. 165
Śīlakulaka by Devendrasūri with Guj. comm. 166
Jīvavicāra by Śāntisūri with Guj. comm. 167
Jīvavicāra by Śāntisūri with Guj. comm. 168
Bhāva-prakaraṇa by Vijayavimala with Guj. comm. 169
Laghu-kṣetrasamāsa by Ratnaśekhara with Guj. comm. 170
Caityavandana-bhāṣya by Devendra 171
Ekaviṁśati-jina-sthānaka by Siddhasena with Guj. comm. 172
Puṇyapāpasvarūpa-kulaka with Guj. comm. 173
Catuḥśaraṇa-prakīrṇaka with Guj. comm. 174
Catuḥśaraṇa-prakīrṇaka with Guj. comm. 175
Set of five Karmagranthas with Guj. comm. 176
Set of three Karmagranthas with Guj. comm. 177
Vicāraṣaṭtriṁśikā by Gajasāra with Guj. comm. 178
Vicāraṣaṭtriṁśikā by Gajasāra with Guj. comm. 179
Upadeśamālā by Dharmadāsagaṇi with Guj. comm. 180
[Verses from the Saptatikā & from Malayagiri's comm. on the Saptatikā with Guj. comm.] 181
Bhāṣyatraya with Guj. comm. 182
Sambodha-saptatikā by Ratnaśekharasūri with Guj. comm. and [jīva-dayā jiṇa-dhammo] with Guj. comm. 183
Lokanālikā-dvātriṁśikā by Dharmaghoṣa with Guj. comm. 184
Navakāra-mantra followed by nine hymns (Navasmaraṇa) with Guj. comm. 185
Sārasvata-vyākaraṇa by Anubhūtisvarūpācārya 186
tuma tajakara Rājula nāra! by Jinadāsa 187
Aticāra-formula 188
amalakalpa udyānamāṁ Devācī nārī by Rāmavijaya 189
Anāgata-covīsī-vandana by Jñānavimala 190
[191][1]
[Śānti jiṇinda avadhārīe] by Ratnavijaya and [merā nehā lagyā Nābhinandana] 192
[Pārśva-jina-stavana] by Śubhavīra 193

[1] For an unknown reason no manuscript numbered Or. 15633/191 and /194 could ever be found (checked several times, again in July 2005).

[	194]
Uttarādhyayanasūtra with Guj. comm., beg. only	195
[Mauna-ekādaśī-stavana] by Jñānavimala	196
Ratnākara-pancaviṁśatikā by Ratnākara with Guj. comm.	197

Oriental collections

Harley collection

A collection of Jain texts	Harley 415

Sloane collection

Anekārthasaṁgraha (fragment)	Sloane 4090

Bhagavandas Kevaladas / Ratnavijaya collection

Uttarādhyayanasūtra with Skt. comm.	Or. 2094
Uttarādhyayanasūtra with Skt. comm.	Or. 2095
Uttarādhyayanasūtra with Sukhabodhā	Or. 2096
Uttarādhyayanasūtra with Sukhabodhā (incomplete)	Or. 2097
Praśamarati by Umāsvāti with comm.	Or. 2098 (A)
Praśamarati by Umāsvāti	Or. 2098 (B)
Praśamarati by Umāsvāti with Skt. comm.	Or. 2098 (C)
Sthānānga (1-10) with Abhayadeva's comm.	Or. 2099
Upāsakadaśāḥ with Abhayadeva's comm.	Or. 2100 (A)
Upāsakadaśāḥ (1-8) with Abhayadeva's comm.	Or. 2100 (B)
Antakṛddaśāḥ with glosses	Or. 2100 (C)
Aupapātikasūtra with Abhayadeva's comm.	Or. 2100 (D)
Daśavaikālikasūtra and -niryukti with Haribhadra's comm.	Or. 2101
Āvaśyaka-niryukti with Jñanasāgara's comm.	Or. 2102 (A)
Āvaśyaka-niryukti with Tilakācārya's comm.	Or. 2102 (B)
Viśeṣāvaśyakabhāṣya of Jinabhadra with Hemacandramaladhārin's comm.	Or. 2103
Ṣaḍāvaśyakavṛtti (Vandāruvṛtti)	Or. 2104
Gurutattvapradīpa	Or. 2105 (A)
Ṣaḍāvaśyaka-bālāvabodha by Hemahaṁsagaṇi	Or. 2105 (B)
Āvaśyaka-niryukti	Or. 2105 (C)
Bhāṣya-traya	Or. 2105 (D)
Catuḥśaraṇa-panjikā	Or. 2105 (E)
Piṇḍaviśuddhi with Udayasiṁha's Dīpikā	Or. 2105 (F)
Śrāddha-jītakalpa-sūtra by Dharmaghoṣasūri	Or. 2105 (G)
Āgamasāroddhāra by Devacanda muni	Or. 2105 (H)
Karma-grantha-ṣaṭka	Or. 2106 (A)
Karma-grantha-pancaka of Devendrasūri with Skt. comm.	Or. 2106 (B)
Karmavipāka by Devendrasūri with Guj. comm.	Or. 2106 (C)
Karma-grantha-ṣaṭka with Guṇaratna's comm.	Or. 2106 (D)
Bandhahetūdaya-tribhangī by Harṣakula with Vijayavimala's comm.	Or. 2107 (A)
Pancasaṁgraha by Candrarṣi with auto-comm.	Or. 2107 (B)

Pravacanaparīkṣā by Dharmasāgara with auto-comm.	Or. 2108
Pravacanaparīkṣā by Dharmasāgara	Or. 2109 (A)
Caityavandana-mahābhāṣya by Śāntisūri	Or. 2109 (B)
Śrāddha-pratikramaṇa-sūtra with Guj. comm.	Or. 2109 (C)
Sukhaprabodhinī by Maheśvarācārya on Municandrasūri's Āv.-saptatikā	Or. 2109 (D)
Pravacanasāroddhāra by Nemicandra with Siddhasena's comm., frag.	Or. 2110
Anekāntajayapatākā by Haribhadra with the auto-comm.	Or. 2111
1. Navatattva-prakaraṇa - 2. Navatattva-prakaraṇa with a Guj. comm.	Or. 2112 (A)
Tattvaprabodha-prakaraṇa by Amaracandra	Or. 2112 (B)
Tattvataranginī by Dharmasāgara with auto-comm.	Or. 2112 (C)
Tattvataranginī by Dharmasāgara with auto-comm.	Or. 2112 (D)
Jīvavicāra by Śāntisūri with Bhāvasundara's comm.	Or. 2112 (E)
Śīlopadeśamālā by Jayakirti with Skt. comm.	Or. 2113 (A)
Śīlopadeśamālā by Jayakīrti with Merusundara's Guj. comm.	Or. 2113 (B)
Upadeśamālā by Dharmadāsa-gaṇi	Or. 2114 (A)
Upadeśamālā by Dharmadāsagaṇi with Guj. comm.	Or. 2114 (B)
Upadeśamālā by Dharmadāsagaṇi with Skt. comm.	Or. 2114 (C)
Puṣpamālā by Hemacandramaladhārin	Or. 2115 (A)
Upadeśataranginī by Ratnamandira-gaṇi	Or. 2115 (B)
Saṁgrahaṇī by Śrīcandra with Skt. comm.	Or. 2116 (A)
Saṁgrahaṇī by Śrīcandra	Or. 2116 (B)
Saṁgrahaṇī by Śrīcandra with Guj. comm.	Or. 2116 (C)
Saṁgrahaṇī by Śrīcandrasūri with Devabhadra's comm.	Or. 2116 (D)
Jaṁbūdvīpa-saṁgrahaṇī by Haribhadrasūri with Skt. comm.	Or. 2116 (E)
Kṣetrasamāsa by Ratnaśekharasūri	Or. 2117 (A)
Kṣetrasamāsa by Ratnaśekharasūri with a Guj. comm.	Or. 2117 (B)
Kṣetrasamāsa by Ratnaśekhara with auto-comm.	Or. 2117 (C)
Kṣetrasamāsa by Ratnaśekhara with auto-comm.	Or. 2117 (D)
Kṣetrasamāsa by Ratnaśekhara with Pārśvacandra's Guj. comm.	Or. 2118 (A)
Kṣetrasamāsa by Ratnaśekhara with Dayāsiṁha's Guj. comm.	Or. 2118 (B)
Kṣetrasamāsa by Jinabhadra-gaṇi with Malayagiri's comm.	Or. 2118 (C)
Kṣetrasamāsa by Somatilakasūri with Skt. comm.	Or. 2118 (D)
Yogaśāstra (1-4) by Hemacandra	Or. 2119 (A)
Yogaśāstra (1-4) by Hemacandra	Or. 2119 (B)
Yogaśāstra (5-12) by Hemacandra	Or. 2119 (C)
Yogaśāstra by Hemacandra with auto-comm.	Or. 2119 (D)
Yogaśāstra by Hemacandra with Guj. comm.	Or. 2119 (E)
Yogaśāstra by Hemacandra with Somasundara's Guj. comm.	Or. 2119 (F)
Śrāddhavidhi-prakaraṇa by Ratnaśekhara with auto-comm.	Or. 2120 (A)
Śrāddhavidhi-viniścaya by Harṣabhūṣaṇa	Or. 2120 (B)
Śrāddhavidhi-viniścaya by Harṣabhūṣaṇa and [Aṣṭāhnikā-mahiman]	Or. 2120 (C)
Śrāvakavidhi-prakaraṇa or Dharma-tattva-vicāra-huṇḍi	Or. 2120 (D)
1. Śrāvakavidhi-prakaraṇa or Dharma-tattva-vicāra-huṇḍi - 2. Prajñāpanā-sūtra with Malayagiri's vṛtti (frag.)	Or. 2120 (E)
Śrāvaka-vrata-bhanga-vicāra	Or. 2120 (F)
Sūtra-vyākhyāna-vidhi-śataka with Skt. comm.	Or. 2120 (G)
Kalpāntarvācya	Or. 2120 (H)
Śrāddha-dina-kṛtya	Or. 2120 (I)

Bhagavad-arhad-abhiṣeka-vidhi by vādivetāla Śāntisūri	Or. 2121 (A)
Guru-tattva-pradīpa by Dharmasāgaragaṇi	Or. 2121 (B)
Guru-tattva-pradīpa	Or. 2121 (C)
Citrarūpakāryakāraṇabhāvarahasya	Or. 2121 (D)
Ātmānuśāsana by Pārśvanāga	Or. 2121 (F)
Ṛṣidattā-rāsa by Jayavantasūri	Or. 2122 (A)
Prajñāpanā-tṛtīya-pada-saṁgrahaṇī with Kulamaṇḍana's Avc.	Or. 2122 (B)
Jñātā-upanaya-kathāḥ	Or. 2122 (C)
[Āvaśyaka ritual of the Ancalagaccha]	Or. 2122 (D)
1. Paryantārādhanā by Somasūri with Guj. comm. - 2. [Darśana-bheda]	Or. 2122 (E)
Ātmabodha-kulaka by Jayaśekhara with Guj. comm.	Or. 2122 (F)
Panca-nirgranthī by Abhayadevasūri	Or. 2122 (G)
Kṣullaka-bhavāvalī-prakaraṇa by Dharmaśekharagaṇi with Mauktikasaubhāgya's comm.	Or. 2122 (H)
Bhuvanabhānu-kevali-carita with Harikalaśagaṇi's Guj. comm.	Or. 2122 (I)
Triṣaṣṭiśalākāpuruṣacaritra (I.1-6) by Hemacandra	Or. 2123 (A)
Triṣaṣṭiśalākāpuruṣacaritra (VIII) by Hemacandra	Or. 2123 (B)
1. Triṣaṣṭiśalākāpuruṣacaritra (VIII) by Hemacandra - 2. [Virāṭa-parva] by Śālisūri	Or. 2123 (C)
Triṣaṣṭiśalākāpuruṣacaritra (VIII.1-12) by Hemacandra	Or. 2124
Śatrunjayamāhātmya by Dhaneśvara, incomplete	Or. 2125
Sirivālakahā by Ratnaśekhara	Or. 2126 (A)
Jambūsvāmi-caupāī by Depāla	Or. 2126 (B)
Merutrayodaśīkathā	Or. 2126 (C)
Ratnaśekharanṛpa-Ratnāvatī-kathā and two other texts	Or. 2126 (D)
Vimalanāthacarita by Jñānasāgara	Or. 2127
Śāntināthacarita	Or. 2128 (A)
Bṛhacchāntistavana with Harṣakīrti's comm.	Or. 2128 (B)
Uttamakumāracarita by Cārucandra	Or. 2129 (A)
Śālibhadracarita by Dharmakumāra	Or. 2129 (B)
Hanūmaccaritra by Brahma Ajita	Or. 2129 (C)
Samarādityasaṁkṣepa by Pradyumnasūri	Or. 2130 (A)
Poṣadaśamīkathā	Or. 2130 (B)
Rohiṇīkathā	Or. 2130 (C)
Bhaktāmara-stotra with comm.	Or. 2131 (C)
Kalyāṇamandira-stotra with Māṇikyacandra's comm.	Or. 2131 (D)
Mahāvīra-stavana by Jinavallabha with comm.	Or. 2131 (E)
Śobhana-stuti with comm.	Or. 2131 (F)
Śobhana-stuti with comm.	Or. 2131 (G)
Vīra-stotrāvalī by Nemiratnagaṇi	Or. 2131 (H)
Vītarāga-stotra by Hemacandra	Or. 2131 (I)
Ajita-Śānti-stotra with comm.	Or. 2132 (A)
Bhayahara-stotra	Or. 2132 (B)
Upasargahara-stotra with Laghuvṛtti	Or. 2132 (C)
Ṛṣimaṇḍala-stotra with comm.	Or. 2132 (D)
Ṛṣimaṇḍala-stotra	Or. 2132 (E)
Vicāraṣaṭtriṁśikā	Or. 2132 (F)
Pratiṣṭhākalpa-stavana	Or. 2132 (G)
Alpabahutva-stavana	Or. 2132 (H)
Dīpālikākalpa with Guj. comm.	Or. 2133 (A)

Dīpālīkalpa with Guj. comm.	Or. 2133 (B)
Sambodhasaptatikā with Amarakīrti's comm.	Or. 2133 (C)
Sambodhasaptatikā	Or. 2133 (D)
Guruguṇaṣaṭtriṁśikā with auto-comm.	Or. 2133 (E)
Vairāgyaśataka with Guj. comm.	Or. 2133 (F)
Siddhapancāśikā with comm.	Or. 2133 (G)
Siddhapancāśikā with comm.	Or. 2133 (H)
Jinaśataka by Jambūguru with comm.	Or. 2134 (A)
Jinaśataka by Jambūguru with Samba Kavi's comm.	Or. 2134 (B)
Jinaśataka by Jambūguru with comm.	Or. 2134 (C)
1. Pramāṇamīmāṁsā by Hemacandra - 2. Pramāṇamīmāṁsāvṛtti by Hemacandra - 3. Parīkṣānāmaprakaraṇa (by Māṇikyanandin) 4. Sarvajñasiddhi-prakaraṇa (by Haribhadra)	Or. 2134 (D)
Vivekavilāsa	Or. 2316 (A)
Praśnottaraṣaṭtriṁśajjalpanirṇaya by Śrutasāgara	Or. 2136 (B)
Siddhāntālāpaka 1. Sangrahaṇīratna - 2. Karmavipāka - 3. Karmastava by Jinavallabha -]4. Karmastavabhāṣya - 5. Āgamikavastuvicāraprakaraṇa 6. Ṣaḍaśīti-laghubhāṣya - 7. Bandhasvāmitva - 8. Śataka 9. Śatakabhāṣya - 10. Sārdhaśatakaprakaraṇa - 11. Sārdhaśatakabhāṣya - 12. Saptatikā - 13. Sattarīsāra - 14. Sattarībhāṣya	Or. 2137 (A)
	Or. 2137 (B)
Setruṁja Udhāra by Premavijaya	Or. 2137 (C)
1. Sūktāvalī - 2. Śāntistavana by Vimalakevala	Or. 2138 (A)
Sūktāvalī	Or. 2138 (B)
Dhanarājaprabodhamālā by Dhanarāja	Or. 2138 (C)
Ārambhasiddhi	Or. 2139
Ārambhasiddhi with an Avacūrṇi	Or. 2140 (A)
Vṛttaratnākara with Kṣemahaṁsagaṇi's comm.	Or. 2140 (C)
Chandoratnāvalī by Amaracandrasūri	Or. 2140 (D)
Chando'nuśāsana with auto-comm., incomplete	Or. 2140 (E)
Śrutabodha	Or. 2140 (F)
Abhidhānacintāmaṇi	Or. 2141
Abhidhānacintāmaṇi, incomplete	Or. 2142 (A)
Pancavargasaṁgrahanāmamālā	Or. 2142 (B)
Śabdānuśāsana with Laghuvṛtti	Or. 2142 (C)
Vākyaprakāśa with Jinavijaya's comm.	Or. 2143 (B)
Vākyaprakāśa with comm.	Or. 2143 (C)

Bendall collection

Śāntināthacaritra	Or. 3347 (A)
Āvaśyaka-niryukti	Or. 3347 (B)
Karma-vipāka and 16 other texts	Or. 3347 (C)
Ācārasārasaṁgraha by Vīranandin	Or. 3348 (A)
Neminātha-purāṇa	Or. 3348 (B)
Daśavaikālikasūtra	Or. 3349 (A)
Kālikācārya-sambandha	Or. 3349 (B)
Kalpāntarvācya	Or. 3349 (C)
Harivaṁśa-purāṇa by Jinasena	Or. 3350
Damayantīkathā-vṛtti	Or. 3351
Tājikasāra by Haribhaṭṭa	Or. 3354

Miles collection

Abhidhānacintāmaṇi	Or. 4530
Daśavaikālika	Or. 4531
Ṣaḍāvaśyaka	Or. 4532
Dravyaguṇaparyāya no rāsa	Or. 4533
Prabandhacintāmaṇi	Or. 4778
Pannavaṇā	Or. 7619
Ṣaḍāvaśyaka	Or. 7620
Śramaṇasūtra	Or. 7621 (A)
Vicāraṣaṭtriṁśikā	Or. 7621 (B)
Pañcanamaskāra	Or. 7621 (C)
Pañcanamaskāra	Or. 7621 (D)
[Paṭṭāvalī-saṁgraha]	Or. 7621 (E)
[Sketches of the lives of five Jinas]	Or. 7623 B

Jacobi collection

Ācārāngasūtra	Or. 5115
Ācārānga-pradīpikā by Jinahaṁsa	Or. 5116
Ācārānga-ṭabo by Pārśvacandra	Or. 5117
Sūtrakṛtānga	Or. 5118
Sūtrakṛtānga	Or. 5119
Sūtrakṛtānga-dīpikā by Harṣakula	Or. 5120
Sthānānga	Or. 5121
Sthānānga-dīpikā by Megharāja	Or. 5122
Bhagavatīsūtra	Or. 5123 (A)
Bhagavatīsūtra fragment	Or. 5123 (B)
Bhagavatī-vṛtti by Abhayadeva	Or. 5124
Jñātādharmakathāḥ	Or. 5125
Jñātādharmakathā-ṭīkā by Abhayadeva	Or. 5126
Upāsakadaśāḥ	Or. 5127
Upāsakadaśāḥ	Or. 5128
Antakṛddaśāḥ comm. by Abhayadeva	Or. 5129
Anuttaropapātika-daśāḥ comm. by Abhayadeva	Or. 5130
1. Antakṛddaśāḥ comm. by Abhayadeva - 2. Anuttaropapātikadaśāḥ comm. by Abhayadeva	Or. 5131
Praśnavyākaraṇa	Or. 5132
Praśnavyākaraṇa	Or. 5133
Praśnavyākaraṇa comm. by Abhayadeva	Or. 5134
Aupapātikasūtra	Or. 5135
Aupapātikasūtra	Or. 5136
Aupapātikasūtra comm. by Abhayadeva	Or. 5137
Rājapraśnīya	Or. 5138
Rājapraśnīya	Or. 5139
Rājapraśnīya comm. by Malayagiri	Or. 5140
Jīvābhigama comm. by Malayagiri	Or. 5141
Prajñāpanāsūtra	Or. 5142

Sūrya-prajñapti	Or. 5143 (A)
Candra-prajñapti	Or. 5143 (B)
Jambūdvīpa-prajñapti	Or. 5144
Nirayāvaliyāo	Or. 5145
Nirayāvaliyāo	Or. 5146
1. Bhaktaparijñā - 2. Saṁthāraka-prakīrṇaka	Or. 5147
Bṛhatkalpasūtra	Or. 5148
Kalpasūtra	Or. 5149
Kalpavṛtti-vācanā	Or. 5150
Kalpasūtra with Kalpadruma	Or. 5151 (1)
Kālikācārya-sambandha	Or. 5151 (2)
Kalpasūtra with Sandehaviṣauṣadhi	Or. 5152
Nandīsūtra	Or. 5153
Anuyogadvārasūtra	Or. 5154
Anuyogadvārasūtra with Hemacandra's Skt. comm.	Or. 5155
Uttarādhyayanasūtra	Or. 5156
Uttarādhyayanasūtra with Devendra's Sukhabodhā	Or. 5157
Uttarādhyayanasūtra with Devendra's Sukhabodhā	Or. 5158
Uttarādhyayana-kathāḥ	Or. 5159
Āvaśyaka-niryukti	Or. 5160
Daśavaikālika-sūtra & niryukti	Or. 5161
Daśavaikālikasūtra	Or. 5162
Daśavaikālikasūtra with Sumatisūri's comm.	Or. 5163
Upadeśamālā-kathāḥ	Or. 5164
Upasthāna-vidhi	Or. 5165
Ṛṣimaṇḍala-stotra by Dharmaghoṣasūri	Or. 5166
Ṛṣimaṇḍala-stotra with Padmamandira's Skt. comm.	Or. 5167
Panca-karma-grantha by Devendrasūri with auto-comm.	Or. 5168
Kalyāṇamandira-stotra with vṛtti	Or. 5169
Guṇasthānākramaroha by Ratnaśekharasūri with auto-comm.	Or. 5170
Caturviṁśati-Jina-stava by Jinaprabhasūri with comm. + Neminātha-stavana in six languages with comm.	Or. 5171
Jīvavicāra by Śāntisūri with Ratnākara's comm.	Or. 5172
Vicāraṣaṭtriṁśikā by Gajasāra with auto-comm.	Or. 5173
Tattvārthasūtra with Bhāṣya	Or. 5174
Dravyasaṁgraha by Nemicandra with Brahmadeva's comm.	Or. 5175
Dvādaśa-kulaka by Jinavallabha with comm.	Or. 5176
Navatattva with Skt. comm.	Or. 5177
Kṣetrasamāsa by Somatilakasūri with Guṇaratna's comm.	Or. 5178
Kathāsancaya (in Jacobi's list: Nānāvicāra-saṁgraha (incomplete))	Or. 5179
Pariśiṣṭaparvan by Hemacandra	Or. 5180
Pravacanasāroddhāra	Or. 5181
Karmastava and Bandhasvāmitva	Or. 5182
Bhaktāmara-stotra with Śāntisūri's comm.	Or. 5183
Bhaktāmara-stotra with comm.	Or. 5184
Bhavabhāvanā by Hemacandra Maladhārin	Or. 5185
Yogaśāstra by Hemacandra with Guj. comm.	Or. 5186
Vardhamānadeśanā	Or. 5187

Pancakarmagrantha by Devendrasūri with Skt. comm.	Or. 5188
Śatrunjaya-māhātmya by Dhaneśvarasūri	Or. 5189
Śobhana-stutayaḥ with Skt. comm.	Or. 5190
Saṁgrahaṇīratna with Skt. comm.	Or. 5191
1. Bhaktāmara-stotra with Harṣakīrti's comm. - 2. Laghuśānti-stava with Harsakīrti's comm. - 3. Ajita-Śānti-stava by Nandiṣeṇa with Guj. comm. 4. Ullāsika-stava by Jinavallabha-sūri with Guj. comm. - 5. Bhayahara- stavana by Mānatuṅga with Guj. comm. - 6. Taṁ-jayau-stotra by Jinadatta-sūri with Guj. comm. - 7. Guru-pāratantrya-stotra by Jinadatta-sūri with Guj. comm. 8. Siggham-avaharau-stotra by Jinadatta-sūri with Guj. comm. 9. Upasargahara-stotra with Guj. comm. - 10. Navagraha-stotra by Jinaprabha-sūri - 11. Sarvajina-stotra by Ratnākara with a Skt. vṛtti - 12. Jina-stuti with Skt. comm. - 13. Tijaya-pahutta-stotra by Abhayadeva with Harṣakīrti's Skt. comm. - 14. Jaya-tihuyaṇa-stotra by Abhayadeva, with Skt. comm. - 15. Bṛhacchānti-stavana by Mānadeva with Harṣakīrti's comm.	Or. 5192 (A)
Ṣaḍāvaśyaka-bālāvabodha	Or. 5192 (B)
Syādvādamanjarī by Malliṣeṇasūri	Or. 5193
Bhāṣya-traya by Devendrasūri	Or. 5194
Abhidhānacintāmaṇi by Hemacandra	Or. 5196
Abhidhānacintāmaṇi by Hemacandra with auto-comm.	Or. 5197
Ārambhasiddhi by Udayaprabhadevasūri	Or. 5199
Uṇādināmamālā by Śubhaśilagaṇi	Or. 5200
Karaṇakutūhala by Bhāskarācārya with Sumatiharṣagaṇi's comm.	Or. 5201
Kriyāratnasamuccaya by Guṇaratna	Or. 5204
Jātakakarmapaddhati by Śrīpati with Sumatiharṣagaṇi's comm.	Or. 5208
Ratnamālā by Śrīpati (Jain scribe)	Or. 5209
Jyotiṣasāroddhāra by Harṣakīrtisūri	Or. 5210
Tarkataranginī by Guṇaratna	Or. 5211
Dhāturatnākara by Sundaragaṇi	Or. 5222
Dhruvabhramayantra by Padmanābha with auto-comm.	Or. 5223
Anekārthadhvanimanjarī	Or. 5224 (A)
Nighaṇṭusamaya by Dhanañjaya	Or. 5224 (B)
Nyāyāmanjūṣā-nyāsa by Hemahaṁsagaṇi	Or. 5227, 5228
Praśnottara by Jinavallabhasūri with Kamalamandira's comm.	Or. 5231
Śatakatraya by Bhartṛhari with Dhanasāra's comm.	Or. 5236
Lingānuśāsana by Hemacandra	Or. 5240
Vāgbhaṭālamkāra	Or. 5241
Śabdaprabheda by Maheśvarakavi with Jñānavimala's comm.	Or. 5246
Śabdānuśāsana by Hemacandra with Laghuvṛtti	Or. 5247
Śabdānuśāsana by Hemacandra with Laghuvṛtti	Or. 5248
Hetugarbha-pratikramaṇa-vidhi	Or. 5255
Vicāraratnasaṁgraha by Kulamaṇḍana-sūri	Or. 5256
Uttarādhyayana-sūtra (ill.)	Or. 5257
Vicāraṣaṭtriṁśikā by Gajasāra with auto-comm.	Or. 5258

W. Erskine collection

Pārśvanātha-caritra by Udayavīra	Add. 26,362
Śrīpāla-rāsa by Vinayavijaya and Yaśovijaya	Add. 26,363
Saṁgrahaṇīratna by Śrīcandra	Add. 26,365
Dīpāvalī-kalpa by Jinasundara-sūri	Add. 26,366

Samyaktva-kaumudī with Guj. comm.	Add. 26,367
Līlāvatī by Lālacandragaṇi	Add. 26,373
Laghu-Kṣetrasamāsa by Rājaśekhara	Add. 26,374
Śatrunjaya-māhātmyôllekha by Haṁsaratna	Add. 26,375
Prajñāpanā-sūtra	Add. 26,378
Kalpasūtra with Vinayavijaya's Subodhikā	Add. 26,379
Anekārthadhvanimanjarī and Anekārthasaṁgraha	Add. 26,424 (E)
Śabdānuśāsana by Hemacandra with Laghuvṛtti	Add. 26,434 (B) and (C)
Lingānuśāsana by Hemacandra	Add. 26,434 (D)
Anekārthadhvanimanjarī	Add. 26,434 (E)
Sanghapaṭṭaka by Jinavallabha with Guj. comm.	Add. 26,435 (B)
Abhidhānacintāmaṇi by Hemacandra with glosses	Add. 26,436 (A)
Hemacandra's Grammar	Add. 26,443
Naiṣadhīyacarita with comm.	Add. 26,446 (A)
Gajasiṁhakumāra-caritra by Namikuñjara	Add. 26,450 (C)
[Campaka-Līlāvatī-kathā] by Paramasāgara	Add. 26,450 (D)
Navatattva-vicāra with Guj. comm.	Add. 26,452 (A)
Vidagdhamukhamaṇḍana by Dharmadāsa	Add. 26,452 (B)
Kalpāntarvācya	Add. 26,452 (C)
Vaidyavallabha	Add. 26,452 (D)
Pramāṇa-manjarī by Śarvadeva	Add. 26,452 (E)
Uttarādhyayanasūtra Adhy. 2, Guj. comm.	Add. 26,452 (F)
Kalpasūtra, fol. 176	Add. 26,452 (G)[1]
Fragment of a Guj. comm. to some Kṣetrasamāsa-text	Add. 26,452 (H)
Ekonatriṁśad-bhāvanāḥ	Add. 26,452 (I)
Kalpasūtra, fol. 210	Add. 26,452 (J)[2]
Sārasvata-prakriyā by Anubhūtisvarūpâcārya and [Sandhi-prakriyā] frag.	Add. 26,452 (K)
[Nāma-rūpâvali]	Add. 26,452 (L)
[Śālibhadra nī sajjhāya] by Sahajasundara and Kāya-jīva-gīta by Samayasundara	Add. 26,452 (M)
[Sthānakavāsī-paṭṭāvalī]	Add. 26,452 (N)
Kṛd-vṛtti	Add. 26,452 (O)
Nemīśvara-bhāsa and Sthulībhadra-bhāsa by Ṛddhivijaya	Add. 26,452 (P)
Aupapātikasūtra with Rājacandra's Guj. comm.	Add. 26,453 (A)
Bhaktāmara-stotra by Mānatunga	Add. 26,453 (B)
Jñātādharmakathāḥ with Guj. comm.	Add. 26,454 (B)
Vaidyamanotsava by Nayanasukha	Add. 26,454 (E)
Kalpāntarvācya	Add. 26,454 (G)
Keśi-Pradeśī-vicāra and [Guru-stavana]	Add. 26,455 (AI)
Anāthī-sādhu-gīta by Samayasundara	Add. 26,455 (AP)
Jambūcarita by Padmasundarasūri with Guj. comm and Kalpasūtra with Sukhasāgara's Guj. comm.	Add. 26,459 Add. 26, 459
Upadeśa-mālā by Dharmadāsa-gaṇi with Rāmavijaya's comm.	Add. 26,460
Ādinātha-abhiṣeka by Ratnākara and sixteen other texts See the section 'Description of composite manuscripts' for details	Add. 26,461
Rājapraśnīyasūtra with a Guj. comm.	Add. 26,462

[1] = fol. 176 of the *Kalpasūtra* ms. Add. 26,463.

[2] = fol. 210 of the Kalpasūtra ms. Add. 26,379.

Kalpasūtra with Sukhasāgara's Guj. comm.	Add. 26,463
Catuḥśaraṇa with Guj. comm.	Add. 26,464 (A)
Chandaḥ-prastāra-vidhi with Guj. comm.	Add. 26,464 (B)
Navatattva-prakaraṇa with Guj. comm.	Add. 26,464 (C)
Ṛṣabha-vivāhalo by Sevaka	Add. 26,464 (D)
Saṁthārā-vidhi with Guj. comm.	Add. 26,464 (E)
Dvādaśabhāvanā by Sakalacandra	Add. 26,464 (F)
Śukasaptati and Jina-stavana	Add. 26,519
Vikramāditya-kathā	Add. 26,542 (B)
Neminātha-bhramaragītā	Add. 26,542 (D)

British Museum

Illustrated folio	BM 1926-3-16-01
Kalpasūtra folio	BM 1947-7-12-02
Kalpasūtra folio	BM 1947-7-12-03
Kalpasūtra folio	BM 1948-10-9-0159
Kālakācārya-kathā	BM 1959-4-11-04
Kalpasūtra folio	BM 1959-4-11-05
Kalpasūtra folio	BM 1966-10-10-05 (1)
Kalpasūtra folio	BM 1966-10-10-05 (2)
[Samyakcaritra yantra], copper plate	OA 1880-4057

Victoria and Albert Museum

[Source: *Art of India. Paintings and Drawings in the Victoria & Albert Museum. Catalogue & Microfiche Guide*. Emmett Publishing, 1992, pp/ 8-10: Western India. Abbreviations: IM = Indian Museum; IS = Indian Section; Circ. = Circulation. Followed by shelf-number and year of acquisition]

Illustrated folios from the Kalpasūtra	IM 161-1914 & IM 161A-1914
Illustrated folios from the Kalpasūtra	IM 6-1931 & IM 7-1931
Illustrated folios from the Kalpasūtra	IM 8-1931, 9-1931, 10A-1931, 11A-1931, 12-1931
Victory banner	IM 89-1936
Illustrated Kalpasūtra with a lacuna	IS 46-1959
Illustrated folio from the Kalpasūtra	IS 83-1963
Illustrated folio from the Kalpasūtra	IS 84-1963
Illustrated Uttarādhyayana with a lacuna	IS 2-1972
The 7 Chakras of the Subtle Body	Circ. 321-1972
Personification of a planet	Circ. 325-1972
Personificatio of a planet	Circ. 326-1972
Game of snakes and ladders	324-1972
Jain manuscript cover	IS 20-1978
Manuscript cover	IS 50-1983
The seven armies of the Bhavanavāsins	IS 2-1984